Current Trends and Future Practices for Digital Literacy and Competence

Antonio Cartelli
University of Cassino, Italy

Managing Director:	Lindsay Johnston
Senior Editorial Director:	Heather A. Probst
Book Production Manager:	Sean Woznicki
Development Manager:	Joel Gamon
Development Editor:	Heather A. Probst
Acquisitions Editor:	Erika Gallagher
Typesetter:	Russell A. Spangler
Cover Design:	Nick Newcomer, Lisandro Gonzalez

Published in the United States of America by
Information Science Reference (an imprint of IGI Global)
701 E. Chocolate Avenue
Hershey PA 17033
Tel: 717-533-8845
Fax: 717-533-8661
E-mail: cust@igi-global.com
Web site: http://www.igi-global.com

Library of Congress Cataloging-in-Publication Data

Current trends and future practices for digital literacy and competence / Antonio Cartelli, editor.
p. cm.
Includes bibliographical references and index.
Summary: "This book offers a look at the latest research within digital literacy and competence, setting the bar for the digital citizen of today and tomorrow"--Provided by publisher.
ISBN 978-1-4666-0903-7 (hbk.) -- ISBN 978-1-4666-0904-4 (ebook) -- ISBN 978-1-4666-0905-1 (print & perpetual access) 1. Digital divide. 2. Computer literacy. 3. Digital media. 4. Information society. I. Cartelli, Antonio, 1954-
HM851.C874 2012
004--dc23

2012000029

British Cataloguing in Publication Data
A Cataloguing in Publication record for this book is available from the British Library.

Associate Editors

Table of Contents

Detailed Table of Contents

tizing, and producing different kinds of texts in critical and creative ways, through the use of all means, languages and technologies available. Considering that media cannot be excluded from literacy programs, it is essential to reflect on the definition of "literate" today. These reflections examine the resignification of concepts like literacy, media literacy, digital literacy and information literacy.

The paper is made of two parts. The first part discusses the importance of informal education environments supported by IT/ICT in students' learning, followed by reports of some international competitions and the role they have in improving students' interest and use of Informatics and related disciplines. At the end of the section, it describes the Bebras contest, an international competition supporting students' Information and Communication Technology competences with emphasis on cross discipline competences, which are useful to solve real life problems. In the second part of the paper, the outcomes of a research study on the features of a framework for digital competence assessment are reported. Based on this, some criticisms emerging from the analysis of the answers that students gave to a questionnaire built on the guidelines of the mentioned framework are analysed. They are integrated by the comments that teachers, colleagues and researchers made on the structure of the hypothesized framework. At last, a new model for digital literacy assessment is proposed. In the conclusion, the necessary elements for making the last framework effective are outlined and its suitability for the construction of the yearly questionnaire of the Bebras contest is discussed.

Today, life is more complex and difficult due to uncertainties in society. Liquid life (Bauman, 2006) is frenetic, rapidly changing and highly influenced from information and communication technologies, and forces subjects to adapt to group behavior avoiding exclusion. Human beings are experimenting in the digital age the pervasiveness of computers and IT/ICT equipment deeper than in the past, because learning and knowledge construction are strongly influenced by digital media. This raises questions in regard to a privileged role for digital competences in the knowledge society, whether or not there is a framework for digital competence assessment, and possible hints, suggestions, experiments, protocols, or curricula helping teachers in hitting this target with students. This paper answers these questions, describing the evolution of psycho-pedagogical paradigms and their comparisons. A framework for digital competence assessment is proposed and teaching activities are suggested. A proposal of a teaching-learning process called OTS (Open Teaching Process) is also presented.

Information and communication technologies have changed the way in which citizens interact with Public Administrations. Digital literacy is key for the development of the Liquid Society, and Public Administrations must take the lead in promoting more efficient, universal, and user oriented public services. The migration to open source standards allows Public Administration to offer more democratic, universal, and efficient channels for establishing relationships with citizens. In this article, the authors present international experiences that show how certain Public Administrations have migrated to open source software to promote digital literacy in the contexts they are operating. The final results depend on contextual and organizational factors, including the need to change, the political support and the existence of available technological resources, the organizational climate, motivation levels of human resources, and the kind of leadership for the project or the organizational complexity. Change efforts have strategic and organizational impacts that the organization must evaluate beforehand.

A community made up of a group of individuals becomes a "community of practice" when a mutual engagement is established between its members. The mutual engagement unites the participants in the carrying out of a common task (Wenger, 1998). The main aim of a community of practice is to find the solution to a problem by sharing experiences (Midoro, 2002). This paper examines the definition, characteristics, management and effectiveness of communities of practice. They are understood as being communities of self-managed learning where professional development is not based on a pre-set training course but on sharing experiences, identifying best practices and helping each other face the daily problems encountered in one's profession (Trentin, 2000). Such communities are useful in particular working environments as an opportunity to improve digital competences. In communities of practice, it is possible to encourage ways of co-building knowledge through teaching methods such as cooperative learning. Until now cooperative learning has been limited to traditional training contexts, but it can be realised via Web technologies.

The aim of this study was to examine the differences among harassed teachers and un-harassed ones, regarding coping strategies, self-efficacy, and locus of control. Participants were 255 teachers (163 women and 92 men) who completed a set of three questionnaires, the Mobbing Perceived Questionnaire, a battery of control expectancies, and the Brief COPE to assess, respectively, mobbing perceived at work, self-efficacy, locus of control, and cooping strategies. The results showed differences in self-efficacy,

Preface

It is almost obvious today to say that digital technologies and the Internet have changed our life, less evident is the path through which this occurred. During last decades (since late '70s and early '80s), soon after the development of PCs and the birth of distributed computing, computers evolved and became user friendly due to the introduction of special input devices (e.g., mouse and joystick) and graphics user interfaces (GUIs); but it has been the introduction and the spreading of digitization and of the Internet, to produce the most relevant changes in data acquisition and communication. Both the above phenomena forced people to use computers more and more frequently, because most part of the information they sent and received from other people had to be managed by digital equipment (Heffernan, 2011).

The described digital revolution followed another revolution, which occurred in human and social communication for the development of mass media. The phenomena associated with the growth of communication equipment and mass media were essentially analogical, due to the physical phenomena they were based on, and they induced deep changes in mankind. M. McLuhan (1968), for example, stated that media determine the structural features of communication and produce pervasive effects on people imagination, independently from the information contents they transport (by using the words of McLuhan "the medium is the message").

Recently, while referring to Popper (2002), and especially to the metaphor of the television as a "bad teacher", G. Sartori has proposed the definition of *Homo videns* (looking people), for his contemporary generation. Sartori (1997) says that children, and more generally people, when looking at the television receive an imprinting, which is the result of an educational action mostly centred on looking and seeing with respect to acting.

Different perspectives have also been adopted in sociology while studying the effects of digitization and of the Internet on mankind. M. McLuhan (1989), before all, said that new media (i.e., digital media) could induce very useful and positive effects on mankind, by increasing the level of democracy all over the world, so that a "global village" could be created.

Psycho-technologists, on another hand, suggested deeper changes on human cognition and intelligence by means of the Internet. P. Levy (1996) suggested the construction of "collective intelligences", which are the result of high levels of collaboration among people, so that their actions look like the result of a single mind; communities of people connected on the Internet can build group intelligences, these intelligences emerge from the cooperation and competition among the subjects belonging to the community. De Kerckhove (1996), started from Lévy's ideas and adapted them to the technological environment of computer networks, as a result his attention was centred on the connection of people intelligences for the hitting of a common and unique target, more than on the collaboration among individuals. Digital media and especially the Internet are for De Kerckhove psycho-technologies which modify McLuhan definition of "global village"; he says in fact: "it is no more the village to be global but the people living in it, who have satellite and Internet connections, so that they can reach every place and everyone at any time". As a result, globalization is not for De Kerckhove a phenomenon pertaining to finance and economy, it is the field of psychology, because it is the expression of mental stages and subjects' perceptions when people are connected on the Net.

Nowadays the different media described above (i.e., analogical and digital media, transmitting and interactive media etc.) are mixing together; as a result the Internet is often and often the vehicle for multimedia messages coming from last generation mobile telephones (i.e., smartphones) and TV broadcasting, while the television uses the Internet to get information and discuss about it.

The effects of the intertwining of the different media described above cannot be considered as the sum of former effects described until now, and evidences for new implications on human mankind have been recently reported by many scientists. P.C. Rivoltella (2006), for example, has proposed the definition of "multi-screen society" for today society, which is highly populated by new technologies, where the spaces of vision are multiplied, and traditional television is accompanied by computer screens, portable consoles (e.g., Nintendo and Mobile PS), public equipments (like those in stations and airports), palmtops, mobile phones, smart-phones etc. Main result of the visual multiplication, depending on the multiple screens is the re-definition of the individuals' seeing, which features are now:

- To be intermittent (it is a mosaic of not contextualized visual stimuli),
- To be mobile (i.e., it no more refers to the time passing for what is seen, but it is connected to the looking time of the people who transfer their look from one screen to another one) and
- To be interactive (what is seen is exactly what people likes to see, because people select it among many different screens).

For Rivoltella the multiplication of human seeing acts on at least the following two human dimensions:

- Knowing, which is no more stored and mono-visual, but is shared and multi-access,
- Living, which is no more situated in a physical space but is social (which means: to be in touch with the others while being connected on the Internet).

The most relevant implications are for mankind focused on the categories of being, which are much more involved in the above changes than the categories of perception: otherwise stated, there is no more contrast between real and virtual experiences (the last ones were always considered imaginary, before the digital revolution), and virtual life is a possible life at all, not less real and concrete than physical life.

Far from any reduction or simplification, the great deal of the hypotheses reported until now on the changes affecting mankind in the evolving world, ask for different questions:

- do different people react the same way to stimuli coming from digital equipment and digital environments?
- do new technologies impact the same on young people and elder people?
- do digital technologies influence the ways people learn and the connections between traditional education and virtual environments?
- do the above considerations apply to single subjects only, or analogous changes can be found in different contexts like communities, organizations and corporate?
- are there instruments and/or processes to be adopted which can help people, communities and organizations to overcome the difficulties they can meet in the knowledge society?

It is very important to remark here that most part of the above questions is not new and some scholars already tried to answer to them, but new and different explanations can be suggested today, and all of them give us different perspectives and frameworks for the description of the world we are immersed in.

M. Prensky (2001) has been one among the visionary interpreters of the new millennium society, because he remarked the difference between young and elder generations, and gave a possible explanation for the second question before it was asked for. He called "digital natives" the people born in a world populated of digital technologies, able in using them since their earliest instant of life, and called on the contrary "digital immigrants" those who had to learn the language and the use of new technologies, had to face the multiplicity of the contexts of interaction with digital equipments but never metabolized them.

Prensky definitions lead to hypothesize a positive answer for the second question, but do not explain the reasons for the differences detected in children and adults behaviours, when they are using new technologies and differently react to them.

Furthermore, the analysis of learning environments in the changing society, reported by many educators, tell us that formal education still is important for the growth of young generations, but the results from non formal and informal educational experiences, cannot be discarded, and are today much more important than in the past for the cultural growth of young generations.

On this side, a special attention must be given to the scheme reported in figure 1, proposed by M. L. Conner (2004), where possible displacements in the relevance of different learning environments on youth education and more generally people learning is drafted.

Undoubtedly the importance of informal education and unexpected learning has notably grown during last decades for the spreading of digital technologies, and new technologies have also deeply modified the ways of teaching and learning in traditional classes.

One of the consequences of the above issue has been the growing of the relevance that public institutions assigned to digital literacy and the changes in its meaning and definition in the last decades.

Figure 1. Map of different learning environments and learning strategies in today's society

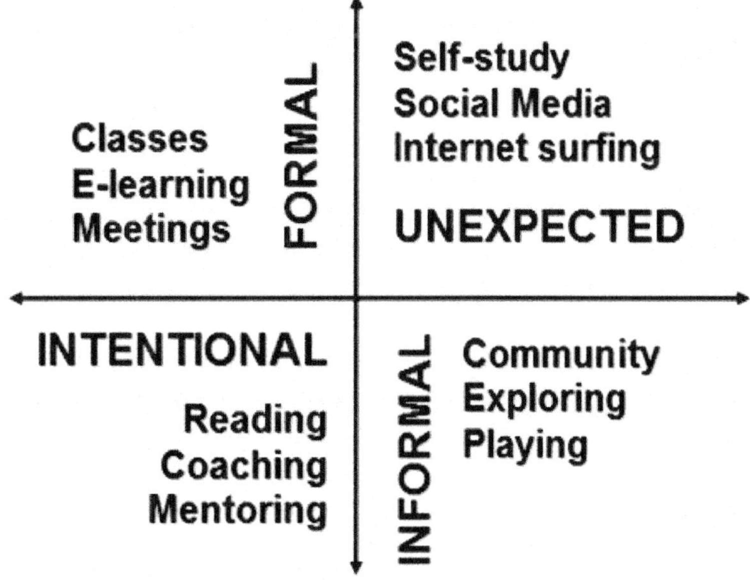

Many conceptual models have been developed to describe the features of new literacy proposals involving IT and ICT and some among the most relevant ones are reported below.

The Committee on Information Technology of the Computer Science and Telecommunications Board on the US National Research Council (1999), published the report "Being fluent with Information Technology"; as a result of this report educational institutions were explicitly invited to propose to the students training activities on the abilities specifically needed for the information society.

The Association of College and Research Libraries (2000) proposed the following definition for information literacy: "the group of skills needed for individual development in modern-day societies" and described the features of these skills.

The UNESCO (2002), on another hand, defined media education as that education allowing people to develop the understanding of the means of communication used in the society they live and setting them along the path for the acquiring of the necessary skills which are needed to use these means in relation to others. UNESCO considers these skills as an essential part of the civic training.

The ETS (2002) by working at the International ICT Literacy Panel developed a framework within which ICT literacy was defined and provided the foundation for the design and conduct of large-scale assessments and diagnostic tests. For ETS the literacy in ICT has the following meaning: "digital technology, communications tools, and/or networks, to access, manage, integrate, evaluate and create information in order to function in a knowledge society".

The basic differences between the above proposals can be grouped in the following two categories (Tornero, 2004):

- Scope: The ACRL proposal refers to information in general, regardless of the means through which it may be accessed; UNESCO refers to the means of communication in a broader sense; ETS confines itself to digital means;
- Framework of applicability: UNESCO makes its proposal within a framework of democratic society, and therefore within a collective context; the ACRL and the ETS make their proposals within the framework of individual competence, which is cognitive and technological.

Furthermore, if a sound digital literacy is important for people living in the knowledge society, much more important is considered today the development of a "digital competence" in those people.

Recently a great attention has been devoted to the impact that new technologies have on mankind, when passing from the discussion on how people use digital resources and processes, to the analysis of what they must know and be able to do with technologies. Otherwise stated, there has been a shift in the focus attention, from a discipline centered paradigm to a human centered paradigm: competences as active involvement of subjects with their representations of reality, their knowledge and skills are considered today much more important than the knowledge of instruments and processes (Le Boterf, 1990).

Notwithstanding the efforts reported above the following issues remain emblematic for the understanding of the contradictions present in our life, and they show how difficult it can be to try answering to the questions asked before:

- The gap existing between "digital natives" and "digital immigrants" (both in learning styles and knowledge development) (Prensky 2001); otherwise stated, young people can use digital equipments to better perform in getting information and communicating with respect to elders, and, what is more, new generations have different perception of reality and, usually, are more ready to act than to think about phenomena,

- The permanence, or the lowering, of the already low basic skills and competences in reading, writing and computing for students at different school levels (OECD 2009). This result seems to contradict what is reported in the item above, because it is usually recognized that the use of digital equipment implies the development of good information management skills (meta-cognitive skills),
- The basic skills and competences for lifelong learning, which are considered essential to let people be the citizens of the knowledge society. On this regard the Commission of the European Community approved a recommendation for all member countries, reporting the set of these competences. Digital competences, the fourth among them, are considered especially important because of their cross cultural features with respect to language (reading / writing) and calculus competences (Council of European Parliament 2005).

It can be easily deduced from the above issues that today, more than in the past, the acquisition of better knowledge, skills and meta-cognitive features from people, go hand in hand with the analysis of the environment people are immersed in, both on the sociological and technological sides.

Furthermore, when passing to communities and organizations, the role of digital technologies in the development of organizational knowledge and the influence they have on the evolution and transformation of tacit and explicit knowledge in individuals (Nonaka and Takeuchi, 1995), needs explanations and claims for deeper analysis.

New disciplines like Knowledge Management have been developed to let corporate and organizations build their own instruments and strategies for getting, retrieving, maintaining and sharing information and knowledge, and studies have been carried out to analyze the influence of the presence of management information systems (MISs) on communities. In some cases good results have been evidenced and the hope for future developments in the implementation of community practices into MISs has spread out, but no final answer on the instruments and the strategies to be adopted for the generalized use and application of digital equipments in these contexts has been found.

The attempt to answer the above questions and the need to deepen clarify new problems resulted in the writing of this book, and the issues reported until now induced to create five different sections for it.

The first section is devoted to the analysis of the problem of digital divide, and the need of new literacies. The second section discusses the connection between digital literacy and digital competence, and shows how relevant can be complex environments and social networks in education, when centered on the development of digital competences. The third section focuses on the application of the considerations developed before in some experiences of lifelong learning. The fourth section displaces the attention on the organizations and the fifth and last section on the whole society and some cultural aspects depending on IT/ICT.

The first section is made of three chapters. The first chapter, by P. Ferri (Digital and Inter-Generational Divide), discusses the digital and inter-generational divide, reports of the separation between the North and the South of the World and shows how great the problem still is also in the developed countries, especially in the field of education.

The second chapter, by L. Cervi, O. Paredes and J. M. P. Tornero (Current trends of Media Literacy in Europe: an Overview), gives an overview of media literacy in Europe. The authors map current practices in the implementation of media literacy in Europe and recommend measures to increase the level of media literacy.

In the third chapter, M. Fantin (Perspectives on Media Literacy, Digital Literacy and Information Literacy) says that the cultural landscape poses different challenges for teachers. Together with the development of reading and writing skills, it is necessary to emerge in the digital culture and master the different codes of the different languages. As a consequence, media cannot be excluded from literacy programs, it is essential to reflect on the definition of "being literate" today. The meanings of concepts like literacy, media literacy, digital literacy and information literacy need deeper analysis and re-signification.

The second section is made of five chapters. The first chapter, by A. Cartelli, V. Dagiene, and G. Futschek (Bebras Contest and Digital Competence Assessment: Analysis of Frameworks) focuses on the importance of IT/ICT supported informal education environments for students' learning, and especially for students' development of skills and competences. It starts from the description of the international competition "Bebras" and its features, and soon after discusses the structure of a framework for digital competence assessment, so that a double correspondence between them can be hypothesized:

- first, the framework can help the committee of the "Bebras" contest to create questions better facing the problem of assessing digital competences,
- second, the analysis of students' answers can suggest changes and improvements for the framework.

The second chapter, by A. Cartelli, (A Framework for Digital Competence Assessment), better explores the features of the framework reported in second chapter and suggest some improvements for it. While doing this job the following elements emerge:

- the privileged role of digital technologies in today society,
- the possible influence of the hypothesized framework on the people, who can be helped to become better persons and citizens,
- the research for hints, experiments, protocols and curricula, helping teachers in the design of better teaching activities.

The third chapter, by C. Giovannella (Beyond the Media Literacy: Complex Scenarios and New Literacies for the Future Education - The Centrality of Design), states that the advent of new media and web technologies has made "contents" and "containers" more liquid, and deeply reflects on the multi facets concept of literacy. He then proposes an experiential definition of literacy in education. According to such reflection, in the present scenarios, the "Design" becomes central to education, and underlines the need of educational activities which should include among their objectives the dissemination of what can be called "design literacy".

The fourth chapter in the section is by C. Petrucco (Wikipedia as Training Resource for Developing Digital Competences), and it discusses whether Wikipedia can be considered a valid resource for educational institutions like schools and Universities, or not. Undoubtedly, Wikipedia brings with itself the risk of incurring in mistakes, inaccuracies and plagiarism, but it is reliable and can be used in the curriculum as new approach for social and collaborative construction of knowledge. It can fully enter in educational contexts as an opportunity to reflect on the verification of information, on the ethical use of technology and on the role of democratic participation in social networking. Otherwise stated the creation and the maintenance of articles of Wikipedia as classroom activities, gives the opportunity for the activation of higher processes in cognitive development and on-line relationship, allowing the development of essential digital competences for life-long learning.

The fifth and last chapter by A. Pozzali and P. Ferri (The Medial Diet of University Students in Italy: An Exploratory Research), analyzes digital skills and competences of university students in Northern Italy. The starting point of the authors' analysis is the increase in the inter-generational digital divide accounting between "digital natives" and "digital immigrants", they evidence that, even if university students are familiar with digital technologies, the general possession of high level skills in accessing and using the Internet should not be taken for granted.

In the third section the development of digital competences is seen in a perspective of lifelong learning and five chapters discuss the different aspects of the problem.

The first chapter by L. Tateo and P. Adinolfi (Integrating Educational and ICT Innovations: A Case Study of Master Course), the effectiveness of new computer-supported collaborative problem solving educational approach in higher education at a master's course level is discussed. After outlining the technological and pedagogical characteristics of a new digital cooperative environment, as well as the constructivist, learner-centred philosophy of the Daosan Master (Management of Health-care Services) at the University of Salerno, the integration of the educational approach and the technological support is reported and discussed in an exploratory case-study. The authors observe that many post-graduate students are able to participate in a dense collaborative problem solving activity within a relatively short lesson period, working and reflecting on a real problem of healthcare management.

In the second chapter by A. Jimoyiannis and M. Gravani (Digital Literacy in a Lifelong Learning Programme for Adults: Educators' Experiences and Perceptions on Teaching Practices) some aspects of digital literacy in the context of a lifelong learning programme for social cohesion in Greece are analyzed. It especially explores the experiences and perceptions of eight adult ICT educators who used flexible instructional practices and adjusted them to adult learners' needs and interests. Additionally, the chapter reveals the difficulties that adults faced in the course while developing ICT literacy skills.

The third chapter by L. Corazza (Information Communication Technologies for Lifelong Learning: The Multimedia Documentation of Best Practices in Education), shows how self-instruction and lifelong learning are acquiring an increasing role due to Information Communication Technologies. These learning opportunities are connected to the worker ability of learning in autonomy throughout the entire span of life. Documentation of experiences, as a form of communication that allows tacit, unexpressed, informal knowledge, provides evidence that can be widely shared. In the conclusion of the chapter it is shown how audiovisual and multimedia documentation has proved to be a useful and efficient means of recording the experiences to be shared in knowledge management.

In the fourth chapter by F. Lazarinis and D. Kanellopoulos (E-Skills and ICT Certification in Greek Cultural and Travel Agencies: An Exploratory Study) the importance of the ICT skills for the enhancement and development of productivity in everyday work is analyzed. The authors report data on the demand for professionals with ICT skills, and show that it still exceeds the supply, especially in travel industry. Soon after they present the results of the study describing the impact of ICT certification on people working in travel agencies in Greece and consider the relevance and practical value of the e-skills acquired during training from tourist employers. It clearly emerges that the ECDL ICT certification plays a crucial role in cultural and travel agencies as their employees being technologically skilful can offer better services to their customers.

The fifth and last chapter, by E. Klekun (Digital Literacy for Health: The Promise of Health 2.0), outlines and challenges expectations and promises regarding the potential of the Internet and in particular Web 2.0 for empowering patients and citizens. The chapter focuses on the literacies required to make a meaningful (to the individual) use of these technologies for health and health care related purposes, and briefly discusses how these should be taught. The main conclusion is that digital literacy and health literacy are complex and challenging to many, and that the empowering claims are over-stated. As a result many traditional sources of information and advice will remain essential to maintaining quality of health care without a sound development of better digital competences.

The fourth section is made of three chapters and discusses the role of digital literacy in organizations and corporate. The first chapter is by C. De Pablos Heredero (Framework for the Experiences in Digital Literacy in the Spanish Market). The author starts by considering the information society as the society made by people, where the priority for the society development is the acquisition of knowledge in the digital society. But, being digitally literate means to have the technological capabilities letting persons survive in the information society; for that reason the chapter offers real examples of digital literacy development in a variety of areas of application: education, social inclusion and firms. Three main projects are described to support the contribution of digital literacy to the growth of Spanish people: the Educared, which promotes the spread of the Internet for innovation and pedagogical training amongst teachers, parents and students in primary and secondary schools; the Dana Project, which identifies good practices to reduce the digital gap based on gender; and the Competic, a program offering good practices for the promotion of information and communication technologies in small and medium size firms.

The second chapter is by A. Cartelli (Frameworks for the Benchmarking of Digital and Knowledge Management Best Practice in SME and Organizations), and discusses the effects that IT/ICT have on subjects and organizations. The proposal of frameworks for digital competence assessment and the construction of suitable instruments helping students in the acquisition of this competence are the main reason for the transfer to Small and Medium Enterprises (SME) and organizations of analogous instruments and processes. To hit the target the author compares knowledge phenomena in the subjects, with the strategies of knowledge management in the organizations. Soon after he describes the features of the framework for the benchmarking of best practices in SME and organizations on the basis of the results formerly obtained with virtual campuses. At last the instruments to be adopted for the acquisition of further information from all stakeholders and from the best practices to be shared are analyzed, and possible interventions towards the improvement of digital processes in SME and organizations are discussed.

The third and last chapter is by C. De Pablos Heredero and D. López (Free Software Implementation Experiences for the Promotion of the Liquid Society), and discusses the changes induced by information and communication technologies on citizens inter-operation with Public Administrations. By following the authors' ideas digital literacy is the key for the development of the "Liquid Society" and, public administrations must lead the actions for promoting more efficient, universal and user oriented public services. The migration to open source standards allows public administration offering more democratic and efficient channels for establishing relationships with citizens and the authors support their idea by showing the results of some international experiences which describe the migration of Public Administrations towards open source software, in order to promote digital literacy in the contexts they operate. They also report that the results depend at a great extent on contextual and organizational factors, as for example the need to change, the political support, the existence of available technological resources, the organizational climate, the motivation of the human resources and the kind of leadership for the project or the organizational complexity.

The fifth and last section is made of three chapters and analyzes the relationship between digital technologies and tradition, or more generally culture. The first chapter is by E. Lastrucci and A. Pascale (Cooperative Learning Through Communities of Practice) In this chapter the authors first recall what a community is, a group of individuals building a "community of practice" when a mutual engagement is established between themselves. Soon after the authors explain that main aim of a community of practice is to find the solution to problems by sharing experiences. As a conclusion they state that communities of practice can be seen as communities of self-managed learning, where professional development is not based on preset training courses, but on the sharing of experiences, on the identification of best practices and on the help that people give each other while facing daily problems. At last the authors remark that until now cooperative learning, which is recognised as one of the best teaching methods and an effective strategy, has been limited to traditional training contexts, but it can also be carried out on teaching work by involving the Web, and especially by using online teaching.

The second chapter is by I. Cantón and C. Morán (Levels of Self-Efficacy among Harassed Teachers). The authors first examine the differences among harassed teachers and unharassed ones, as regards coping strategies, self-efficacy, and locus of control. They conduct a survey over 255 teachers (163 women and 92 men) with a set of three questionnaires: the Mobbing Perceived Questionnaire, a battery of control expectancies, and the Brief COPE to assess, respectively, mobbing perceived at work, self-efficacy, locus of control, and coping strategies. The authors explain that the efforts made by educational organizations for preventing mobbing need to be intensified, and new technologies must play a more relevant role in collecting data, monitoring processes and making available all information on those phenomena.

The third and last chapter is by A. I. T. Kiser, T. Porter, and D. Vequist (Employee Monitoring and Ethics: Can They Co-Exist?). The paper shows that advanced technologies that make possible the monitoring of employees in the workplace have led to controversies on both legal and ethical grounds. Employers can now easily monitor emails, Internet usage and sites visited, and keystrokes, as well as use GPS systems to track employees' movements throughout the day. At one end of the spectrum is the employer who claims that monitoring not only improves productivity but is a legal necessity that assists in keeping the company from becoming legally liable for employees' misuse of technology. Employees, on the other hand, want their privacy protected, and many believe that it is more a matter of them not being trusted. In this chapter, a survey is presented that describes various forms of workplace surveillance and monitoring, viewpoints of both employers and employees, policies that companies have implemented, and the ethical and legal implications of such policies.

Antonio Cartelli
University of Cassino, Italy

REFERENCES

ACRL. (2000). *Information literacy competency standards for higher education.* Chicago, IL: Association of College & Research Libraries.

Committee on Information Technology Literacy. (1999). *Being fluent with information technology.* Washington, DC: National Academy Press.

Conner, M. L. (2004). Andragogy and pedagogy. *Ageless Learner*, 1997–2004. Retrieved Dec 7th 2011, from http://agelesslearner.com/intros/andragogy.html

Council of European Parliament. (2005). *Recommendation of the European Parliament and of the council on key competences for lifelong learning*. Retrieved June 1, 2010, http://ec.europa.eu/education/policies/2010/doc/keyrec_en.pdf

De Kerckhove, D. (1996). *La pelle della cultura: Un'indagine sulla nuova realtà elettronica*. Genoa, Italy: Costa & Nolan.

Educational Testing Service. (2002). *Digital transformation. A framework for ICT literacy. A report from the ICT Literacy Panel*. Princeton, NJ: ETS.

Heffernan, V. (2011). *The digital revolution. La clé des langues*. Retrieved October 27, 2011, from http://cle.ens-lyon.fr/93744078/0/fiche___pagelibre/

Le Boterf, G. (1990). *De la compétence: Essai sur un attracteur étrange*. Paris, France: Les Ed. de l'Organisation.

Lévy, P. (1994). *L'Intelligence collective. Pour une anthropologie du cyberespace*. Paris, France: La Découverte.

McLuhan, M., & Powers, B. (1989). *The global village*. New York, NY: Oxford University Press.

McLuhan, M., & Quentin, F. (1968). *Il medium è il messaggio*. Milan, Italy: Feltrinelli.

Nonaka, I., & Takeuchi, H. (1995). *The knowledge-creating company: how Japanese companies create the dynamics of innovation*. New York, NY: Oxford University Press.

OECD. (2009). *PISA 2006 technical report*. OECD. Retrieved June 1, 2010, from http://www.pisa.oecd.org/document/41/0,3343,en_32252351_32236191_42025897_1_1_1_1,00.html

Popper, K. (2002). *Cattiva maestra televisione* (G. Bosetti Ed.). I libri di Reset. Venice, Italy: Marsilio.

Prensky, M. (2001). Digital natives, digital immigrants. *Horizon*, *9*(5). doi:10.1108/10748120110424816

Rivoltella, P. C. (2006). *Screen generation. Gli adolescenti e le prospettive dell'educazione nell'età dei media digitali*. Milan, Italy: Vita e Pensiero.

Sartori, G. (1997). *Homo videns. Televisione e post-pensiero*. Rome, Italy: Laterza.

Tornero, J. M. P. (2004). *Promoting digital literacy: Understanding digital literacy*. Final report (EAC/76/03). Barcelona, Spain: UAB. Retrieved December 4, 2007, from http://ec.europa.eu/education/archive/elearning/doc/studies/dig_lit_en.pdf

UNESCO. (2002). *Recommendations addressed to the UNESCO*. Youth Media Education conference. Seville, 15-16 February 2002.

Section 1
Introduction

Chapter 1
Digital and Inter-Generational Divide

Paolo Ferri
University of Milan Bicocca, Italy

ABSTRACT

Digital divide can be considered a macro economical index representing the social differences and the separation between the North and the South of the world. Since the first definition of digital divide, it has been shown that it is also a great and unrecognized problem in the developed countries, especially in the field of education. "Digital disconnection" is a key problem for School and University as institutions. In this paper, the above questions are widely analyzed with a special attention on the spreading gap between digital natives (i.e., young students), and digital immigrants (i.e., parents, teachers and policymakers in the school).

THE GLOBAL CHALLENGE OF THE DIGITAL DIVIDE

We are aware that the more developed forms of capitalism are moving towards a new form of social configuration, the "information society" or the "access society" (Castells, 1996, 1997, 2000; Rifkin, 1995, 2000). This change is based on digital communication as "key technology" of the new millennium. G8 countries in the past twenty years have had continuous economic and social growth, despite the Gulf war, September 11 and the "new economy" crash in 2001 and the present Financial Global Crisis. This evidence is surely true for the G8 countries and perhaps for the OECD ones, but is it also true for the remaining 5/6ths of humanity? What about the effects and consequences of this mega change (Ferri, 2004), on this percentage of the population of the world? As Primo Levi said, it is strictly inherent the structure of the world, and represents the line up of the "doomed" but certainly not that of the

DOI: 10.4018/978-1-4666-0903-7.ch001

"saved", even if it is obviously impossible to give a complete answer to the pressing questions posed here. The issue of the *Digital Divide* is a worldwide theme and unfortunately not well known about in Italy (Zocchi, 2003; Tarallo, 2003).

Through the analysis of Arjun Appadurai's ideas we can evoke the "divergent globalization" concept (Appadurai, 1996), and at the same time Manuel Castells warns us about: "The problem of the internal differentiation of what was once the "third world", in the newly industrialized countries (the Pacific Rim area), relatively self-sustaining (China, India) and decomposing societies (Africa, Sub-Saharan, fourth world) have a lot to do with the different degrees of integration or adaptation of these societies for the processes of the information economy" (Castells, 1999, p. 44).

At the same time the phenomenon of mass migration from countries in "rapid decomposition" towards rich countries is correlated to the development of the information economy, just as the topics of the intercultural integration, internal security of developed countries and even of international terrorism is. For example, the January 9, 2002 issue of the Italian newspaper "Corriere della Sera" published an insightful article written by the ex US President, Bill Clinton. The article began: "This new century poses an important question: is the era of interdependence (or we could say of digital globalization) for mankind good or evil? The answer depends on several factors: on the fact that we rich nations today diffuse the advantages and reduce the tribulations of the world; on the fact that the poor nations make the necessary changes for progress to take place; on the fact that we all are able to develop a high enough level of conscience to understand what our reciprocal obligations and responsibilities are". Clinton's reasoning centers the question of the relationship among the international crisis, globalization, security and "access" as the benefits of the digital revolution, which the attack on the Twin Towers September 11 dramatically showed us.

A few lines later, Clinton writes: "The terrorist attacks on September 11 were a manifestation of globalization and interdependence as much as the explosion of the economic growth was. We cannot insist on having all the advantages without also seeing the other side of the story. It is very important therefore, to consider the war against terror in the broadest context of the question of how to manage our worldwide interdependence".

The question which we should ask ourselves therefore is the following: how is it possible to use the new technologies to decrease and not increase the divide between rich and poor countries? How is it possible therefore, to give to the 5/6ths of humanity access to the huge quantity of information, communication and opportunities for emancipation, which global content providing has circulated inside the "second Minneapolis flow economy". And these global questions are challenging also for the second topic we will try to point out in this essay: how we can manage the intergenerational divide.

In the "fortress of the west", in fact, the end of the mass media era and the dawn of the digital media era, create great opportunities for economic, cultural and civil growth which are available to the social organization and the political choices; but what happens outside our cities which are more and more networked and informationalized? And what happens "inside the western fortress" to the people with socio-economic disadvantages or to the elderly who we will define "digital immigrants" (Prensky, 2001)?

THE DIGITAL REVOLUTION AS A GLOBALIZATION FACTOR

Let us try to analyze the question from a global point of view. Information Communication Technology constitutes the *condition sine qua non* and the backbone of globalization (1). That the development of *Information Communication*

Technology is a central factor in establishing globalization has been shown, years ago, from the data made available by UNO and published in their 2001 report dedicated to the Digital Divide, entitled *Making New Technologies Work for Human Development* (UNO, 2001). And the data we report are still effective now except for some areas in India and China:

a. First, it is essential to consider technological growth, with regard to the speed and quantity of exchanged data: a greater quantity of information could be sent on a single optic fiber cable in 2001 than on the entire Internet network in one month in 1997.
b. Second, the transmission cost of a Gigabit (a billion bit) of information from Boston to Los Angeles was about US$150 in 1970 and is US$.12 cents today (AA. VV., 2001). This trend will certainly continue and there are some empirical laws that describe this phenomenon; Moore's law forecasts the doubling of computer power every 18-24 months, while Gilder's law forecasts, thanks to fiber optic technologies, the doubling of the transmission capacities of the telecommunication networks every 6 months. And these laws are realistic also today in 2008.
c. Third, Internet diffusion: in 1995 there were 16 million users, growing to about 400 million in 2000. In 2005, according to the research of Forrester and Gartner, there were over a billion users; and in 2008 the unbelievable value of 1.5 billion users was hit, as shown in Table 1. 1.5 billion is the number of people present in the developed and affluent nations; they will rapidly become a *connected society*. (In March, 2008 there were more than 1,407,000,000 Internet users worldwide. Considering the estimated world population at 6,676,000,000, about one in six people today use Internet. www.internetworldstats.com/stats.htm)
d. Fourth, as Noam Chomsky (1998) showed, the volume of financial transactions reached and exceeded about $200 billion a day; the types of transactions have changed over time: 30 years ago 90% of the trade was tied to volume "real" economy (commerce, long term investments), today the trade is short term (often lasting less than a day) of currency and interest rates. A conspicuous volume of the shares of financial operations is often speculative which takes place integrally in a "molecular" immaterial manner. (See Figure 1)

Now, the new information economy, or the new cultural capitalism, is based on two factors. On one hand, there is the increased ability to elaborate and exchange data and information. On the other hand, there is the exponential growth of hi-tech companies with respect to companies with a medium or low technological impact. Furthermore the new economy depends on the passage from a material exchange economy to an "experience economy" (Rifkin, 2000), and therefore on the exchange of services with a highly symbolic, cultural and informational contents.

The UNO data corroborated by recent Forrester, Gartner and IWS statistics show that digital technologies were an exponential growth factor for the economic and productive inequality between the rich and poor nations. As reported in Table 1 more than 1.3 billion users of Internet live in the OECD countries or in parts of China and India which are exponentially growing.

The table very eloquently shows the asymmetry in the access to the contents of the system of global *content providing;* the quick exchange of huge quantities of data is probably the main factor for the birth of the new economic and the social configurations which have been analyzed above.

Furthermore the figures show the enormous "divide" between rich and poor nations, between democratic nations and "scoundrel nations". They

Figure 1. World internet penetration rates by geographic regions

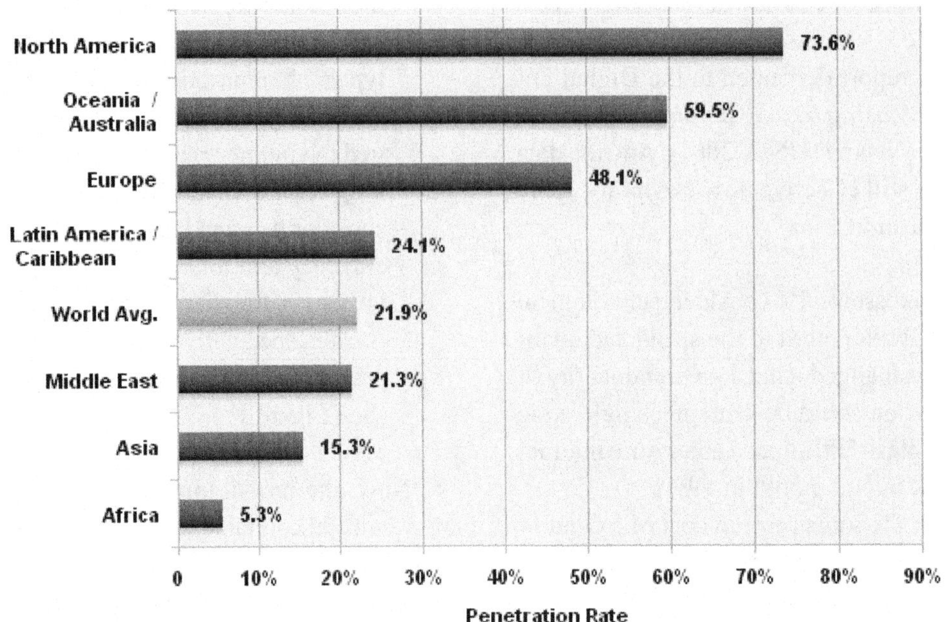

Source: Internet World Stats - www.internetworldststs.com/stats.htm
Penetration Rates are based on a world population of 6,676,120,288 for mid-year 2008 and 1,463,632,361 estimated Internet users.
Copyright © 2008, Miniwatts Marketing Group

Table 1. World Internet users and population stats

World Regions	Population (2008 Est.)	Internet Users Dec/31, 2000	Internet Usage, Latest Data	% Population (Penetration)	Usage (% of World Pop.)	Usage Growth 2000-2008 %
Africa	955,206,348	4,514,400	51,065,630	5.3	3.5	1,031.2
Asia	3,776,181,949	114,304,000	578,538,257	15.3	39.5	406.1
Europe	800,401,065	105,096,093	384,633,765	48.1	26.3	266.0
Middle East	197,090,443	3,284,800	41,939,200	21.3	2.9	1,176.8
North America	337,167,248	108,096,800	248,241,969	73.6	17.0	129.6
Latin America/ Caribbean	576,091,673	18,068,919	139,009,209	24.1	9.5	669.3
Oceania / Australia	33,981,562	7,620,480	20,204,331	59.5	1.4	165.1
WORLD TOTAL	6,676,120,288	360,985,492	1,463,632,361	21.9	100	305.5

(Source: World Internet Statistics, http://www.internetworldstats.com/stats.htm, 24 August 2008).

can be read through a form of *lateral thinking,* which clearly shows how the regions and the nations that support today's international terrorism are those which are more underdeveloped and where new technologies are less diffused. Societies which are more open are therefore exposed to greater risks, while societies closed to development are open to fundamentalism and terrorism. Democracies or "info-cracies" against totalitarianisms, hierocracies and autocracies: is this the future scenario?

It is not possible to determine if the above issue is completely right, but the above ideas are confirmed by an UNO data report which presents a "worldwide classification" of the most developed societies and takes into consideration four parameters:

- the degree of technological innovation and the development attained in the ICT area
- the diffusion of innovation in the high tech sector
- the diffusion of innovation in traditional sectors (telephone and energy sectors)
- the relative parameters that are defined by UNO as "human advancement and training" which corresponds to the level of well-being and education of a nation

Here it is also easy to observe how all the areas of the world "in decline", using a colorful expression of Castells, belong to "marginalized" countries or they are not even present in the classification, a sign that the necessary data is not available in order to be put into this table (Castells, 1996).

THE ECONOMY OF EXCLUSION

The difference which marks the globalized economy, the *digital divide,* represents the main obstacle to overcome, in order to transform the network age into an opportunity for everyone.

Until today, the globalization era has meant the concentration of access in economically developed countries, the oligopoly of the production of software and hardware by a few companies (with the exception of some distributed communities like that working on the Linux Open Source Operating System) up until the "imposition" of some Microsoft standards and protocols (see the EU Anti-trust case against Microsoft http://europa.eu/rapid/pressReleasesAction.do?reference=IP/08/318&guiLanguage=de).

Up until now, hi-tech globalization has paradoxically created more closure than opening on the part of the underdeveloped societies and inside the developed countries (economical and intergenerational divide), while has served as an economic and democratic multiplier for the "happy few" connected people in the developed West. It has therefore generated a further block and a restriction of communication and information spaces, other than survival.

An example on this regards can be the iconoclast hate and the violence against the western culture and the information spreading manifested by the past Taliban regime in Afghanistan or the Iranian regime today. The same violent animosity against the West also favored the affirmation of a "resistance identity" (Castells, 1997; Rikfin, 2000, ch. 10) which increased the real and imaginary antagonism of underdeveloped countries towards western and developed nations. They are considered, in fact, a source of oppression, both from the economic and the cultural front. Thus, "digital globalization" has favored and not contrasted the most violent impact of the religious or ethnic fundamentalisms. Does this reaction also affect the digital "immigrant" in the developed country, in terms of reaction to the use and dissemination of the digital tool inside the classroom and the institutions not directly connected with the business world?

NEW ACCESS POLITICS?

As Clinton said in the article after September 11 in 2001, "We have to create more opportunities for those who have been left behind from progress ... to convince new partners that the wealthy world has to accept its own obligation to promote more economic opportunities and to contribute to reduce poverty"; and we may add, to reduce the socio-economical and intergenerational divide in developed countries.

This possibility exists, as some indications in the UNO report and recent scholarly literature show (Papert, 1996; Aptech, 2001; Cheung, 2000; Mehra, Merkel & Bishop, 2004); otherwise stated we can answer positively, though cautiously, to the above requests. Through appropriate international policies, the use of two intrinsic characteristics of the digital media is favored: their molecular media and the fact that they are particularly capable of creating a collaborative network economy. As regards the first point, or the characteristic which distinguishes *digital media* from *mass media,* it is the difference which Pierre Lévy identifies between the *molar media* and the *molecular media.* The first are based on a one to many communicative structure, and are addressed to the individuals to the masses, each one the same as the other; the second are based on a many to many model of interactive bidirectional communication. In this sense, the network can come about; it can be an effective instrument of actions aimed at the local development of underdeveloped countries. As Pierre Lévy affirms, "The minimum ability to navigate in cyberspace is probably acquired in less time than the time it takes to learn how to read. Like literacy, navigating in cyberspace will be associated with other social economic and cultural benefits, with respect to the simple right to citizenship" (Lévy, 1994, p. 76). Furthermore, the big difference between molar and molecular media is based on the necessary cost scale and investments (financial, technological, human resource). To install, for example, a television network, the necessary investments are quite considerable; on the contrary, the molecular media economy, when implemented through open systems like Linux and other *open source* software, can be managed at the local level with relatively reduced costs. Therefore, it is possible to create activities which favor the birth of a network of small manufacturers and of local training institutions which create a small network of "personal or molecular entrepreneurs" (Bonomi, 1997).

The necessary cooperation of OECD countries could then be a "qualifying" intervention, according to the logic of Amartya Sen, Nobel Prize winner for economics, (Sen, 1999) whose logic we completely agree with. According to Sen, development is inseparably tied to freedom; in this perspective, the attention should be concentrated on all the measures which can increase the autonomous ability of the southern part of the world to grow and develop.

And the Amartya Sen issues, as we will show afterwards, are also effective against the generational divide inside the developed countries; setting up contexts, where youth digital native and older "digital immigrants" learn from each other and share digitally their memories, as we propose in our research project, are a good example on this regard. Going back to a global perspective we have many examples of this kind on international cooperation.

a. through the policies, like the promotion of the "molecular" diffusion of the digital technologies which can broaden the possibilities of individual undertakings (the reasoning developed by Sen on microcredit is analogous),
b. on the training, like the creation of an environmental context favorable to the extension of the market, without which neither development nor liberty can exist (Sen, 1999, p. 19-21).

A concrete example from the UNO report shows how it is possible to use the new technologies supporting what we explained. In India a series of experiments of this type have been

Figure 2. The OLPC device

developed to create a graphic interface which can allow illiterate people to navigate in cyberspace. It bypasses the problem of literacy that in third world countries is crucial. To overcome the barriers of the text based interfaces, several scholars of the Indian Institute of Science and Engineering of the Ancore Software design company in Bangalore designed a *touch-screen* application for Internet which costs less than $200 and is based on the Linux open source operating system. The first versions of the Simputer (http://www.simputer.org/simputer/about/) make it possible to access Internet and email in the local languages, through functions activated by a touch screen and also micro-banking applications. Future versions of the system use vocal recognition and software for the text trans-codification of the spoken word for illiterate users. Another more recent and exiting example is the OLPC project by Nicholas Negroponte, with Charles Kane, Jim Gettys, Seymour Papert, Alan Kay, and Antonio Battro. The One Laptop Per Child Association, Inc. (OLPC) is an American non-profit organization set up to oversee the creation of a cheap, affordable educational device for use in the third world (see Figure 2).

The current focus of OLPC project is the development, production and dissemination of the XO-1 software and OLPC device to promote children's education in developing nations. One Laptop Per Child is a 501(c)(3) organization registered in Delaware, USA. OLPC is funded by a number of sponsor organizations, including AMD, Bright Star Corporation, eBay, Google, Marvell, News Corporation, SES, Nortel Networks, and Red Hat. Each company has donated two million dollars.

The goal of the foundation is to provide children around the world with new opportunities to explore, experiment, and express themselves. For this reason OLPC has designed a cheap laptop, OS educational software, manufacturing base, and distribution system to provide children outside of the first-world with otherwise unavailable technological learning opportunities. The OLPC Organization gives children the OLPC and sets up training session to make access to Internet easy for children in disadvantaged countries. OLPC lists five core principles:

1. Child ownership
2. Low ages. Both hardware and software are designed for elementary school children ages 6-12
3. Saturation
4. Connection
5. Free and open source

These examples show how the connection between technologies and liberties, education and civil rights is concrete. This is because one of the biggest advantages of the new digital communication technologies is the huge contribution of information and training per time and cost unit with respect to the analogical media.

The access to the benefits of the information economy can mean not only inclusion but also economic, cultural, religious and political opportunity. If concrete international policies are brought about, it can mean greater democratization of the social development processes and greater respect for reciprocal diversities.

Also from this point of view the services of the new economy of digital *content providing* can become a lever to knock down the digital divide which they created. It is a possibility, a choice with risky implications. It is the choice which favors radical free trade at the global level, which does not define fair rules for the subdivision of natural resources, like the information and technological ones. This approach will only widen the divide, and not only the digital one between all the North and South of the world.

The choice is in our hands and it is a crucial one, as our fathers in the NCP Protocol affirmed, the ancestor of the Internet in 1968: "if the network remains confined to a privileged elite population, the network will only exasperate the differences between intellectual opportunities. Instead, if the idea of the network should remain, like we hoped when we designed it, an aid for education, and if all minds should react positively, then the benefit for mankind will certainly be immense" (Licklider & Taylor, 1968).

INTERNAL DIGITAL DIVIDE AND THE INTERGENERATIONAL DIGITAL DIVIDE

The digital divide is not only a macro economical and social North-South issue, but it is also a big and mostly unrecognized problem inside the developed countries, as we pointed out before. We know at least two other forms of "internal digital divide"; the divide between the center (megalopolis, towns and well connected cities) and the peripheral areas (countryside, mountains, disadvantaged areas and ghettos) that is well designed in Castells and Himanen works (Castells, 1996, 1999, 2000, 2001; Castells & Himanen, 2002) and the second and less known form of divide that was focused on first by Seymour Papert in his work *Connected Family* (1996). Papert's prophetical essay can help us outline the key points of the generational digital divide problem. What does Papert mean with the word connected or disconnected family? Let's hear Papert's voice: "I use that term 'connected family' as the name of a book, playing on two meanings of connected, of course. Talking about the fact that we connect through the Internet, but also about whether we connect or don't connect inside the family" (Schwartz, 1999). Papert goes on to point out that there's a widespread fear, more or less justified, about the possibility that computers inside the home and classroom are going to disconnect the family and the schools itself. The almost justified fear is that digital technology can create a deep generational gap between the young digital kids and their "Gutenberg" teachers and parents. "Already the television was a conversation killer in the home. This can be more so" (Schwartz, 1999). The following step of Papert's way of describing the way of handling and trying to solve this "new" problem—in 1996 it was new—is the analysis of the presence of computers and digital networks inside society, families, and classrooms and how they can strengthen rather than weaken the connection between kids and adults. In Papert's, almost optimistic view, computers and digital networks can help to overcome the intergenerational divide if parents and teachers are going to connect with children, playing the digital play with them, as it happens in Mamamedia (www.mamamedia.com) the large community (2) (5.4 million young subscribers) that Papert founded together with Idit Harel Caperton (the today CEO of the project) in 1995. MaMaMedia.com is a pioneer Internet dot-com that focuses on promoting digital literacy and creative learning skills for children and their parents. Basing itself on the educational principles of constructivism, the site's goal is to allow children and their parents and teachers to access a vast selection of "playful learning" activities and projects. In applying Papert's constructivist theories, the site seeks to allow children worldwide the opportunity to grow creatively at their own pace, starting from a young age. For example, children using the site can create, save, and share their own animations, cartoons, stories, digital art and games with dynamic tools provided on the website, thereby creating a global exercise in experiential education. Papert believes that overcoming the inhibition and the fears parents and teachers have, often solicited by vendors of software which promise better results for their children, they can participate in the digital learning experiences of the kids, be more sympathetic and learn from the kids to better handle technology, sharing with children their experience, memories and knowledge in a language that the toddlers understand better. Papert has, in fact, the aim to encourage "Gutenberg native" to think about the technology in a new and friendlier way for their kids.

ARE THEY DIFFERENT? THE DIFFUSION OF DIGITAL TECHNOLOGY IN YOUNG AND VERY YOUNG CHILDREN

What Papert understood first in 1996 in *The Connected Family* is the fact that "digital natives" show a passionate and growing enthusiasm for computers and digital technology and this enthusiasm scares teachers, parents and scholars. Papert's 1996 statement today is a matter of fact also confirmed by a large amount of recent social, psychological and pedagogical research. We can quote the recent OECD New Millennium Learner report (Pedrò, 2008), which clearly points out Papert's previous intuition. "The speed at which technology penetrates children's and young people's lives mimics the rate of adoption at the home level, which runs very fast. According to the last PISA survey (2006), 86% of pupils aged 15 frequently (3) use a computer at home. As a matter of fact, in 21 out of the 30 OECD countries the actual percentage is higher than the mean, and in five countries it is higher than 95%. Based on the growth experienced in these rates since the previous PISA survey in 2003, it can be projected that by 2009 the frequent use of a computer at home will become a universal feature of young people aged 15 in most OECD countries" (4) (Pedrò, 2008). These kinds of data are coherent also with media preferences of the youth. In a UK recent research that is based on a questionnaire which asks the youth to express their preference in using six media, one-third of children aged 8 to 17 chose the Internet as their only choice if they could not have any other, surpassing TV, telephone and radio (BBC Monitoring International Reports, 2002). According to the OECD New Millennium Survey we can find serious evidence about the fact that very young children (0-6) also experience a great deal of exposure to computers. As quoted in the research of Calvert, Ridout, Woolard, Barr, and Strouse (2004), in the US there is a constant linear increase in the use of computer and digital devices in children aged 6 months to 6 years. Children start to handle computers modeling their parent's way of using them at the age of 2.5 years; and they start with an autonomous and quite finalized use of software and devices, such as simple video games or painting tools - at the age of 3.5. Obviously the socio-economic context is very relevant "already in 2006 children in the United States under the age of 6 almost universally lived in homes with television (98%), with a vast majority having computers (80%) and nearly half having videogame consoles as well (Rideout & Hammel, 2006, quoted in Pedrò, 2008). These data are also coherent with the results of the University of Milan-Bicocca "Children and Computers" qualitative research (Mantovani & Ferri, 2006, 2008) and they clearly show that "digital native" or, speaking in terms of the OECD report, New Millennium learners are very different from us, "Gutenberg native", for the simple fact that the they handle information and communication digital devices in a very natural way, when we have learned to use them as a second language. Using ICT tools for them is as natural as for us, when we were children, opening an illustrated book. What about digital immigrants? Marc Prensky, famous consultant in new technology and author of "Don't bother me Mom—I'm learning!" (Prensky, 2006) synthesizes the phenomenon in this way: "Today's students—K through college—represent the first generations to grow up with this new technology. They have spent their entire lives surrounded by and using computers, videogames, digital music players, video cams, cell phones, and all the other toys and tools of the digital age. Today's average college grads have spent less than 5,000 hours of their lives reading, but over 10,000 hours playing video games (not to mention 20,000 hours watching TV). Computer games, email, the Internet, cell phones and instant messaging are integral parts of their lives" (Prensky, 2001).

NOTE THE DIFFERENCE: THE DIGITAL NATIVE WAY OF THINKING

Following Wim Veen, the Netherlander scholar who wrote the brilliant essays *Homo Zappiens* (Veen & Vrakking, 2006) we can note that the way the digital native learns is in some way different from the way we, Gutenberg native, think and learn.

We can summarize the difference between digital native and Gutenberg Native in Figure 3 (modified from Veen & Vrakking, 2006).

In other words, what we can underline is the fact that the learning skills of digital native have evolved and they have a new form of understanding of the world, which is very unusual for us digital immigrants. In the Digital background instead of internalizing knowledge, "put memory first" and reflection, we can see the growing importance of social and communication skills. Moreover, the process of externalizing knowledge is more and more important. Scholars in education have stressed this social activity of learning even before technology became predominant in the lives of young learners; and this kind of skill is now really insisted on with the astonishing growth of digital devices for communication and learning (Ferri, 2008). The other very important difference between digital native and digital immigrants is the nature of the code they use to communicate and learn with. Our digital immigrant way of learning and communicating was mostly devoted to the alphabetic writing code, the book was the king, and the text had monumental authority (as McLuhan pointed out in the sixties). Now out of the Guttenberg Galaxy things are changing. The digital native lives, at least in developed countries, in a "multi-screen" society. When they are toddlers they see their parents using ICTs and also they begin to use ICTs very early. They get in touch with this new socio-technological environment in the first days of their lives; and this really changes their way of seeing, learning, and constructing their internal and social world. They are

Figure 3. Digital immigrants and native communicating and learning skills

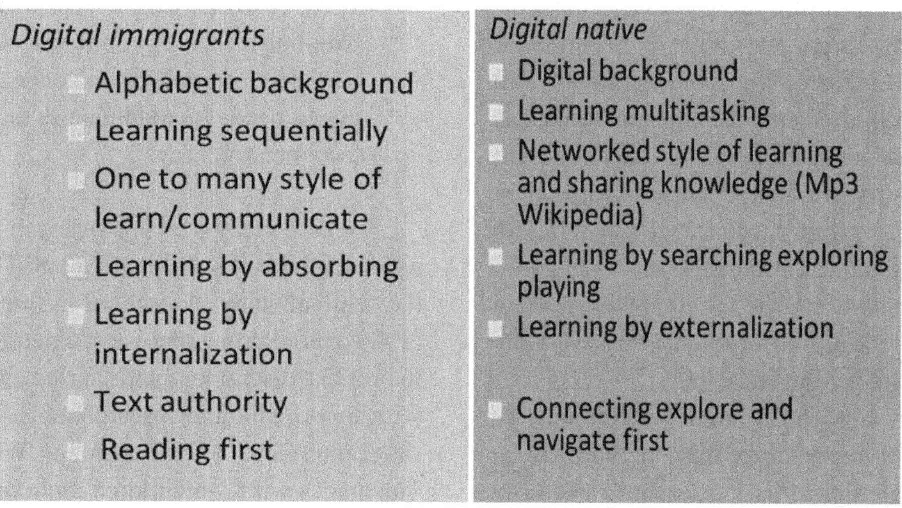

used to a multimodal approach to communications and learning. They experiment knowledge in a digital multimedia way, and in contrast with our Gutenberg native experience which is mostly alphabetical, their brain frame is audio visual, graphic, iconic and "also" alphabetic. Their brain frame (De Kerchove, 1991) is digitally augmented, also digitally deprived and is focused on these attitudes (Veen & Vrakking, 2006):

- high speed
- multi tasking
- non linear approaches
- iconic skills first
- connected
- collaborative and creative
- learning by searching and playing
- learning by externalizing

Lots of parents and teacher understand the need for a mega change in schools and education systems, but very few especially in Italy, Southern Europe, understand what to do practically; in England and Northern Europe it is different: "In the Netherlands, a variety of innovative schools have started recently to work along new lines. In addition, parents who no longer accept traditional schools have started schools that are based on the ideas and ideals of the Sudbury Valley School in the USA and the Summer Hill School in the UK. When comparing these educational experiments it is interesting to see that all of them have adopted four major organizational, pedagogical and curricular changes" (Veen, 2007). These experiments are based, according to Veen experience, on a new organization of school curricula: longer lessons and training time (4-hour periods), interdisciplinary themes, new set up of the scholastic building (Ferri, 2008) with working areas for 1 to 100 students and continuous individual learning paths (all inside a digital augmented classroom).

The Veen statements are also confirmed by the research project "Children and Computers" carried out by the University of Milan-Bicocca and led by Susanna Mantovani and myself (Mantovani and Ferri, 2006, 2008). The goals of the research are to explore the ways in which preschool children (3-6 year olds) approach the use of new technologies in educational environments, both at home and at school, by observing their first spontaneous approaches to computers, the changes in their constant use of this tool, their cognitive strategies and relational modalities. Our research aims are:

1. to observe the ways in which preschool children (3-6 year olds) approach computers both at home and at school. In particular we will focus on the spontaneous ways in which children approach the tool as well as on those mediated by adults/other children;
2. to identify children's behavior while they interact with new technologies in different educational environments such as:
   a. at home, where the computer is both a working tool for adults and an everyday tool for the family;
   b. in educational environments outside the home, where the computer will be introduced as the teacher's working tool, and if necessary, as an exploratory tool for the child or group of children (individual or shared exploration);
   c. in educational environments outside the home, where computers are already used as pedagogical tools (observations will be targeted at the identification of children's behavior when they use both computers and the Young Explorer multimedia workstations);
3. to learn the knowing, exploring and learning strategies activated during the children's interaction with these tools (for example, by recording a dialogue between a child and an adult or between different children in front of a computer, and introducing challenges which alter the interaction and thus prompt reactions in the single child, in the interaction between children, etc.);
4. to call in parents and teachers to discuss the observational data (video recordings and observations) regarding both the environments where the observation took place and many others in order to prompt comparisons, comments and interpretations;
5. to develop support pathways for parents and educators. The findings we get after a five year project are very interesting and confirm that the differences between "native" and immigrants are huge (Mantovani & Ferri, 2006, 2008). Directly observing the children handling technology and exploring their potential, we particularly note these emerging phenomena: the toddlers use technology in a cooperative way.

The core method of this research follows the approach taken by Tobin, Wu and Davidson in the seminal study "Preschool in three cultures" (1989) and combines the use of video as a 'stimuli' to provoke discussions and sharing among adults with some qualitative research tools, such as narrative interviews and focus groups. We have done videotapes with 3-6 children and computers (at home and in preschool) and we have used them not "primarily" as data, but as tools to stimulate a multi-vocal dialogue (Bove, 2004). Three municipal preschools have been involved in our research and others will be involved in the future (*Scuola Comunale Clericetti, Milan; Scuola Andersen, Vimercate, Scuola Costa, Milan; these schools are also part of the "Bambino autore project",* www.bambinoautore.org*)*. So far, videotapes have been discussed with teachers and the discussion will be extended to parents in the second phase of our research (Bers, New & Boudreau, 2004).

We assume that the way in which children explore and use computers (individually, with other children or with adults) is strictly linked to the adults' ideas and beliefs, and to their educational models and representations. In our study the voices of parents and teachers will therefore enrich our interpretations and extend the repertoire of possible educational practice with technologies. We also assume that by studying the way in which children approach computers we will promote higher awareness of how children can be considered as "scaffholders" of a broader collaborative experience of learning based on the use of digital technologies.

We will also conduct some micro-experiments using our previous findings as the starting point for creating settings of "semi-experimental observations"; this will help us create educational settings for cooperative learning and e-learning with children. The results of our research add interesting "field evidence" to our comprehension of the digital native way of constructing the world. The data of our research on Italian children and the others researches we have quoted allow us to hypothesize that the use of ICT changes the cognitive skills of children and young people in many ways. According to our Italian research data:

a. The use of digital devices stresses a multitasking use of media. Our research parents and teachers' focus group results prove that they strongly agree with this idea. Their children use a multitasking approach in gaming, playing and learning. Sometimes they feel this difference with fear, they are not able to act this way.
b. Cooperative learning is the way children adopt also when they are very young, 3-6 year olds, in approaching computers and ICT. As our observation testifies, they very rarely stay alone when they are using a computer at school.
c. Learning by doing ICT and learning with ICT is strongly preferred by the children we observed, emphasizing the need for meta-reflection on practical experience led by teachers.
d. On-line communication, especially instant messaging, messaging etc. has a very widespread pattern of use of ICT (mobile phone Instant messaging) also in the 6-10 year old age group. In Italy the use of the mobile phone is a tool used by particularly all children, both to communicate with peers (mostly with text, SMS) and with parents (voice communication). In Italy parents use mobile phones with children not only to communicate but also as control/care tool. Mobile phones, in Italy have become a mediated tool for parental care. In school the mobile phone is forbidden and teachers are very concerned about the children's use of such a technological tool. In the same way they are very concerned about video game and video User Generated Content.
e. The children at home, as testified from our observation, learn from parents using a modeling style; at school this style is very rarely adopted by the teachers.
f. In Italy immigrant children are particularly fond of ICT (Skype at the Internet café, e-mail, etc.) because they are useful for them to keep in touch with relatives. They can help with their integration in school because they have excellent skills to share with peers and teachers.
g. In our view children often dislike educational software because these software are far worse designed and low budget than video game and commercial web sites on the Internet.

Other hints that have come up from our qualitative research are the following:

In Italy the digital native (Prensky, 2001) phenomenon begins relatively late. It starts with children born after 1993, not earlier. This is probably because of the gap with the US and Northern Europe in the spread of computers at home and in schools. The first serious government plan for new media introduction in schools began in 1996 PSTD (Plan for the development of instructional technology).

In Italy the use of ICT is a domestic phenomenon, the use in school is rare and only a few days per month. In fact, there's a big divide between the family and social appropriation of ICT and the primary and secondary schools use.

To conceptualize this phenomenon we can speak of "multiple intelligence" at work for digital natives (Gardner, 1993) through multimedia devices: the digital kids show a variety of way of constructing and reframing the world, with strong emphasis on video, graphical and musical intelligence (Caron & Caronia, 2007). We don't know if this means the end of the alphabetic world, but we can say that the digital natives are moving from an "only alphabetic" paradigm in learning and teaching (Bolter & Grusin, 1999). And are the adults aware of this problem? Are they really aware of the challenge of the "natives" to our cultural heritage and traditions? Are they conscious of the huge relevance of the generational divide problem? Let's analyze this last problem.

WHAT DOES GENERATIONAL DIGITAL DIVIDE MEAN?

To better understand the generational divide it is necessary to understand what digital immigrants feel and think about the technology of the digital immigrants. "The importance of the distinction is this: As Digital Immigrants learn—like all immigrants, some better than others—to adapt to their environment, they always retain to some degree, their "accent," that is, their foot in the past"(Prensky, 2001). The "digital immigrant accent" can be detected in many ways; for example, turning to the Internet for information second rather than first, or in reading the manual for a program rather than assuming that the program itself will teach us to use it. Most of the digital immigrants had to learn this second language to maintain their job in the age of the "digital revolution" (1996-2000). They learn, except for a small amount of advanced knowledge workers, to use ICT for making money and to better organize their work They do not consider first ICT a communitary and identitary medium. The elders, inside a Gutenberg Mass society, were "socialized" differently from their kids; and are now in the process of learning a new language. And a language learned later in life goes into a different part of the brain. "There are hundreds of examples of the digital immigrant accent. They include printing out your email (or having your secretary print it out for you – an even "thicker" accent); needing to print out a document written on the computer in order to edit it (rather than, just editing on the screen); and bringing people physically into your office to see an interesting web site (rather than just sending them the URL). I am sure you can think of one or two examples of your own without much difficulty. My own favorite example is: 'Did you get my email?'" (Prensky, 2001).

Form Gartner Research analysis (www.gartner.com) an interesting new paradigm in studying this phenomenon emerges, which we can synthesize in Figure 4.

In the same way we can split the population of OECD countries into:

1. Native
2. Generation V
3. Pure Emigrant

We have already spoken about the first group. The third group, the pure immigrants, is made up of people mostly over fifty years old who grew up without digital technology and adopted it later. A digital native might refer to their new "camera"; a digital immigrant might refer to their new "digital camera". This kind of immigrant has an instrumental or low use of the net, and the computer is difficult; except for the "silver surfer" who may understand properly the new frame of communications. But not all the immigrants are the same, especially the so called V generation. The Virtual generation is a generation of digital immigrant who can do something to manage the generational divide. They are immigrants who have understood the relevance of the problem. They are the baby boomers or younger immigrants who in their general behavior, attitudes and interests start to blend together in an online environment. The idea of Generation X (and later Generation Y) was conceived as a way of understanding new generations that appeared not to have connections to the culture icons of the baby boomers. However, as more baby boomers (who are living longer) and the younger generations go online and participate/communicate in a flat virtual environment, the

Figure 4.

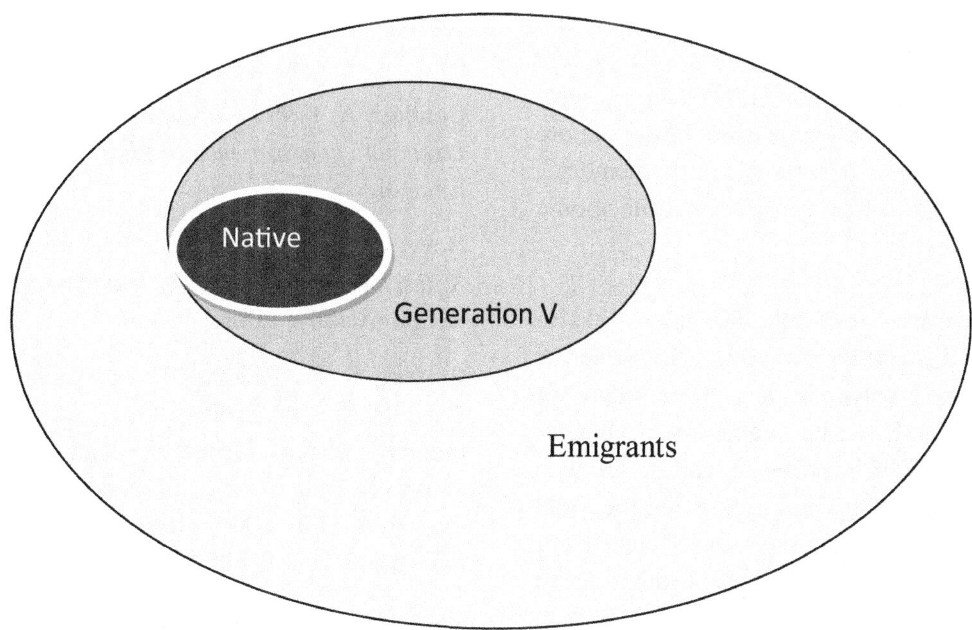

generational distinctions break down. Generation V hops across segments at various times of life for various reasons and is likely to act like several generations at any given time. "For Generation V, the virtual environment provides many aspects of a level playing field, where age, gender, class and income of individuals are less important and less rewarded than competence, motivation and effort", said Adam Sarner, principal analyst at Gartner. We are generation V members; what does that make the rest; what can we do to overcome the digital generational divide inside our home or classroom or society? How can those of us who were not born into the digital generation handle the problem?

CONCLUSION: DON'T BREAK THE MEMORY LINE!

We work with the aim to contribute to outline better the different dimensions of the digital generational divide problem. The goal of our qualitative action research project from a theoretical, methodological and experimental point of view, is to construct a bridge between digital native and digital immigrants. In more detail: the Memory Line project aims to train groups of elderly and young citizens, living in the project's partner countries, to collect records (stories, songs, poems, experiences, etc.) in order to ensure their conservation and dissemination. We aim to create a model of cooperation and inter-regional and intergenerational learning based on memory and communication, and to promote innovative experiences within the area of lifelong training. The main research issues are:

- How can the relationship between memory, knowledge and communication be affected by the passage from an analogical civilization to a digital civilization?
- How can this be translated into practice?

There are two intertwined topics in the project:

- Intergenerational digital divide: how do old and young people relate to new digital technologies? Are there relevant differences? Why? How can we "bridge the generational gap?"

- How can digital ICTs help to keep and hand down memories between generations? Is the "digitalization" of our culture leading to a general "loss of memory", or to the decrease in personal mnemonic abilities?

We have tried to accomplish these tasks in our research, working directly in the atelier of each country involved in the project, where we collected and shared the memories of younger people and elders in presence, and on the web (http://www.memoryline.org/). After the field phase we analyzed the data and sketched our theoretical framework and possible solutions to save the "memory line" from the generational digital storm. If we have succeeded or not, is up to the readers of the study.

REFERENCES

Appadurai, A. (1996). *Modernity at large: Cultural dimension of globalization.* Minneapolis, MN: University of Minnesota Press.

Aptech, E. (2001). Minimizing the digital divide and the intergeneration gap. *Ubiquity.* Retrieved June 12, 2009, from http://www.acm.org/ubiquity/

BBC Monitoring International Reports. (2002). *Coverage: April 2001 to date.* Retrieved July 15, 2009, from http://ds.datastarweb.com/ds/products/datastar/sheets/bbcm.htm

Beck, U. (1998). *Was ist Globalisierung? Irrtümer des Globalismus, Antworten auf Globalisierung.* Frankfurt am Main: Suhrkamp.

Bers, M. U., New, R. S., & Boudreau, L. (2004). Teaching and learning when no one is expert: Children and parents explore technology. *Journal of Early Childhood Research and Practice, 6*(2), 60–75.

Bolter, J. D., & Grusin, R. (1999). *Remediation. Understanding new media.* Cambridge, MA: MIT Press.

Bonomi, A. (1997). *Il capitalismo molecolare. La società al lavoro nel nord Italia.* Torino, Italy: Einaudi.

Bove, C. (2004). *Le idee degli adulti sui piccoli. Riflessioni e ricerche per una pedagogia culturale.* Bergamo, Italy: Edizioni Junior.

Calvert, S. L., Rideout, V. J., Woolard, J. L., Barr, R. F., & Strouse, G. A. (2004). Age, ethnicity, and socioeconomic patterns in early computer use: A national survey. *The American Behavioral Scientist, 48*(5), 590–607. doi:10.1177/0002764204271508

Caron, A. H., & Caronia, L. (2007). *Moving cltures. Mobile communication in everyday life.* Kingston, Ontario, Canada: McGill-Queen's University Press.

Castells, M. (1996). *The information age: Economy, society and culture. Vol. I: The rise of network society.* Malden, MA: Blackwell Publishers.

Castells, M. (1997). *The information age: Economy, society and culture. Vol. II: The power of identity.* Malden, MA: Blackwell Publishers.

Castells, M. (1999). Flows, networks, identities. In P. McLaren (Ed.), *Critical education in the new information age* (pp. 37- 64). New York: Rowman & Littlefield.

Castells, M. (2000). *The information age: Economy, society and culture. Vol. III: End of millennium.* Malden, MA: Blackwell Publishers.

Castells, M. (2001). *The Internet galaxy. Reflections on the Internet, business, and society.* New York: Oxford University Press.

Castells, M., & Himanen, P. (2002). *The information society and the welfare state. The Finnish Model.* Oxford, UK: SITRA.

Cheung, C. (2000). Identity construction and self-presentation on personal homepages: Emancipatory potentials and reality constraints. In D. Guantlett & R. Horsley (Eds.), *Web studies* (pp. 53-68). London: Arnold.

Chomski, N. (1998, December). Finanza e silenzio. In *Le monde diplomatique*.

De Kerckhove, D. (1991). *Brainframes: Technology, mind and business*. Utrecht, The Netherlands: Bosch & Keuning.

Drotner, K. (2000). Difference and diversity: Trends in young Danes' media use. *Media Culture & Society*, *22*(2), 149–166. doi:10.1177/016344300022002002

Ferri, P. (2004). *Fine dei Mass Media. Le nuove tecnologie della comunicazione e le trasformazioni dell'industria culturale*. Milano, Italy: Guerini & Associati.

Ferri, P. (2008). *La Scuola Digitale. Come le nuove tecnologie cambiano la formazione*. Milano, Italy: Bruno Mondadori.

Gardner, H. (1993). *Frames of mind: The theory of multiple intelligences*. New York: Basic Books.

Lévy, P. (1994). *L'intelligence collective: Pour une anthropologie du cyberspace*. Paris: La Découverte.

Licklider, J. C. R., & Taylor, R. W. (1968). Computer as communication device. In *Science and Technology* (pp. 61-87).

Mantovani, S., & Ferri, P. (2006). *Bambini e computer. Alla scoperta delle nuove tecnologie a scuola e in famiglia*. Milano, Italy: Etas.

Mantovani, S., & Ferri, P. (2008). *Digital kids. Come i bambini usano il computer e come potrebbero usarlo genitori e insegnanti*. Milano, Italy: Etas.

Mehra, B., Merkel, C., & Bishop, A. P. (2004). The internet for empowerment of minority and marginalized users. *New Media & Society*, *6*, 781–802. doi:10.1177/146144804047513

Papert, S. (1996). *The connected family: Bridging the digital generation gap*. Atlanta, GA: Longstreet Press.

Pedrò, F. (2006). *The new millennium learners, what do we know about the effectiveness of ICT in education and what we don't*. Retrieved July 15, 2009, from http://www.oecd.org/dataoecd/52/4/37172511.pdf

Pedrò, F. (2008). *The new millennium learner a project in progress*. Retrieved June 2006, from http://www.olis.oecd.org/olis/2008doc.nsf/ENGDATCORPLOOK/NT0000310E/$FILE/JT03245474.PDF

Prensky, M. (2001). Digital natives, digital immigrants. *Horizon*, *9*(5), 50–72.

Prensky, M. (2006). *Don't bother me mom—I'm learning*. Minneapolis, MN: Paragon House Publishers.

Rideout, V. J., & Hammel, E. (2006). *The media family: Electronic media in the lives of infants, toddlers, preschoolers and their parents*. Menlo Park, CA: Henry J. Kaiser Family Foundation.

Rifkin, J. (1995). *The end of work: The decline of the global labor force and the dawn of the post-market era*. New York: Putnam's Sons.

Rifkin, J. (2000). *The age of access: the new culture of hypercapitalism, where all of life is a paid-for experience*. New York: Tarcher/Putnam.

Schwartz, D. (1999). *Ghost in the machine: Seymour Papert on how computers fundamentally change the way kids learn* (Interview with Seymour Papert by Dan Schwartz). Retrieved May 1, 2009, from http://www.papert.org/articles/GhostInTheMachine.html

Sen, A. K. (1999). *Development as freedom*. Oxford, UK: Oxford Oxford University Press.

Tarallo, P. (2003). *Digital divide. La nuova frontiera dello sviluppo globale*. Milano, Italy: Franco Angeli.

Tobin, J. J., Wu, D. Y. H., & Davidson, D. H. (1989). *Preschool in three cultures: Japan, China, and the United States*. New Haven, CT: Yale University Press.

UNO. (2001). *Making new technologies work for human development*. Retrieved July 15, 2009, from http://www.undp.org/hdr2001

Veen, W. (2007). *Homo Zappiens and the need for new education systems*. Retrieved July 10, 2009, from http://www.oecd.org/dataoecd/0/5/38360892.pdf

Veen, W., & Vrakking, B. (2006). *Homo Zappiens, growing up in a digital age*. London: Network Continuum Education.

Zocchi, P. (2003). *Internet. La democrazia possibile. Come vincere la sfida del digital divide.* Milano, Italy: Guerini e Associati.

ENDNOTES

1. Most scholars agree on considering the ICT revolution as a fundamental element of globalization, Castells says: "the complete economic globalization can advance only thanks to new information and communication technologies" (Castells, 1996, p. 147). In the same way Beck: "... it is necessary to distinguish the many globalization dimensions: every list [of them] should include, without pretenses of being complete, the dimensions of the technologies of information, ecology and economy of the organization of work, culture and civil society" (Beck, 1998, p. 19).
2. In partnerships with leading Internet content providers, including AOL, StarMedia, EarthLink, Disney's GO Network, Time Warner's Road Runner, Netscape's Netcenter KidZone, and Microsoft's WebTV.
3. Defined in PISA as daily or a few times a week.
4. In fact, the presence of children in the home may be a primary reason for the adoption of computer technology in the household. As Drotner pointed out as early as in 2000, access to digital technologies is greater in homes with children than in those without (Drotner, 2000).

This work was previously published in International Journal of Digital Literacy and Digital Competence, Volume 1, Issue 1, edited by Antonio Cartelli, pp. 1-23, copyright 2010 by IGI Publishing (an imprint of IGI Global).

Chapter 2
Current Trends of Media Literacy in Europe:
An Overview

Laura Cervi
Universitat Autonoma de Barcelona, Spain

Oralia Paredes
Universitat Autonoma de Barcelona, Spain

José Manuel Pérez Tornero
Universitat Autonoma de Barcelona, Spain

ABSTRACT

In this paper, the authors give an overview of the current trends of media literacy in Europe. The study titled "Current trends and approaches to media literacy in Europe", commissioned in the second half of 2007 by the European Commission to the Universitat Autonoma de Barcelona, maps current practices in implementing media literacy in Europe and recommends measures to increase the level of media literacy in Europe. Starting with information from the study, this paper will examine the evolution of media literacy in Europe, its orientation, and its relationship with other related fields, such as media education and digital literacy to explore the emerging trends, innovations, changes, crisis points, alternatives, and so forth.

INTRODUCTION

"To become the most competitive and dynamic knowledge-driven economy in the world, capable of sustainable economic growth with more and better jobs and greater social cohesion", as the Lisbon European Council[1] (Lisbon European Council, 2000) established, the European Union, both the Parliament and the Commission, have played an active role in the development of media literacy in Europe.

Among these initiatives we find the study titled *Current trends and approaches to media literacy in Europe*[2] (Pérez Tornero & Celot, 2007) commissioned, in the second half of 2007, by the European Commission to the UAB, *Univer-*

DOI: 10.4018/978-1-4666-0903-7.ch002

Table 1. Models of media literacy (adapted from Pérez Tornero & Celot, 2007)

Model	Technology	Focuses	Privileged actors	Premises	Objectives	Priorities
Protection	MASS MEDIA	Moral protectionism	Tutors and Educators	Media represent risk to the moral development of children and young people	Condemnation of abuses. Protection of children and young people	Creation of control mechanisms
		Ideological Protectionism	Social activists	Media have power of manipulation and ideological control.	Acts of resistance, suggestions for alternative reading.	Social debate: condemnation and criticism
Promotion (awareness and appropriation)	INTERACTIVE MEDIA (Small and social media)	Proposal of critical reading	Educators Education Authorities Regulatory_authorities	Different ways of reading media messages can be developed.	Critical reading Awareness	Critical thinking Media education in the curriculum Regulation/ self-regulation
		Production proposal	Education authorities Industry Professionals	New media facilitate the liberty to produce messages	Autonomy and personal initiative Creation of standards Innovative Production	Individual appropriation of the media Improvement of production quality
	Web 2.0	Cooperative action proposal	Communities and associations Industry teamwork	Network communication boosts cooperative media	Mediation between citizens/media Social appropriation of media	Active_citizenship Participation Cooperative production *Co-regulation* Corporate responsibility

sitat Autonoma de Barcelona. Using document analysis, case studies and the analysis of media literacy in representative countries, the study maps current practices in implementing media literacy in Europe and recommends measures to be implemented in Europe to increase the level of Media Literacy.

The aim of this paper is to give an overview of the current trends of ML in Europe. Starting from the information given by the mentioned study, we will look at the evolution of media literacy in Europe, its orientation and its relationship with other related fields, such as media education and digital literacy to explore the emerging trends of the current situation: innovations, changes, crisis points, as sells as alternatives, etc. All these aspects allow us to draw a panorama of Media Literacy y Europe.

EVOLUTION OF MEDIA EDUCATION AND MEDIA LITERACY

Educational interest in the media, which has centered on media education, or media literacy, has had different stages or origins which we will describe below, but these phases often correspond to specific focuses and models of media literacy (Table 1) and which, therefore, can coexist at the same time and in the same setting. We will still, however, present the phases in stages to facilitate comprehension and to explain the dynamic orientation of the media literacy.

- During the 1960s and a large part of the 1970s

The movie captured the attention of European teachers. Its rising influence and the emergence of new aesthetic and cultural trends boosted the interest in bringing films into schools.

- During the 1970s and the beginning of the 1980s

The interest was focused on television, discussion about the emerging consumer society and in particular, criticism of advertising. Media education became more critical and took advantage of the critical experience of French Semiology and proposals made in British Cultural Research.

- During the 1980s

Media education was enriched by the effort for seeking alternatives to mass communication. It was during this time that the video as a didactic tool appeared with the meanwhile development of local or close communication. This trend was particularly strong in France, Italy, Spain, etc.

- The end of the 1980s the beginning of the 1990s

This is the era of the end of public television's monopoly: private television appears thanks to the de-regulation of the market. Media education and media literacy turned to the debate on the impact of the media and its contents. Discussions and debates began on public communication services and independent regulatory authorities started to appear, regulation and self-regulation codes were proposed and citizens were invited to participate in the configuration of the new electronic media services. The unprecedented strength of electronic media and the need to connect schools with current information led to the first systematic links being formed between schools and the media.

- During the mid-1990s

The appearance of digital media had a huge impact on communicative systems, in particular Internet and the web. The novelty of these new media, and the need for digitalisation that they brought, changed the focus of literacy to the need to acquire instrumental skills, and above all to combat the digital divide, which developed into serious levels of inequality in access to new media.

- At the beginning of the 2000s

Media convergence began, thus the perception of the need for a synthesis of digital literacy and the tradition of audiovisual literacy (media education), which began to be known as *media literacy*. The skills required for success in the new media environment should, in fact, include old skills related to conventional media, as well as those related to digital technologies. However, the convergence between policies that promote audiovisual and digital literacy is not moving as quickly as that of the media themselves, as well as the convergence of the theoretical, pedagogical and methodological focuses of media education and digital literacy. That is to say, the call for a new media literacy is relatively recent, and is based on several research initiatives, both academic and institutional.

EMERGING TRENDS

While media literacy has evolved, as described in the previous section, since the 1970s some European trends have been identified, which have had a deep effect on the development of media literacy models. We will look at these trends below.

It is important to note that, in many cases, these are emerging trends, which although not dominant, are significant. Observed as a whole, they allow us to portrait a complete picture of the situation.

1. Media convergence: new research, new experiences

Media convergence and multiplication of media platforms is creating a new multimedia environment in which citizens move. This is particularly true for young people, able to easily switch from their television screens to their games consoles or computers. As a result, besides these experiences, there are a rising number of research projects in Europe looking into the effects and consequences of this new environment.

Media literacy, as a result of these experiences and studies is tending to focus and pay particular attention to the new media environment. Many of these studies describe the new multimedia environment, and when faced with the question of media literacy, support the encouragement of the critical abilities of communication users, and their abilities of appropriation in the new environment.

2. Shift from focus on protection to focus on promotion: shared responsibilities (emissary and receptor)

The idea of the need for protection was associated with theoretical models within the theory of the effects of the media and its power[3], while the idea of promotion was associated with models that concentrated on how the user uses the media, and his or her ability to search, select and evaluate[4].

One of the emerging features of media literacy in Europe is the emphasis on promotion and an increase in the media skills of citizens. This is leading to a gradual reduction in the attention paid to policies focused exclusively on protection. It is becoming more evident that activities aimed at protection (particularly those involving children and young people) are being compensated with strategies of empowerment and promotion.

3. Growing sensitivity of citizens to commercial communication

Advertising and commercial communication have changed a great deal in recent years, adapting themselves to the new media environment. They have become more intense, more precise, have explored new techniques and, at times, have become more aggressive. This has led, on occasions, to excesses, saturation and the transgression of certain limits or standards which until now have been the norm. With this in mind, the over-riding feeling in Europe is that any self-regulation or standardisation strategy must be accompanied by an increase in the critical skills of citizens who must be able to select, adequately interpret and appropriate the contents of commercial communication. To this end, educators, families and many citizens' associations are taking part in workshops, seminars, and debates on advertising. And many of these activities demand an active commitment from advertisers and communication and publicity companies.

Meanwhile, some advertising companies and associations, aware that they must maintain the trust of citizens for their messages to be effective, are trying out strategies in which self-regulation plays a fundamental role[5]. The addition of criticism on advertising, public debate on commercial communication and self-regulation by businesses are creating a new context for media education and for media literacy in this area.

4. Increasing presence of media literacy in the compulsory education curriculum

European educational reforms have tended to include the introduction of new ways of dealing with media education and media literacy in the curriculum. Attention to the mass media and ICT is present in the new curriculums that have been introduced following reforms of recent years.

Initially, media education in the curriculum was focused on mass media (press, radio, film and television). With the development of ICT, interest was redirected from mass media to digital media. More recently, a balance has been established between mass media and digital media and there has been more educational interest in the new digital environment which includes new and old media. This is a rising phenomenon in Europe.

The inclusion of the media in the curriculum has risen with the educational reforms of the 1990s and 2000s. Until then, the media was rarely and unsystematically approached via different subjects, but the situation seems to have changed over the last decade. Many countries have included the acquisition of media and digital skills as among the final objectives of their curriculum (Finland[6], Slovenia[7], France, Spain[8], see Ley Orgánica, 2006); and some have linked these skills to civic education and active citizenship (France, Spain). Some have created optional subjects (some in Spain and France) on the media. Others have established evaluation systems for such skills (France).

In general, there is a clear trend for linking skills related to new digital media with critical and creative skills related to mass media. Technological evolution has an important effect on this evolution, though it does not wholly determine it. Cultural and political attitudes are also huge influences.

But everything seems to suggest that the most likely evolution is a convergence of models, which would allow for a combination of active participation in media production, with critical thinking, that is, the conjunction of the values of traditional media education, centred on mass media, and the current direction of media literacy, centred on production in the new digital environment.

5. School media: media production skills

Digital technologies facilitate the access, production and circulation of contents. These technologies are being gradually introduced into European educational centres, and are not only leading to innovations in teaching and learning methods, but are also facilitating the creation of local media.

As a result of these new opportunities, an infinity of school media produced in education centres are appearing, and are being circulated beyond the limits of the centres themselves. By "school media" we mean the media that arise within the context of the school and which are produced by the students themselves: newspapers and magazines, websites, school radio and television stations, etc. They provide the students with true experiences of mediated communication, thus bringing them closer to the logic of the major media and to take part in the social life of their immediate surroundings.

On the whole, school media can constitute new ways of projecting the school within its immediate – and distant – environment, and can be transformed into platforms for interaction and contact that require (and, consequently, foster) media education skills. It is possible that the systematic promotion of these media by educational authorities, along with the new possibilities brought about by new technologies – which are becoming lighter and more accessible – may make school media one of the best tools in education media within the near future.

6. Media industry more interested in media literacy

Newspaper editors launch International and National initiatives promoting the introduction of the press into schools. The medium-term objective is the consolidation of a reading public related to the press, but the short-term objective is to increase skills and abilities in reading media and the development of critical abilities. Therefore, these initiatives are directly involved in the development of media literacy. So all over Europe, agreements have been made between educational authorities and press editors. There are also many alliances between education and industrial sectors for the launch of campaigns and projects related to reading and the promotion of books.

In regard to cinema, activities promoting ties between film and education are becoming common. Authorities and businesses finance festivals and fairs aimed at bringing young people closer to the world of film and encouraging new attitudes towards the audiovisual heritage. Film is also the subject of workshops, seminars or activities that take place in education centres. So there are many campaigns, pedagogical programmes and other initiatives which link audiovisual and media professionals with children, young people and students.

To a lesser extent, it is also common for the world of television, especially public television, to launch initiatives related to media literacy in the areas of audiovisuals, television itself, and more frequently, new media. The same is occurring among companies involved with digital media. In Europe, there are a rising number of initiatives aimed at extending the media skills of young people. There is also an increase in contents and audiovisual programmes aimed at media education in Europe: television programmes that analyse advertising or that discuss the content of television programmes themselves, which explain the key aspects of information production or that provide information on new technologies.

The possible connection between this type of programme and curricular objectives in the field can be taken great advantage of in the future.

7. New active participation by stakeholders

In the early stages of development, media education seemed to be the exclusive responsibility of the educational system and of teachers. This responsibility has progressively been extended to reach families (parents), teachers in general, media, public institutions, professionals, associations, etc.

The "third social sector" called civil society, which is not the State and does not intervene in the market, has played a fundamental role in media education. Throughout Europe there is a growing presence of professional educators' associations, and associations of parents, professionals, political and religious movements, and young people that protest media related risk situations and encourage the raising of awareness on the media and education.

In general, each of these associations has its own style and tends to focus on different aspects, but together they manage to constitute an increasing systematic and comprehensive network of concerns and attitudes toward the media. These associations are increasing their influence over the media. They are beginning to form a kind of lobby on specific topics (education, violent content, sexism, etc.) and are gradually becoming more powerful.

Lately, there has been a noticeable trend towards creating platforms for interaction among these groups and to participate when given the opportunity in any instance of guidance or regulation. It is obvious that their ability to denounce risks or abuses, to initiate debates and controversies, and to present proposals and suggestions for action is contributing in this process to the creation in public opinion of a type of media education curriculum. Despite the fact that they are not yet very well known, their participation, documents and declarations are undoubtedly going to represent one of the areas of greatest activity in media education in the very near future.

It is important to mention here the rising participation in the field of family and children's associations. Recent studies carried out in many European countries (see the model by Sonia Livingstone demonstrate that in homes with ever more access to the media, parents tend to ignore their children's media consumption, intervening little in the selection of programmes, and they tend to spend less time with their children in media consumption. However, it is this very lack of action on a domestic level that is paradoxically leading to increased sensitivity by family and parents' associations. This is an emerging trend in the majority of European countries.

8. Involvement of authorities in regulation

In recent years, regulatory authorities from the world of communication in Europe, which tend to separate themselves from government influence to become independent authorities, have launched, although unsystematically, initiatives related to increasing the autonomy and critical abilities of citizens. At the same time, they have on occasions used different mechanisms to promote civic participation in some of the decisions and standards that affect the communication sector.

Nevertheless, only a few of these authorities, such as OFCOM, have systematically supported the promotion of media literacy. It is not however, an isolated case. On the contrary, its example has spread and many authorities now promote media literacy or are beginning to recommend its promotion as a result of the research and investigations that they have carried out.

Currently, almost every European country has some form of body or authority in charge of supervising the implementation of broadcasting or telecommunication legislation. Broadcasting regulation usually encompasses the power to license broadcasters, to monitor whether broadcasters are fulfilling their legal obligations, to impose sanctions if they fail to carry out those obligations and to protect the audience.

Almost all of these authorities recognize the safeguarding of plurality and the protection of audiences as fundamental tasks. Promoting media literacy should be among the duties of these institutions along these lines: the development and preservation of independent, pluralistic and responsibly minded media requires citizens to be aware and to support this process, as well as being actively involved. Only media literate people will be able to exercise informed choices, understand the nature of content and services, be able to take advantage of the full range of opportunities offered by new communications technologies and be better able to protect themselves and their families from harmful or offensive materials.

It seem that a emerging trend in the system of communication in Europe is for regulatory authorities to participate in the field of media literacy and advance the development of media literacy in all sections of society, as well as conducting regular research to monitor it.

GAPS, BARRIERS AND DEFICIENCIES

Considering the dynamic aspects and trends, as well as factors that favour the development of media literacy policies from a European point of view, we have identified many factors that make it difficult to achieve a wider and deeper development.

- **Lack of shared vision.** Regarding objectives, concepts, methods, resources, research, and results evaluation, etc., there is not a shared common framework to work with. This makes it more difficult for exchanges, comparisons, joint strategies and in general any state or European policy.
- **Cultural barriers to innovation.** Barriers can be due to lack of technological knowledge, lack of critical analysis, or lack of specific culture in the field. Beyond the difficulties of a material and technological nature, it is the institutional inertia and routine that cause problems and slow down the development of innovation that media literacy policies bring with them.
- **European visibility of national, regional and local initiatives.** Very often initiatives in the field do not achieve a proper media visibility. There are many good and successful examples
- **Dispersion and lack of coordination among European stakeholders.** There is a kind of dispersion and lack of coordination among stakeholders. No European network dedicated to the field of Media Literacy: that leads to a lack of co-operation and interchange of information among different actors, whose are working in isolated effort. So, stakeholders who are active in the field are disperse, that is to say most initiatives remain unique and unknown because there is scarce co-operation among actors.

FACTORS THAT CONTRIBUTE TO MEDIA LITERACY

By contrast, we have identify some elements that could help in the development of media literacy: the treatment of media literacy in the educational curriculum of each country; the policy of training teachers on the subject; the policy of assessing media literacy; the existence of teaching material on the subject; the existence of systems of assistance and orientation in the field; the existence of public campaigns of media literacy; the existence of stable public departments of media literacy; the activity of civic associations in the sector; the activity of regulatory activities in the sector; specific contents and programmes; the participation of the media industry in the; the visibility in questions related to media literacy in the public sphere; the existence of incentives and promotion policies for media production by citizens; Media literacy research; participation in networks of international co-operation; family participation; and finally, initiatives in media literacy in relation to commercial.

THE EUROPEAN AUDIOVISUAL MEDIA SERVICES DIRECTIVE (AVMSD)

Finally, it is important to emphasize the all the efforts of the stakeholders, some authorities, some educational system leaders, etc., to make digital and media literacy a key element of the development of the information society in Europe have concluded successfully in the enactment of the European Audiovisual Media Services Directive[9] which was incorporated on December 2009, into legislation in all Member States of the EU, introducing the need to promote media literacy into a regulation of the media system for the first time[10].

REFERENCES

Aguaded Gómez, J. I. (Ed.). (2007). Media Education in Europe. *Comunicar, 28*.

CLEMI/Academie De Bordeaux (Ed.). (2003). *Parcours médias au collège: approches disciplinaires et transdisciplinaires*. Aquitaine, France: Sceren-CRDP.

D'Amato, M. (2006). *Le pubblicazioni del Centro nazionale*. Retrieved from http://www.minori.it/pubblicazioni/quaderni/pdf/quad_38.pdf

EAVI. (2004). *Advancing European Viewers Interests*. Brussels, Belgium: Author.

Ley Orgánica. (2006). *Disposiciones generales*. Retrieved from http://www.boe.es/boe/dias/2006/05/04/pdfs/A17158-17207.pdf

Lisbon European Council. (2000). *Presidency Conclusions*. Retrieved from http://www.europarl.europa.eu/summits/lis1_en.htm

Livingstone, S., & Bovill, M. (2001). *Children and the changing media environmental, an European comparative study*. Mahwah, NJ: Lawrence Erlbaum Associates.

Mediappro. (2006). *The appropriation of new media by the youth*. Retrieved from http://www.mediappro.org/publications/finalreport.pdf

Pérez Tornero, J. M. (2005). *Media education in Spain*. Media Education Journal.

Pérez Tornero, J. M., & Celot, P. (2007). *Current trends and approaches to media literacy in Europe*. Retrieved from http://ec.europa.eu/culture/media/literacy/studies/index_en.htm

ENDNOTES

1 Lisbon European Council 23 and 24 March 2000, Presidency Conclusions, http://www.europarl.europa.eu/summits/lis1_en.htm

2 Pérez Tornero, J.M., & Celot P. (2007), Current trends and approaches to media literacy in Europe. EC, http://ec.europa.eu/culture/media/literacy/studies/index_en.htm

3 Within the field of research on communication, these studies have referred to "impact" or "effects".

4 Here we are closer to the models linked to the paradigms of "uses and gratifications" and, above all, of the new models of social appropriation of the media.

5 Consider advertising self-regulation codes applied in almost the whole Europe.

6 Cf. The Ministry of Education's expert report on media literacy, 2007.

7 Media literacy was included in the curriculum in 2003.

8 The Royal Decree 1513/2006, of 7 December.

9 Audiovisual Media Service Directive 2007/65/EC of the European Parliament and the Council of December 11th 2007), Retrieved at: http://ec.europa.eu/avpolicy/reg/avms/index_en.htm

10 The article 37 institutionalises media literacy as one of the measures to be boosted. It therefore makes media literacy a vital element of the regulation of the European audiovisual industry and provides a less detailed definition of media literacy than previous definitions: "It includes the skills, knowledge and understanding that allow consumers to use the media effectively and safely".

This work was previously published in International Journal of Digital Literacy and Digital Competence, Volume 1, Issue 4, edited by Antonio Cartelli, pp. 1-9, copyright 2010 by IGI Publishing (an imprint of IGI Global).

Chapter 3
Perspectives on Media Literacy, Digital Literacy and Information Literacy

Monica Fantin
Universidade Federal de Santa Catarina, Brazil

ABSTRACT

The cultural landscape poses different challenges for teachers. Beyond developing reading and writing skills, it is necessary to emerge in the digital culture and master the different codes of different languages. In this context, media education studies discuss the educational possibilities of interpreting, problematizing, and producing different kinds of texts in critical and creative ways, through the use of all means, languages and technologies available. Considering that media cannot be excluded from literacy programs, it is essential to reflect on the definition of "literate" today. These reflections examine the resignification of concepts like literacy, media literacy, digital literacy and information literacy.

INTRODUCTION

Concepts such as media literacy, digital literacy and information literacy are being used with greater frequency in the field of education and communication. But what is the specificity of each literacy and its concept? This article will discuss this issue based on the understanding of scholars from the field of media education.

DOI: 10.4018/978-1-4666-0903-7.ch003

Many authors consider media-education to be a synonym for literacy or media literacy. Buckingham differentiates these concepts, arguing that literacy involves reading and writing, while media literacy necessarily involves interpretation and production of media.

Media education, then, is the process for teaching and learning about the media; media literacy is the outcome – the knowledge and the skills learners acquire. (...) Media literacy neces-

sarily involves 'reading` and `writing` media. Media education therefore aims to develop both critical, understanding and active participation. It enables young people to interpret and make informed judgments as consumers of media; but it also enables them to become producers of media in their own right. Media education is about developing young people's critical and creative abilities (2005, p. 4).

Understanding that media literacy "refers to the knowledge, skills and competencies that are required to use and interpret media," Buckingham (2005, p. 36) highlights that the different literacies demanded by the different media involve specific abilities of analysis, evaluation and reflection, and imply an understanding of the social economic and institutional context of the communication, to understand how it affects the experiences and uses of the media and their interpretations on micro and macro levels. Since different media have distinct narrative structures and elements, the production of meanings is based on the abilities to operate with the codes of different languages and their instruments, such as photographic cameras, video cameras, computers, cell phones, etc.

From this perspective, media literacy involves the capacity to decipher, appreciate, criticize and compose, but also requires a broad understanding of the historic, economic and social context in which these texts are produced, distributed and used by audiences, as Silverstone (2005) emphasizes. To assure this form of appropriation, the learning of the medias should be dynamic and involve reflexive approaches combined with critical analyses, creative productions and critical consumption.

Working for quite some time with the concept of media literacy, Hobbs (1994) defines it as "the ability to access, analyze, evaluate and produce communication in a variety of forms" (Aufderheide apud Rivoltella, 2005, p. 69). This definition is also found in the works of Livingstone (2003) and Rivoltella (2005), who understand that it involves an ability to read, write, speak, listen, and see critically and create messages using the broadest range of technologies.

Media literacy is "literacy for the information era," according to Hobbs (1994, p.2) for whom it means essentially learning to formulate questions about what one sees, observes and reads. To do so, it is possible to use the most varied types of messages and products: television drama, newspapers, films, news programs, documentaries, mini-series, advertising, photography, video-clips, online services, etc.

The essential focus of this media literacy approach is anchored in the presumptions of Masterman, which Hobbs appropriates by synthesizing his fundamental ideas: all messages are constructed; messages are representations of reality; messages have proposals related to social, political and economic, ethical, and aesthetic contexts; individuals construct meanings for the messages that they receive; each media, form and genre of communication have specific characteristics.

The focuses of media literacy correspond to a demand for greater semantic amplitude of the concept of literacy, and for Hobbs (2003) concern the possibility of knowing how to:

- *access messages*: read with a good level of understanding; recognize and understand different types of languages; develop strategies to look for information in different sources; select relevant information, process and analyze it; use various technological tools;
    - *analyze messages*: develop a reflexive and critical reception; analyze the form, structure and construction of meanings; know how to use categories, concepts and ideas; interpret messages based on basic concepts such as intentions, audiences, points of view, formats, genres, arguments, themes, languages, contexts; compare and contrast infor-

mation; identify fact from opinion; differentiate cause and effect;

- *evaluate messages*: relate to the experience itself by evaluating its quality, veracity and relevance; interpret it according to the origin of the sources; respond and debate the message according to content and complexity; analyze the message according to its production context; evaluate the form and content of the message;
- *create and/or communicate messages*: learn to write, speak, and create texts and images, for a variety of purposes and audiences; use ideas and express them clearly; use different types of language; select codes and resources that allow the message to reach its objectives; understand the grammar and syntax of the various media and of communication technologies to know how to use them in the construction of messages and in post-production.

If the understanding of media literacy is plural and continues to be difficult to define, according to Livingstone (2003), it can be understood as a characteristic of the technology or of the individual, and the difficulty in its conceptualization also resides in the demarcation of these frontiers. Thus, we can ask to what degree the concept of media literacy is distinguished from digital literacy.

Upon contextualizing the economic and social reasons for digital literacy, Pérez-Tornero (2004), affirms that digital literacy is a response to a technological process known as digitization. He maintains that, digitization can be understood as an encounter amongst many different languages: audio, visual, linguistic, numerical, spatial... This has brought about the emergence of a veritable multimedia universe. Thus, digitization involves giving potential to the convergence of different communication and broadcast media, producing a hybrid media, whilst the importance of certain conventional supports diminishes.

This is, then, a complex process of linguistic and media hybridisation with the appearance of a multimedia universe that revolves around the possibilities of digitization. This phenomenon requires new skills, new expertise, new ways of thought and action, and new forms of social relation. In short, it demands a new digital culture, a new literacy (Perez-Tornero, 2001, p. 2)

To adjust the similarity of the concept of digital literacy to that of media education as defined by UNESCO, Pérez-Tornero highlights that we need to recognize the fact of this convergence, because practically all of the media today are based on the use of digital technologies. He affirms that, "digital literacy and media education refer to individual and collective skills and abilities that transcend mere technical and operational know-how. They require semiotic, cultural and civic skills and mere technical knowledge does not enable us to acquire true literacy".

According to Pérez-Tornero, digital literacy has four dimensions:

- *operational*: the ability to use computers and communication technologies;
- *semiotic*: the ability to use all of the languages that converge in a new multimedia universe;
- *cultural:* a new intellectual development for the society of information;
- *civic*: a new repertoire of rights and responsibilities related to the new technological context.

As we can see, it appears that the dimensions of digital literacy proposed by Pérez-Tornero are similar, in semantic terms, to the fundamental focuses of Hobbs' media literacy approach, which have inspired various syntheses and reflections, such as Rivoltella's (2005).

Reaffirming the need to adopt a new perspective for literacy, which allows going beyond the limits set by traditional schooling, Rivoltella criticizes the still prevalent idea of understanding literacy as a set of relatively independent abilities and competences that concern only the forms of printed reading and writing, and not as a range of social practices related to various media. The author finds support in Hart to emphasize that:

It is necessary to extend this concept of literacy beyond written forms to include the vast range of other media, and in addition to "the how" (ability and competencies), include "the what" (genres, styles, formats, codes, registers). In other words, the development of a new literacy must expand from the teaching of the mother tongue to the awareness of language and, consequently to the awareness of media (Rivoltella, 2005, p. 69).

The idea of literacy for Rivotella implies an ability to access, analyze, evaluate and communicate messages of various forms that can be shared from a didactic-pedagogical perspective, converging as a "an educational guide that is attent to innovation: the centrality of learning, the importance of research, problem solving and cooperative work, research of alternative forms of evaluation and an integrated curriculum" (2005, p. 69).

Upon working with this idea related to digital media, Rivoltella (2008) affirms the specificity of digital media (internet, mobile phones, palms, iPods) locating the challenges faced by the traditional media education approach to the media. For Rivotella, digital media implies interaction and convergence and the problem involves both the question of critical thinking about passive use and consumption, as well as the question of production and sharing of content that children and youth produce when they interact on their own and with peers in the digital media, which implies the need for mediation. The author affirms that "The aim of digital literacy is to help people to become active and conscious citizens of the Information Society" and proposes a new paradigm for media education, a digital literacy, because the traditional forms of media education must be upgraded to digital literacy because of the possibility that "digital literacy will really be the education of our near future" (2008, p. 217).

More recently, Rivoltella (2010) defines Information Literacy as a skill that in the information society indicates the possibility that people seek, select and validate information found on the net. As part of the field experience of Media Literacy, mainly the ability of people to evaluate critically the sources of information, these skills are increasingly necessary in a society where information is increasingly abundant and knowledge becomes increasingly uncontrollable.

In this discussion, appears the idea of media literacy as an element of support for democracy, participation and active citizenship; the knowledge economy, competitiveness and choice; and lifelong learning, cultural expression and personal fulfillment (Livingstone, 2007) and this idea is related to information literacy.

The concept of information literacy is worked with by Sharkey and Brandt (2008) and involves different domains of skills and knowledge that involve finding, retrieving and using information. The authors highlight that "specific information literacy approaches include identifying standards, goals, objectives, or outcomes. For the American Library Association (ALA), information standards include accessing, using, and evaluating information "critically and competently" (American Association of School Librarians, 2004; Sharkey & Brandt, 2008, p. 88).

For some scholars, while media literacy has been defined in relation to the audiovisual media, information literacy has been defined in relation to the new digital media and systems (Vieira, 2007, p. 8). In this case, the first is focused on cultural expression as a strong critical dimension, which for the author would be nearly absent from the concept of information literacy, which focuses on the "technical" competencies needed for using Information and Communication Technologies; finding, bringing together and distributing information.

Considering the convergence of the media and technologies, the idea of information literacy is related to questions of democracy, citizenship and participation. From this results a need to combine media literacy and information literacy (*e-strategy, e-culture, e-learning*) in a broader framework to promote other forms of participation in society, as Livingstone (2005) emphasizes.

From the concept of information literacy can emerge another consequence: Internet literacy, which according to Veira (2007, p. 10), involves:

- *analytical competence:* understanding the formal qualities, for the use and operation of the Internet, for the construction of web sites, links, hypertexts, and the symbolic codes of the *web*;
- *contextual knowledge:* understanding of the socio-cultural, political and economic contexts in which Internet information is produced, distributed and consumed;
- *canonic knowledge*: a frame of reference about "classic" web sites, their importance, utility, reliability and veracity;
- *productive competence:* creation of Internet pages and content, interpretation, consumption and appreciation of the Web, participation in chats, groups, e-mails and mailing lists, which are essential for individual expression and collective production.

Given the situation presented above, it is clear that "each media has its own alphabet and uses it to construct symbols that inhabit our world, and compete to structure perception, building our culture" according to Rivoltella (2005, p. 125). Thus, it appears natural that each media requires its own learning process due to its particularities. Nevertheless, if the idea of "information literacy" can be understood as an organic part of the dimension of understanding any literacy process, to what degree is knowledge fragmented even more by the specificities and detailed nature of each literacy?

After all, if all media require literacy and if all language needs to be appropriated, we can think of a broad concept of literacy. This concept should be updated according to the demands of social practice and different socio-cultural contexts and should dialectically consider the micro and macro dimensions of these processes in their specificities and generalities. We see some pillars that can be used as a reference guide to the different forms and contents in the process of appropriation of knowledge and of the practices that the multiple literacies involve. This approximates us to the concept of multiliteracies, which will be considered in the following article.

REFERENCES

Buckingham, D. (2005). *Media Education: literacy, learning and contemporary culture*. Cambridge, UK: Polity Press.

Fantin, M. (2007). Alfabetização midiática na escola. In *Proceedings of the Anais do16 Congresso de Leitura do Brasil, COLE*. Campinas, Brazil: Unicamp.

Fantin, M. (2008). Os cenários culturais e as multiliteracies na escola. *Revista Comunicação e Sociedade, 13*.

Hobbs, R. (1994). *Teaching Media Literacy – Yo! Are you Hip to This*? Retrieved December 16, 2007, from http://reneehobbs.org/renee's%20 web%20site/Publications/Yo%20Are%20you %20 Hip.htm

Hobbs, R. (2003). *Lo que docents y estudiantes deben saber sobre los medios*. Retrieved November 10, 2007, from http://reneehobbs.org/renee's%20 web%20site/Publications/lo_que_docentes_y_estudiantes_de.htm

Livingstone, S. (2003). *What is media literacy?* Retrieved November 10, 2007, from http://www.lse.ac.uk/collections/media@lse/pdf/What_is_media_literacy.doc

Livingstone, S. (2005). *Adult Media Literacy. A review of the research literature on behalf of Ofcom*. London: Department of Media and Communications, London School of Economics and Political Science. Retrieved October 14, 2010, from http://www.ofcom.org.uk/advice/media_literacy/medlitpub/medlitpubrss/aml.pdf

Menduni, E. (2000). *Educare alla multimedialità*. Florence, Italy: Giunti.

Pérez-Tornero, J. M. (2004). *Digital Literacy and Media Education: An Emerging Need.* Retrieved October 16, 2010, from http://www.elearningeuropa.info/directory/index.php?page= doc&docid =4935&doclng=6

Rivoltella, P. C. (2005). *Media education: fondamenti didattici e prospettive di ricerca*. Brescia, Italy: La Scuola.

Rivoltella, P. C. (2008). From Media Education to Digital Literacy: A Paradigm Change? In *Digital literacy: Tools and Methodologies for Information Society* (pp. 217-29). Hershey, PA: IGI Publishing.

Rivoltella, P. C. (2010). *Métodos e Técnicas da Pesquisa Educativa em Ambientes Digitais*. Florianópolis, Brazil: UFSC.

Sharkey, J., & Brandt, D. S. (2008). Interating Technology Literacy and Information Literacy In Rivoltella, P. C. (Ed.), *Digital literacy: Tools and Methodologies for Information Society* (pp. 85–97). Hershey, PA: IGI Publishing.

Silverstone, R. (2005). *Por que estudar a mídia* (2nd ed.). São Paulo, Brazil: Loyola.

Vieira, N. (2007, September). *As literacias e o uso responsável da Internet*. Paper presented at V Congresso SOPCOM.

This work was previously published in International Journal of Digital Literacy and Digital Competence, Volume 1, Issue 4, edited by Antonio Cartelli, pp. 10-15, copyright 2010 by IGI Publishing (an imprint of IGI Global).

Section 2
Digital Literacy and Digital Competence in Formal Education

Chapter 4
Bebras Contest and Digital Competence Assessment:
Analysis of Frameworks*

Antonio Cartelli
University of Cassino, Italy

Valentina Dagiene
Institute of Mathematics and Informatics, Lithuania

Gerald Futschek
Vienna University of Technology, Austria

ABSTRACT

The paper is made of two parts. The first part discusses the importance of informal education environments supported by IT/ICT in students' learning, followed by reports of some international competitions and the role they have in improving students' interest and use of Informatics and related disciplines. At the end of the section, it describes the Bebras contest, an international competition supporting students' Information and Communication Technology competences with emphasis on cross discipline competences, which are useful to solve real life problems. In the second part of the paper, the outcomes of a research study on the features of a framework for digital competence assessment are reported. Based on this, some criticisms emerging from the analysis of the answers that students gave to a questionnaire built on the guidelines of the mentioned framework are analysed. They are integrated by the comments that teachers, colleagues and researchers made on the structure of the hypothesized framework. At last, a new model for digital literacy assessment is proposed. In the conclusion, the necessary elements for making the last framework effective are outlined and its suitability for the construction of the yearly questionnaire of the Bebras contest is discussed.

DOI: 10.4018/978-1-4666-0903-7.ch004

INTRODUCTION

Information Technologies (IT) and Information and Communication Technologies (ICT) have produced many changes in our society and especially in students' learning; new technologies greatly increased the influence of informal learning on students approach to knowledge construction and made deeper the difference between what they learn at school and what they learn outside it. The above phenomenon is not limited to students, it can be recognized in every kind of people and more generally in firms, corporate and whole organizations; it can be considered an integral part of the transformation process affecting our society, where the role and the importance of non formal and informal educational environments in people's knowledge development is continuously growing and in many cases has overcome formal contexts.

It can be easily recognized that the problem is not with technology but in their use (i.e., computers, laptops, mobile phones etc. are the same in whatever context people use them); process management, process organization and people involvement in the phenomena where IT/ICT play a relevant role are in fact responsible for the described changes. As an example the case of school and extra-school experiences are described in what follows: different topics, tools and strategies have been used in formal education to develop students' computing skills and let people autonomously interact with automatic systems to solve problems, create documents, communicate and, more generally, make with computers what they did in a different way (i.e., to digitally manage information being conscious of the operations they carried out). Outside school, edutainment tools and computer games created special environments where people usually learn by immersion and interaction with a virtual context. Edutainment is a form of entertainment designed to educate as well as to amuse. It typically seeks to instruct or socialize its audience by embedding lessons in some familiar form of entertainment. Otherwise stated virtual environments, simulation contexts, educational games as well as computer games have been and still are an important part of people's life and modern education and they are also responsible for the development of computing skills. The success of these last experiences is usually attributed to the motivation people have in the interaction with digital media and the corresponding tools and in the feedback they have from them (Vasilyeva, 2007).

Many questions are connected to the above issues:

- first, are the reasons for the reported changes the consequence of the natural evolution of society?
- second, how much the above changes are influenced by the approach people have with technology at school and outside it?
- third, are there strategies helping students, their families and teachers develop and use common IT/ICT based teaching-learning processes?

In what follows an attempt is made to answer the above questions and two different kinds of experiences are discussed: first, the features of the "Bebras" (beaver) International Contest on Informatics and Computer Fluency are described, second, the analysis of digital literacy and the development of frameworks for digital competence assessment are analyzed.

BEBRAS INTERNATIONAL CONTEST AND DIGITAL LITERACY

Since many years different multimedia and edutainment tools have been developed to help young people to improve their thinking skills. Furthermore many instruments have been planned to find students with good mathematical and computing skills and let them develop their natural talent. Problem solving has been the main principle underlying those experiences, because it was considered the best way to develop thinking skills. On this side the Olympiads of Mathematics (http://www.imo-official.org/), the Olympiads of Informatics (http://ioinformatics.org/index.shtml), the Kangaroo competition (http://www.mathkangaroo.org/) and other international contests had a great role since they started, because they involved many thousands of young students all over the world.

More recently V. Dagiene and her colleagues developed the idea of a new contest in IT/ICT, devoted to school students (http://www.bebras.org). The basic ideas underpinning the new contest were:

a. interest and engagement are very important in problem solving (Dagiene, 2006; Dagiene & Skupiene, 2004),
b. problem solving is the individual capacity of using cognitive processes to compare and solve real, cross-disciplinary situations where the solution path is not immediately obvious (Casey, 1997).

As reported by V. Dagiene the activity of beavers on trees' branches and strands was so noticeable, that the beaver was suggested as symbol and name of the contest, therefore the word "Bebras" (the Lithuanian word for beaver) has been used for the name of the contest.

One could ask for the reasons of one more competition, but the main answer to this question comes from the organizing committee of the contest, who stated that cognitive, social, cultural and cross-cultural aspects are very important in the use of technology. Otherwise stated these aspects had to be clear in the minds of those who prepared the questions so that the competition had to focus on the following aspects:

- put strong emphasis on the influence of IT/ICT on culture and language,
- help educational community to support school students who can use IT in most creative and profound way,
- develop students' ability to derive pleasure and satisfaction through intellectual life while thinking about efficient and effective use of applications of IT/ICT in everyday experience.

The main principles for the structure of the "Beaver" contest have been borrowed from the international mathematical contest "Kangaroo". Since the first contest, in 2004, it does not restrict participation, so that everyone who is willing can participate. The main goal of the contest is to evoke interest in larger and larger numbers of students around the world.

The rules of the "Beaver" contest are very simple:

a. the contest takes place in every country during the same time period,
b. there exists a common problem set that is translated into the different native languages,
c. the time limit for answering the whole questionnaire is fixed and the format of every question is closed and structured as interactive task or multiple-choice test.

The students taking part in the contest are grouped into three age groups called: Benjamins (primary school students, i.e., pupils), Juniors (students with some IT/ICT basic knowledge) and Seniors (upper secondary school students). The age of the students' groups was progressively adjusted to consider the differences in the national school systems and the increase in the number of the countries and students taking part in the contest. During the contest, each participant has 45-60 minutes to solve 18-27 problems of various complexity and different scores (i.e., time allocation and number of problems depends on countries). The problems are distributed on the following three different score values: 3 points, 4

Table 1. Classification of Bebras contest questions

INF	Information comprehension	Representation of data (symbolic, numeric, visual), coding, encryption
ALG	Algorithmic thinking	Everything including programming aspects
USE	Using computer systems	Search engines, email, spread sheets, etc. general principles, but no specific systems
STRUC	Structures, patterns and arrangements	Combinatories, discrete structures (graphs, etc)
PUZ	Puzzles	Puzzles and games (e.g., mastermind, minesweeper, etc.)
SOC	ICT and Society	Social, ethical, cultural, international, legal issues

points and 5 points. Students answers are evaluated as follows:

- when they are correct they add as many points as specified to the total amount,
- when they are wrong they diminish the total amount of 25% of the given points (i.e. – 0,75, – 1, and – 1,25 points, respectively),
- when not given (unanswered), they do not add or subtract any point to the total amount (i.e., 0 points are given).

To avoid negative results, each participant starts with the amount of points equal to the total number of the questions (e.g., 18 points if 18 questions are given).

As can be easily deduced the choice of the problems to submit to the students requires much more attention, because interest and engagement are very important in problem solving. It is well known, in fact, that most part of the textbooks and teaching materials used by the students in their class-work and at home do not propose problems but in the best cases they offer just exercises. When teaching computer programming and more generally IT/ICT via problem solving, it is very important to choose interesting tasks (problems) to motivate students in the search of possible solution/s. Therefore, one should try to present problems from various spheres of science and life, as close as possible to real life and with suitably chosen situations.

Problems can be of different types, starting from the most common questions on IT/ICT and their applications in everyday life or including specific integrated problems related to history, languages, arts, and, of course, mathematics. It is also very important to choose the problems so that the participants in the competition are not influenced by the operating systems or the computer programs they are experienced with.

At the second international Bebras workshop, a brainstorming session was held to generate ideas for different types of tasks that could be used in the contest. Also the classification of tasks was started and some topics groups were suggested (Opmanis *et al.*, 2006).

The work on problem classification continued in next Bebras workshops and in discussions between the members of the Bebras Organizing Committee. In September 2007, some active members of the Committee during the meeting in Potsdam proposed the classification reported in Table 1 for the topics in the Bebras contest (Dagiene & Futschek, 2008).

After that meeting the members of the Bebras Organizing Committee agreed on the need of using all the types of the questions in Table 1 in every competition, they also confirmed an elective method for mandatory tasks and proposed a format (reported in Table 2) for the structure of the questions to be submitted to the committee for approval and inclusion in the competition.

Table 2. Format for the proposal of problems for Bebras contest

TASK ID.	Made by nation code and progressive number (e.g., LT_19)
TITLE	Short title that characterizes the task most properly, max. 3 words.
QUESTION	Cover-story with definitions, metaphors, mini-world description, pictures, graphics etc. followed by the question to be answered
ANSWERS	Four alternative answers (one among them must be correct)
EXPLANATION	Explanation for the right answer and the wrong ones
INFORMATICS	The principles and concepts of informatics that are involved in the problem
REMARKS	Cultural remarks for translations
CATEGORY	One among the categories in Table 1
AGE GROUP / DIFFICULTY	One among the students' families (Benjamin, juniors, seniors) and difficulty: low, medium, high
AUTHOR/S	Name of the people who developed the question
FILES	Name of the task file and additional files
COPYRIGHT	Suggested the Creative Common 3.0 BY-NC-SA Licence

Furthermore it has been emphasized that each Bebras task has to involve concepts of informatics and/or information management (Futschek & Dagiene, 2009). The Bebras organizing committee is persuaded in fact that pupils and students can learn advanced informatics concepts by solving Bebras problems when a good and age adequate formulation of the task is adopted (Dagiene & Futschek, 2008).

At last it must be remarked that the questionnaire could be submitted to the students in two different ways: by using an online testing system or a pdf-based system where the students can download, compile and send back the tasks to the national committee.

DIGITAL LITERACY AND DIGITAL COMPETENCES

In addition to what has been reported until now on the instruments today available for improving computing/communication skills, and more generally digital skills in young generations, the outcomes of many studies on the difficulties people manifest in the acquisition of those skills must be considered.

The digital divide is probably the most important reason for digital illiteracy because it features today not only the presence or not of computing/communication instruments (like in the difference between developed and underdeveloped countries), but reports of at least two more complex problems affecting people's IT/ICT skills (Bindé *et al.* 2005; Guidolin, 2005):

a. the gap for pre-existing personal differences between people who are able in the use of technologies and people who are not,
b. the gap in the content management between people who master it (i.e., subjects who are able in the use of IT/ICT to manage information, knowledge, know how etc.) and people who don't.

The pedagogical emergency of digital divide, in all its aspects, is dramatically present all over the world and induced many private and public institutions, like Associations of Libraries, OECD and UNESCO, to act in two steps: first, to propose different hypotheses and strategies for the description of information literacy, computing literacy, digital literacy and media education, second, to suggest possible educational solutions for the improvement of those literacy.

The European Commission in 2005 issued the Recommendation on key competences for lifelong learning and stated the features of digital competence: the fourth among them (Commission of the European Parliament, 2005). The definition of this competence, which can be considered the most comprehensive until now adopted among those taken to date, like informatics literacy, information literacy, media literacy etc. is reported below:

> This competence is based on the confident and critical use of Information Society Technology (IST) for work, leisure and communication and is underpinned by basic skills in ICT: that is the use of computers to retrieve, assess, store, produce, present and exchange information, and to communicate and participate in collaborative networks via the Internet.

The presence of digital competences is intertwined with:

a. the understanding and knowledge of the nature, role and opportunities of IST in everyday contexts: in personal and social life as well as at work. It includes main computer applications, a sound use of the Internet and the communication via electronic media for leisure, information sharing and collaborative networking, learning and research,
b. the understanding of the support that creativity and innovation can receive from IST, the development of sound understanding skills helping state if information is valid, reliable and affordable enough and the knowledge of the ethical principles for the interactive use of IST.

The analysis of the connections between digital literacy (Tornero, 2004) and the development of digital competences for lifelong learning induced a group of Italian researchers and scholars in the Universities of Florence, Turin, Salerno and Cassino, to search for the features of a framework for the assessment of digital competence.

People in the research group agreed on the following features for digital competence:

- it is multidimensional, because it implies the integration of cognitive, relational and social abilities and skills,
- it is complex, because it cannot be completely measured by single tests and very difficultly can be verified in a short run, because it requires more time and different contexts before becoming evident,
- it is interconnected, because it is not independent from other key competences like reading, numeracy, problem solving, inferential skills etc.
- it is sensitive to the socio-cultural context, because its meaning can change over time, according to context and to different educational settings.

FRAMEWORKS FOR DIGITAL ASSESSMENT

The mentioned features looked general and wider enough to be the basis for the sound development of a framework for digital competence assessment (Calvani *et al.*, 2008). Three levels of analysis have been proposed within that context: search for information, problem solving, and collaborative knowledge building. The last item was intertwined with students' skills which govern their movement in the cyberspace, in order to protect themselves from possible dangers and responsibly interact with others.

The hypothesized model for the framework for digital competence assessment is based on the co-existence of three different dimensions intersecting one another (Figure 1):

- the technological: that is, being able to explore and face new problems and new technological contexts in a flexible way;

Figure 1. Digital competence assessment framework

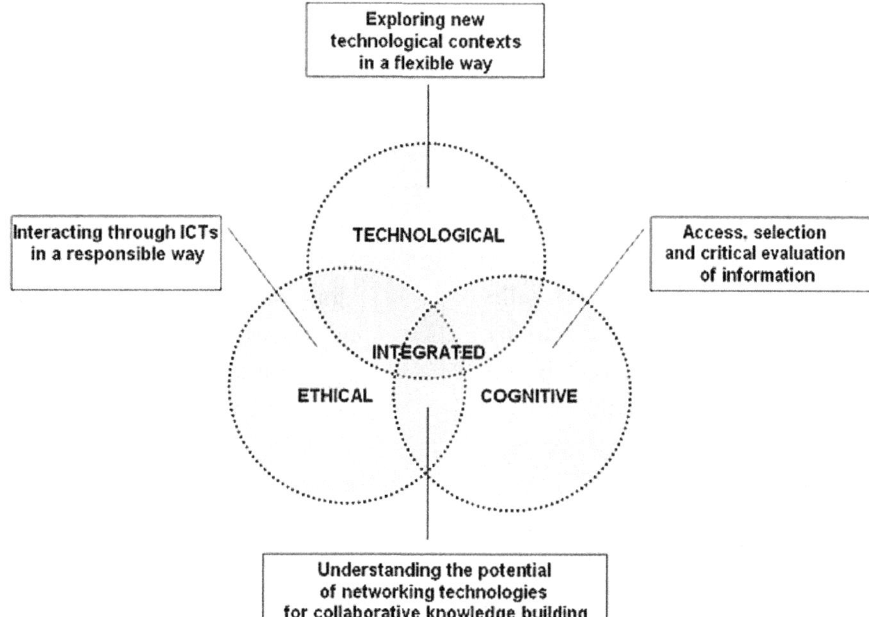

- the cognitive: which means reading, selecting, interpreting and evaluating data and information, while considering their pertinence and reliability;
- the ethical: which is expressed by the interaction with other individuals in a constructive way and with sense of responsibility (by using the available technologies).

The integration of the three mentioned dimensions is also possible and is based on the understanding of the potential offered by technologies, which let individuals share information and collaboratively build new knowledge.

By starting from the proposed framework, a test system with different kinds of analysis instruments has been hypothesised. First of all, the questionnaire called instant Digital Competence Assessment (iDCA), has been developed; its "instantaneous" feature is the consequence of its ease of use and application and its immediateness. Within it the following aspects are investigated (the Roman numbers stay for each of the three dimensions):

I) recognizing environments and interfaces,
I) recognizing possible solutions for technological troubles,
I) selecting the most suitable technical solutions to problems,
I) dealing with logical operators and operations,
I) charting out processes,
I) recognizing the difference between real and virtual phenomena,
II) dealing with texts (summarizing, representing, analyzing),
II) organizing data,
II) selecting and interpreting texts,
II) selecting and evaluating relevant information,
II) evaluating reliability of information,
III) safeguarding oneself,
III) respecting others on the net,
III) understanding social and technological inequalities.

Once ready, the questionnaire has been submitted on paper to students of different school levels and their answers have been analyzed. This first experience led researchers to adjust the structure of the questionnaire: it clearly emerged, in fact, that some questions had to be removed because they didn't produce any useful information; i.e., almost all the students selected the right answers or, on the contrary, the questions were too much difficult (i.e., in this last case more than 95% of the students selected the wrong answer or didn't answer at all).

After the suggested changes the Moodle platform was used to implement the questions and an invitation was sent to the schools in the neighbourhood of the Universities in the project, to let teachers and students take part in the collection of the answers to the questionnaire.

Until now only a little number of school have been involved in the study and the researchers in the university of Florence decided to extend the invitation to participate to the schools on the whole nation.

The data collected with the paper version of the questionnaire and the discussions of the results that the members of the research group had with teachers and colleagues working on similar problems, in national and international workshops and conferences, evidenced different needs and problems.

First of all, the questionnaire couldn't be the same while time passing due to the learning effect it had on teachers (i.e., classes of the same teacher answering the questionnaire at different times had better results if they participated in the experiment later than the others). Furthermore some criticisms concerning the model of the framework reported in Figure 1 explicitly emerged:

1. The ethical dimension looked much more normative than descriptive (i.e., most part of the aspects under analysis could only be present or absent in students), and it was very difficult, if not impossible, to measure and assess the competences it dealt with; a thorough analysis of this dimension showed also that it was inappropriate to describe any ethical student aspect, it aimed in fact at describing people compliance with rules for the use of technology and tools more than individual behavioural principles.
2. Both technological and cognitive dimensions produced questions in the cognitive domain and it looked suitable to join the two cognitive aspects in a unique dimension; otherwise stated, knowing how to use an instrument or a tool, recognizing an interface, developing an algorithm were considered knowledge and skills which could be immersed in real life situations and problems and could be investigated in a wider cognitive dimension.
3. The absence of the affective and social-relational dimensions negatively influenced the efficacy of the whole model, due to the effects the IT/ICT have on these spheres of individuals' life; as suggested from Ong (2002) and Olson (1991), for example, digital technologies led mankind to new forms of orality and social interaction. A possible remark supporting this criticism came from the observation that despite the lack of a social-relational taxonomy many questions concerning this issue were already present in the questionnaire (i.e., they mostly appeared in the ethical and cognitive dimensions of the framework).

The mentioned criticisms led to rethink the dimensions better featuring the interaction each individual has with IT/ICT and, what is more important, to bring the individual at the core attention of the analysis for the presence of digital competences and their assessment. Three dimensions, as emerged from the discussions, looked essential:

- the cognitive,
- the affective,
- the social-relational.

For the first two among them the psycho-pedagogical literature and the corresponding educational taxonomies suggested suitable instruments of analysis, the last one needed a taxonomy to be made from the scratch. By hypothesizing the existence or the definition of a taxonomy for this last dimension a new framework was possible.

The cognitive dimension in the new framework unifies the cognitive and technological dimensions of the former framework. Main elements governing the assessment for this dimension come from Bloom categories: knowledge, comprehension, application, analysis, synthesis, evaluation (Bloom *et al.*, 1956). A finer breakdown of the elements to be intertwined with digital competences in this dimension depends on the following elements: the verbal-linguistic and the logical-mathematical competences (deduced from the corresponding Gardner intelligences) and the skills derived from the construction and evolution of the concepts of space, time and causality (Piaget 1964, 1967). This last issue is the consequence of different needs:

a. the compliance of the questions to be created in this dimension with the problems usually adopted from the Bebras Organizing Committee, due to the identification of their aims,
b. the need of recovering the categories of space, time and causality that the use of the web, and more generally new technologies, modified; everyone can experiment in fact the contraction of spaces, the dilatation of times, and the loss of any causality when interacting with virtual worlds, using social networks and collecting results from search engines.

The use of the Krathwohl taxonomy (Krathwohl *et al.*, 1973) for the affective domain aims at extending the application of its categories to the interaction of the individual's affective sphere with digital technologies. The affective taxonomy, as derived from Krathwohl, is in fact based on the following categories: receiving phenomena, responding to phenomena, evaluating, organizing and internalizing phenomena.

The lack of a taxonomy for the social-relational taxonomy does not affect the new model which can be already used to assess the digital competences in the other dimensions. Once ready the last taxonomy will be added to the others and will better profile individuals' digital competences.

These considerations are well synthesized in the framework reported in Figure 2 (Cartelli, in press). In the figure, cognitive competences are split into three areas: technological, verbal-linguistic and logical-mathematical, all under the umbrella of space, time and causality categories. In the same figure the affective and the social-relational dimensions are reported; the last one is also proposed under the influence of the intrapersonal and interpersonal intelligences (Gardner, 1993).

As in the previous model (Figure 1), the area in the intersection of all the dimensions can be thought as depending on the understanding and use of the potential of networking technologies for collaborative knowledge building. More generally the common area can be considered responsible for the ability of being able in the creation and development of communities of learning and practices.

CONCLUSION AND FUTURE WORK

The state of work in progress for the framework reported in Figure 2 does not lead to final conclusions for the structure of the instruments to be used for digital competence assessment. First of all, there is the need of collecting the ideas today available on the influence that digital equipments have on social-relational features of mankind and a taxonomy for the assessment of the corresponding

Figure 2. The synthesized digital competence assessment framework

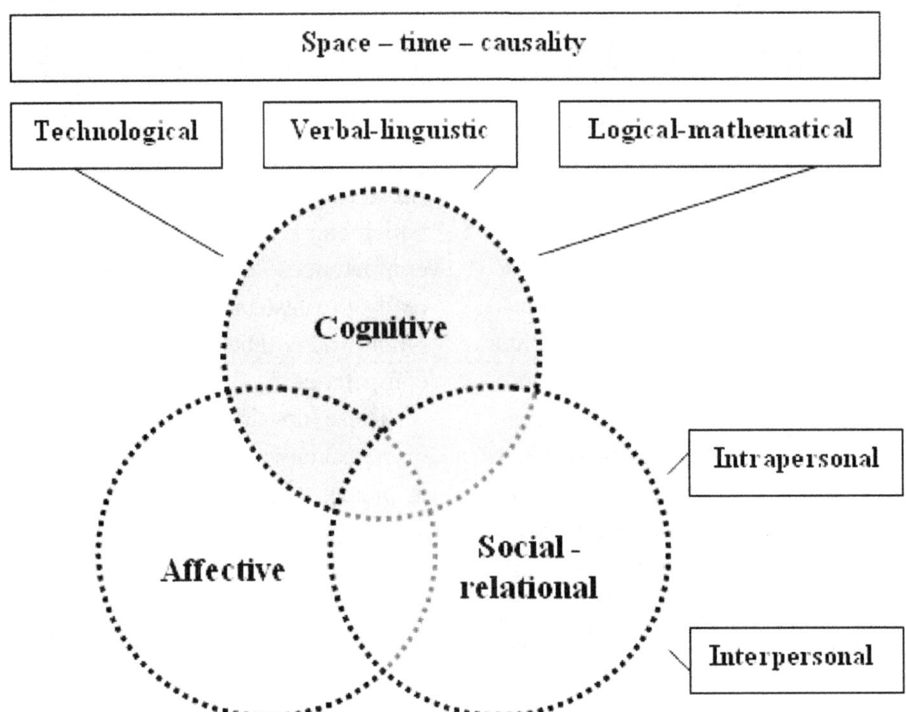

competences must be defined. Once this target is hit, the correctness of the whole framework has to be verified and deeper analyses for the evaluation of the instruments to be used for digital competence assessment would be needed.

After these assumptions one could ask if it is still possible to use any instruments for the assessment of digital competences. Some answers to the above question come from the following statements:

a. The aims of the "Bebras contest" can be considered very close to the ones of the framework for digital competence assessment and the questionnaire, with the questions structured as described in Table 2, can be the instrument to be used for digital competence assessment,
b. The comparison of the families of questions in Table 1 with the dimensions of the model in Figure 2 suggest that:
   - many questions in the iDCA (instant digital competence assessment) questionnaire can be recycled and included in the new questionnaire,
   - all the questions in the "Bebras" contest can be considered a subset of all the possible questions in the final questionnaire,
c. The new synthesized framework is completely centred on the individual in his/her interaction with digital technologies (i.e., the individual is the subject of investigation), and some dimensions within it already have taxonomies which can help in the investigation of students' competences; as a consequence, at least the digital competences in the cognitive and affective dimensions can be analyzed.

In addition to what has been reported until now it has to be noted that further elements suggest the choice of a questionnaire structured like the ones in the "Bebras" contest:

a. a rigid questionnaire, made of fixed questions which don't change over time, is not compliant with people evolution and different students' generations; today students are in fact considered to belong to the net generation and to be digital natives, their knowledge and communication strategies, are showed to change quickly every school year, and the questionnaire must consider these changes as much as possible,
b. the questionnaire must change every year to avoid the training-effect on the teachers, which has already been experimented with the instant digital competence assessment questionnaire; it has been shown in fact that students of the same teacher in subsequent classes perform better than former ones, because they have been trained to face those questions.

At last, when the model will be verified and a final structure for the questionnaire decided, could we state that the answers from the students will suggest to teachers how develop suitable instruments and strategies for the improvement of digital competences?

The results that one of the authors had when submitted the instant digital competence assessment questionnaire to the students in the schools in the neighbourhood of his university suggest a negative answer for the above question (Cartelli, 2008). In the meeting he held at the end of that experience, in fact, when teachers were invited to discuss and comment students' answers, they asked for support to improve their teaching strategies.

Until now no final strategy has been developed to hit the target of passing from teaching technologies to teaching with technologies in teachers in service training. The best results come from the involvement of teachers in the creation of learning objects for everyday teaching; those teachers who reorganize their teaching by using digital equipments and IT/ICT strategies perform better than the others in motivating the students and creating suitable learning environments. It is probably too early to say how much these results will influence the use of the questionnaire for digital competence assessment but it could be expected that the analysis of students answers will guide the process of planning and development of suitable learning objects to be used at school.

ACKNOWLEDGMENT

* The authors contributed in the realization of the paper by working all together on the introduction and the conclusion. V. Dagiene and G. Futschek mostly developed the paragraph on the Bebras competition, A. Cartelli specifically discussed digital literacy, digital competence assessment and the corresponding frameworks (section three and four in the paper).

REFERENCES

Bindé, J., Cotbett, J., & Verity, B. (2005). *21st-century talks: Towards knowledge society*. Paris: UNESCO.

Bloom, B. S. (1956). *Taxonomy of educational objectives: Handbook I: The cognitive domain*. New York: David McKay Co. Inc.

Calvani, A., Cartelli, A., Fini, A., & Ranieri, M. (2008). Models and instruments for assessing digital competence at school. *Journal of E-learning and Knowledge Society*, *4*(3), 183–193.

Cartelli, A. (2008). *T.I.C. e alfabetizzazione digitale* (Issue no 3 of the Faculty Centre for ICT and online teaching). Cassino, Italy: Idea Stampa by Ivo Sambucci.

Cartelli, A. (in press). Frameworks for digital literacy and digital competence assessment. In *Proceedings of the European Conference on E-Learning (ECEL 2009)*, Bari, Italy.

Casey, P. J. (1997). Computer programming: A medium for teaching problem solving. *Computers in the Schools*, *XIII*, 41–51. doi:10.1300/J025v13n01_05

Dagiene, V. (2006). Information technology contests – introduction to computer science in a attractive way. *Informatics in Education*, *5*(1), 37–46.

Dagiene, V., & Futschek, G. (2008). Bebras International Contest on Informatics and Computer Literacy: Criteria for good tasks. In *Informatics education – supporting computational thinking* (LNCS 5090, pp. 19-30).

Dagiene, V., & Skupiene, J. (2004). Learning by competitions: Olympiads in informatics as a tool for training high grade skills in programming. In T. Boyle, P. Oriogun, & A. Pakstas (Eds.), *2nd International Conference on Information Technology: Research and Education,* London (pp. 79-83). Washington, DC: IEEE Computer Society.

European Parliament and Council. (2005). *Recommendation on key competences for lifelong learning.* Retrieved December 4, 2008, from http://ec.europa.eu/education/policies/2010/doc/keyrec_en.pdf

Futschek, G., & Dagiene, V. (2009). A contest on informatics and computer fluency attracts school students to learn basic technology concepts. In *Proceedings 9th WCCE 2009, Education and Technology for a Better World*, Bento Goncalves, Brazil (No. 120).

Gardner, H. (1993). *Multiple intelligences: The theory in practice*. New York: Basic Books.

Guidolin, U. (2005). *Pensare digitale. Teoria e tecniche dei nuovi media*. Milan, Italy: McGraw-Hill.

Krathwohl, D. R., Bloom, B. S., & Masia, B. B. (1973). *Taxonomy of educational objectives, the classification of educational goals. Handbook II: Affective domain*. New York: David McKay Co.

Olson, D. R., & Torrence, N. (1991). *Literacy and orality*. Cambridge, UK: Cambridge University Press.

Ong, W. J. (2002). *Orality and literacy: The technologizing of the word*. New York: Routledge.

Opmanis, M., Dagiene, V., & Truu, A. (2006). Task types at "beaver" contests standards. In V. Dagienė & R. Mittermeir (Eds.), *Proceedings of the 2nd Internatioanl Conference on Informatics in Secondary Schools: Evolution and Perspectives*, Vilnius (pp. 509-519).

Piaget, J. (1964) *Six études de psychologie*. Paris: Gonthier.

Piaget, J. (1967). *La construction du réel chez l'enfant*. Paris: Delachaux & Niestlé.

Tornero, J. M. P. (2004). *Promoting digital literacy: Final report (EAC/76/03). Understanding digital literacy*. Barcelona, Spain: UAB. Retrieved September 25, 2009, from http://ec.europa.eu/education/archive/elearning/doc/studies/dig_lit_en.pdf

Vasilyeva, E. (2007). Towards personalized feedback in educational computer games for children. In *Proceedings of the Sixth IASTED International Conference on Web-Based Education*, Chamonix, France (Vol. 2, pp. 597-602). Anaheim, CA: ACTA Press.

This work was previously published in International Journal of Digital Literacy and Digital Competence, Volume 1, Issue 1, edited by Antonio Cartelli, pp. 24-39, copyright 2010 by IGI Publishing (an imprint of IGI Global).

Chapter 5
A Framework for Digital Competence Assessment

Antonio Cartelli
University of Cassino, Italy

ABSTRACT

Today, life is more complex and difficult due to uncertainties in society. Liquid life (Bauman, 2006) is frenetic, rapidly changing and highly influenced from information and communication technologies, and forces subjects to adapt to group behavior avoiding exclusion. Human beings are experimenting with the digital age and the pervasiveness of computers and IT/ICT equipment, which are influencing learning and knowledge construction. This raises questions in regard to a privileged role for digital competences in the knowledge society, whether or not there is a framework for digital competence assessment, and possible hints, suggestions, experiments, protocols, or curricula helping teachers in hitting this target with students. This paper answers these questions, describing the evolution of psycho-pedagogical paradigms and their comparisons. A framework for digital competence assessment is proposed and teaching activities are suggested. A proposal of a teaching-learning process called OTS (Open Teaching Process) is also presented.

INTRODUCTION

It is straightforward to note that IT/ICT and especially the Internet have deeply modified, during the last thirty years, the approach that subjects and society have to learning, knowledge construction and communication. Less evident is the impact that the analysis of the above situation has on the planning and carrying out of the activities leading to the improvement of subjects' features and to better society. It is probably for this reason that makes sense to question about the features of education and teaching in today society, better known as the "knowledge society".

DOI: 10.4018/978-1-4666-0903-7.ch005

It is behind the aims of this paper a deeper discussion of the features of knowledge society, and what has led to the transformation of industrial, post-industrial and information society into the new one. But the following issues, emblematic for the understanding of the contradictions in our life and very important for the discussion of what follows, merit to be analyzed here:

- The gap existing between "digital natives" and "digital immigrants" (both in learning styles and knowledge development) (Prensky, 2001); otherwise stated, young people can use digital equipments to better perform in getting information and communicating with respect to elders, and, what is more, new generations have different perception of reality and, usually, are more ready to act than to think about phenomena,
- The permanence, or the lowering, of the already low basic skills and competences in reading, writing and computing for students at different school levels (OECD, 2009), at least in Italy. This result seems to contradict what is reported in the item above, because it is usually recognized that the use of digital equipment implies the development of good information management skills (meta-cognitive skills); recent works show on the contrary that students have problems in the use of computers and other digital equipment, when high level operations with information are required (Pozzali & Ferri, 2010),
- The basic skills and competences for life-long learning, which are considered essential to let people be the citizens of the knowledge society. On this regard the Commission of the European Community recently approved a recommendation for all member countries, reporting the set of these competences. Digital competences, the fourth among them, are considered especially important because of their cross cultural features with respect to language (reading / writing) and calculus competences (Council of European Parliament, 2005).

It can be easily deduced from the above issues that today, more than in the past, the acquisition of better knowledge, skills and meta-cognitive features from subjects, go hand in hand with the analysis of the social environment and its.

Also if different perspectives and theories can explain the changes today happening, the metaphors of liquid and solid modernity will be adopted here to obtain a better vision of the social change; they have recently been developed together with the concept of post-modernity (Bauman, 2006), under the influence of the continuous growing of information production and transmission and the effects of pervasive computing and digital equipment explosion. These phenomena are the basis of the uncertainty of today society and of the transformation of human beings; furthermore, they state that the most important reason for the change in the society is the destruction of the certainties, because liquid life is more and more frenetic than in the past and forces the subjects to adapt to group behavior to avoid exclusion.

In this context the following questions claim for urgent answers:

- Is there any privileged role for digital competences in the knowledge society?
- Is there a framework for digital competence assessment helping people harmonize their competences and helping them become better persons and citizens in this society?
- Are there hints, suggestions, experiments, protocols and/or curricula helping teachers in hitting the above target with their students?

In the following paragraphs these questions will be discussed by starting with the description and the comparison of the psycho-pedagogical paradigms describing learning phenomena, soon after the analysis of a framework for digital competence assessment will be proposed and some teaching activities based on the author last experiences will be reported.

DIGITAL COMPETENCES AND PSYCHO-PEDAGOGICAL PARADIGMS

When debating on the role of digital competences for lifelong learning it is essential to focus on the ideas which describe the connections between the use of digital technologies and the different teching-learning theories.

They also suggest instruments and methods to be used in everyday teaching and lead to the analysis of the competences that students must develop in today educational systems. For the above reasons the main features of learning and educational theories (i.e., behaviorism, cognitivism, costructivism and connectivism) and their implications on the construction of e-learning environments will be discussed in what follows.

Behaviorism

Gredler (2001) states that behaviorism is the result of several theories, and makes three basic assumptions about learning:

1. Observable behavior is more important than understanding internal activities,
2. Behavior should be focused on simple elements: stimuli and responses,
3. Learning expresses a behavior change.

Skinner (1953), among other behaviorists, developed the theory of the operant conditioning which is based on the sequence: stimulus, operant response and reinforcement; following his ideas people, and more generally teachers, could always plan and design instruction with success.

The principles of behavioral theories have been positively applied to many teaching strategies influencing curricula development, like Mastery Learning, Programmed Instruction, Personalized System of Instruction, Teaching to Test etc., all sharing the following features-steps, derived from the principles of behavioral theory: assessment, intervention and evaluation.

Mastery learning, as proposed by J. B. Carroll (1963), assumes that all students have aptitude to learn and can master the presented educational materials. In mastery learning the main sequence of operations in behavioral theory is applied: first, the instructional design focuses on the assessment of the instructional needs of the learner; second, the intervention focuses on conceptualizing the learner's performance into goal and tasks (i.e., every task is split into smaller components, subtasks, which must be mastered before the learner can pass to the next task); finally, the learner's achievement is evaluated.

Since their first origin almost all behavioral hypotheses used computing to support teachers in their work or to develop self contained learning systems; good examples on this side are CAI (Computer Aided Instruction), CAL (Computer Aided Learning), CAE (Computer Aided Education) Systems, or Test Systems and, more recently, due to the introduction of Artificial Intelligence, ICAI (Intelligent Computer Aided Instruction) systems and ITS (Intelligent Tutoring Systems). An interesting example of learning environment developed under the above guidelines, built on the web and freely accessible at the URL http://virtualskies.arc.nasa.gov/, is the *Virtual Skies* website by NASA (Gillani, 2003).

Cognitivism

In cognitive theories learning is viewed as a process of data input, managed in short term memory, and coded and stored for long-term recall. Like in behaviourism, knowledge is considered external to learner, and learning is the process of internalization of knowledge in the subject.

Piaget (1952), the first developmental cognitivist, stated that the process of intellectual and cognitive development is the result of the mental adaptation to environmental demands; the development is the result of a spiral process based on assimilation, accommodation and construction of new equilibriums. Other scientists who influenced the development of curricula and teaching are Ausubel (1968), Bruner (1966), and Flavell (1985). Ausubel, hypothesizes a hierarchical structure in each discipline and proposes a new teaching approach, the Advance Organizer, by which students are presented with the structure of the discipline so that they can better learn. Bruner educational theory is based on the scaffolding, where students are presented with concrete subjects and mentors provide great support; when children learn more and begin to think abstractly (i.e., they pass through the enactive, iconic and symbolic phases), the support fades away. Flavell hypothesizes the development of the adolescents by means of the acquisition of three operations: combinational reasoning, propositional reasoning and hypothetical-deductive reasoning.

Cognitive theories have been positively applied to teaching and have produced fruitful teaching-learning methods. The inquiry-training model and the discovery learning, for instruction in the school are recalled here. The inquiry-training is based on five phases: 1) puzzlement or intellectual confrontation (started by the teacher), 2) first proposals of explanations for the puzzlements (by students), 3) gathering of new information in regard to the original hypotheses, 4) analysis of gathered and organized data and proposal of final hypotheses answering to the original puzzlement, 5) evaluation. Discovery learning emphasizes exploring, experimenting, doing research, asking questions and seeking answers.

Cognitive theories influenced e-learning by leading teachers to the use of editing and authoring tools in everyday class work. The first step in this revolution, directly involving students in the production of documents, is based on the use of office automation suites (especially word processors, spreadsheets and presentation managers), suddenly Hypercard, Flash, HTML editors and Quicktime led to the development of simulation environments and educational games. An interesting example of learning environment developed under the above guidelines, built on the web and freely accessible at the URL http://astroventure.arc.nasa.gov/, is the *Astroventure* website by NASA (Gillani, 2003).

Constructivism

Constructivism assumes that learners are not empty vessels to be filled with knowledge. Instead, learners must be actively involved in the knowledge creation processes. At least two separated branches of constructivism have developed and will be discussed here: interactive and social constructivism.

Interactive constructivism has its roots in cognitivists' ideas, that is J. Piaget, D. P. Ausubel and J. H. Flavel cognitive development. S. Papert (1993), Piaget's disciple, is one of the best representatives of interactive constructivism; he invented the LOGO programming language, which allows children to construct their own knowledge by means of the *Turtle Geometry* (i.e., it creates one micro-world in which children can explore the learning environment and restructure it or even add new micro-worlds to it).

L. Vygotsky (1978) is usually considered the founder of social constructivism. He developed the socio-cognitive theory, by which human development and learning originate and develop out of social and cultural interaction, within the zone of proximal development. It is the distance between the actual developmental level, as determined by individual problem solving, and the level of potential development, as determined through problem solving under adult guidance or in collaboration with more capable peers.

With respect to former learning theories it is now more difficult to describe the influence of constructivist ideas on teaching strategies; first, there is a great multiplicity of teaching-learning experiences (usually based on different learning environments), second, each experience is mostly experimental and strictly connected to studies and researches on higher level students. Most relevant features of these experiences are: they are situated and have local character and they are usually based on communities of practice and of learning.

As regards communities of practice the Laboratory of Comparative Human Cognition (LCHC) (1982) and M. Cole (1996) considered the context in the analysis of learning experiences and hypothesized the presence of a shared elaboration system connecting the individuals' learning experience to the corresponding performances, by means of special schemas. J. Lave and E. Wenger (1991) analyzed membership and especially legitimate peripheral participation (LPP) in communities; they concluded that all members of a community have the same rights and are legitimated in participating to all resources and practices of the community.

A. L. Brown and J. Campione (1994), focused on communities of learners (CoL). Students, teachers, tutors, and experts contribute to make the community and work together: they analyze previous knowledge, verify and discuss it, and build new knowledge and theories. Some years later the same authors suggested a change in their idea of CoL, and proposed the concept of fostering community of learners (FCL), which is based on a system of interactive activities within a learning environment, where conscious and reflexive works are made (Brown & Campione, 1996): research, information sharing, and suitable exercises are for the authors the basic elements for the development of reflection and deepen learning.

Constructivist principles acknowledge that real-life learning is messy and complex. Classrooms which emulate the "fuzziness" of this learning are more effective in preparing learners for life-long learning. On this side an example of learning environment built on the web and freely accessible at the URL http://quest.nasa.gov/aero/planetary/welcome.html, is the *planetary flight* site developed by NASA (Gillani, 2003); other sites of NASA which can engage students in authentic scientific and engineering processes can be found at the URL http://quest.nasa.gov/index.html.

Connectivism

Connectivism, as proposed by Siemens (2005), has its bases on the integration of the principles explored by chaos, network, complexity and self-organization theories, to design new ways of interpreting learning and knowledge phenomena.

Some remarks are needed before a deeper analysis of connectivism:

- D. de Kerckhove (2000), defined connective intelligence as the set of strategies and cognitive skills emerging while being in the Internet, or contextually to ICT use, but his definition did not flow up in a theory on knowledge construction,
    - There is no general agreement on connectivism as a developmental learning theory,
    - Connectivist ideas have been proposed to overcome the difficulties of the other psycho-pedagogical paradigms in the digital era,
    - There are just a few examples of applications of connectivism to teaching.

Following Siemens ideas on connectivism, learning is a process that occurs within nebulous environments of shifting core elements – not entirely under the control of the individual. Learning (defined as actionable knowledge) can reside outside of subjects (within an organization or a database), it is focused on connecting specialized information sets, and the connections that enable us to learn more are more important than our current state of knowing.

Connectivism is driven by the understanding that decisions are based on rapidly altering foundations. New information is continually being acquired. The ability to draw distinctions between important and unimportant information is vital. The ability to recognize when new information alters the landscape based on decisions made yesterday is also critical.

Where connectivism differs from other theories, argues Downes (2007), is that connectivism denies that knowledge is propositional. Otherwise stated, the other theories are 'cognitivist', in the sense that they depict knowledge and learning as being grounded in language and logic. Connectivism is, by contrast, 'connectionist'. Knowledge is, in this theory, *literally* the set of connections formed by actions and experience. It may consist in part of linguistic structures, but it is not essentially based in linguistic structures, and the properties and constraints of linguistic structures are not the properties and constraints of connectivism.

As regards teaching experiences based on connectivism there are a few examples to refer to, if all the constraints of the founders of the theory are applied. Downes (2007) states in fact that: "to teach is to model and demonstrate, to learn is to practice and reflect". Siemens and Downes have proposed a course on "Connectivism and Connective Knowledge" in 2008, this model course has been repeated in 2009.

On the contrary, some elements of connectivism can be found in the teaching experiences of J. S. Brown, who worked with technicians and researchers on training and updating courses; the main concepts emerging from his work are: 1) the construction of knowledge assets, which make effective learning in a community of practice, 2) the web as a medium for an ecology of learning, where everyone can be producer and consumer of information and knowledge and 3) the construction of a regional learning repository, where a social knowledge is built and made available (Brown, 2000).

Conclusion

Final remarks accompanying what has been reported until now are:

a) The different psycho-pedagogical paradigms are used from teachers depending on the contexts and topics to be faced in the class; otherwise stated, they all can be present in today teaching praxis at all school levels, also in the work of the same teacher and in the same teaching module,
b) The levels of digital competence required to students and teachers, to fully benefit of the application of a given psycho-pedagogical paradigm, vary considerably when passing from a learning theory to another; a remarkable increase in the level of the needed digital competences can in fact be easily detected when passing from behaviorism to connectivism.

Roughly speaking, the association to each learning theory of a value, ranging from low to high, for the level of the digital competence to be held from students and teachers in that context, leads to the graphic in Figure 1.

It is probably too early to say if being "digital natives" is a sufficient condition to hypothesize the use of the different psycho-pedagogical paradigms in the school, where digital equipments are in every class if not for every student, without any further work; recent studies suggest caution in the application of the simple equation "digital native" = "digital competent" (Mantovani & Ferri, 2008). Furthermore, it cannot be hypothesized that all teachers are able in the use of digital equipments and especially in their proper

Figure 1. Digital knowledge and skills to be possessed in the different learning theories

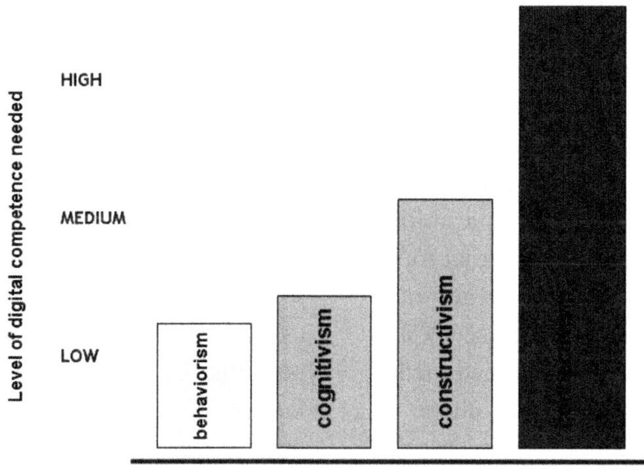

application to the different learning theories in the digital age (as shown from the many training programs for in-service teachers and from the myriad of teaching innovation projects continuously approved and funded by Education Ministries).

The DULP paradigm (Design inspired learning, Ubiquitous learning, Liquid learning places, Person in place centered design), as developmental learning context able in suggesting answers to the above problems, can probably give a contribution in this direction (http://www.mifav.uniroma2.it/iede_mk/events/dulp/index.php?s=9).

THE FRAMEWORK FOR DIGITAL COMPETENCE ASSESSMENT

In the above section a first attempt of connecting digital competences and the application of the different learning theories in everyday class work has been made. It has also been questioned whether a good digital literacy is enough or not to guarantee students and teachers the full access to the resources available on the Internet and the mastery of computing for the management of the information and the construction of new knowledge.

In the author opinion basic computing and information management skills, or more properly digital competences, must be guaranteed in educational systems and in what follows a sound framework for digital competence assessment will be presented.

The Need for Digital Competence Assessment

Since twenty five years ago, when personal computing became a reality, many organizations and institutions tried to specify the features of the literacy needed in the society; the increasing presence of computers and digital equipments in all aspects of our life induced many changes in the ideas from time to time emerging.

The introduction of a suitable literacy at school or, more generally, for every citizen in a perspective of lifelong learning, has been considered the best choice for the creation of a sound digital culture. On this side public institutions like the Associations of Libraries, OCSE and UNESCO, worked at the definition of different "literacies", needed in the information/ knowledge society:

information literacy, computing literacy, IT and ICT literacy, digital literacy and media education, were the results of their efforts.

Recently a comprehensive definition for digital literacy has been proposed by Martin (2005), when working on the European research project DigEuLit (http://www.jelit.org/): "Digital Literacy is the awareness, attitude and ability of individuals to appropriately use digital tools and facilities to identify, access, manage, integrate, evaluate, analyze and synthesize digital resources, construct new knowledge, create media expressions, and communicate with others, in the context of specific life situations, in order to enable constructive social action; and to reflect upon this process".

What is changed in these years to induce the passage from "digital literacy" to "digital competence"? A different approach to the analysis of the impact that new technologies have on mankind has emerged, when passing from the discussion on how people use digital resources and processes, to the analysis of what they must know and be able to do with technologies. Otherwise stated, there has been a shift in the focus attention, from a discipline centered paradigm to a human centered paradigm: competences as active involvement of subjects with their representations of reality, their knowledge and skills are considered much more important than the knowledge of instruments and processes (Le Boterf, 1990).

On the basis of the data reported until now A. Calvani et al. (2008) decided to better analyze these competences and to create the instruments for their assessment, to let people know the levels of their abilities and help teachers plan suitable activities to improve students' competences.

They all agreed on the following features for digital competences:

- They are interconnected, because they are not independent from other key competences like reading, numeracy, problem solving, inferential skills etc.
- They are sensitive to the socio-cultural context, because their meaning can change over time, according to the context and to different educational settings.

A First Hypothesis of Framework for Digital Competence Assessment

By assuming an anthropocentric perspective for the development of the digital competence assessment framework, the results from psycho-pedagogical literature and especially the well known educational taxonomies for the assessment of learning and for knowledge construction and evolution (Bloom *et al.*, 1956), have been adopted. The model for that framework has been hypothesized based on the following dimensions: cognitive, affective and social-relational.

The assessment of the competences in the new cognitive dimension was based on the Bloom's categories: knowledge, comprehension, application, analysis, synthesis, evaluation (Bloom *et al.*, 1956). A finer breakdown of the elements to be intertwined with the competences in that dimension led to the specification of the following elements:

a) The verbal-linguistic and logical-mathematical competences, deduced from the corresponding Gardner intelligences (Gardner, 1993), to be seen as special sections in the cognitive dimension; they are very important together with technological competences when people use digital equipment for the construction of new knowledge, the creation of media expressions, and communication with others, in the context of specific life situations, as suggested by Martin (2005),
b) The skills derived from the construction and evolution of the concepts of space, time and causality (Piaget, 1970); which act as categories on the above sections in the cognitive dimension. This last issue has been derived from the space dilatation

Figure 2. The first hypothesis for a digital competence assessment framework

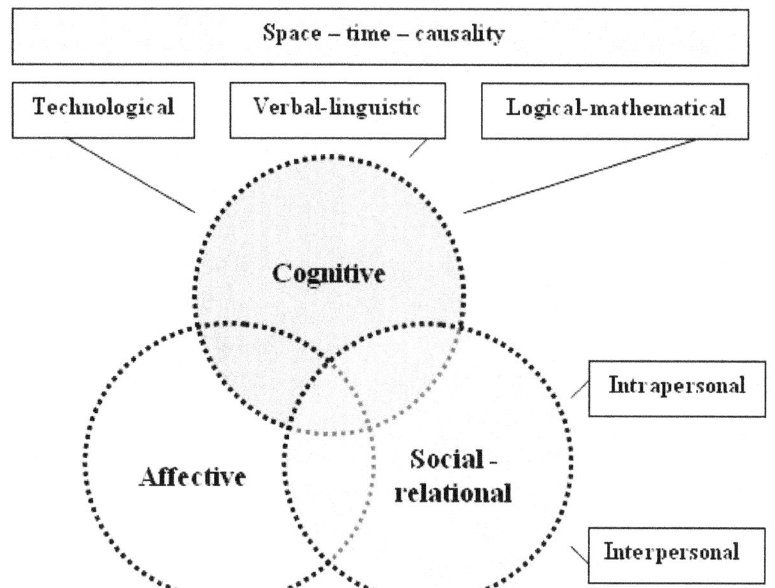

and time contraction usually experienced by people interacting with information on the web, and can also be found in the loss of causality, especially experienced in the answer that search engines give to people queries, when word matching strategies are adopted.

- In the affective dimension the Krathwohl taxonomy (multidimensional, because they imply the integration of cognitive, relational and social abilities and skills,
- They are complex and evolve with time,

Krathwohl et al., 1973) has been adopted. It is based on the following categories for the assessment of facts and experiences: receiving phenomena, responding to phenomena, evaluating, organizing and internalizing phenomena.

At last the social-relational dimension has been hypothesized to assess human and social interactions and relations in the digital age; the problem with this dimension has been the uncertainty on the categories to be adopted for the taxonomy.

The final framework is reported in Figure 2 (Cartelli et al., 2010). It can be easily recognized that cognitive competences are split in three sections: technological, verbal-linguistic and logical-mathematical, all under the umbrella of space, time and causality categories. In the figure are also reported the affective and the social-relational dimensions; this last one, still to be deeply studied, analyzed and described, is thought under the influence of interpersonal and intrapersonal interactions of the subjects.

The Final Framework for Digital Competence Assessment

Although the framework was not complete in all its details (for the lack of a detailed social-relational taxonomy), an attempt has been made to evaluate the goodness of what hypothesized, and a questionnaire has been submitted to students of different school levels (Primary and Junior High School). A good help in this direction has indirectly come from the work of many colleagues, who yearly cooperate in the development of the questionnaire for the "Beaver" international competition. The questionnaire made up for the competition is usually devoted to the analysis of computing competences, but its questions (or those suitably selected from the international repository collecting all the questions approved for the competition), have the right features to analyze the technological, logical-mathematical and verbal-linguistic sections in the cognitive dimension (they usually explore situations and phenomena simultaneously pertaining to one or more sections in that dimension), and evidence clear dependences from the space, time and causality categories governing them (Cartelli et al., 2010).

As regards the affective dimension the following aspects have been analyzed by means of some questions in a section of the questionnaire: 1) student – questionnaire interaction, 2) student – discipline interaction, 3) student – digital technology interaction.

The analysis of students' answers (Cartelli, 2010a) shows that:

- In the cognitive dimension, when a specific section is involved in the solution of a problem and one or more categories intervene in the description of the corresponding phenomenon, students' performances can change accordingly (otherwise stated one or more sections in the cognitive dimension can be more developed with respect to the others in the students and their answers reflect this different development),
- In the affective dimension all the categories have been detected:
    - The "receiving" was present in all the students who took part in the competition,
    - The "responding" emerged together with good scores in the answers to a given section of the cognitive dimension,
    - The "valuing" was present in the answers to questions asking for an opinion on the cognitive dimension (student – questionnaire interaction),
    - The "organizing" appeared in the answers to questions asking for an opinion on the student – discipline interaction,
    - The "characterizing" could be found in the answers to the question asking for an opinion on the student digital technology interaction.

From a deepen analysis of the students' answers in the cognitive dimension it was difficult to identify the higher categories of that taxonomy (i.e., analysis, synthesis and evaluation). The suggestion for a revision of the structure of the Bloom's cognitive taxonomy came from A. Churches (2008), who applied the revised formulation of Bloom's cognitive taxonomy (Anderson & Krathwohl, 2001) to ICT use. Due to the features of the revised cognitive taxonomy it looked suitable to transfer the results of Churches to all the sections in the cognitive dimension (i.e., technological, verbal-linguistic and logical-mathematical). The result, with the translation of each level in the corresponding actions, is reported in Table 1.

Progresses in the interpretation of students' answers could be obtained with the application of the above table, but also in the best cases (i.e., when the students made their own computations to find the right answer to a given question) the highest categories in the taxonomy (i.e., evaluating and creating) could not be detected.

At last the psychological literature on relational domain, and especially the work from A. R. Brandhorst (1976), suggested the structure of the taxonomy for the social-relational dimension in the framework for digital competence assessment.

By adopting Brandhorst's ideas, a taxonomy conceptualizing some interpersonal skills, in terms

Table 1. Application of Churches' qualification of Bloom's categories to the cognitive dimension of the digital competence assessment framework

Bloom's categories	Technological	Verbal-linguistic	Logical-mathematical
Remembering	Recognizing, listing, describing, identifying, retrieving, naming, locating, finding		
Understanding	Interpreting, summarizing, inferring, paraphrasing, classifying, comparing, explaining, exemplifying		
Applying	Implementing, carrying out, using, executing		
Analyzing	Comparing, organizing, deconstructing, attributing, outlining, finding, structuring, integrating		
Evaluating	Checking, hypothesizing, critiquing, experimenting, judging, testing, detecting, monitoring		
Creating	Designing, constructing, planning, producing, inventing, devising, making		

of observable behaviors amenable to measurement, could be draft.

In this taxonomy six categories representing six different sets of capabilities are present: one of them cognitive (conceptualization), one cognitive-affective (evaluation), and four cognitive-affective-behavioral (leadership, followership, role exchange - yielding, role exchange - asserting). Each category has to be thought broken down into three subcategories, reflecting three different bases of order in a task oriented group: control of sanctions, control through persuasion, and control through the exercise of expert knowledge.

Main assumptions of Brandhorst's taxonomy are:

- No one should be a leader on a continuous basis, and in a given set of circumstances another individual might most appropriately lead, so that being a follower would be more appropriate for the first subject,
- Followership is a learned behavior, and should accordingly be included in a taxonomy of educational objectives,
- The learned dispositions of follower are psychologically unique, and hence must be identified and pursued as unique categories of objectives.

The application of Brandhorst relational taxonomy to the social-relational dimension of the digital competence assessment framework required a deeper analysis of its categories; they are discussed below:

1. *Conceptualization* refers to the capacity to relate to leader and follower roles on a class basis, to specify the relevant variables which determine a class of role orientations; it also refers to the capacity to recognize and classify leader-follower relationships as power, influence or interdependence orientations,
2. *Evaluation* refers to the ability to identify criteria for making judgments about ego's capacity for leadership in given situations and to apply those criteria objectively, to self and relevant others in the given group - situation, in order to determine who should most appropriately be leading in a group task situation,
3. *Leadership* is the ability to direct and coordinate task- relevant group activities.

In power orientations it is the ability to direct and coordinate task relevant group activities through the resource of control over positive and negative sanctions.

In social orientations it is the ability to direct and coordinate task relevant group activities through the resource of persuasion.

In interdependent orientations it is the ability to direct and coordinate task relevant group activities because of group-acknowledged superior capabilities (i.e., the influence of specialized knowledge).

4. *Followership* is the ability to accept and acknowledge the leadership of another in the pursuit and culmination of task relevant group activities. For measurement purposes, followership is defined as the ability to participate as an integral part of the group without being the leader.

In power orientation it is the ability to remain in a group and participate in it under conditions when another controls through the use of positive and negative sanctions.

In social orientations it is the ability to remain in a group and participate in it under conditions when another controls through persuasion.

In interdependent orientations it is the ability to remain in a group and participate in it under conditions when another directs and controls through the influence of specialized knowledge or expertise.

5. *Role exchange in a yielding direction* is the capacity to transfer the leadership of a task relevant group activity to another group member, without either disrupting the group activity or withdrawing from the group.

In power orientation it refers to the capacity to acknowledge the superior control of another over positive and negative sanctions and withdraw from the leadership position without either leaving the group or disrupting the activity of the group.

In social orientation it refers to the capacity to recognize the superior position of another in terms of group loyalty and withdraw from the leadership position without either leaving the group or disrupting the activity of the group.

In interdependent orientation it refers to the capacity to recognize the superior qualifications (knowledge and experience) of another and withdraw from the leadership position without either leaving the group or disrupting the group activity.

6. *Role exchange in an assertive direction* is defined as the capacity to claim the leadership position from another without unnecessarily disrupting the group activities and/or necessitating the former leader's leaving the group.

In power orientation it refers to the capacity to use superior control over positive and negative sanctions to assert one's leadership in replacing an incumbent leader, without disruption of the group.

In social orientation it refers to the capacity to use the personal loyalty of group members to assert one's leadership and replace an incumbent one without disrupting the group activities or necessitating the former leader's departure from the group.

In interdependent orientation it refers to the capacity to demonstrate one's superior knowledge and skills relevant to a group task, and thereby assume the leadership of the group from an incumbent leader.

All the above categories looked suitable enough to analyze the relational phenomena both in the real communities and the virtual communities, especially in these last ones, where digital competences have a prominent role in determining interpersonal relations and the CMC (Computer Mediated Communication) can make difficult communication (identity masking, gender swapping and other side effects, depending on the CMC have been widely studied).

As regards the detection and measurement of the different categories in the above taxonomy, a situation very similar to that of cognitive taxonomy has to be noted. As suggested from Brandhorst, only for conceptualization and evaluation, the first two categories, written tests seem to be used without any problem. Special environments allowing the learner to explore social relationships through direct experience, either in simulated formats or 'real world work experience' would seem to be superior to verbal or mechanically mediated experience.

The framework for digital competence assessment emerging from the inclusion of the new features into the old ones is reported in Figure 3.

It has to be noted, in the lower part of the draft, the presence of a meta-category the "ethic-moral behavior / judgment", covering both the affective and social-relational taxonomies; it is the result of the recovering of the ethical dimension hypothesized in the framework by Calvani et al. (2008), which was no more present in the scheme reported in Figure 2 due to the criticisms expressed from many colleagues (i.e., they opposed to the presence of regulatory more than descriptive issues which pertained to that dimension). This meta-category, in the author opinion, intervenes in determining different behaviors in the highest categories of the affective and social-relational taxonomies, because digital equipments and especially the web and social networking have been

Figure 3. The final framework for digital competence assessment

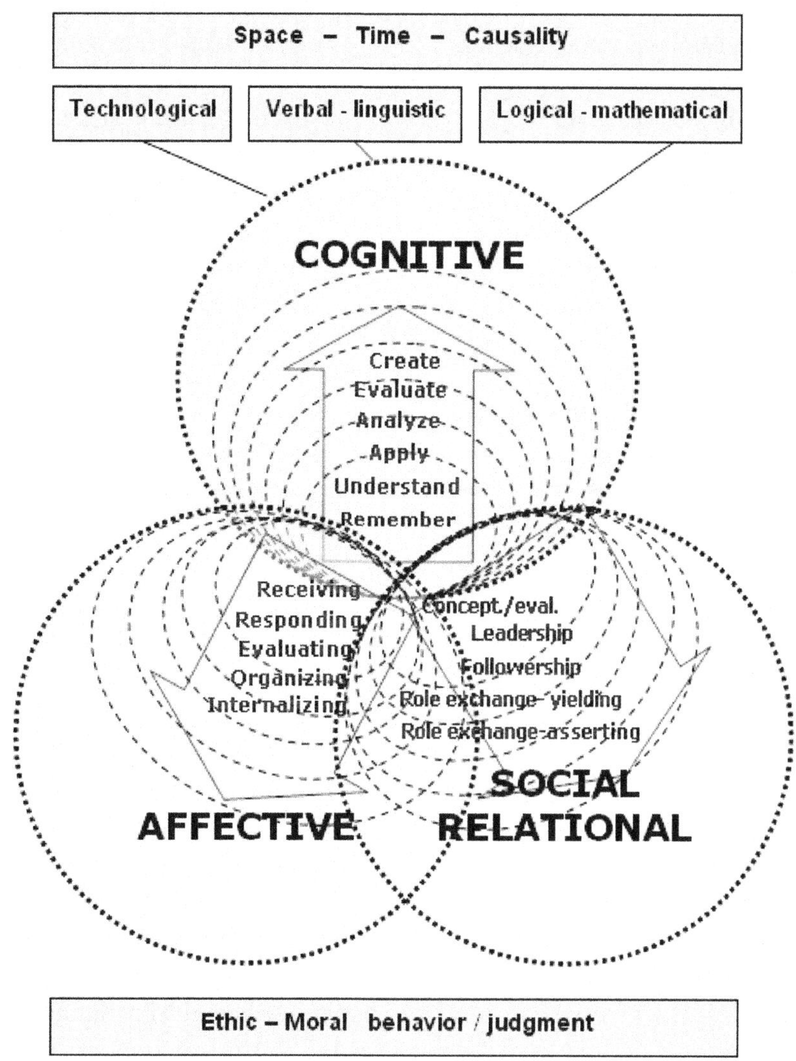

proven to alter the perception of ethical behaviors in the subjects.

CONCLUSION, TEACHING SUGGESTIONS AND FUTURE STUDIES

In the above section a framework for digital competence assessment has been proposed as the result of successive transformations and integrations. Main questions are:

1. Is the new framework the final one?
2. Will the instruments used so far, be sufficient to assess the students' digital competences?
3. What suggestions can be given to teachers to improve the students' digital competences and more generally their teaching?

The answers to the first two questions are not independent; since now the structure of the framework has in fact evolved by virtue of the results obtained from the instruments used. It can be stated that:

a. The framework in Figure 3 is probably the most comprehensive one, and can be considered in its final form until the need for a revision coming from new results,
b. The questionnaire from the "Beaver" contest, when suitably completed with questions on the affective and social-relational categories, can still be used for the assessment of digital competences, or at least for the first categories in all the dimensions;
c. Whether projective or situated tests can be used to obtain a measure for the higher categories in all the taxonomies, or virtual environments can be made up to simulate real phenomena, it is too early to say (i.e., this is one of the research lines to be followed and developed).

As regards the last question, the following results from the most recent experiences carried out by the author must be reported:

1) The Open Source instruments for the management of documents and the creation of Learning Objects, have been positively used from teachers in their everyday work,
2) The questionnaire developed under the guidelines of the framework for digital competence assessment (especially its cognitive dimension), has been considered very useful from teachers, to discover undeveloped or less developed languages (i.e., sections) and skills in the students (Cartelli, 2010b),
3) The use of instruments involving students and families in the continuous monitoring of school processes and in the updating of students learning and educational data, had positive effects on the evolution of teaching-learning activities (Cartelli, 2010c),
4) The planning of teaching activities, based on problem finding, problem searching and problem building, has been considered essential for students' successful learning, due to the development of problem solving features; the hypothesis underlying this issue is that contextual and situated learning can be reconciled with scientific/discipline learning and, what's more, students can be helped to overcome the problems they usually show when approaching scientific knowledge.

The main suggestion for teachers when they submit to their students both discipline topics or modular units, is the adoption of a spiral teaching-learning process, passing through the recourse to the different learning theories and the teaching-learning strategies reported in the first part of the paper. In Table 2 the phases of the suggested process are reported with the main psycho-pedagogical paradigm used.

Table 2. Hypothesis of the structure of a teaching route

Psycho-pedagogical paradigm	Activity to be started
Behaviorism / Cognitivism	using a platform for making transparent the teaching-learning processes to create a snapshot of the teaching-learning work which can be easily seen from everyone (i.e., to make clear and available to all stakeholders - students, families, teachers etc. the aims, the instruments, the strategies, the targets to be hit and the evolution of the learning unit),
Behaviorism / Cognitivism	planning and building up of Learning Objects to be used for presenting the topics / module to the class,
Cognitivism	using an e-learning platform where to put the materials proposed to the students and start self – group work and discussions (i.e., management of documents, authoring, blogs, wikis and forums),
Constructivism	planning and carrying out of class work with an IWB (Interactive White Board), both for self and group work,
Connectivism	soliciting the collaborative work for the research of more information on different sources and especially on the web and using freely accessible online resources for the construction of shared documents,
Connectivism	proposing and guiding the use of online instruments for the production of shared documents on the web (Wikipedia?), as suggested from C. Petrucco in another contribution in this book.

There are at least two notices to avoid confusion and misleading in the interpretation/application of the process highlighted in Table 3, and they are reported below:

a. To make the process easier and more efficient, the continuous connection / communication with all stakeholders has not been reported in the steps following the first, but it is hypothesized the intervention from relatives, experts, researchers, social offices etc. in all process phases; as a consequence adjustments to planned activities must be possible,
b. The spiral process can be triggered by requests for deepening of special topics and processes, from all stakeholders, but it is neither necessary not binding,
c. The involvement of all or part of the different psycho-pedagogical paradigms and the hypothesized sequence of events may depend on the topic, the theme, the situation (i.e., the unit of learning) proposed to the students; it means that the process can stop before the end of the trail is reached.

It seems plausible to introduce a specific term to describe the highlighted process and in the author opinion the best one is: Open Teaching System (OTS).

The openness in the acronym comes from many sides: the Open Source Software to be used, the recourse to different psycho-pedagogical paradigms depending on the topics and the processes, also in the same learning unit, the openness to all stakeholders of the educational process and the creation of an open network, whose contribution can help students in growing in the knowledge society.

REFERENCES

Anderson, L. W., & Krathwohl, D. (Eds.). (2001). *A Taxonomy for Learning, Teaching and Assessing: a Revision of Bloom's Taxonomy of Educational Objectives*. New York: Longman.

Ausubel, D. P. (1968). *Education psychology: A cognitive view*. New York: Holt, Rinehart & Winston.

Bauman, Z. (2006). *Vita liquida*. Rome-Bari, Italy: Laterza.

Bloom, B. S. (1956). *Taxonomy of Educational Objectives, Handbook I: The Cognitive Domain*. New York: David McKay Co. Inc.

Brandhorst, A. R. (1976). Toward a Taxonomy of Educational Objectives in the Relational Domain. In *Proceedings of the Annual Meeting of the National Council for Social Studies*, Washington, DC. Retrieved August 4, 2010, from http://www.eric.ed.gov/ERICWebPortal/search/detailmini.jsp?_nfpb=true&_&ERICExtSearch_SearchValue_0=ED134505&ERICExtSearch_SearchType_0=no&accno=ED134505

Brown, A. L., & Campione, J. (1994). Guided discovery in a community of learners In McGilly, K. (Ed.), *Classroom lesson: Integrating cognitive theory and classroom practice* (pp. 229–270). Cambridge, MA: MIT Press.

Brown, A. L., & Campione, J. (1996). Psychological theory and the design of innovative learning environments: On procedure, principles and systems In Schaube, L., & Glaser, R. (Eds.), *Innovation in learning* (pp. 289–375). Mahwah, NJ: Lawrence Erlbaum.

Brown, J. S. (2002). *Growing Up Digital: How the Web Changes Work, Education, and the Ways People Learn. United States Distance Learning Association*. Retrieved July 31, 2010, from http://www.usdla.org/html/ journal/FEB02_Issue/article0 1.html

Bruner, J. (1966). *Towards a theory of instruction*. Cambridge, MA: Harvard University Press.

Calvani, A., Cartelli, A., Fini, A., & Ranieri, M. (2008). Models and Instruments for Assessing Digital Competence at School. *Journal of E-learning and Knowledge Society*, *4*(3), 183–193.

Carroll, J. B. (1963). A model of school learning. *Teachers College Record*, *64*, 723–733.

Cartelli, A. (2010a). Frameworks for Digital Competence Assessment: Proposals, Instruments and Evaluation. In E. Cohen & E. Boyd (Eds.), *Proceedings of the Informing Science + Information Technology Education International Conference (InSITE 2010)* (pp. 561-574).

Cartelli, A. (2010b). Digital Competence Assessment and Teaching Strategies in the Knowledge Society. In *Proceedings of the 7th Pan-Hellenic Conference with International Participation (HCICTE 2010)*, Korinthos, Greece.

Cartelli, A. (2010c). Digital Competences in Online Classes. In *Proceedings of the European Conference on E-Learning (ECEL 2010)*, Porto, Portugal.

Cartelli, A., Dagiene, V., & Futschek, G. (2010). Bebras Contest and Digital Competence Assessment: Analysis of Frameworks. *International Journal of Digital Literacy and Digital Competence*, *1*(1), 24–39.

Churches, A. (2008). Bloom's Taxonomy Blooms Digitally. *Tech&Learning online Journal*. Retrieved August 4, 2010, from http://www.techlearning.com/article/8670

Cole, M. (1996). *Cultural psychology*. Cambridge, MA: Belknap.

Council of European Parliament. (2005). *Recommendation of the European Parliament and of the Council on key competences for lifelong learning*. Retrieved June 1, 2010, from http://ec.europa.eu/education/policies/2010/doc/keyrec_en.pdf

De Kerckhove, D. (1995). *The skin of culture*. Toronto, Canada: Somerville House.

Downes, S. (2007). *What Connectivism Is*. Retrieved August 18, 2010, from http://halfanhour.blogspot.com/2007/02/what-connectivism-is.html

Flavell, J. H. (1985). *Cognitive development*. Englewood Cliffs, NJ: Prentice Hall.

Gardner, H. (1993). *Multiple Intelligences: The Theory in Practice*. New York: Basic Books.

Gillani, B. B. (2003). *Learning Theories and the Design of E-learning Environments*. Lanham, MD: University Press of America.

Gredler, M. E. (2001). *Learning and Instruction: Theory into Practice*. Upper Saddle River, NJ: Pearson Education.

Krathwohl, D. R. (2002). A Revision of Bloom Taxonomy: an overview. *Theory into Practice, 41*(4), 212–218. Retrieved August 2, 2010. doi:10.1207/s15430421tip4104_2

Krathwohl, D. R., Bloom, B. S., & Masia, B. B. (1973). *Taxonomy of Educational Objectives, the Classification of Educational Goals. Handbook II: Affective Domain*. New York: David McKay Co. Inc.

Laboratory of Comparative Human Cognition (LCHC). (1982). Culture and intelligence In Sternberg, R. J. (Ed.), *Handbook of human intelligence*. Cambridge, MA: Cambridge University Press.

Lave, J., & Wenger, E. (1991). *Situated learning. Legitimate peripheral participation*. Cambridge, MA: Cambridge University Press.

Le Boterf, G. (1990). *De la compétence: Essai sur un attracteur étrange*. Paris: Les Ed. de l'Organisation.

Mantovani, S., & Ferri, P. (2008). *Digital Kids*. Milan, Italy: Etas.

Martin, A. (2005). DigEuLit – a European Framework for Digital Literacy: a Progress Report. *JeLit, Journal of eLiteracy, 2*(2). Retrieved July 31, 2010, from http://www.jelit.org/65/01/JeLit_Paper_31.pdf

OECD. (2009). *PISA 2006 Technical Report*. Retrieved June 1, 2010, from http://www.pisa.oecd.org/document/41/0,3343,en_32252351_32236191_42025897_1_1_1_1,00.html

Papert, S. (1993). *The children's machine*. New York: Basic Books.

Piaget, J. (1952). *The origins of intelligence in children*. New York: International University Press. doi:10.1037/11494-000

Piaget, J. (1970). *Lo sviluppo mentale del bambino*. Turin, Italy: Einaudi.

Pozzali, A., & Ferri, P. M. (2010). The Medial Diet of University Students in Italy: An Exploratory Research. *International Journal of Digital Literacy and Digital Competence, 1*(2), 1–10.

Prensky, M. (2001). Digital Natives, Digital Immigrants on the Horizon. *MCB University Press, 9*(5).

Siemens, G. (2005). Connectivism: A Learning Theory for the Digital Age. *Instructional Technology and Distance Learning, 2*(1). Retrieved July 31, 2010, from http://www.itdl.org/Journal/Jan_05/article01.htm

Skinner, B. F. (1953). *Science and human behaviour*. New York: Macmillan.

Vygotsky, L. S. (1978). *Mind in Society: The development of higher psychological processes*. Cambridge, MA: MIT Press.

This work was previously published in International Journal of Digital Literacy and Digital Competence, Volume 1, Issue 3, edited by Antonio Cartelli, pp. 1-17, copyright 2010 by IGI Publishing (an imprint of IGI Global).

Chapter 6
Beyond the Media Literacy: Complex Scenarios and New Literacies for the Future Education– The Centrality of Design

Carlo Giovannella
University of Rome Tor Vergata, Italy

ABSTRACT

The advent of new media and web technologies made both contents and "containers" more "liquid" and requires an in depth reflection on the multi-facets concept of literacy in which the author tries to develop from an education point of view that can be defined as "experiential". According to such reflection, in the present scenarios, the "design" becomes central to education, underlining the need of educational activities, which should include among their objectives the dissemination of what one may call "design literacy".

THE COMPLEXITY IS NOT JUST IN THE "MEDIA"

The bursting development of last decade technologies, usually referred to as "digital," accompanied us during a transition from "disorder" to "order" - rather than from "continuous" to "discrete" - that made all informations easy to virtualize and to associate/organize in vectors and matrices. On one hand, then, contents have become easily to reproduce and transmit, on the other mathematically manipulable and mixable, with no limits and barriers. All this, as well known, thanks to a single "little box" whose size is getting smaller and smaller, a single "meta-medium" that once we were used to call "computer" and that today, in its multiple transformations and reductions,

DOI: 10.4018/978-1-4666-0903-7.ch006

has become a technological appendix of the human brain with multiple forms/faces, not always easily identifiable.

For our "life-style" even more relevant than the transition from "disorder" to "order" appeared to be, however, the possibility to organize the flow of contents in "containers" characterized by a familiar look and feel. The development of nets to distribute the information can be considered a "sine qua non" but not the killing factor; in fact, it has been only with the release of the first hypermedial browsers - Mosaic ® and Netscape ® - and even more when the browser become a mass application - with Internet Explorer ® (thanks to the penetration of the Windows ® OS) - that one begun to realize what dimension could had taken the "digital divide", and its consequences. At that point it was necessary to take actions for the dissemination of an appropriate "media literacy" (see for example Tornero, 2004).

But technology continued to be unceasingly and inevitably developed, so before one could win the battle for a reasonable spread of "media literacy" the front widened. Since several years, indeed, are no longer only information flows to be virtualized, but also environments and functions/activities associated with them. Nowadays it is obvious to all the global nature of market places and e-commerce, and even more of the access to information through search engines and social networks. Their use is now part of everyday life of the most advanced component of the population of those nations whose economic power is consolidated, or emerging.

At the same time, inevitably, the meaning of "media literacy" changed and cannot any longer limited to the ability to manage and treat arrays/matrices of information by means of applications having more or less user-friendly interfaces, but had to include the ability to orient oneself within environments and applications (Prensky, 2001) that opens new possibilities, provide competitive advantages and new opportunities, also in terms of potentially new professional qualifications. In other words, the media-literacy makes a quantum leap in which: a) the ability to process information became a basic one, as it was once writing, reading and numeracy; depending of the level of such ability, the individuals started to be represented in a continuum "classification space" that ranges from consumer to prosumer of the 'digital universe' b) the professional treatment of the "digital" information was delegated, however, to experts who developed specific skills, c) higher level skills, like knowledge and efficient use of the "environments" that populate the net, gradually became indispensable components of the personal background of the "digital human".

Beside the most evident aspects, there were also less obvious consequences of the transformation described above:

i) The individual achieved a higher degree of centrality although s/he was considered as "user" rather than "person" (inevitably, together, became central also the so called "experience of use");
ii) It started to be clear that each one had to reinforce her/his critical skills that cannot be delegated solely to the "intelligence" of search engines or to the spread of fads which too often prove to be ephemeral (e.g., the Second Life ® effect, the most recent Wave ® effect, and many others that have marked the development of the Web). The essentiality of a critical ability becomes even more evident in the presence of the magmatic reconfigurability of both content and containers, either for the "inflow" rate of new contents, either for the increasing level of "intelligence" that started to be embedded in the applications, in the attempt to profile the users and to satisfy her/his presumed needs.

When attention to the individual is not equivalent - and almost never coincides - with the attention to the whole kaleidoscope of qualities that make significant human experiences and, instead, focus on the satisfaction of customers' individualism and their need to feel at the center of the media stage (in other words when the media try to satisfy craving to be present, offering them what we metaphorically may call the "five minutes of fame" on the Web) one observes also another phenomenon: containers and contents lose their "character", become digital "no-place" (Augé, 1993) and dissolve in the indifferentiated "mare magnum" of the net, dominated by the" void for excess", requiring to reflect on the meaning of "digital places" (Tuan, 1977; Giovannella, 2006, 2008c).

This framework, however, will change again in the near future.

The "machine", indeed, is progressively hybridizing with artifacts and environments of the everyday life (Weiser, 1993; Dourish, 2004) and its presence will manifest only through the perception of"computability". The interaction, in fact, is becoming so natural (by means of voice, gestures, emotions, etc ...) that, in the future, there will be no need to learn new interaction techniques: we are moving away from the "mouse" era and entering the "organic" era of interaction (Giovannella, 2008a), an era that at mass-market level has been anticipated by pioneering products such like the iPhone/iPad ® and other of the same class.

A more natural interaction will then bring individuals to give less relevance to functional aspects and more to the so called "use qualities" (Löwgren, 2006) that will contribute to define the one's personal EXPERIENCE. Physical and virtual environments will hybridize, become able to perceive individual's conditions and to co-evolve to respond to each one's personal needs and to provide, thus, more personalized "experience":

Liquidity, not only because of the pathological society described by Bauman (Bauman, 2000), will become a dominant characteristic of our life (Giovannella, 2009).

Looking ahead, therefore, we can only expect a further transformation of the concept of "media literacy". It will be not any longer limited to the ability to "play" with the media, to orient oneself in the virtual environments provided by the network, but it will include also the ability to design her/his own destiny, its trajectory within the physical-virtual liquidity: the dissemination of the "design literacy" will become the educational challenge of the future.

The above scenarios raise some questions on which we will try to reflect in the following paragraphs

- What is an "experience" ? Is there any definition of "experience" that applies also to educational processes?
- In what respects the "design" can play a central role in education?
- Is it possible to develop an operational framework that can be adopted to design and manage educational processes having among their purposes also the dissemination of a "design literacy" (in order to prevent the spread of what in future could configure as a "design devide") ?

EDUCATION AS AN EXPERIENCE

Regardless of whether the educational process will be conducted face-to-face, in blended or fully on-line configurations, the framework described above requires the development of complex PB3 - problem, project and process based (Giovannella & Spinelli, 2009) - educational processes, as 'organic' as the era we are living in.

Such processes, which cultural background can be found in the activism, should be regarded as "experiences", characterized by their own "experience's qualities".

Although the identification of all the dimensions of an "experience" is still a very open issue, in a very general manner, one can say that every "experience", including the educational ones, is based on interactions, or communicative acts,

Figure 1. Representation of the time dimension and of the interaction levels involved in an experience

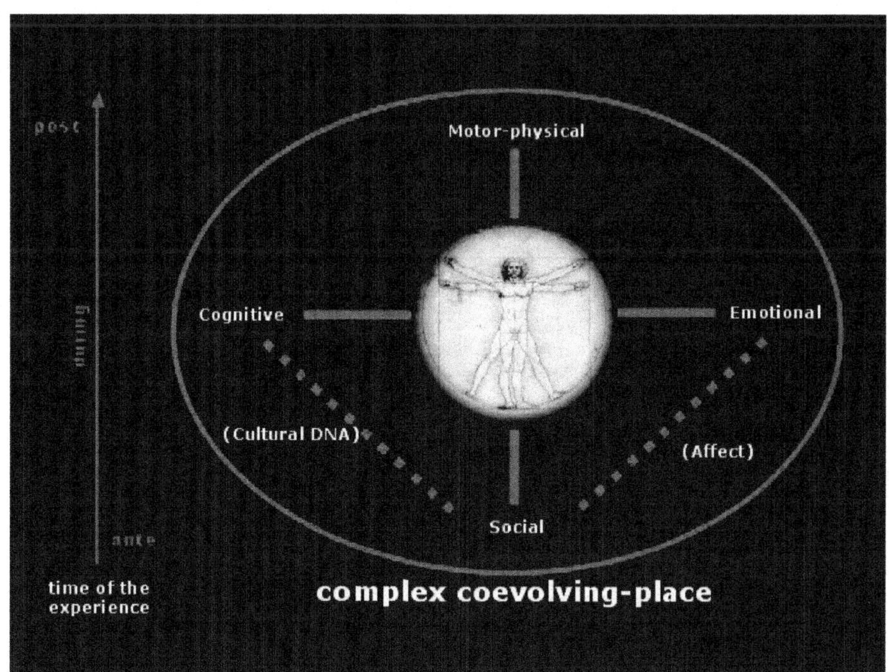

performed by the individuals simultaneously on multiple levels, see Figure 1, the main fuels being the personal motivation. It is not possible, therefore, to describe an "experience" separately from the personal characteristics of each individual, because this latter is at the same time focus and active element of the "experience".

To define the "experience", then, one has to define a multidimensional space that integrates the characteristics of the educational process with the personal characteristics (e.g., learning styles) (Coffield et al., 2004), the specific dimensions of the human interaction and any further dimension that can help to describe as completely as possible an "experience" (e.g., use qualities).

Because of this, recently we have introduced the set of "Experience styles" (Giovannella et al., 2010a) resumed by Table 1, that help to describe the multidimensional space of the one's personal "experience".

Such a framework has been developed starting from a model of process, sufficiently flexible to describe any experience, including education: the "Organic process" (OP) (Giovannella, 2007). OP,

Table 1. Set of experience styles

		Experience Styles					
				Interaction			
Organic Process	Explore Learning	motiva-tional	perceptive (exploring)	physical cognitive	creative, in-novative	subjective time	ludic (alea, ilinx, mim-icry, agon)
	Elaborate Design		info processing, working, design	cognitive emotional, social			
	Actuate Communicate		extroversion introversion	social, emotional, cognitive			

Figure 2. Blob representation of the "organic process"

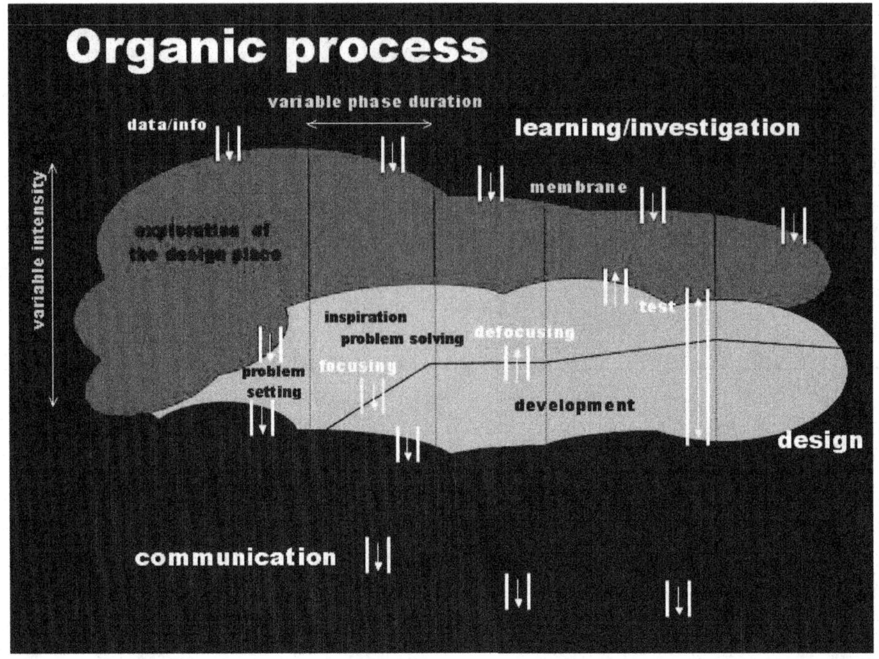

Figure 2, is a process inspired by the "living organisms" that, at any scale, fulfill three basic functionalities:

- Investigate the environment to collect information & learn;
- Elaborate the information to design/produce;
- Communicate the "products" by means of "actions" and "behaviors" that, in the case of very complex organisms, can make use of highly structured and conventional languages.

The three parallel functional layers - 'explore/learn', 'elaborate/design', 'actuate/communicate' - should be kept always active (as described more in depth further on).

Coming back to Table 1, to the 'explore/learning' layer, thus, one may associate the perceptual preferences; for example, the preferences on the use of the multi-sensory channels of input, or about the cultural forms through which we communicate (images, text, sounds, etc.). Each of these preferences may be, then further specified by adding what we call 'exploring styles' (used to visualize an image, reading, listening, handling, etc.). This first set of experience styles is certainly related to the physical layer of interaction and, inevitably, also to the cognitive one, for what concern attention, memory, interpretive strategies, self-control, etc. The latter of these elements involve clearly the emotional level too. Emotions affect the sensory inputs also because of individual propensities toward specific emotional colorings. Actually none of the levels of the human interaction is completely unrelated from OP's layers, but it is clearly different the intensity of involvement of each of them.

To the 'elaborate/design' layer belong both the personal styles of information processing (e.g., analytical and sequential or intuitive and global, more or less emotionally colored), work (active or reflective, individual or collaborative) and design (abstract or concrete, propensities toward creativity, divergence and innovation).

The prevailing interaction level in this layer is no doubt the cognitive one, that can be more or less 'colored' by emotional and social implications.

The third and last layer of the OP, 'actuate/ communicate', can be linked to the propensities toward extroversion/introversion combined with the preferences about social interaction and communication modalities that, of course, may partially overlap to the perceptual preferences (do, say, write, produce images, etc.) and being strongly colored by the ability to generate emotion.

As shown in Table 1 there is at least one transverse dimension of the EXPERIENCE that one has to consider when defining the experience styles: time. The 'ante', 'during' and 'post' of an EXPERIENCE are often perceived in a very subjective manner. The subjectivity of the experience shows itself at the perceptual level (duration of time intervals), as differences in the expectation of the experience and, as well, in its memory. The time dimension is clearly related also to motivation. Another cross-cutting dimension of the EXPERIENCE is the ludic one and can be related to the propensity of individuals towards the game that, although not completely independent of the other styles already discussed above, introduces the propensities to 'alea', competition ('agon'), vertigo ('ilinx') and 'mimicry' (Callois, 1958/2001).

The framework described above may also be linked to the 'use qualities', developed within the digital design, but whose validity extends well beyond the limits of that field: 'anticipation' is related to the time dimension, motivation and subjective creativity; the playability to the 'agon' facet of the game and motivation; the ambiguity and randomness to the 'alea' facet of the game dimension; the 'connecteness' to the social level of the interaction, etc..

The identification of all the dimensions of the EXPERIENCE is, in any case, an issue still very open. For example, another important aspect of the EXPERIENCE is the 'sense' that it takes for the learner. However, intensity, breadth and perceived meanings of the EXPERIENCE are closely related to the motivation, to many of the styles already introduced above and, as well, to the design and management of the process that, in principle, should take into account the experience's styles of each individual. This is the reason because we have not included the 'sense' in the scheme of Table 1. Similarly, 'seductivity' also can be put in relation with strategic issues related to motivation and, as well, with the emotional level of interaction and the cultural background of the learner. And so the 'identity', that being relevant for both individual and process, involves, probably, a relationship between motivation and the characteristics of each process, besides the mimicry.

At this point it should be quite evident that in our opinion the technological progress have the duty to support the harmonious development of all the so call experience's qualities that make the experience meaningful for the individual.

THE CENTRALITY OF DESIGN IN EDUCATION

In the framework just outlined the goal of the education is no longer the transmission of predefined patterns but, rather, the support to the self-determination of individuals to make them able to chose and manage their own "trajectory", to grasp the opportunities that the progressive liquefaction of the "structures" offers them to originate new sedimentations. Liquidity, indeed, does not mean lose of any cultural substrate but, rather, the possibility to redefine the skylines, the reference points. In such scenario individuals must learn not only to design (design ability) in a creative and innovative manner but also to flexibly readapt on fly, if needed, their design strategies to different contexts (metadesign ability).

The practices of design and meta-design, thus, although readapted to the new situation, may become the cornerstone of all educational processes. Indeed the Design, as compared to the fluctuations that have characterized the history of education (Cambi, 2003) - nature/culture, utopia/pragmatism, humanities/sciences, theoretical/practical activities - places itself in a central location that can integrate the various opposites.

We believe that the centrality of design (here we do not refer to any specific design sector but rather to the interdisciplinary integration of all its facets) can be claimed on several levels:

i) **Educational:** for what concerns the purpose of training processes; the ultimate aim, indeed, should be to enable learners to acquire reflective and meta-design skills in order to be able to continuously readjust the design process and, even, their own project of life; in other words learner should be able to put into practice the critical method (Horkheimer & Adorno, 1976) that makes the so-called reflective practitioner (Schön, 1983) a sort of a reference model in the complexity of contemporary society;
ii) **Process:** because the design is able to respond to complexity by structuring flexible processes that can, from one side acquire the organicity of the natural systems and on the other include the iterativity typical of the scientific method; to this latter, the design adds the pragmatic aimed at finalizing a modification of the world (not only its understanding); therefore the design processes are not only problem-based, but also project and process based, i.e., P3BL;
iii) **Methodological:** for the ability to absorb the best of what is expressed by various disciplines and to integrate it within the processes mentioned above; consider, for example, the methodologies derived from cultural anthropology, that suitably readjusted, are used in the process of problem setting; those derived from cognitive science used in the design and implementation of the tests; those derived from the engineering reused in the medium- and high-fidelity rapid prototyping, etc. (Moggridge, 2007; Benyon et al., 2005);
iv) **Didactic:** as demonstrated by the continuous tension in readapting the methods outlined above and in developing tools and procedures that allow their practical implementation in different contexts and situations, in other words by the effort to be at the same time general and flexible (Jones, 1980; Lidwell et al., 2003).

At the end of this paragraph we wish to emphasize that the recognition of the pedagogical centrality of design automatically leads to the need of an effort to spread among the new generations a sufficient level of "design literacy".

GUIDE LINES FOR THE ORGANIC PROCESS

At this point it lasts to define in more details the operational framework associable to the OP.

Dealing with processes, whose level of complexity might be similar to those characterizing organisms living in a co-evolving environment, does not mean that one cannot identify appropriate guidelines, as reference for educational processes inspired by the OP. Indeed, in the past, I have been engaged in the definition of either general guidelines and, as well, guidelines specific to each functional layers of the OP (Giovannella, 2008b). They are reported hereafter for those may wish to set in place educational processes OP-inspired.

Let us start with the general guidelines of the OP:

a) Consider the educational process as a "design place" whose features can be continuously redefined according to characteristics and dynamics of the contexts and of the process by itself - ***principle of metadesign***

b) Keep the three functional layers constantly active during the entire educational process - ***principle of parallelism***
c) Expose the participants to an as larger as possible number of methods (or their mixing), consistently with the time-window provided for the process - ***principle of methodological flexibility***
d) Encourage collaborative work, the scaffolding and the development of a high degree of social awareness - ***principle of aware collaborative construction***
e) Use technological environments to host creative and enjoyable processes and to make feel educational processes as valuable personal experiences - ***principle of the value of the experience.***

Going on with the guidelines appropriate to each functional layer of the process:

A) *Guidelines for the 'explore/learn' layer:*
   i) Don't start an educational process from a statement that could imply a designer-driven process but start from the analysis of the reference place/domain in order to understand its organization and dynamics and, as well, needs of the the interacting entities;
   ii) Acquire the information taking into consideration eventual scaling-lows that the place /domain might be submitted to;
   iii) Identify the spacial and temporal extension of the "interaction field" generated by the place/domain taken into consideration, and individuate all useful information for the study of such interaction;
   iv) Try since the beginning to identify the elements that might be used as "traces" during both the analysis phase and the monitoring one, and start to collect data;
   v) Involve the entities that populate the place/domain into the generation of a continuous flow of information (opinions, behaviors, etc...) to be used in whatever phase of the project;
   vi) Carry out a proper technological benchmarking;
   vii) Constantly monitor the process by tracking the "traces" identified in iv)

B) Guidelines for the 'elaborate/design' layer:
   i) Try to achieve a shared vision highlighting possible scaling lows, universalities and peculiarities that characterize a specific place/domain;
   ii) Create a narrative representation of the place/domain and of the interactions that are carried out in there; summarize all this by highlighting points of strength and of weakness of such scenario; show the potentialities of intervention over places/domains and scenarios;
   iii) Elaborate in a diverging manner ideas for possible interventions;
   iv) Create conceptualizations and diagrammatic representations of the places/domains showing the variation that maybe induced by possible intervention;
   v) Study and define the implications of what has been designed with respect to the experience stiles and phases of the processes;
   vi) Elaborate a vision of the possible long range consequences that may derive from the design proposals;
   vii) Elaborate prototypes with different level of fidelity;
   viii) Perform tests, record traces and elaborate them to work out meaningful indicators;

C) Guidelines for the 'actuate/communicate' layer:

i) Work on the representation modalities to work out the most appropriate ones to communicate in an immediate manner the results derived from data analysis;
ii) Open a design diary in which ideas and advancements may be clearly annotated along the whole process
iii) Supply periodic reports on the advancements achieved;
iv) Collect materials to prepare adequate presentations of the project and, as well, adequate technical documentations diversified according to characteristics of various possible stakeholders.

To conclude this paragraph, it may be worthwhile nothing that:

a) Since the three parallel functional layers of the OP should be always on - although with different intensity - during the whole development of the educational processes, deliverables, or at least most of them should be regarded as constantly in progress;
b) The above guidelines have been applied in several educational processes that I designed and carried on since 2005 (see for example Giovannella et al., 2010b).

AN IMPORTANT COROLLARY: MONITORING LITERACY

In a very general manner one can say that "experience" is a complex process that cannot be assessed exclusively in terms of effectiveness and efficiency and/or on the bases of its outcomes, especially when the main focus is on persons participating in it, and not on the process itself.

The logical consequence of increasingly complex educational processes is that assessment and evaluation should converge, and integrate the monitoring of the educational experience's quality. It is not an easy task, which, usually one tries to accomplish by defining grids and rating scales containing both qualitative and quantitative criteria derived upon her/his own personal idea of training experience.

Being well aware of the objective difficulty in defining the relevant qualities of an experience and what may be their weight in the learning processes (see the second paragraph), we may wonder whether it would be possible to equip the teachers/tutors with tools able to help them in the quantitative and qualitative monitoring of the activities that are carried on during the processes. A request that becomes even more stringent in on-line processes which lack multimodal face-to-face interaction.

Fortunately, the educational processes mediated by the machine, like those taking place on-line or in blended configuration, generate copious amounts of electronic traces that, when properly channeled and analyzed, can come to our aid.

Whatever the tools and methodologies used, a shrewdness of those who design educational processes should be to pay attention that each activity leaves at least some traces in a given place. Ideal from this point of view is the forum because it is particularly suited to collect analysis, brainstorming, storytelling, design diaries, etc.

Texts, in fact, are still the traces that are left more likely by the learners in their training and the text analysis is still the most ecological way to obtain information on individuals, their socio-relational skills, and the learning process.

Of course, once that traces have been collected we must ask ourselves what aspects of the educational experience we intend to monitor and which indicators are the most appropriate to use. This is a very wide and quite new field of investigation!

In the past we have already shown how it is possible to monitor the cognitive evolution by mean of a quantitative evaluation of concept maps (Giovannella et al., 2007); more recently, moreover, we have shown how, starting from an analysis of the interaction occurred in a forum, it would be possible to monitor the social and emotional characteristics of educational processes (Spadavecchia & Giovannella, 2010) by integrating social network analysis (SNA) (Wasserman & Faust, 1994) and automatic text analysis (ATA) (Bolasco, 1999). Other attempts are also under the way (see for example: Calvani et al., 2008; Cartelli et al., 2010)

This is not the place in which we can dwell on the details of such monitoring methods for which we refer the reader to articles listed in the bibliography. Here it is enough to stress that:

a) The final goal will be the definition of a multidimensional space of indicators to be used in monitoring the qualities of the educational experiences, according to the "experience styles" defined in Table 1.
b) The complexity of processes requires to include among the new "literacies", even digital, that relating to the monitoring of educational processes.

CONCLUSION

The development of technology that has accompanied the advent of the new millennium, is inducing an epochal change in our relationship with the "machine" and, of course, in the forms of the mediation this latter plays in the development of all our activities, including of course the educational processes.

The complexity of the systems, their tendency to become liquid, places the individual more than ever, at the center of educational processes and asks us to rethink

- Processes (goals, strategies, methods) in terms of experiences
- Significant qualities of these processes in terms of experience styles
- Capabilities that all players participating in these processes should possess and/or acquire; among these stand out design, meta-design and, as well, the ability to monitor the progress of the process and, also, the personal ones.

New skills implies new competencies and literacies, that become necessary to prevent the opening of new "divides".

Recently we synthesized all this - and more - in a acronym that represents, at the same time, a vision and an operational framework for the future, the DULP (Giovannella, 2009; Giovannella & Graf, 2010):

Design Inspired Learning - Ubiquitous Learning - Liquid Learning Places - Person in Place Centered Design.

DULP, therefore, can be considered the Grand Challenge of the XXI century within which to consider and work on the transformation of digital literacies and competencies discussed above.

REFERENCES

Augé, M. (1992). *Non-lieux. Introduction à une anthropologie de la surmodernité*. Paris: Le Seuil.

Bauman, Z. (2000). *Liquid Modernity*. Cambridge, UK: Polity.

Benyon, D., Turner, P., & Turner, S. (2005). *Design Interactive Systems*. Harlow, UK: Pearson Education.

Bolasco, S. (1999). *Analisi Multidimensionale dei dati*. Roma, Italy: Carocci.

Callois, R. (2001). *Man, Play and Games*. Champaign, IL: First Illinois. (Original work published 1958)

Calvani, A., Cartelli, A., Fini, A., & Ranieri, M. (2008). Models and instruments for assessing digital competence at school. *Journal of E-learning and Knowledge Society*, *4*(3), 183–193.

Cambi, F. (2003). *Manuale di storia della pedagogia*. Rome, Italy: Editori Laterza.

Cartelli, A., Dagiene, V., & Futschek, G. (2010). Bebras contest and Digital Competence Assessment. *International Journal of Digital Literacy and Digital Competence*, *1*(1), 24–39.

Coffield, C., Mosely, D., Hall, E., & Ecclestone, K. (2004). *Learning styles and Pedagogy in Post-16 Learning* (Tech. Rep.). London: University of Newcastle upon Tyne, Learning and Skill Research Centre.

Dourish, P. (2004). *Where the Action is: The Foundation of Embodied Interaction*. Cambridge, MA: MIT Press.

Giovannella, C. (2006). From 'Learning Space' to 'Design Place': transforming the present and challenging the future. *Metamorfosi*, *62*, 62–65.

Giovannella, C. (2007). An Organic Process for the Organic Era of the Interaction. In P. A. Silva, A. Dix, & J. Jorge (Eds.), *Proceedings of the HCI Educators 2007: creativity3: Experiencing to educate and design*, Aveiro, Portugal (pp. 129-133).

Giovannella, C. (2008a). L'uomo, la macchina e la comunicazione mediata: evoluzioni di paradigmi e design per le esperienze nell'era organica dell'interazione. In Graphics, B. A. (Ed.), *Machinae: tecniche arti e saperi del novecento* (pp. 471–490). Bari, Italy.

Giovannella, C. (2008b). 'Personal-in-place centered design' per formare gli attori dei 'Learning places' del futuro. In *E-learning tra formazione istituzionale e life-long learning*. Trento, Italy: Educare al.

Giovannella, C. (2008c). 2.0? In *E-learning tra formazione istituzionale e life-long learning*. Trento, Italy: Learning.

Giovannella, C. (2009). DULP: complessità, organicità, liquidità. *IxD&A*, *7/8*, 11-15.

Giovannella, C., Camusi, A., & Spadavecchia, C. (2010a). From learning styles to experience styles. In *Proceedings of the ICALT*, *2010*, 732–733.

Giovannella, C., & Graf, S. (2010). Challenging Technologies, Rethinking Pedagogy, Being Design-Inspired. The Grand Challenge of this Century. *eLearn Magazine*. Retrieved from http://www.elearnmag.org/subpage.cfm?section=articles&article=114-1

Giovannella, C., Selva, P. E., & Fraioli, S. (2007). MapEvaluator in action: a comparative test on the efficiency of the quantitative concept map evaluation in a primary school. In *Proceedings of the ICALT2007, Distributed social and personal computing for learning and instruction* (pp. 566-569). Washington, DC: IEEE.

Giovannella, C., Spadavecchia, C., & Camusi, A. (2010b). Educational complexity: centrality of design and monitoring of the experience. In *Proceedings of UXFUL2010*. New York: Springer.

Giovannella, C., & Spinelli, A. (2009). Grand Challenge per il TEL: Design Inspired Learning. In Andronico, A., & Colazzo, L. (Eds.), *DIDAMATICA 2009*. Trento, Italy.

Horkheimer, M., & Adorno, T. W. (1976). *The Culture Industry: Enlightenment as Mass Deception*. London: Continuum International Publishing Group.

Jones, J. C. (1980). *Design Methods* (2nd ed.). New York: Wiley.

Lidwell, W., Holden, K., & Butler, J. (2003). *Universal Principles of Design*. Beverly, MA: Rockport.

Löwgren, J. (2006). Articulating the use qualities of digital designs. In *Proceedings of the Aesthetic computing* (pp. 383-403). Cambridge, MA: The MIT Press.

Moggridge, B. (2007). *Designing Interactions*. Cambridge, MA: The MIT Press.

Prensky, M. (2001). *Digital Natives, Digital Immigrants on the Horizon*. Bradford, UK: MCB University Press.

Schön, D. A. (1983). *The Reflective Practitioner: How professionals think in action*. New York: Basic Books.

Spadavecchia, C., & Giovannella, C. (2010). Monitoring learning experiences and styles: the socio-emotional level. In *Proceedings of the ICALT, 2010*, 445–449.

Tornero, J. M. P. (2004). *Promoting digital literacy: Under- standing digital literacy (Rep. No. EAC/76/03)*. Barcelona, Spain: UAB.

Tuan, Y. (1977). *Space and Place. The Perspective of Experience*. Minneapolis, MN: University of Minnesota Press.

Wasserman, S., & Faust, K. (1994). *Social network analysis: methods and applications*. Cambridge, UK: Cambridge University Press.

Weiser, M. (1993). Some Computer Science Problems in Ubiquitous Computing. *Communications of the ACM*, 7(36), 75–84. doi:10.1145/159544.159617

This work was previously published in International Journal of Digital Literacy and Digital Competence, Volume 1, Issue 3, edited by Antonio Cartelli, pp. 18-28, copyright 2010 by IGI Publishing (an imprint of IGI Global).

Chapter 7
Wikipedia as Training Resource for Developing Digital Competences

Corrado Petrucco
University of Padua, Italy

ABSTRACT

It seems improbable that Wikipedia could be considered a valid resource for educational institutions like schools and universities because of the risk of incurring mistakes, inaccuracies, and plagiarism. The bad reputation of the free encyclopedia is false, Wikipedia is reliable and can be used in the curriculum as a new approach for social and collaborative construction of knowledge. It can enter fully into educational contexts, which will represent an opportunity to reflect on the verification of information, the ethical use of technology, and the role of democratic participation of people that use social software. In fact, the creation and maintenance of the articles of Wikipedia as classroom activities offer higher processes of cognitive development and on-line relationships, allowing the development of essential digital competences for life-long learning, like Information Literacy, Participation Literacy, and Ethical Literacy.

INTRODUCTION

Today social software and instruments of Web 2.0, allow the sharing and construction of knowledge by using a complex network of social interaction. A particular example of constructive collaboration is the Wikipedia project, the "Free Encyclopedia" that gives anyone the possibility to contribute to the writing of articles. From a typical point of view of social software and Web 2.0, it doesn't represent an innovation, looking as practically all the applications of this type which are open to editing, comments and mash up by the users. From the epistemological point of view, instead,

DOI: 10.4018/978-1-4666-0903-7.ch007

it represents a real and true breaking point (Fallis, 2008).

Indeed, Wikipedia has caused a crisis within the concept of authoring and the "principle of authority", concepts on which the traditional encyclopedia has always been based on, since the eighteenth century's famous *Encyclopédie ou Dictionnaire Raisonné des Sciences, des Arts et des Métiers* of Diderot and Alembert. In Wikipedia, in fact, contributions are spontaneous, anonymous and/or are the result of modifications by many people: their identity and competence with regards to the subject, remaining unknown.

When we consult a traditional encyclopedia, it goes without saying, that we rely implicitly on the authors and the processes of updating and editing the articles. Wikipedia doesn't have a true editing process. It doesn't possess a classification system which attempts to give a significance to the world (Eco, 1990). It doesn't highlight and prioritize certain opinions rather than others; it is based mainly on the concept of emergent semantics. No one can establish priority on its worthiness, in being an encyclopedic article or not, and how in depth it could be developed.

IS WIKIPEDIA A RELIABLE RESOURCE FOR SCHOOLS?

From the introduction, it seems improbable that Wikipedia could be considered a valid resource for Educational institutions like schools and Universities. Indeed, they need to guarantee, within their teaching and learning processes, the access to a body of organized knowledge. Knowledge that is reliable and relevant, and respects the principles of accuracy, completeness, and that of being updated and comprehensive (Fox, 1994). This therefore explains the wariness that teachers expressed initially, with regard to Wikipedia. Wariness aggravated from the fact, that the students used it as a resource for their homework, copying and pasting their text, without verifying the contents, and thereby running the risk of incurring mistakes and inaccuracies. An example of this is the History Department of the Middlebury College, which banned students from citing Wikipedia (Cohen, 2007).

Nevertheless, contrary to what may be seen as unreliable in its contents, further studies illustrate the real problem of Wikipedia (Giles, 2005; Magnus, 2006; Bragues, 2007). The problem doesn't lie in the inaccuracy and comprehensiveness of its articles, but rather in the completeness of its entries. In certain areas of knowledge it seems to be more profound (Mathematics, Physics, Medicine and science in general) than in others, where it's feasible there is a "stub". This is a rough draft of a few lines, which no-one has developed yet, and in which there aren't quotations of the source yet.

In fact in Wikipedia reliability/verification of an argument dealt with, is related to the concept of a secondary source. In its own rights it is itself a secondary source, which must anyway quote in each of its articles the primary influential source, in which it refers to. From this point of view, the necessity to validate the source is however not only a problem of Wikipedia, but of all the resources found on the Internet.

Wikipedia has also a bad reputation because of "vandalism". That is to say the cancelling and modifying not relevant to the entries. Actually, these problems are in most cases solved in a short time span. A more subtle and interesting problem, on the contrary, is that of the continual changing of entries. This occurs with regard to a non-neutral point of view, (NNPOV) from political and social groups, opposing contributors which are the cause of heated arguments or "edit wars". In this case, the administrators invite the participants to choose the compromised route. In extreme cases the entries become blocked waiting for reconciliation.

However, Wikipedia doesn't give a guarantee of absolute neutrality, like all other resources, no resource – digital or paper can. The reason being that every encyclopedic entry is however an artifact generated from a specific culture, and group of people within that culture, which have potentially different visions of the world. These are attempts at imposing structures of knowledge-power, as defined by Foucault, or of interpretations of reality. The discussions that are created are within "sensitive" cultural entries of Wikipedia, they are not therefore a problem. They are rather an interesting sign, which has the honor of allowing to emerge and highlight "bias", otherwise hidden. The same community of editors of the encyclopedia represents the guarantee to treat every theme with a greater objectiveness and tolerance as possible.

On the basis of these considerations, we can then answer the question with a "yes", Wikipedia certainly can be a reliable source for schools. Its educational importance is however in a dimension which exceeds the simple use of a traditional encyclopedia. It moves it to other levels of social and collaborative construction of knowledge, on meta-cognitive reflection and on Information Literacy.

WIKIPEDIA AS A CONSTRUCTIVE AND COLLABORATIVE LEARNING ACTIVITY

Schools and other educational institutions, in this sense, could take the responsibility of an important role in the Wikipedia project and vice versa. Wikipedia, in turn, could provide an important support to the didactic and educational processes. The schools experience with *free encyclopedia* is now numerous all around the world. They have supplied a starting point at an institutional level for its direct introduction in the didactic practice. A recent school reform proposal in an English Primary School, for example, highlights the importance of having the necessary competence to judge the accuracy and reliability of the source of information, quoted the case of Wikipedia (Rose, 2009; Becta, 2009).

Generally, the most frequent experiences in the schools and Universities, want that the students, with the help of their teachers of a specific subject, modify some entries of the encyclopedia. They go into more depth and verify its reliability, or else they create new entries. This research process, based on scientific method, permits to individualize objective and reasonably reliable sources to quote. These are all activities that favour learning connected to constructive collaboration and dialogic knowledge (Bereiter & Scardamalia, 2005). At the end of the research process, there is a creation of shared artifacts on the web that can be perceived as a useful service to others.

One of the most interesting experiences in this sense was the Department of Wildlife Ecology of the University of Florida. Here, the students were requested to evaluate the contents of some entries about ecology and natural science, and to edit the articles while working together to improve it (Callis et al., 2009). The outcome was very positive, although the interaction with other editors of Wikipedia wasn't always without friction. The students appreciated the exercise, and they perceived it as a formative and educational experience, with a superior value to that of a simple report or written exercise.

A similar experience occurred, in The Faculty of Educational Science of the University of Padua, with the students in 2009 Course on Educational Technology. A part of the assignment consisted of a group activity that aimed at critically editing some entries on "e-learning" and "tutoring on line" in Italian language. Also, here the "dialogic interaction" with the community of Wikipedians wasn't always easy and in some cases appeased notably initial enthusiasm. In the end, however, the students' efforts, that implied depth study and accurate methods of research, were rewarded by the final entries published. It also gave them greater satisfaction, in comparison with traditional written assignment. Many other existing experiences can be found quoted in Wikipedia under the apposite entry "Schools and University Projects" (Wikipedia, 2010).

These practices of interacting with on line encyclopedias modify the old model of reference use from encyclopedic source. They transform them in a participating and dialogic-based approach to knowledge (Jonassen, 2000). It is interesting to note that, in this way, the objectives of the subject taught are pursued on an educational and social level. It puts the school in contact with the community of authors, and editors of Wikipedia, that comes from an informal world and from contexts which places an emphasis on the use of knowledge.

In this sense, an action research undertaken by the author research group at the Department of Education of the University of Padua, in collaboration with IPRASE - Provincial Institute of Educational Research of Trento - Northern Italy, attempts to investigate learning processes in informal and non-formal environment examining Wikipedia entries about subjects relevant to local community. The research analyze their possible integration within the formal school curriculum, using active learning environments: students and teachers seek to collaborate to create digital artifacts, highly contextualized in the real world, and making them useful to the whole community. For example one was developed by two secondary school teachers from the Institute Comprehensive Bassa Val di Sole, who edited with their children in classes, the article "Museum of Solandra" in the Italian Wikipedia (http://it.wikipedia.org/wiki/Museo_civilt%C3%A0_solandra). Another project was carried out by pupils of lower secondary school level including the Institute of Cles along with two of their teachers. By taking the overall aim of constructing a historical memory of the country, the working group implemented the Wikipedia entry on Cles (http://it.wikipedia.org/wiki/Cles). They ventured into the photo collection trips constructed on the ground, interviews with elders to gather personal knowledge about the country, research in books and other documents and finally the publication of selected photos and news on Wikipedia. Indeed, the publication of the articles was the latest step in work that lasted months and included the training of students on search strategies, editing and evaluating Wikipedia entries.

It is important to say that every Wikipedia article is a *shared digital artifact*, and the methods of revision and updating are codified in rules. These rules must be respected if one doesn't want to run the risk of being excluded from the community. Therefore, a sense of membership or belonging is created, by a collective process of knowledge construction. A community project and decentralized cognitive places (entries in Wikipedia) are created where each participant finds his/her "work niche" and competence (Geser 2007). However, it is necessary to highlight that there exists an important distinction between the practical community that spontaneously collaborates, and those "forced", which result in academic or University learning. This could bring with it significant differences in attitude and motivation (Wannemacher, 2009).

The advantages of an educational activity which involves editions from Wikipedia can be summarized in the following six points:

- You are more motivated in your study especially if you can see your contribution posted online. (i.e., "global audience")
- You promote the use of the language by adopting it
- You improve dialogue-based skills, negotiation skills (Wannemacher, 2009) and collaborative skills
- You acquire technical skills by using search engines
- You develop critical behavior with regard to evaluating information sources, and finally
- You learn to respect rules and ethical principles as regards information management.

Moreover, a significant percentage of students continue to edit the entries in the encyclopaedia also after the assigned exercise from the teacher has been completed. Consequently they become long term contributors, participating actively in the community and contributing to words improving and extending the scope of Wikipedia.

THE DIGITAL COMPETENCES WITH WIKIPEDIA

On the basis of these experiences, it is important to try to understand if the ability acquired during the practical use of Wikipedia can then evolve through a process of active transfer, in a series of organic and complementary abilities encountered in everyday life and work. This is referred to, for example, in the "Recommendation of the European Parliament and the Council (2008) on the establishment of the European Qualifications Framework for lifelong Learning. In the context of the European Recommendation, "skills" means the ability to apply knowledge and use know how to complete tasks and solve problems. Skills are described as cognitive (involving the use of logical, intuitive and creative thinking) or practical (involving manual dexterity and the use of methods and materials, tools and instruments). On the other hand, "competence" is described in terms of responsibility and autonomy and means the proven ability to use knowledge, skills and personal, social and / or methodical abilities, in work or study situations and in the professional and personal development.

From this point of view, Digital Competences should be part of the skills required for digital citizenship (e-citizenship) and for the world of work, which now tends to exclude those who can't use social software to continuously update their professional profile. There are three dimensions referred to and they depict particular kinds of Literacy: Participation Literacy, Information Literacy and Ethical Literacy (Figure 1).

Today every aspect of learning, teaching and working in the job place, requires the gathering, processing and communication of information. While in the past there was a reliance only on the textual medium, now the most important source is the networked information.

Information Literacy includes technological and methodological skills which allow the person to be able to know how to find information, to efficiently filter it, so as not to be subjected to information overload and above all to evaluate it adequately (Eisemberg, 2008). Therefore, this literacy includes also the development of meta-cognitive and critical skill. The teacher must become a point of referral: he helps the students to decide if the resources retrieved online are valuable and reliable, stimulating the use of appropriate methods of research (Garvoille & Buckner, 2009). The attention given to the source should support the development of critical thinking, which is how to think critically, evaluating and verifying continuously paper resources or online resources. Evaluating the authority, and the objectiveness of the source of information, signifies to determine not only that the author of a certain document is present on the net, but also that the opinions expressed are validated by concrete facts.

Participation Literacy (Giger, 2006), regards the relational aspects of the participants using social software; people can exploit the knowledge of others and share information in online communities of practice. You are participation literate if you work actively to invite everyone into a discussion and consider everyone's discourse valuable. It is also a crucial competence when it allows developing the ability to dialogue, to argue ones own ideas. To be participation literate signifies not only to know how to share ones knowledge with others, but also how to manage appropriately ones privacy and virtual identity.

Figure 1. The main digital competences using Wikipedia in educational settings

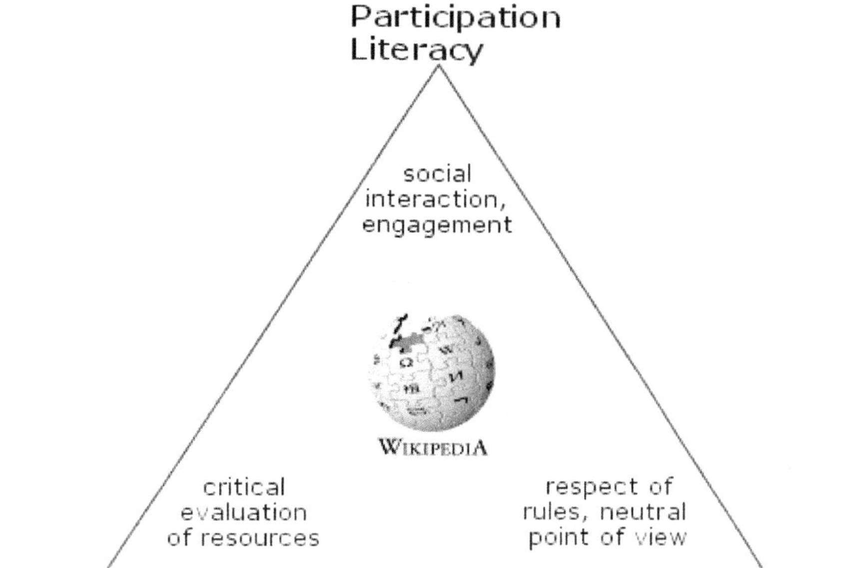

Ethical Literacy, examines the competence to respect people and the rules defined by a community, to which one belongs, (i.e., mutual respect) (O' Sullivan, 2009) and the privacy of others. The exchange of knowledge takes place in the moment in which there exists respect and trust among people. If this is missing, it is highly improbable that people can have useful and significant experiences on-line. Also, the honest use of information to contrast for example problems like "Plagiarism" is a part of this literacy.

CONCLUSION

Wikipedia can fully enter in educational contexts representing a stimulating occasion to reflect on the verification of information, ethical use of technology and the role of democratic participation of people which use social software. The prohibition of quoting Wikipedia, in schools and Universities tasks and assignments doesn't encourage the development of the student, and doesn't represent an answer to the problem of finding, evaluating, sharing and critically discussing the information which can be retrieved on the Web. In intentional, collaborative and dialogue-based learning situations the students are occupied in actively confronting with the source of the problem. This process is certainly more educational than focusing on what is an acceptable resource rather than a banned one. This could also offer the opportunity to activate higher processes of cognitive development and relations. The student could experience in a context of real life situation, abilities which more than ever seem to be required of the adult in the digital society. Wikipedia could then become an efficient instrument for the acquisition, and development of reflection, participation and ethical competences, in the vision of lifelong learning.

REFERENCES

Bateson, G. (1984). *Verso una ecologia della mente* (p. 207). Rome, Italy: Adelphi.

Bereiter, C., & Scardamalia, M. (2005). *Technology and Literacies: From Print Literacy to Dialogic Literacy. Ontario Institute for Studies in Education of the University of Toronto* (p. 10). http://www.oise.utoronto.ca/projects/impacton-policy/pdfs/bereiter_edited_Feb_20_04.pdf

Callis, (2009). Improving Wikipedia: educational opportunity and professional responsibility. *Trends in Ecology & Evolution, 24*(4), 177–179. doi:10.1016/j.tree.2009.01.003

Codogno, M. (2009). Wikipedia, i Pokémon e la teoria della complessità nei sistemi emergenti. In *Proceedings of the conference "From Diderot to Wikipedia: an epistemological revolution"*? University of Padua, Italy.

Cohen, N. (2007). A history department bans citing Wikipedia as a research source. *The New York Times*. Retrieved from http://www.nytimes.com

Eco, U. (1999). *Kant and the Platypus*. London: Secker and Warburg.

Eisenberg, M. (2008, March). Information Literacy: Essential Skills for the Information Age. *DESIDOC Journal of Library & Information Technology, 28*(2), 39–47.

European Parliament Council. (2008). *Recommendation of the European Parliament and of the Council of 23 April 2008 on the establishment of the European Qualifications Framework for lifelong learning*. Retrieved from http://eur-lex.europa.eu/LexUriServ/LexUriServ.do?uri=OJ:C:2008:111:0001:0007:EN:PDF

Fallis, D. (2008). Toward an Epistemology of Wikipedia. *Journal of the American Society for Information Science and Technology, 59*(10), 1662–1674. doi:10.1002/asi.20870

Fox, C., Levitin, A., & Redman, T. (1994). The notion of data and its quality dimensions. *Information Processing & Management, 30*, 9–19. doi:10.1016/0306-4573(94)90020-5

Freire, P. (1971). *La pedagogia degli oppressi* (new ed.). Milan, Italy: Mondadori.

Garvoille, A., & Buckner, G. (2009). Writing Wikipedia Pages in the Constructivist Classroom. In *Proceedings of World Conference on Educational Multimedia, Hypermedia and Telecommunications 2009* (pp. 1600-1605). Chesapeake, VA: AACE.

Geser, H. (2007, June). From printed to "wikified" encyclopedias: Sociological Aspects of an incipient revolution. *Sociology in Switzerland: Towards Cybersociety and "Vireal" Social Relations*. Retrieved from http://socio.ch/intcom/t_hgeser16.pdf

Giger, P. (2006). *Participation Literacy: Part I: Constructing the Web 2.0 Concept Series*. Karlskrona, Sweden: Blekinge Institute of Technology.

Giles, J. (2005). Internet Encyclopaedias Go Head to Head. *Nature, 438*, 900. IARD e IPRASE. (2009). *Insegnare in Trentino. Seconda indagine Istituto IARD e IPRASE sui docenti della scuola trentina*. Provincia Autonoma di Trento - IPRASE.

Lave, J., & Wenger, E. (1991). *Situated Learning. Legitimate peripheral participation*. Cambridge, UK: Cambridge University Press.

Magnus, P. D. (2009). On trusting Wikipedia. *Episteme, 6*, 74–90. doi:10.3366/E1742360008000555

Report, B. (2009). *Contribution's to the Rose Review*. Retrieved from http://publications.becta.org.uk/download.cfm?resID=40240

Rose, J. (2009). *Primary Curriculum Review*. Retrieved from http://www.dcsf.gov.uk/primarycurriculumreview/

Star, S. L., & Griesemer, J. R. (1989). Institutional Ecology, 'Translations' and Boundary Objects: Amateurs and Professionals in Berkeley's Museum of Vertebrate Zoology, 1907-39. *Social Studies of Science*, *19*(4), 387–420. doi:10.1177/030631289019003001

Wannemacher, K. (2009). Articles as assignments - Modalities and experiences of wikipedia use in university course. In M. Spaniol, Q. Li, R. Klamma, R. W. H. Lau (Eds.), *Proceedings of the Advances in Web Based Learning (ICWL 2009), 8th International Conference*, Aachen, Germany (pp. 434-443). Berlin: Springer.

Wenger, E., McDermott, R., & Snyder, W. M. (2002). *Cultivating Communities of Practice*. Boston: HBS press.

This work was previously published in International Journal of Digital Literacy and Digital Competence, Volume 1, Issue 3, edited by Antonio Cartelli, pp. 29-35, copyright 2010 by IGI Publishing (an imprint of IGI Global).

Chapter 8
The Media Diet of University Students in Italy:
An Exploratory Research*

Andrea Pozzali
University of Milano-Bicocca, Italy

Paolo Ferri
University of Milano-Bicocca, Italy

ABSTRACT

Developments in information and communication technologies have raised the issue of the intergenerational digital divide that can take place between "digital natives" and "digital immigrants". Despite emphatic claims concerning how educational systems must take into account the specific characteristics of "digital natives", sound empirical research on these topics is lacking, especially for Europe. This paper presents the results of research performed during the course of 2008, studying how university students in Italy use digital technologies. The research is based on a survey of 1086 undergraduate students at the University of Milan-Bicocca, complemented by focus groups and in-depth interviews. The results of our research show that, even if university students are familiar with digital technologies, the general possession of high level skills in accessing and using the Internet should not be taken for granted.

INTRODUCTION: THE "DIGITAL NATIVES" DEBATE

It has become sort of a common sense to think that the new generations of students, that are currently entering into the school system, present some characteristics that contribute to make them completely different from their parents. This has to be reconnected, as it is well known, to the fact that the accelerated rate of technological progress is deeply changing our world. The "Net generation" (Tapscott, 1998) indeed, is the first generation to grow up in a world where the presence of things such as personal computers, mobile devices, the

DOI: 10.4018/978-1-4666-0903-7.ch008

World Wide Web and so on does not represent "something new", but is part of the normal, everyday life. In a couple of well known papers, Mark Prensky (2001a, 2001b) referred to the generation born after 1980 by defining them as "digital natives", as they are all "native speakers" of the digital language of computers, video games and the Internet" (Prensky, 2001a, p. 1).

The diffusion of new digital technologies was defined by Prensky as a *singularity* – an event that introduces so great a discontinuity with the past that no coming back is possible. Educational systems throughout the world urge to find a way to cope with this type of change: "*... the single biggest problem facing education today is that our Digital Immigrant instructors, who speak an outdated language (that of the pre-digital age), are struggling to teach a population that speaks an entirely new language*" (Prensky, 2001a, p. 2). Following Prensky, the intergenerational divide that separate digital natives from "digital immigrants" (i.e., all those people who did not grow up in a digital world, but still embrace many aspects of it in their work and their everyday life) has become a popular subject for discussion, not only in the scholarly literature (Gaston, 2006; Long, 2005; McHale, 2005), but also on mass media (1).

As a recent critical review of all the "digital natives" debate reports (Bennet et al., 2008), notwithstanding the great popularity of the topics, sound empirical basis in support of the idea that young people *in general* are marked by strong familiarity with digital technologies still is largely lacking. Indeed, the number of studies in the literature is quite limited, and the available data are quite ambivalent. Research on post-compulsory education performed in the United States (Kvavik et al., 2004) and in Australia (Oliver & Goerke, 2007; Kennedy et al., 2006) seem to show that, even if digital technologies are widely diffused among university students, a significant proportion of the overall population may not have such high level skills as may be expected. In particular, even if personal computers and mobile phones are of common use among young students, activities such as having an own blog, using social-networks sites and creating new content for the Web seem to concern only a limited proportion (around 20% on average) of the sample considered in the different studies. As the authors commented:

In summary; though limited in scope and focus, the research evidence indicates that a proportion of young people are highly adept with technology and rely on it for a range of information gathering and communication activities. However, there also appears to be a significant proportion of young people who do not have the levels of access or technology skills predicted by proponents of the digital native idea. (...) It may be that there is as much variation *within* the digital native generation as *between* the generations. (Bennet et al., 2008, pp. 778-779)

In this paper, we try to contribute to the current debate on digital natives by presenting the result of an empirical research on how university students in Italy access to and use the Internet and the related digital communication technologies. This study was based on a survey on a sample of 1086 undergraduate students of the University of Milan-Bicocca (2). The survey was performed between January and May 2008 by the Observatory on New Media "nuMediaBios" of the University of Milan-Bicocca, as part of a broader research program that seeks to provide on a regular basis data on the diffusion and use of new media among university students (at the time we are writing this paper a second survey, based on a similar approach but concerning a different sample, is going on; further details can be found on the website of the Observatory: www.numediabios.eu) (3). The paper is organized as follows: in the next paragraph we present the general framework that is at the basis of our approach, by making references also to the available literature. It follows the section where we present the methodology and the results of our research; at last the paragraph focusing on the lessons learned and on suggestions for future research follows.

UNIVERSITY STUDENTS AND DIGITAL MEDIA

The study of how University students make use of information and communication technologies has been developing soon after the introduction and the diffusion of the Internet, but available data are still scarce, especially for what concern the European context. One of the first exploratory studies was performed by Wilson in 1996 and was limited to "five small, independent, residential, undergraduate colleges in central Pennsylvania" (Wilson, 1999, p. 1). The methodology was based on focus groups and among the main findings the author reported that the average time spent on the Internet amounted at 2.6 hours per week. E–mailing and "course–related research" seem to be the primary uses of the Net, followed by other activities such as communicating in online groups or playing games, researching scholarships, completing online applications and preparing for job interviews by researching companies. More extensive surveys performed by Kvavik and Caruso (2005) on a sample of 18.039 respondents coming from 63 higher education institutions in the United States confirmed these trends, with the great majority of students using technology for e-mail (99.7 percent), for course-related activities and for their own pleasure. In 2002, the Pew Internet & American Life Project issued the report "The Internet Goes to College" (Jones, 2002) showing that college students were indeed heavy users of the Internet, with 74 percent of the sample using the Internet for four or more hours per week. Some studies soon started also to raise concerns about the possibility that excessive use of the Internet can lead to a kind of "dependence". Anderson (2001) performed a survey on eight colleges and universities (seven in the U.S. and one in Ireland), finding that "Internet dependent" students spent more than three times as much time online (229 minutes/day) than the others students in the sample (73 minutes/day) and were more likely to have disrupted sleep, as well as disarrayed social and academic lives.

With the development of new communication tools and with the recent burst of social networking sites (SNS, cfr., boyd & Ellison, 2007; Ellison et al., 2007), the typology of possible usages of the Internet has widened to a considerable level, and the sheer number of hours spent on line has increased consequently. Surveys performed on college students in the U.S. (Cotten & Jelenewicz, 2006; Peluchette & Karl, 2008) and in Canada (Quan-Haase, 2007) found strong preference for online social interaction activities and in particular underlined a massive use of instant messaging (IM). The 97 percent of the sample in Cotten and Jelenewicz survey "reported accessing the Internet several times a day", and the time spent online for "communicative purposes" (28 hours per week) was twice the time spent for "non-communicative purposes" (14 hours per week). It is not surprisingly, then, that rates of usage of SNS by college students seem to be significantly higher than those of the average population: a report of the Pew Research Centre found that these sites are used by the 22 percent of the general U.S adult population, but the data rise significantly to 67 percent if we consider only users aged 18-29 (Kohut et al., 2008).

An extensive survey performed in 2005 on 29 college and universities in the United States confirm these trends (Jones et al., 2009), showing that the amount of time spent online is constantly on the rise: one student out of three reported an increase in the rate of use of the Internet in the six months preceding the survey, and only the 9 percent of the sample declared that the rate of use has actually decreased in the same period. The 94 percent of the sample spent at least one hour on the Internet every day, and the 53 percent reported being online three or more hours per day. Concerning the type of uses, social communication purposes were mentioned by 40 percent of the sample, while 28 percent of the students reported using the Internet mainly for entertainment and 22 percent to engage in work related to their classes. Blogging seems to be much more diffused among college students than in the general population, with one third of the students involved in the sample maintaining an own blog, compared to eight percent of all U.S. Internet users. Not surprisingly, Facebook seems to be one of the more popular SNS: 36 percent of students uses it every day, and 21 percent of the sample log on to their profile several time a day. However, a consistent part of the sample (37 percent) never or almost never logged on to Facebook: this once again warns us against the possibility of drawing general conclusions on the propensity of university students to engage in on line communication and social networking activities.

The brief review we have presented so far concerned studies and research that were performed almost exclusively in the U.S., with partial exceptions represented by a couple of work done in Australia and Canada and by Anderson's work (2001), that concerned both the U.S and Ireland. As a matter of fact, data on the European context are very hard to find in the literature. As far as the Italian context is concerned, the only data available on the level of new media access and consumption are those included in periodical reports such as the ones issued by the *Osservatorio permanente sui contenuti digitali* (Permanent observatory on digital contents) (www.osservatoriocontenutidigitali.it), that anyway present some well known limitations, as they come from a private source and they are not always disaggregated by age cohort. Useful as they may be to have a general snapshot of the Italian context, this type of data clearly are not enough to support an analytical sound discussion of university students behaviours and attitudes toward new media. In order to start filling this gap in data availability, that in our view seriously constraints the possibility of developing a more consistent debate on these topics, we have started in 2008 to perform a series of yearly research on the Media diet of university students. In this paper we present some of the most relevant findings coming out of the first research, performed between January and May 2008 on a sample of undergraduate students at the University of Milan-Bicocca. At present, we are completing the second edition of this research, on a different sample of undergraduate students at the same University, and we are planning to extend our work to include other universities and institutions for higher education.

METHODOLOGY AND RESULTS

During the first months of 2008, the research team of the Observatory on New Media "nuMediaBios" of the University of Milan-Bicocca started to develop a comprehensive research on the "media diet", and more specifically on university students (18-22 years old) styles and profiles of media consumption and usage. The decision of focusing on this particular population was driven by some specific reasons, linked to our main research interests. While there are, in the literature, some evidences available concerning the relationships between ICTs and pupils and adolescents (Pedrò, 2006), there seem to be, as already mentioned, quite a lack of available data focusing on university students. This holds in particular for the Italian situation. Another reason is linked to the fact that one of the variables on which we would like to focus our attention is the diffusion and the profiles of use of SNS such as Facebook, MySpace, Twitter. As it is well known, and as many statistics available on the Net seem to confirm, on average the use of this type of sites is more diffused among people from 18 to 25 years old. Furthermore, we also wanted to confront rates of usages of "traditional" and "new" media, and once again university students seem to provide the more interesting field of research to study this type of topics.

The methodology of our research was based on a mix of quantitative and qualitative approaches. A survey research was done, on a sample of undergraduate students of the University of Milan-Bicocca, based on a questionnaire that was accessed through the Intranet of the University. To avoid selection sample biases, we choose to administrate the questionnaire when students accessed the Intranet in order to complete their test on informatics, a compulsory examination that all students need to pass if they want to go on in the course of their study (also for this reason, we choose to restrain our analysis to undergraduate students, as older students might already have completed the test). The submission of the questionnaire took place in different sessions, in the months of March and April 2008. As the students' registration number was recorded, we were able to avoid the possibility of double answers. Moreover, we also controlled if the sample obtained was statistically significant as far as the distribution of students in different faculty was concerned, and we corrected the biases with a second, more focused, administration of the questionnaire. This was done in order to assure that our final sample of 1086 students was indeed representative of the overall population of undergraduate students of the University of Milan-Bicocca.

Some of the students were also involved in a series of focus groups and in-depth interviews, which were performed in order to collect more information on the motivations that make people connect to the Net, the diffusion of different instruments of social networking, the ways in which digital media are replacing traditional ones and so on. To address the theme of the intergenerational digital divide, we also realized a series of focus groups with some students' parents. A different series of focus groups was furthermore performed, involving a set of qualified experts and practitioners operating in the new media sector, that was instrumental in helping us to understand the point of view of people that are currently involved "from the inside" into the current wave of developments. In the following part of this paragraph we focus in particular on the quantitative part of our research, by presenting the most relevant findings coming out from the questionnaire data analysis; we will refer sometimes to data coming out from our qualitative analysis too, as supporting evidence, in order to underline some specific points worth mentioning.

Our questionnaire was divided in three main parts: a preliminary section, focused on general data concerning the use of digital technologies and the access to the Internet (What kind of technology do students use? Where? When? For how much time? etc.). The second part was specifically focused on the "media diet": we collected data concerning the usage of different media, both in the "analogic" (books, newspapers, television, radio) and in the "digital" version (e-books, on-line news, web-tv and web-radio, etc.). In the last part of the questionnaire, we specifically focused on a series of tools and platforms for social networking, trying to analyze their diffusion among the population of students and the reasons that could be at the basis of their use.

By comparing the quantitative results drawn from the questionnaire with the evidence arising from the focus groups and the interviews, we can underscore a few relevant points. First of all, as it was largely expected, it seems that generally speaking university students are quite familiar with technologies: 97,2 percent of students in our sample uses a computer, the 88,7 percent uses an Mp3 player and the 83,3 percent uses a digital camera. On another hand, only 7.7 percent of the students' sample uses a smart phone or a palmtop. On average, students can be considered heavy Internet users: 68.7 percent of our students' sample connects to the Internet more than 5 hours a week, with more than a student out of four who connects to the Internet for more than 20 hours a week and 24.6 percent who connects between 10 and 20 hours a week. Only 6.8 percent of the students connect to the Internet less than one hour a week. If we compare this result with data concerning the rate of use of other media, we see that the Internet seems to play the lion's share in the media diet of our students. Almost three students out of four listen to the radio less than five hours a week, with the 31.7 percent of students listening less than one hour a week and only the 2.6 percent listening more than 20 hours a week. The same seems to hold for what concerns television, even if in this case the rates of use are a little bit higher: 53.8 percent of the students watch TV less than five hours a week, with more than one student out of ten watching less than one hour and only 4 percent watching more than 20 hours a week. For what concerns reading, finally, 13.7 percent of our students never reads a book (except the ones required for studying) and almost one student out of two (49.3 percent) reads less than 5 books in a year. Maintaining an own blog is an activity that concern 42 percent of students, while 78 percent of the students read others' blogs.

Taken together, these results seem to confirm that for university students, the computer and the Internet are quickly becoming one of the preferred media. Evidences coming from the focus groups and the interviews clearly confirmed this point, also adding some more qualifications, in particular for what concerns the digital divide between generations; for example, we think that this excerpt from an interview is highly representative of the type of relationship that some students are developing with their PC: "I think that my all life could be easily confined within a 4x4 square meter room, with a bed, a WC, a little kitchen and a computer... I wouldn't need anything else". On the contrary, many parents have confessed the great difficulties and discomfort encountered when they have to revert, for reasons mainly linked to working necessities, to the use of computers. Quite curiously, one of the points in which discrepancies between students and parents appear more evident is based on the different use of e-mail and instant messaging: while parents still largely prefer the e-mail, students are more and more shifting towards IM. Indeed, only a student out of four uses the e-mail every day, while more than half of the sample uses IM every day.

Entering more in detail into the kind of use students make of the Internet, some mixed evidence come out. While sites such as YouTube, Wikipedia and Google Maps are commonly known and frequently used by our sample of students (only 2.6 percent of the sample doesn't know about YouTube, while Wikipedia is not known by the 4.4 percent of the sample and another 2.5 percent doesn't know about Google Maps), other SNS seem to be not so well known. Almost three students out of four (75.2 percent) do not know Flickr, 77.6 percent does not know Slideshare and 57.4 percent does not know Amazon. Even more impressive seem the fact that the 82.4 percent of students doesn't know Twitter and 80.2 percent doesn't know Linkedin. Data on Facebook need to be taken with particular caution: almost a student out of two (50.4 percent of the sample) did not know this SNS at the time we performed the survey, and more than a student out of four knew it but did not use it. It must be underlined that at the time we submitted our questionnaire (March-April, 2008) Facebook as a social phenomena still was not diffused in Italy. The penetration of Facebook in the Italian context started to grow considerably soon after we completed our research, and it was also driven by substantial mass media coverage. Provisional data coming out from the second edition of our research (carried out between April and July 2009) seem to provide evidence in favour of this fact: even if at the time we are writing this paper this research still has to be completed, a quick look at our first, uncorrected sample of 1126 undergraduate students shows that more than 60 percent of this sample make constant use of Facebook, and only 2.2 percent of the sample does not know about it. Anyway, Facebook seems to represent a kind of separate case, as far as data concerning other SNS seems to be quite comparable between the two editions of our research.

A further point we wanted to explore concern the propensity of students to engage actively in the creation of new original content on the Web. It is often argued that the new media are completely different from old media inasmuch as they have the potential to bread individual creativity and self-expression (Jenkins, 2006; O'Reilly, 2005). With the development of new tools and platforms that allow to easily assemble, create and upload new original contents on the web, it is often argued that traditional media consumers can somehow transform themselves into active "prosumers" (Tapscott & Williams, 2007), capable of developing their own "personal media" (Lüders, 2008). Once again, evidence on this topic seems to be somehow mixed. Almost a student out of four (24.9 percent of the sample) reported having uploaded original content on MySpace, and 21 percent of the sample actively contributed to YouTube. Anyway, the rate of active contribution decreases sensibly if we consider other sites such as Wikipedia (12.3 percent of the sample), and falls dramatically for Flickr and Slideshare (2.1 percent each). A cluster analysis performed on the data coming from the questionnaire allowed us to split our sample in three groups, depending on the overall rate of use of the Internet and on the propensity to engage actively in the creation of new contents. The results of this analysis showed that "active and creative users" of the Internet and all the related technologies make up only 26.3% of our overall sample, while the great majority of our students (more than the 40 percent) can be somehow considered as "passive users" and a significant proportion (almost the 20 percent of the total) do not seem to show a particular high level of global involvement with the Internet and new media, all things considered.

CONCLUSION

In this paper we have presented the results of a survey on the media diet of undergraduate students at the University of Milan-Bicocca. This survey was done by the research team of the Observatory on New Media nuMediaBios, as part of a wider program of research attempting to provide on a regular basis data and analysis on the ways in which university students approach the Internet and the new digital media. Our attempt aims at starting to fill what we believe to be a serious gap in data availability concerning the actual attitudes of University students toward the Internet and the new digital technologies.

As a matter of fact, notwithstanding the high level of concern and public debate on "digital natives" and on the very peculiar characteristics of the "Net generation", sound empirical research on these topics are not easily to find in the literature. Furthermore, the great majority of the available studies concern research carried out in the United States, and very few evidences can be found for what refers to the European context. This seems to apply in particular to college and university students. Another significant problem is represented by the fact that available data often come out of individual, isolated research, and are not the result of systematic research programs. The possibility of making compared analysis is thus severely constrained. This in turn does not allow gaining a deeper understanding of how contextual and time variables can affect the phenomena under scrutiny: are there significant differences in the attitudes toward the use of Internet and the new media in different countries? How can we explain the role of national and context-specific variables in orienting individual behaviours towards these technologies? How does the use of the Internet evolve in the course of time? Can we identify specific discontinuities, linked to particular social and technological evolutions, in the ways subjects approach the Internet and the related technologies?

The data we present here obviously don't allow us to approach these kinds of problems, that in our view represent some suggestions on which future research in this field might concentrate. What we have done so far was mainly intended as a preliminary study in what seems to be a still unexplored field, one in which, quite paradoxically, the scarcity of sound empirical research somehow seem to go hand in hand with the abundance of general statements and common sense analysis. By summing up the main results of our study, some kind of very broad general trends start to come out with a certain clarity.

First of all, it is true that university students present a sort of general familiarity with the computer and with the Internet. This familiarity must be, however, interpreted with some caution, because only a very tiny percentage of our sample of student makes regular uses of things such as palmtops and smart phones. Secondly, it seems that the Internet is somehow replacing other traditional media, especially if we consider activities such as listening to radio or reading books. Anyway, data concerning the propensity to read newspapers are more difficult to make sense of, as the traditional, paper format still seems to be somehow preferred to the online version (more than six students out of ten never or rarely read on-line newspapers, while almost a student out of two sometimes read traditional newspapers, and two students out of ten read them every day). As far as television is concerned, our data seems indeed to show that students no longer consider it as the preferred medium (more than half of our sample watches TV less than five hours a week, and more than a student out of ten watches it less than one hour per week), but this is clearly not enough to say that the transition from the passive, broadcasting model of watching TV to the active, net-casting model of the Internet has been completed. This is a topic that still deserves further scrutiny, and that will require also a sort of diachronic monitoring over a more extended time range.

Finally, interesting findings seem to come out for what concerns the propensity of students to use SNS and to actively create and upload original content on the web. Our data here seems to somehow converge with some of the international evidence we have reviewed in the introduction to the present paper, and that seems to be interesting, given the diversity in the contexts considered. All things considered, we can in fact sum up that the active creation of new content on the Web, and the extensive involvement in social communication activities, far from representing general features of the Net generation, seem to characterize only a limited part of our sample (from 20 to 30 percent, depending also on the specific activity we are considering). What seems to be particularly surprising here is that even sites that we would have expected to be quite popular (Flickr in particular, but also Amazon and Twitter) are known by only a minority of our sample.

An interesting point here concerns Facebook: for a mere coincidence, we were able to perform our research immediately before the explosion of what we can label as a real "Facebook hype", as far as the Italian context is concerned. As a matter of fact, in March-April 2008 Facebook was not known by the majority of our sample. An informal exploration of the new data coming from the second edition of our research, performed between April and July 2009, seems to show that at the time we are writing this paper Facebook has become by far the favourite SNS, while other sites such as Twitter, Flickr, FriendFeed and so on still are almost completely unknown. This in turn raises the question of why Facebook was able to gain such an immediate and quick popularity among our samples of undergraduate students. We do not have enough data at the moment to try to answer to this question, but given the great coverage the "Facebook phenomenon" has received on "traditional" media such as newspapers, magazines and even television, one could suspect that the relationship between old and new media could be more complicated than expected, and that traditional means of communication and information sharing retain a substantial importance in the Italian public sphere.

REFERENCES

Anderson, K. J. (2001). Internet use among college students: an exploratory study. *Journal of American College Health*, *50*(1), 21–26. doi:10.1080/07448480109595707

Bennett, S., Maton, K., & Kervin, L. (2008). The 'digital natives' debate: A critical review of the evidence. *British Journal of Educational Technology, 39*(5), 775–786. doi:10.1111/j.1467-8535.2007.00793.x

Boyd, D., & Ellison, N. B. (2007). Social network sites: Definition, history, and scholarship. *Journal of Computer-Mediated Communication, 13*(1). Retrieved October 28, 2009 from http://jcmc.indiana.edu/vol13/issue1/boyd.ellison.html

Cotten, R., & Jelenewicz, S. M. (2006). A disappearing digital divide among college students? *Social Science Computer Review, 24*(4), 497–506. doi:10.1177/0894439306286852

Ellison, N. B., Steinfeld, C., & Lampe, C. (2007). The benefits of Facebook 'friends' Social capital and college students' user of online social network sites. *Journal of Computer-Mediated Communication, 12*(4). Retrieved October 28, 2009 from http://jcmc.indiana.edu/vol12/issue4/ellison.html

Gaston, J. (2006). Reaching and teaching the digital natives. *Library Hi Tech News, 23*(3), 12–13. doi:10.1108/07419050610668124

Jenkins, H. (2006). *Convergence Culture: Where Old and New Media Collide*. New York: New York University Press.

Jones, S. (2002). The Internet goes to college: How students are living in the future with today's technology. *Pew Internet & American Life Project*. Retrieved October 28, 2009 from http://www.educause.edu/Resources/TheInternetGoestoCollegeHowStu/151825

Jones, S., Johnson-Yale, C., Millermaier, S., & Seoane Pérez, F. (2009). Everyday life, online: U.S. college students' use of the Internet. *First Monday, 14*(10). Retrieved October 28, 2009 from http://firstmonday.org/htbin/cgiwrap/bin/ojs/index.php/fm/article/viewArticle/2649/2301

Kennedy, G., Krause, K., Judd, T., Churchward, A., & Gray, K. (2006). *First year students' experiences with technology: are they really digital natives?* Melbourne, Australia: University of Melbourne. Retrieved October 28, 2009 from http://www.bmu.unimelb.edu.au/research/munatives/ natives_report2006.pdf

Kohut, A., Keeter, S., Doherty, C., & Dimock, M. (2008). Social networking and online videos take off: Internet's broader role in campaign 2008. *Pew Research Center for the People and the Press*. Retrieved October 30, 2009 from http://people-press.org/reports/pdf/384.pdf

Kvavik, R. B., Caruso, J. B., & Morgan, G. (2004). *ECAR study of students and information technology 2004: convenience, connection, and control*. Boulder, CO: EDUCAUSE Center for Applied Research. Retrieved October 31, 2009 from http://net.educause.edu/ir/library/pdf/ers 0405/rs/ers0405w.pdf

Long, S. A. (2005). What's new in libraries? Digital natives: if you aren't one, get to know one. *New Library World, 106*(3/4), 187. doi:10.1108/03074800510587381

Lüders, M. (2008). Conceptualizing personal media. *New Media & Society, 10*(5), 683–702. doi:10.1177/1461444808094352

McHale, T. (2005). Portrait of a digital native. *Technology and Learning, 26*(2), 33–34.

O'Reilly, T. (2005). *What Is Web 2.0? Design Patterns and Business Models for the Next Generation of Software*. Retrieved October 28, 2009 from http://oreilly.com/web2/archive/what-is-web-20.html

Oliver, B., & Goerke, V. (2007). Australian undergraduates' use and ownership of emerging technologies: implications and opportunities for creating engaging learning experiences for the Net generation. *Australasian Journal of Educational Technology, 23*(2), 171-186. Retrieved October 28, 2009 from http://www.ascilite.org.au/ajet/ajet23/oliver.html

Pedrò, F. (2006). *The New Millennium Learners: Challenging our Views on ICT and Learning*. Paris: OECD. Retrieved October 28, 2009 from http://www.oecd.org/dataoecd/1/1/38358359.pdf

Peluchette, J., & Karl, K. (2008). Social networking profiles: An examination of student attitudes regarding use and appropriateness of content. *Cyberpsychology & Behavior*, *11*(1), 95–97. doi:10.1089/cpb.2007.9927

Prenksy, M. (2001a). Digital natives, digital immigrants. *Horizon*, *9*(5), 1–6. doi:10.1108/10748120110424816

Prenksy, M. (2001b). Digital natives, digital immigrants, part II. Do they really think differently? *Horizon*, *9*(6), 1–6. doi:10.1108/10748120110424843

Quan-Haase, A. (2007). University students' local and distant social ties: Using and integrating modes of communication on campus. *Information Communication and Society*, *10*(5), 671–693. doi:10.1080/13691180701658020

Tapscott, D. (1998). *Growing up digital: the rise of the Net generation*. New York: McGraw-Hill.

Tapscott, D., & Williams, A. D. (2007). *Wikinomics. How Mass Collaborations Changes Everything*. London: Portfolio.

Wilson, R. A. (1999, April). *Revelry, revelation, or research: What are college students really doing on the Internet*. Paper presented at ACRL's Ninth National Conference: Racing toward Tomorrow, Detroit, MI. Retrieved October 28, 2009 from http://ala.org/ala/mgrps/divs/acrl/events/pdf/wilsonr99.pdf

ENDNOTE

* The paper was developed jointly by the authors. Paolo Ferri wrote the Introduction, Andrea Pozzali wrote the other paragraphs.

1. The original paper by Prensky has currently 1451 citations on Google Scholar (data updated to the 31st of October, 2009), while a research on "digital natives digital immigrants" performed in the same day gave us more than 3.000.000 of results. The terms "digital natives" has entered into the vocabulary of Italian popular press, and references can be easily found on newspapers and magazines: maybe one of the most salient example is represented by the Italian edition of *Wired*, that dedicated the cover page of the October issue to the "iSchool Manifesto", saying with a strong emphasis that: "The school for Digital Natives is already here".

2. The University of Milan-Bicocca was instituted in June 10, 1998, to serve students from Northern Italy and take some pressure off the over-crowded original University of Milan. At present, it has eight faculties covering humanities and sciences (Economics, Law, Medicine and surgery, Psychology, Educational Sciences, Mathematics, Physics and Natural Sciences, Statistical sciences and Sociology).

3. We thank here all the research team of the Observatory, and in particular Nicola Cavalli, Elisabetta Ida Costa, Andrea Mangiatordi, Stefano Mizzella and Francesca Scenini, for the invaluable contribution provided to the carrying out of the research.

This work was previously published in International Journal of Digital Literacy and Digital Competence, Volume 1, Issue 2, edited by Antonio Cartelli, pp. 1-10, copyright 2010 by IGI Publishing (an imprint of IGI Global).

Section 3
Digital Literacy and Digital Competence after Graduation and for Lifelong Learning

Chapter 9
Integrating Educational and ICT Innovations:
A Case Study of Master Course

Luca Tateo
University of Sassari, Italy

Paola Adinolfi
University of Salerno, Italy

ABSTRACT

The paper explores the effectiveness of a new computer-supported collaborative problem solving educational approach in higher education at a master's course level. After outlining the technological and pedagogical characteristics of a new digital cooperative environment, as well as the constructivist, learner-centered philosophy of the Daosan Master (Management of Health-care Services) at the University of Salerno, the integration of the educational approach and the technological support is reported and discussed in an exploratory case-study. The authors show that a large number of postgraduate students have been able to participate in a dense collaborative problem solving activity within a relatively short lesson period, working and reflecting on a real problem of healthcare management. This indicates that the experience is effective in fostering reflexivity, collaboration and situated learning in management training.

1. THEORETICAL FRAMEWORK

In education the idea of problem solving has been long influenced by the traditional representation of schooling, according to which the classroom is a social context in which students have little ownership of decisions (Bruner, 1996). Teaching and learning were considered asymmetrical roles, where students had to make basically individual decisions, such as in problem solving tasks, attempting to choose the correct solution previously established by the teacher. Since Vygotsky, we

DOI: 10.4018/978-1-4666-0903-7.ch009

know that in education, as in any other social or work context, the ability to solve problems is situated and depends upon the interactions, the affordances and the shared knowledge created in classroom (Cole, 1996). This leads to the idea that teaching must improve students ability to make decisions and solve problems, both individually and collaboratively, in order to enable them to better face the real world's situations. Within this general framework, an educational approach has been developed by LEAD project - *Technology-enhanced learning and problem-solving discussions: Networked learning environments in the classroom*, www.coffee-soft.org – funded by the EU VI FP. The basic idea is to use the computer supported collaborative problem solving to foster student's ability to produce new knowledge and creative solutions, instead of re-producing and simply applying what was taught by the teacher. This approach is the outcome of a joint research activity in four EU countries, carried out by psychologists, pedagogists and computer scientists in school, university, R&D and software evaluation.

Although it is broadly accepted that computers can support collaborative problem solving; it is indeed a matter of fact that putting into practice the theoretical concept above stated in a real classroom's problem solving activity is not an easy task to accomplish. The first requirement is to make visible the structure and context of the problem students are required to solve, that is to "embody" the process of collaborative problem solving interaction is crucial. The interaction between different perspectives leads to more in-depth thinking, to manage information but also to participate in the process of sharing information through discussion and argumentation (Ligorio et al., 2009). These requirements also affect the management of time constraints, materials, participation and group-working in classroom. Collaboration requires communication between participants (students and teacher) during their attempts to solve problems, in order to reach shared understanding about what the questions means, about how to answer it and checking answers, and about how to coordinate how they will work together: who will do what and when? Such a coordinated collaboration is actually what a collaborative environment could enhance.

From this perspective, the educational focus is on the development of collaborative, reflective and creative skills rather than on learning the ability to solve specific problems, the latter becoming a conceptual tool to experience those skills. Thus, in this study the concept of collaborative problem solving is used in a broader sense, including a wide range of those collaborative activities in which students must analyze, apply, share, make decisions, argue and discuss, summarize, etc. to achieve a common solution to a real-life problem. This vision has been instantiated in a new collaborative environment, named CoFFEE.

2. A DIGITAL FACE-TO-FACE COOPERATIVE ENVIRONMENT

CoFFEE (Cooperative Face2Face Educational Environment) (De Chiara et al., 2007; Manno et al., 2007) is an open-source suite designed to enhance multi-modal, face-to-face and computer supported, collaborative problem solving. CoFFEE has been already used in several studies, testing a wide range of collaborative problem solving pedagogical activities (Ligorio et al., 2009; Enriquez et al., 2008). A brief overview of CoFFEE tools and features will be now provided in order to describe the digital educational environment in which the case study has been situated.

CoFFEE is a software suite - based on Eclipse Rich Client Platform - made of five main applications (Figure 1). The **CoFFEE Controller** is the teacher application that coordinates class' activities, while each student runs a **CoFFEE Discusser** client application. The classroom activity is described in a XML *session* file (that is a sequence of steps including a set of tools), managed run-time by the CoFFEE Controller. A session can

Figure 1. CoFFEE's architecture

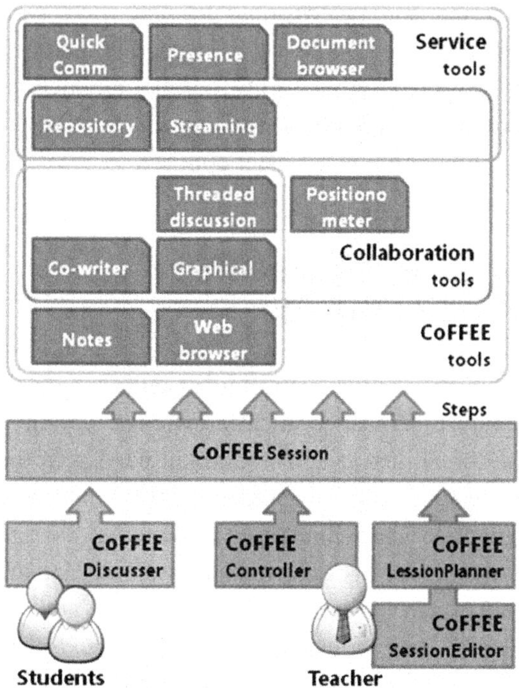

be designed using two different applications: the **Lesson Planner** (a quick and easy design tool that offers a set of sessions templates, including steps and tools configurations, that the teacher can adapt to specific topics); and the **Session Editor** enabling teachers to design a new session from scratch or to modify in detail an existing session. The **Class Editor** is the application to edit the class roster, that is the students' list, setting also user-names and passwords when needed.

CoFFEE provides students with a wide range of collaborative tools to support effective problem solving in classroom (Figure 2). The core tools are: the *threaded chat*; that enables students to post contributions, organize them in threads, categorize and label them; a *graphical tool*, in which posts are placed within a two-dimensional visual space of debate, using boxes, labels and connectors. CoFFEE also provides other collaborative tools, such as a *co-writer*, a *voting tool* (named positionometer), a *streaming and video-conferencing tool*, a *shared repository*, etc.

CoFFEE has been designed to improve the effectiveness and provide scaffolding for face-to-face collaborative problem solving activities in educational contexts along four main dimensions (Ligorio et al., 2009; Enriquez et al., 2008):

- *flexibility*: the software can be used for a wide range of educational activities (problem solving, planning, hands-on activities, brainstorming, etc.), tailored on students of different ages (from primary school, to professional training), and can be used on different subjects (e.g. humanities, science, nurse training, etc.);
- *parallel interaction*: CoFFEE can be used to support parallel discussions, so to en-

Figure 2. The graphical tool (left), threaded chat (right) and positionometer (bottom right)

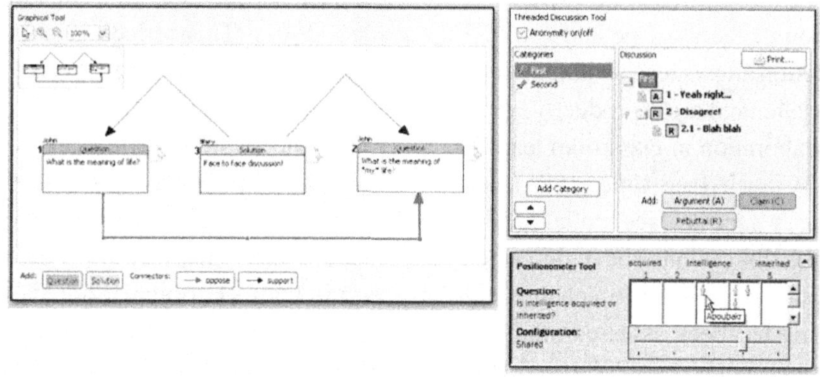

hance participation and knowledge construction. Comparing face-to-face discussions with CoFFEE-enhanced discussions shows that the latter produce a higher number of contributions, in which students can better share their opinions. This is due to the multi-modal nature of CoFFEE-enhanced interaction, exploiting both face-to-face and digital communication channels. Students can indeed come through the limited turns of speech of face-to-face interactions. They can also participate in a more democratic, giving voice also to shy and less dominant students, improving both quantitatively and qualitatively the discussion;

- *productivity:* CoFFEE enhances classroom productivity by keeping permanent trace of the interactions. Everybody can take notes and everything that happens during the computer mediated discussion is recorded, together with the digital artifacts produced. This helps students and teachers to come back to the knowledge and reflect upon it;
- *anonymity*: the last added value of CoFFEE-enhanced collaboration is the possibility of anonymity While the face-to-face speaker is always identifiable, CoFFEE can be configured in anonymous state, in order to reduce students' status inequalities and shyness. Anonymity can be also very useful when discussing sensitive topics, such as those related to health-care.

The integration of face-to-face and CoFFEE supported interaction allows teacher and students to experience a richer and more productive communication. Collaboration in classroom leads to better learning by itself (see Cole, 1996), and CoFFEE enhances face-to-face collaboration with respect to the dimensions above described. The efficacy of using CoFFEE to enhance collaborative learning has been assessed mainly in school context (see Ligorio et al., 2009 for further readings). Less data exist with respect to higher education and professional training. The case study presented in the following paragraphs will thus explore how flexibility, parallel interaction, productivity and anonymity can foster more effective learning in a master course.

3. A LEARNER-CENTRED MASTER COURSE

One of the challenges in higher education is to provide in-depth theoretical knowledge combined with the ability to apply such knowledge to the real contexts, enabling students to go from theory to practice. We will attempt to demonstrate that the endeavor can be carried out by combining the collaborative problem solving approach and the CoFFEE environment into a specific context, such as the DAOSan Master Course (www.daosan.it).

The University Master for Leadership in Health-care Services (DAOSan) is a post-graduate course at the University of Salerno, organized by the Dept. of Business Studies Research, in partnership with the Dept. of Preventive Medical Science of the "Federico II", University of Naples, the Dept. of Analysis of Economic and Social Systems, University of Sannio (DASES) and the Campania's Regional Health Agency (ArSan).

The DAOSan approach is related to a more general ongoing reflection within health-care organizational studies, questioning the technocratic and bureaucratic managerial approach dominating the last two decades of 20th century (Glouberman, 2005). This reflection points out the rays and shadows of the managerial reforms taking place since the 80's that tried to innovate and renew the Western health-care systems, in a sort of *positivist* philosophy both on the medical and the managerial sides. The failure of this endeavor made evident the need for a conceptual change rather than an organizational one. Therefore Daosan promotes a *new health governance* which goes beyond positivist managerialism to enhance a *patient-centered* approach, re-establishes the centrality of the individual, joining means and ends, blending logics of action that differ from those that are strictly of an economic-financial kind, and recovering a reflective role for managers, to enable them to evaluate the consequences of technical-economic-normative productivity and to control the risks of a complexity that surpasses by far the tools available to manage it (Adinolfi, 2005).

In line with the approaches that tend to re-establish the centrality of the individual, the DAOSan Master Course proposes a new learner-centred educational approach, in which educational objectives are not given as such and the goal is not just to acquire knowledge and skills. These are considered means for managing *Change*.

3.1. The DAOSan Educational Approach

It is nowadays widely understood that well-chosen case studies support students in acquiring competence at a higher level than just learning context-independent information and rules. In higher education and in professional schools the case-based teaching approach is becoming central (Flyvbjerg, 2006, p. 222). The DAOSan educational philosophy too is oriented towards the achieving of a context-based professional competence and a more general set of life skills – such as reflection, collaboration, creativity, communication, adaptation, etc. – through a case-based learning (Adinolfi, 2006).

The first requirement for this kind of new educational approach is to have learner-centered training programs, such as Mintzberg's IHML, that support students in developing mind tools (Jonassen, 1999) as well as reflective and planning skills. The second requirement is to go from theory to practice, applying theoretical knowledge to real-life problems and field experience. The third requirement is to set up place for collaboration and collective reflection. Finally, this approach requires a continuous monitoring and evaluation of students' achievements and improvements.

One of the training methods, that seems to fulfill all these requirements, is Problem-based learning (PBL) (Woods, 1994). PBL is one of the most effective constructivist instructional approaches, that enables students to work on authentic tasks, to keep the ownership of the solution process, and to experience the complexity of the environment they should be able to work in at the end of learning (Duffy, Lowyck & Jonassen, 1993). It is also aimed at challenging learners' thinking and pre-conceptions, in order to create and test new ideas (Duffy & Jonassen, 1992).

The PBL approach, developed since the 70's in medical education, has been instantiated in DAOSan teaching methodology, including, for instance different training activities such as: case-study discussions, group-work, classroom exercises, role-playing, simulations - in addition to traditional lectures and seminars with experts from the health-care sector.

The common constructivist ground is what made the encounter between DAOSan and CoFFEE possible. The DAOSan's teaching method, for instance, requires students to carry out independent reflection's group sessions about the lessons topics. The PBL, adopted as main approach in DAOSan, has been easily integrated with the collaborative problem solving approach of CoFFEE. In the next paragraph a case study of such an integration will be described and discussed.

4. INTEGRATING TECHNOLOGICAL TOOLS AND EDUCATIONAL APPROACH: THE DAOSAN CASE

The discussion of the conceptual framework leads us to define some basic propositions about the positive role of collaborative problem solving approach in order to improve students' "life skills", their ability to reflect, to create new knowledge and to link theory and practice. Such life skills become even more relevant in higher education and professional training. The effectiveness of this general approach can be improved by the use of CoFFEE-enhanced collaborative problem solving, which provides more flexibility, parallel interaction, productivity and participation when applied to support master students in argumentative discussion aimed at generating ideas, arguing and reflecting upon them.

4.1. Research Question and Methodology

In order to provide understanding and empirical support to the above stated propositions and to instantiate them in a real educational context, the case-study analysis will try to answer the following research question: how is a collaborative face-to-face and digital educational environment useful to enhance master's students ability to reflect, participate, collaborate, debate and to apply knowledge?

The choice of the case-study methodology is of course driven by the nature of the object to be studied and by the research question. The descriptive case study approach is here used in order to describe the educational intervention and its related phenomena within the real-life context in which it occurred (Yin, 2003).

The data sources for the case study are:

- the students' evaluations of teaching and tutoring: during the course students are required to answer some teaching's evaluation forms, providing information about customer satisfaction, teacher's performance and proposals for improvements. The students notes have been analyzed in order to define their evaluation, needs and requests with respect to collaborative activities;
- the transcripts of CoFFEE-enhanced collaborative problem solving sessions: CoFFEE keeps trace of a session including the participants, the groups' composition, all the messages and the products created. The transcripts of three different sessions carried out during master's courses have been taken into account and analyzed;
- researchers' field notes: one researcher observed all the CoFFEE sessions taking field notes about the classroom's atmosphere, the students' participation and the teaching and tutoring styles. These notes have been used to scaffold the case-study analysis.

First, students' evaluations of the courses before the introduction of CoFFEE are discussed in order to grasp the needs and expectations with respect to classroom's activities. Then, three CoFFEE-supported activities are presented and sessions transcripts are analyzed with respect to the flexibility, parallel interaction, productivity and participation dimensions. The analysis is supported by transcripts of the interaction via CoFFEE. Finally, students' evaluations after the CoFFEE-supported activities are analyzed and discussed.

4.2. The Context

The DAOSan master course enrolls three types of students:

- graduate students from different domains (healthcare, law, economy, engineering, etc.);
- healthcare professionals (i.e. surgeons);
- administration professionals (healthcare managers, administrative staff).

Students can choose between full-time and part-time status. Full-time students must follow all courses and have to graduate in a shorter time, while part-time students, namely professionals, can spread the courses over a longer time span. Each class is made approximately of 40 students, including a 30% of part-time students.

The lectures include healthcare systems, human resource management, marketing, communication and quality management, as well as law, computer systems and case management. Students must also carry out project works and stages in healthcare organizations. During the courses, students achievement are constantly monitored and, in return, students are asked to evaluate anonymously teachers' performances at the end of each lecture. In particular, students are asked to evaluate on a 5 grade scale aspects such as teacher's clarity, completeness, and attention to students' needs. These dimensions generally receive high scoring (4 and 5), proving students' satisfaction with respect to master teaching approach.

Students can also provide free comments with respect to the courses. Such comments are the source for a more in-depth evaluation of the general DAOSan teaching approach. Students' notes highlight both the commitment in debate and the need for a real-case application of knowledge. Students, especially part-time, also point out that during classroom debates there are some colleagues which tend to monopolize the discussion leaving little room for others to contribute.

In order to overcome such problems, it has been decided to experiment the use of CoFFEE in order to improve the quality and participation of collaborative activities in classroom.

4.3. Pedagogical Scenarios

CoFFEE-supported activities are based on a pedagogical scenario, that is a narrative description of what should happen in classroom – a sequence of steps - and of the configuration of CoFFEE tools. For the sake of this study, and in order to make more clear how this kind of activity is carried out, the description of the three pedagogical scenarios used in the master course is now provided.

4.3.1. The Choice of a General Manager

The general learning objective of the activity is to involve students in an argumentative discussion about the criteria to be applied in the choice of the general manager of an health-care institution. In particular, the teacher wants to evaluate student's pre-conceptions about the lesson topic and to foster a reflection about the main dimensions involved in the choice of a manager in healthcare, the outcome of the discussion being later used as a starting point for the front lesson.

The scenario of the activity, co-designed by the teacher and the researcher, is a 50 minutes discussion, organized in 3 steps:

1) Brainstorming: the class is asked to provide a set of criteria that should lead to the choice of a general manager, to categorize them and to argue against or in favor of each specific criterion. Students discuss both face-to-face and by the CoFFEE's *threaded chat tool.* At the end of the step students vote, using the *positionometer tool*, the most relevant criteria that should be kept into the next step. Duration: 20 minutes.
2) Knowledge consolidation and organization: students, divided in five small groups, are asked to draw collaboratively a conceptual map - using the *graphical chat tool* - of the most relevant criteria, individualizing *pros* and *cons* of each one, and to graphically connect them by arrows (Figure 3). Duration: 20 minutes.
3) Restitution: in the final step students are asked, anonymously, to reflect upon the discussion and to synthesize individually the "lesson learnt", using the *threaded chat* again. They are also asked to evaluate the teacher's performance at the end of the lesson using the *positionometer*. Duration: 10 minutes.

Figure 3. Screen-shot of graphical tool's discussion

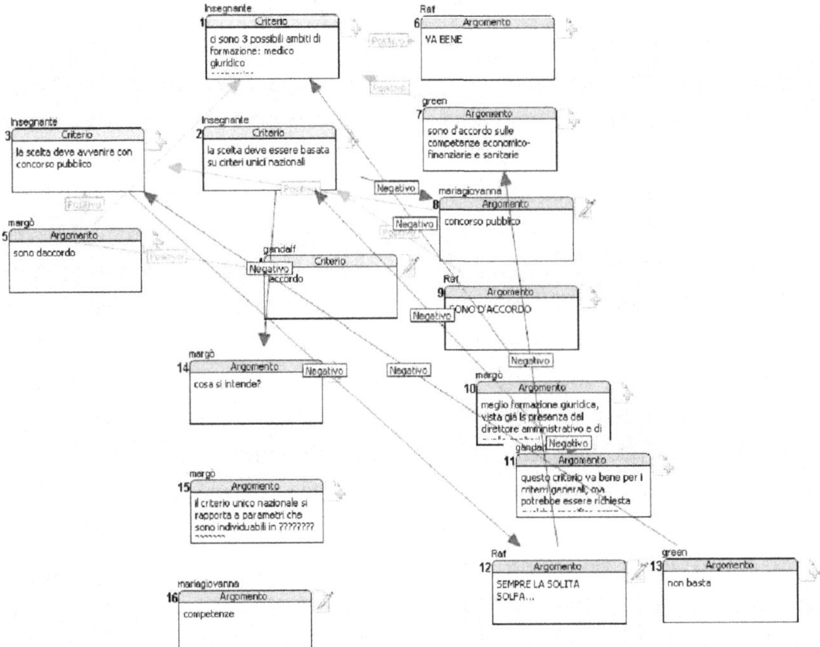

This scenario is a good example of the type of activity to be carried out with CoFFEE. The basic structure of this activity consists of three main phases: brainstorming, knowledge consolidation and organization, restitution (Ligorio et al., 2009). This scenario has been used during a law course as starting point for the lecture about the procedures and criteria to select and hire the general managers.

4.3.2. Marketing for Healthcare Organizations

The pedagogical objective of the scenario is to make students better understand the principles and competences of marketing for an healthcare organization (marketing course) and how to apply these principles to a real case. Students are first asked to define concepts, roles and professional competences of healthcare marketing. Then, they work in small group to write a project of introduction, implementation and assessment of marketing activities in a real organization.

The activity lasts about 50 minutes and is organized in three steps:

1. Organization of knowledge: students work in 4 groups using the *threaded chat tool* to discuss and report the basic principles of healthcare marketing they learned during the previous front lessons. Each group must provide a summary of these principles using the *co-writer tool*. The objective is to make them appropriating the fundamental concepts and characteristics of marketing by the collaborative re-formulation and summary of the knowledge acquired. Duration: about 15 minutes.
2. Building a conceptual model of marketing management: students work in 4 groups using the *threaded chat tool* and the *graphical chat tool* to build a conceptual scheme representing the relationships between the concepts of the marketing management cycle in healthcare. The teacher uses the *Positionometer tool* to ask a stimulus question in order to guide the discussion:

Figure 4. Screen-shot of the conceptual model produced during the step

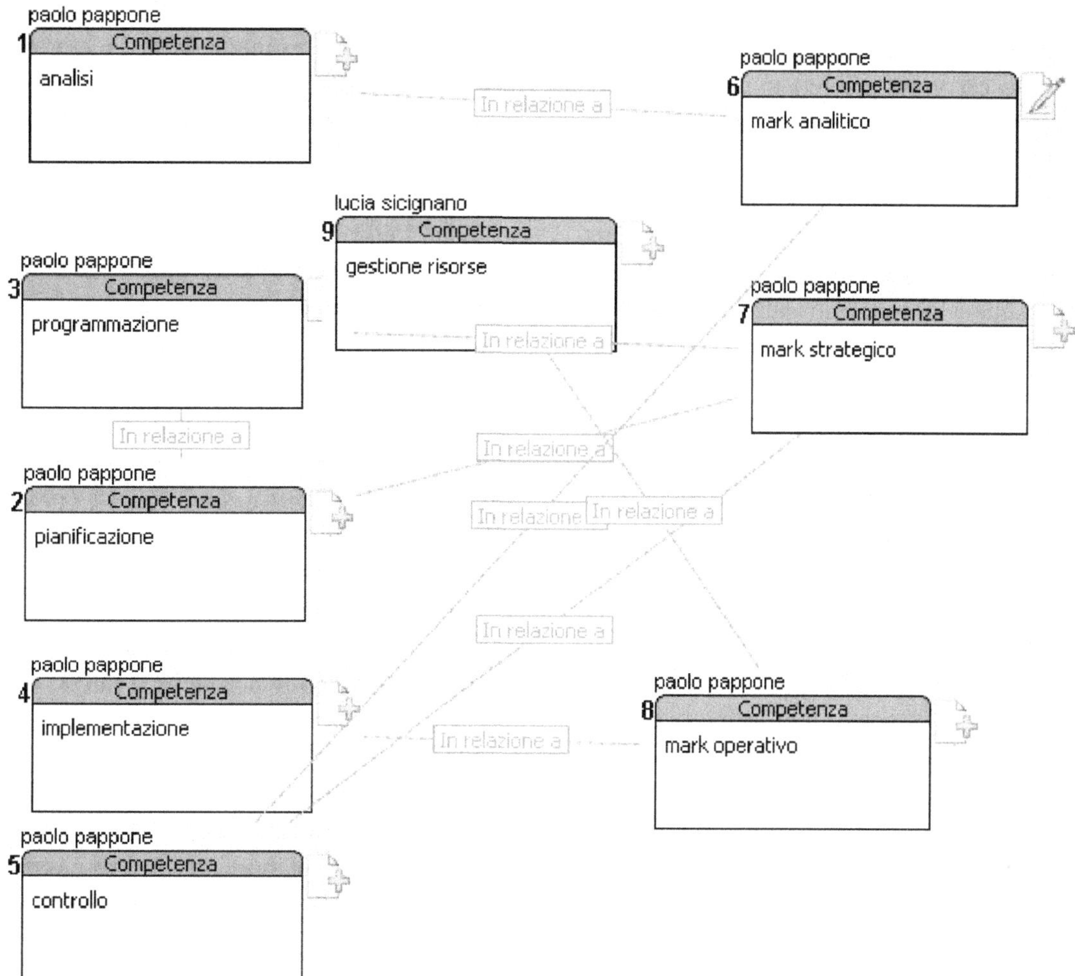

Teacher question: "Actually, it is not possible to apply the marketing management cycle to an healthcare organization. You can just follow a general improvement of the communication in healthcare. How much do you agree or disagree with this statement?"

The students are then asked to motivate their position and build the conceptual model of the management cycle (Figure 4).

The objective is to scaffold students in acquiring an integrated overview of the concept and the professional competences of healthcare marketing. Duration: about 20 minutes.

3. Apply concepts in a real context: students work in plenary discussion in order to provide an individual proposal of application of the marketing cycle to a specific healthcare organization. Students work with the *threaded chat tool* providing their proposals of application and discussing together pros and cons of their proposals. Duration: about 15 minutes.

4.3.3. ICTs in Healthcare Organizations

The third scenario here presented has been designed to discuss and evaluate the project works carried out by the students during the computer science course. One of the characteristics of the DAOSan teaching approach is that students often have to carry out projects in order to apply theoretical knowledge to real situations and to develop their planning skills. At the end of the computer science course focused on the computer supported collaborative work, the four groups of students were asked to write collaboratively a project about how to introduce ICT in their healthcare organizations. Each group choose a real healthcare organization and a service (treatment, emergency service, administration), elaborating a project to introduce and assess ICT technology in order to improve the service. During the final classroom session each group had to present its own project and discuss it with the rest of the class. The scenario is organized in three steps in about 80 minutes:

1. Choosing the spokesman: each group must choose a spokesman that will present the project work to the rest of the class and agree on the way to present the final product. In this case, the discussion is supported by the *threaded chat tool* and the decision is made face to face, benefiting from the two communication modalities. Duration: 5 minutes
2. Presentation: each group by turns presents face to face its own project to the class, while the students are taking individual notes by the CoFFEE's *note tool*. Duration: 40 minutes.
3. Discussion: the teacher sets up four discussion rooms, one room for each project, using the *threaded chat tool*. Students are asked to discuss pros and cons of each project work, providing suggestions for further improvements. In particular, students can ask question to the projects authors, provide comments and make suggestions. Duration: about 35 minutes.

The objective of this scenario is to make students reflect upon their project works by a peer reviewing process that can also provide useful hints for improvement.

The following example is an excerpt of the discussion about one of the four projects presented by the students. Namely, one of the small groups elaborated an idea about a geo-reference system to map and visualize the healthcare services in a given area (i.e. surgeons, hospitals, pharmacies, etc.) to support citizens and stakeholders in choosing the healthcare assistance and planning the distribution of services into the different areas. The idea is quite simple: to show on a virtual map the different healthcare services so that citizens can choose with respect to their needs (proximity, availability, quality, etc.) and accessing the information and the reservation's system just by clicking on it. The idea is also feasible because it is based on GoogleHearth technology. The service is also useful for the stakeholders and the healthcare management because it can be used to visualize the geographic distribution of services and the amount of people using them. It can be then used to reallocate resources and even decide where to start new services.

After the presentation, the class discussed the "geo-reference system" project using the *threaded chat tool*.

5. DISCUSSION

The focus of the paper is how to apply some constructivist educational principles - namely collaborative knowledge construction, its application to real problems and reflexivity – to health-care management training by using a collaborative digital environment. The question how is it possible to enhance master's students' ability to reflect, participate, collaborate debate and to apply knowledge by using a collaborative face-to-face and digital educational environment will be now discussed using the scenario above referred to, in order to describe the compliance with those principles. For the sake of brevity in this exposition, we will present some excerpts of the CoFFEE sessions described above as specimen of the similar processes occurred during the three sessions considered in the present exploratory study.

The first example is drawn from the scenario #1. The collaborative problem solving activity's task was: "*We have to choose a general manager for a health-care institution. What are the suitable selection criteria?*". The CoFFEE-enhanced session was flexible enough to carry out a brainstorming, the building of a conceptual map, an argumentative discussion and a classroom restitution, allowing the teacher to set up a rich problem-based activity. The session was also productive with respect to both students' parallel interaction (e.g. during the 20 minutes brainstorming, 166 contributions were posted) and outcomes (students were able to find by themselves the most relevant dimensions of selection criteria: candidate's training and background, recruitment's procedure and formal criteria, who is going to decide the hiring). In excerpt 1 is presented an example of a discussion thread.

Excerpt 1 (The letters in square brackets indicate the label that the student gave to his/her post [P]=proposal; [A]=argument):

[P] Student 1: the training background must be both management and medical because the organizing choices concern the medical domain.
[A] Student 2: I agree, but management has priority
[P] Student 3: he must come from the management of a large company
[A] Student 3: I mean a private company

The three students are trying to individualize the most suitable training background of a candidate to an healthcare management position. The first point to highlight is that all the students are using the contribution labels provided by CoFFEE threaded chat (see paragraph II.I) in the right way. They are able to build a correct argumentative debate by organizing and supporting their proposals with arguments. Secondly, in just four turns they come to an agreement about the need for a managerial background. This is an example of how the visual representation of the argumentative debate – using threads and labels – can lead to a more productive and parallel interaction in classroom.

The second example (Excerpt 2) is taken from another step of the session #1. Students are asked to re-organize and synthesize the discussion, building a conceptual map of the candidate's profile, using the graphical tool.

The first remark is that the graphical representation of the debate is impressively clear and well-organized (Figure 5).

The group of students has been able to organize concepts and relationships between them in a relatively short time, building a graph of the criteria (yellow boxes), the arguments (light blue boxes), and the pros and cons (respectively, green and red arrows).

Excerpt 2:

[Criterion] Teacher: there are 3 possible educational backgrounds: medical, economic, legal
[Argument] Student 1: do not forget the social aspect of management
[Argument] Student 2: finally we could have national open competitions
[Argument] Student 3: it seems right to me, because it gives the opportunity to everybody to apply, and may the best win
[Argument] Student 4: do not forget the social aspect of management background which will give a soul to the human conduct

Excerpt 2 is an example of how students are able to apply some of the basic principles of DAOSan philosophy – meritocracy and human-centered approach in healthcare – during the classroom debates. They are not directly prompted by the teacher, which instead synthesize the "educational background" issue, nevertheless they can link the practical issue of education with the more abstract concept of human-centered healthcare.

Figure 5. Graphical representation of the argumentation

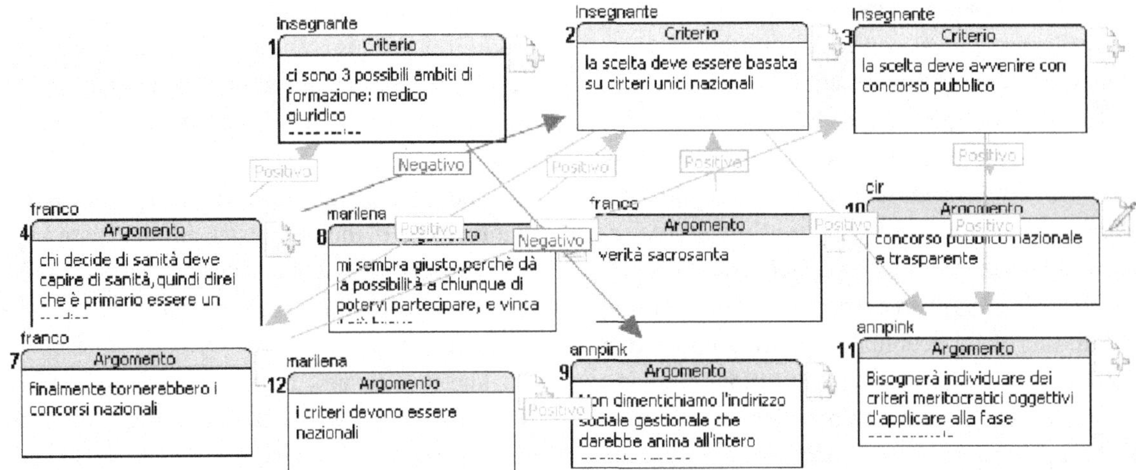

Scenario #2 provides a significant example of parallel interaction and productivity: during about 50 minutes 210 messages were posted, where students made a considerable effort to apply concepts and tools of marketing management to their health care organizations. The recording of the session has been used by the teacher to evaluate (through the analysis of individual proposals) to what extent participants had learnt to manage the theoretical knowledge and to foresee its practical impact. It has been saved on the master's e-learning platform, as a classroom "collective memory", so that students can look it up as didactic material in the prosecution of the course. It has also been considered by the teacher a useful starting point to plan the lesson for the next class.

The third specimen is taken from the activity presented in the scenario #3. The discussion was parallel and productive: during about 35 minutes 59 messages were posted in this single room, more than 150 messages were posted in total during the discussion of the four projects. The second relevant aspect is that students were able to self-evaluate their project works and provide each other with comments and suggestions about how to improve the projects. Last but not least, the discussion has been traced and stored so that students were able to come back on this collective repertoire of ideas, using the suggestions to reflect and improve the projects.

In excerpt 3 is presented a short discussion thread in which students are discussing a particular aspect of the project. The idea is to include in a single geo-system the information, the surgeon assistance and the pharmacies. In this way, the citizen could book a medical service directly into the nearest pharmacy.

Excerpt 3 (The letters in square brackets indicate the label that the student gave to his/her post [D]=question; [S]=suggestion; [C]=explanation):

[D] 1 – Student 1: if the purpose is to enhance the role of the physician, why involving into the reservation system also the pharmacies etc.?

[C] 1.1 – Student 2: Pharmacies are a second phase of development. The opportunity to book healthcare services also from the "pharmacy points" is just a possibility, but it must follow the physician's decision

[C] 1.2 – Student 3: the physician prescribes the medical examination or the medicines, anyway he is always informed about the patient's data

[C] 1.3 – Student 4: the systems takes also into account the availability of the medical services required; the physician can evaluate case by case the service and assign a priority ranking.

Students discuss simultaneously three different topics: which is the role of the physician with respect to the system; how the physician can monitor the patient and the available resources in the area; if the citizen can book medical service of his own into a "pharmacy point". This short excerpt shows how deep can go the discussion supported by CoFFEE. Students have the possibility to reflect upon many different aspects and technicalities that a simple presentation of the projects and a face-to-face only discussion would not allow. Besides, this type of collaborative problem solving scenario let students reflect upon the practical aspects of healthcare management, by linking the project to the practices of everyday life, as for instance how people actually behave with their physician.

Going back from the detailed description of how the educational approach has been instantiated in CoFFEE sessions to a more general evaluation of the scenarios presented, a final remark is about the students' evaluation of such a classroom activities. The evaluation forms after the CoFFEE sessions have been compared with those filled before the introduction of CoFFEE, concerning teachers' performances at the end of each lesson. No relevant difference has been found with respect to teacher performance. Teacher's clarity, completeness, and attention to students' needs received high scoring (4 and 5).

Nevertheless, students free comments put instead in evidence students' self awareness about their "life skills". They claim to feel more adaptive and able to deal positively with real-life situations related to their work. Students also observe an improvement of participation and absence of complaining about the democratic distribution of speech turns. In other words, it now seems that everybody is participating without few students monopolizing the discussion.

6. CONCLUSION

Despite of the exploratory and descriptive nature of this case study, it can be maintained that an educational approach like the one adopted by DAOSan master can foster student reflexivity and involvement, enabling them to fully understand the relationship between both theoretical and case-based knowledge acquired during the course and the real problem that they will face in healthcare organizations. The case study provides empirical evidences in favour of the introduction of CoFFEE in problem-based learning activities in higher education.

It does not proves that ICT *per se* is not sufficient to enhance collaborative problem solving in educational contexts. ICT has in fact been embedded in a suitable learning approach which can deal with the complexity and flexibility of each collaborative type of learning. The examples provided have shown a wide range of different activities and topics carried out by a quite large classroom of master's students. In spite of the high number of participants, the pedagogical scenarios have been able to lead the classroom interaction towards the pedagogical goals in a reasonable amount of time. Besides, the quality of the interaction was high, as showed by the students evaluations and by the quantity and depth of the contribution posted via CoFFEE. The type of collaborative activity, called *CoFFEE-enhanced pedagogical scenario*, seems to be a good deal between the need for managing and pre-designing a lesson - for a large number of students about complex topics – and the flexibility required in a problem-based approach – in which students must be able to discuss and self-organize the group work. Finally, the features and tools provided by CoFFEE – traceability, threaded and graphical chat, notes, etc. – seem to allow a rich parallel interaction. The traces can be used as "collective memory" of the class and as didactic material for reflection and further activities.

To sum up briefly, by the use of CoFFEE and the related pedagogical approach, it has been possible to carry out a dense collaborative problem solving activity with a quite large number of post-graduate students in a relatively short lesson time. The result of this activity has been that of enabling students to work and reflect upon a real problem of health-care management. Students seemed to improve some of those "life skills" that will be part of their professional identity, such as – collaboration, reflection, communication, creativity, etc. They also seemed more aware of the relevant aspects of the human-centered approach in healthcare.

The first positive evaluation of the experience led to the formal integration of CoFFEE-enhanced problem solving approach into the DAOSan curriculum. Obviously, these preliminary results require rigorous evaluative analyses, which will be carried out during the following academic year.

REFERENCES

Bruner, J. (1996). *The culture of education*. New York: Harvard University Press.

Cole, M. (1996). *Cultural psychology. A once and future discipline*. Cambridge, MA: Belknap Press.

De Chiara, R., Di Matteo, A., Manno, I., & Scarano, V. (2007, November). CoFFEE: Cooperative face-2face educational environment. In *Proceedings of the 3rd International Conference in Collaborative Computing: Networking, Applications and Worksharing (CollaborateCom2007)*, New York.

Duffy, T. M., & Jonassen, D. (Eds.). (1992). *Constructivism and the technology of instruction: A conversation*. Hillsdale, NJ: Lawrence Erlbaum Associates.

Duffy, T. M., Lowyck, J., & Jonassen, D. (Eds.). (1993). *Designing environments for constructivist learning*. Berlin: Springer-Verlag.

Enriquez, J., Ainsworth, S., Gelmini Hornsby, G., Buda, M., Crook, C., & O'Malley, C. (2008). Turn-taking and mode-switching in text-based communication in the classroom. In *Proceedings of the International Conference of the Learning Sciences*, Utrecht, The Netherlands.

Flyvbjerg, B. (2006). Five Misunderstandings about Case-Study Research. *Qualitative Inquiry*, *12*(2), 219–245. doi:10.1177/1077800405284363

Glouberman, S. (2005, March 29). *Changing Conceptions of Health and Illness: Three Philosophical Ideas and Health*. Paper presented at the Workshop on Shaping the Future of Home Care, Toronto, ON, Canada.

Jonassen, D. H. (1999). *Computers as Mindtools for Schools: Engaging Critical Thinking*. Upper Saddle River, NJ: Prentice Hall.

Ligorio, M. B., Andriessen, J., Baker, M., Knoller, N., Klonyguy, M., & Tateo, L. (Eds.). (2009). *Talking over the computer: pedagogical scenarios to blend computers and face to face interaction*. Naples, Italy: Scriptaweb.

Manno, I., Belgiorno, F., De Chiara, R., Di Matteo, A., Erra, U., Malandrino, D., et al. (2007). Collaborative face2face educational environment (CoFFEE). In *Proceedings of the First International Conference on Eclipse Technologies (Eclipse-IT)*, Naples, Italy.

Woods, D. R. (1994). *Problem-based Learning: How to Gain the Most from PBL*. Waterdown, ON, Canada: Donald R. Woods.

Yin, R. K. (2003). *Case study research: Design and methods* (3rd ed.). Thousand Oaks, CA: Sage.

This work was previously published in International Journal of Digital Literacy and Digital Competence, Volume 1, Issue 4, edited by Antonio Cartelli, pp. 16-29, copyright 2010 by IGI Publishing (an imprint of IGI Global).

Chapter 10
Digital Literacy in a Lifelong Learning Programme for Adults:
Educators' Experiences and Perceptions on Teaching Practices

Athanassios Jimoyiannis
University of Peloponnese, Greece

Maria Gravani
Open University of Cyprus, Cyprus

ABSTRACT

The study presented explores aspects of adult learning on digital literacy in the context of a lifelong learning programme for social cohesion in Greece. The article outlines the framework of the digital literacy subject and underlines its associated objectives regarding adults' knowledge and competence in Information and Communication Technologies (ICT). The exploration draws upon the experiences and perceptions of eight adult ICT educators. The findings reveal that the educators tried to use flexible instructional practices that were adjusted to adult learners' needs and interests. Common effective instructional practices used were: ICT competence sessions, interdisciplinary and multi-literacy lessons, ICT-based projects, individual instruction sessions. Additionally, the article reveals the difficulties that adults faced in the course of developing ICT literacy skills. The paper ends with implications for the design of adult digital literacy courses in lifelong learning programmes, and for the preparation and development of the ICT educators in the years to come.

INTRODUCTION

The rapid advancement of Information and Communication Technology (ICT) during the last decades has radically affected citizens' individual and social lives and transformed the industrial-centred society to a new, dynamic society described as *information society*, *knowledge society* or *global universal society*. This has presented new challenges to most adults, as they have to constantly keep up with the changes around them. Today, more than ever, adult learners need to update their knowledge for skills improvement, job

DOI: 10.4018/978-1-4666-0903-7.ch010

advancement, personal growth and understanding (Lawson, 2005). Career and job changes are commonplace, and as a consequence adults must be able to acquire new skills so that they succeed and survive.

Since the late 1990s, only literacy and numeracy have been considered to be the basic skills for social and labour success. However, ICT literacy is nowadays considered as being a third important skill for work force and life alongside literacy and numeracy (EC, 2000a, 2001; DfES, 2003; NIACE, 2005). Within Europe, ICT has been identified as a key goal of educational policy and a major strategy aiming at helping EU citizens to participate in the 21st century *knowledge society and* the *knowledge-based economy* (EC, 2000b, 2001).

During the last decade, there has been an extensive discussion about *digital divide*, the divide between people who have access to technology, computers and the Internet and those that do not. Recently, the extension of the digital divide concept beyond mere physical access to computers and the Internet, gains attention and constitutes a central policy and research issue (Selwyn, 2004; Van Dijk & Hacker, 2003; Van Dijk, 2006). The digital divide and the consequent information divide do not only exist between industrialised nations and developing countries. There is also a dichotomy, within individual societies, between those with easy access to digital media and an abundance of information, and those who do not know how and where to find information, and furthermore, do not understand the value of information and how it can help them in their day-to-day lives (Goulding, 2001).

Improving adult digital and ICT literacy levels is fundamental in terms of bridging the digital divide and effectively confronting the issues of exclusion and marginalisation that accompanies the increasing importance of ICT-mediated activities in modern social life. Increasing ICT usage by both young people and adults is considered as a critical factor in reducing inequalities and ensuring people's inclusion in the social, economic and political life of their communities and societies, so that they have an influence over their own life chances. It has become apparent that digital literacy is not just about using the computer and the growing interest about the Internet and mobile technologies. Undoubtedly, ICT training can motivate people to develop literacy, numeracy and language skills. Moreover, ICT competency is necessary not only for citizens to function efficiently on a personal level, but also to develop, advance and succeed in their professional lives, and become active citizens in the information age, thus contributing to the social and economic success.

On the other hand, ICT also impacts on the nature of literacy and numeracy practices in daily life practices, at home and in the social arena. Van Deursen and Van Dijk (2009) have shown that citizens' digital skills level influences the extent to which the latter take up the online public and government services offered to them. Additionally, new digital literacies that involve multi-modal forms of expression are emerging such as the need to widen participation of adults in learning, lifelong learning and distance learning initiatives (Gorard et al., 2003; Mason, 2006), consequently facilitating flexible learning in terms of time and distance, and, thereby, establishing equal opportunities and conditions for a 'learning society' for all (EC 2000b, 2001).

Mere access to technology, however, does not enable one to effectively use it. Research data offer lots of knowledge regarding students' representations about computers and ICT systems, and the barriers encountered in using ICT to solve problems and in integrating ICT in their learning patterns. During the past decade a great number of studies have investigated various types of people regarding their attitudes and beliefs towards computers, such as students, teachers, adults (see Levine & Donitsa-Schmidt, 1998; Knezek & Christensen, 2002; Sugar *et al.,*

2004; Jimoyiannis, 2008; Jimoyiannis & Komis, 2007). A great number of investigations have revealed four correlated dimensions concerning adults' attitudes about computers and ICT (Jimoyiannis & Komis, 2006): a) *anxiety, fear, resistance* or *cautiousness* of using computers; b) *self-efficacy* and *confidence* in the ability to use ICT; c) *liking to use computers* and ICT tools; and d) *value* and *usefulness* of using ICT in personal life. Undoubtedly, young people, who have grown up within ICT environments, namely computers, mobile phones and the Internet, are not fearful of technology and are willing and open for experimentation with new ICT applications and facilities. In contrast, adults' learning habits, their notional barriers about computing systems, their technical difficulties in using ICT, and, finally, their cultural attitudes towards ICT, seem to be different when comparing to those of high-school or university students (Chua *et al.*, 1999; Wilfong, 2006).

The issue of how to teach ICT skills in adult education programmes has not been explicitly addressed (Kambouri, Mellar, & Logan, 2006). Tutors sometimes adopt a purely didactic form when teaching ICT skills and digital literacy skills. There is little research concerning best practices to teach basic ICT skills. This study aspires to contribute into filling this gap. Understanding more about adult learners' difficulties with ICT as well as aspects of adults' instruction on digital literacy, from the perspective of the educators, constitutes the fundamental purpose of the research reported. The research is justified given the importance placed on ICT both by the Commission and the Greek government, the central role of ICTs' in the curriculum of the SCS programme, and the fact that digital literacy in relation to adult learning is an under researched field in Greece (Jimoyiannis & Gravani, 2008). Harnessing a qualitative methodology this research aims at a deeper investigation of adult digital literacy in the context of the Second Chance Schools (SCS) programme in Greece.

This paper addresses two key aspects of adult learning in an attempt to outline a general framework of digital and ICT literacy in adult education programs from the educators' perspective. First, the main common barriers that adult educators faced while teaching digital literacy in the context of the SCS are explored, as well as the ways in which the above can be addressed so that adult learners are successfully supported. Second, the effective teaching practices and learning approaches that educators used in SCS are explored so that adult learners have positive learning experiences and potentially develop their knowledge and digital skills.

THE CONTEXT: SECOND CHANCE SCHOOLS AND DIGITAL LITERACY

The focus of this study is on the Second Chance Schools (SCS), a programme established by the Greek Ministry of Education in 1997, in the framework of the Operational Programme for Education and Initial Vocational Training, and in the light of the European Commission's 1995 White Paper '*Teaching and learning: towards the learning society*' (EC, 1997). One of the aims of the White Paper aims was to propose actions which combat social exclusion. Towards this end, the SCS pilot projects have been initiated in twelve European Countries[1] and a network linking all these schools has been set up enabling an exchange of experience and best practice between different pilot sites and participants. The SCS aim at offering education and training to young people who lack the skills and qualifications necessary to find a job or fully benefit from conventional training. According to the Commission (EC, 1997), at the heart of this initiative is the setting up of long term partnerships between all those concerned at local level with the social and economic integration of young people at risk of social exclusion. SCS have been established initially in cities[2] which have both concentrations of detrimental socio-economic factors and a strong potential for mobilising the local players. The teaching approaches adopted are both integrated and tailor-made and they take into account young people's situation, while the new educational technology plays an important role.

In Greece, the SCS project, funded by the EU and the Greek State, is administered by the General Secretariat for Adult Education (GSAE) through the Institute for Continuing Education of Adults (IDEKE). The first school started its operation, on a pilot basis, in Athens on 2000. Since then 48 SCS have been established and operate all over the country; three of them operate within prisons. Following the above, the SCS in the Greek context constitute a flexible and innovative educational programme which provides lower secondary education to individuals of 18 or over[3], who have not completed the nine-year compulsory education. It aims at the social inclusion of the individuals who lack the qualifications and skills necessary to meet the contemporary needs of the labour market. More specifically, the main objectives of SCS are to re-link individuals who have not completed the basic compulsory education with the educational process and to create networks of cooperation between the school, the local community, the business world and education (Gravani & Marmarinos, 2008). The SCS programme lasts 18 months, and is divided in two stages of nine months each (two academic years). The weekly schedule covers 21 teaching hours taking place in the afternoons (GSAE, 2003). After finishing their studies, adults can obtain a certificate while they are expected to enhance their possibilities for integrating and further participating into social, economic and professional life.

The SCS are characterized by an open and flexible *Curriculum* which is significantly differentiated from the one followed in formal schools, in terms of its principles, content, teaching methods, students' learning activities as well as assessment (Vecris & Hodolidou, 2003). *Multiliteracy* is at the key concept of the programme and forms the basis for the development of the *Programme of Studies* while the adults' interests and the wider social environment are the critical factors determining the written and the oral word (GSAE, 2003). The core of the learning subjects is mainly developed around three dimensions, in other words three interrelated literacies, namely *(language) literacy*, *numeracy* and *digital literacy*.

In particular, the curriculum of SCS is developed around three dimensions:

- To develop adults' skills in language, mathematics and communication, with special emphasis on foreign languages and ICT. The basic subjects are: Greek Language, Mathematics, Information Technology, English, Social Education, Environmental Education, Aesthetic Education, Technology and the Physical Sciences.
- To offer basic training and preparation for their professional life in cooperation with the local authorities. This is mainly done through their orientation or career counsellors, whose role is to re-integrate adult students into social and financial life.
- To develop adults' skills in the domain of their personal interests, such as, sports, music, theatre, etc. (EC, 2003, p. 8). Towards this end, consulting psychologists work to support students and insure a fruitful environment that favours learning as well as the development of social and personal skills.

Within the context of SCS the above courses are not strictly confined to the corresponding field of scholarship. They draw elements from other disciplines instead. SCS are designed to operate on an *open curriculum and oral program*, in which teaching and learning activities are seen as a communication act rather than an effort to achieve pre-determined goals. In each SCS, subjects and learning activities are not drawn up in advance nor are supplied ready-made for the teachers. They rather draw upon the basis of students' individual needs. The above implies teaching methods and practices that, among others, promote personalised teaching, experiential learning, self-motivation, students' active involvement and decision making, critical thinking. The most important methods routinely used are group-centred teaching, team working, brainstorming, case-studies, collaborative learning and project method (GSAE, 2003).

In the light of the above, and according to the founding regulations of the SCS programme, the assessment of studies does not lie in the evaluation of the accomplishment towards predetermined goals, but it is more qualitative in nature placing greater emphasis on the teaching and learning processes and the activities carried out by students in the classroom. In other words, it is not only the result that is assessed but the learning process itself in terms of the extent to which students are provided with opportunities to develop and put in practice their own potential (GSAE 2003). Teaching practice at the SCS therefore is not seen as a process in which knowledge is transmitted via an apprenticeship model of learning (Deem, 2002). It is rather a journey during which knowledge is produced as a shared responsibility of the students and the teachers' community (Bickel & Hattrup, 1995). Educators and students have the opportunity to communicate and collaborate in the synthesis of what each community knows about important learning and teaching processes (Gravani & John, 2005; Gravani, 2007).

The role of the ICT and digital literacy in the curriculum of SCS is vital. As stated in the Programme of Studies (GSAE, 2003), digital literacy aims at helping adult learners to:

- acquire the necessary technical knowledge and skills that make them able to use ICT effectively;
- be competent in using ICT to solve problems of everyday life;
- understand the social dimensions and the impact of ICT in our modern society;
- cultivate positive attitudes regarding ICT and to face the demands of modern age.

In the framework above, digital literacy is seen in a broader view than computer use and familiarization with various ICT environments (hardware devices, software tools and applications, digital content, etc.). In other words, it refers not only to the knowledge and skills of using a wide range of ICT environments but also to those skills related to accessing, processing, analysing, evaluating, applying and communicating information (content) in order that adults will be able to participate as active members in the so called, 'knowledge society' (EC, 2000a).

In the light of having already stated that the field of digital and ICT literacy in the adult education context is under-investigated, especially in Greece, we should draw attention to the fact that the present study is part of a broader study investigating adult teaching and learning of digital literacy in the context of Second Chance Schools in Greece. This particular article focuses on and analyses the experiences and perceptions of the educators who participated in the study with regard to aspects of instruction of adults on digital literacy and the difficulties faced while learning ICT. The main research questions guiding the study evolved around the sorts of learning activities, practices and approaches used in the instruction of digital literacy in regard to both the adults' barriers to learning, and the difficulties faced educators while instructing digital literacy in SCS.

THE STUDY

Since the study uses the experiences and perceptions of the participants to illuminate certain aspects of the SCS programme, a qualitative case study approach, within the phenomenological mode, to the selection and analysis of the data is adopted. According to Bogdan and Biklen (1982), the phenomenological qualitative research brings the study of human beings as 'human beings' to centre stage and represents a fundamental rejection of the ultimately irrational pursuit to quantify

Table 1. Presentation of the adult educators' profile

Adult Educators Profile	Characteristics	Total
Gender	Male Female	7 1
Age	34 - 43 years 44 - 53 years	7 1
Education	Bachelor Computer Science Physics Masters PhD	6 2 4 1
Years of joining the service	after 1994 before 1994	6 2
Experience in secondary Education	1 - 10 years > 10 years	6 2
Experience in Adult Education	< 3 years 3 - 10 years > 10 years	4 2 2

all aspects of human belief and experience. In the case study survey the focus is usually upon a small cohort investigated in an intensive manner. This can be carried out at various levels of complexity (Bromley, 1986). When two or more subjects, settings, or depositories of data are studied, these are known as multi-case studies Bogdan and Biklen (1982).

Four broad case studies were used for the purpose of this research. These were the four oldest SCS programmes run in Greece. The replication logic (Yin, 1984) was followed in the selection of the cases explored. According to this, each case it is selected so that it either a) predicts similar results or b) produces contrary results but for predictable reasons. However, selecting the setting and context of research is not the only decision required. In case studies decisions involve internal sampling as well, which involves among others decisions about 'whom to talk'. With regards to the choice of the participants for the study, it was decided to select all the ICT adult educators teaching digital literacy in the context of the four chosen SCS, two from each of the four schools. Overall, eight educators participated in the study, one woman and seven men. They were all permanent secondary school teachers in ICT and varied in their profile. They ranged in their teaching experience in secondary education schools from 2 to 15 years. Their prior experience in instructing adults in SCS or/ and elsewhere also varied. Similarly, the training they received in adults' education varied. For the purposes of clarity and anonymity educators in the study are referred as educator 1, educator 2… educator 8. Table 1 gives an account of the adult educators' profile.

The tools employed for the collection of the data include in-depth, audio-recorded, semi-structured interviews carried out over a two-month period. The semi-structured approach was chosen due to its advantage to retain its main objective of eliciting equivalent information from a number of informants, thus allowing a comparative analysis of responses between different groups of subjects to be made, while it also provides a more flexible style that can be suited to the personality and circumstances of the persons being interviewed, and permit the researcher to probe and expand the informants' responses (Hitchcock & Hughes, 1989). An interview schedule was prepared for the educators aimed at eliciting data related to their perceptions, experiences, and beliefs of ICT instruction. Examples from the agenda included questions related to: instructing practices, approaches, course content, projects undertaken, interdisciplinary teaching, individualised teaching, laboratory exercises, barriers to learning, difficulties faced. The duration of each interview ranged from thirty five minutes to one and a half hours with an average time of sixty five minutes. Respondents were asked to choose the place of the interview so as to feel comfortable. Prior the interview the researchers had early contacts with the respondents, explaining to them the aims, nature, utility and contribution of the research in order to establish rapport, trust and the respect of the respondents.

The main process of data analysis in the present study was completed in the spirit of hermeneutics which implies a constant interplay between data and conceptualization. Meaning is not self-contained; it comes to realization only in and through the 'happening' of understanding. The analysis of data went through the three concurrent flows of activity: data reduction, data display and thematic interpretation (Miles & Huberman, 1994). Categories and their properties emerged from a detailed sententious analysis of the data. Two main categories were identified: instructing practices and approaches, and learning barriers. These were derived from an iterative reading of the data and guided the validity of the wider emerging themes. For the construction of the categories the following guidelines were born in mind: categories reflect the purpose of the research; are exhaustive and mutually exclusive and derive from a single classification principle (Evans, 2002). The emerging themes in the first category were: ICT competence sessions, interdisciplinary and multi-literacy lessons, ICT-based projects, individual instruction sessions; and in the second category: adult personal factors, adult learning factors, educators' pedagogical factors, school factors. These are clearly presented in Tables 2 and 3. In the analysis, the above themes were discussed and contextualised by being placed in correspondence to the literature through the process of theoretical memoing (Locke, 2001). The final accounts were illustrated by using the most telling pieces of data, which evoked the original words of the participants.

ANALYSIS AND INTERPRETATION

Instructing Practices and Approaches

As findings from the interviews indicate, educators tried to follow flexible instructional prac-

Table 2. Instructional practices and pedagogical approaches followed in adults' digital literacy sessions

Instructional practices	Pedagogical approaches	Objectives
ICT competence sessions	Active learning Constructivist and discovery learning	• ICT knowledge • ICT competence • computer and software usage skills • societal aspects of ICT
Interdisciplinary and multi-literacy lessons	Task-based learning Cross-thematic	• ICT knowledge • two or more literacies involved
ICT-based projects	Project-based learning Collaborative learning	• information skills (search, select and evaluate information) • critical and analytical thinking • strategic and problem solving skills • collaboration skills
Individual instruction sessions	Face to face instruction in the computer lab	• ICT competence • information skills • project related skills

Table 3. Factors determining adults' learning barriers in digital literacy sessions

Item	Specification
Adult personal factors	• negative attitudes toward ICT • lack of confidence in using computers • fear towards ICT and the Internet • personal characteristics (e.g., age, social income, physical condition) • lack of time and ICT usage opportunities at home, work or other places • lack of basic reading and writing skills (in Greek and in English also)
Adult learning factors	• existing learning habits and beliefs • lack of collaborative skills and spirit • lack of effectual representations and notions about computational systems and their operation • pre-existing attitudes about the societal role of ICT • perceptions about the usefulness of ICT in everyday life
Educators' pedagogical factors	• previous experiences and practices at typical secondary schools • inadequate training about adults' education • lack of skills to apply in practice the basic principles of andragogy • lack of collaborative culture to work with other educators in the school (SCS) • lack of knowledge to design and promote interdisciplinary and multi-literacy lessons • lack of knowledge to support ICT-based projects
School factors	• technical and space problems in the computer laboratory • quality of infrastructure in the school (lack of new generation PCs, broadband connections to the Internet, etc.) • lack of computers available in every classroom and subject • lack of appropriate educational software • ICT is not adopted as a learning tool across the SCS curriculum

tices and approaches adjusted to adult learners' profile, needs, ICT prior skills and interests, and preferences. This is in accordance with the adult learning principles (Brookfield, 1986; Knowles, 1990; Jarvis 2006). However, the above was implemented within the framework of the digital literacy in SCS, as stated in the Programme of Studies, namely the ICT knowledge and technical skills; the use of ICT in problem solving; the social dimension aspects of ICT.

Data analysis revealed that in all four schools, and even in the context of the same school, digital literacy was taught in a very different way. This is indicative of the degree of flexibility that characterises the Programme of Studies in the SCS. Illustrative are the following words of an educator in the study who argued that:

"...In all three classes I taught different things. I tried to do the same within one class, but that was impossible".

Educator 1

Similarly, another colleague in the same school underlined that every year he changes the content of the digital literacy subject in the light of the learner's needs. He said

"Every year I am trying not to teach topics that are difficult to comprehend, for instance, the PC units. It depends on the adults' interest".

Educator 2

Despite the diversity and flexibility exhibited to the ICT instruction, some general practices and approaches can be evident in the data. The findings reveal that the following instructional practices were routinely used in SCS: a) ICT competence sessions performed in the computer laboratory; b) interdisciplinary and multi-literacy lessons; c) ICT-based short and long term projects, and

d) individual instruction sessions, focused on adults' specific needs or difficulties. Table 2 summarizes the common instructional practices and pedagogical approaches followed, and the aims to be achieved in adults' digital literacy sessions in SCS. (See Table 2)

a. **ICT competence sessions:** These are instruction sessions and learning activities aiming at developing students' ICT technical skills and competences so that they can use computers and general purpose software. The students were working individually or collaboratively in pairs in the computer laboratory. The ICT competence sessions lasted between 2 to 3 hours per week. In two of the schools studied ICT lessons took the form of a class aiming at preparing adult learners for the exams of the ICT Certification. In the other two schools, digital literacy was taught in conjunction with some other literacy, such as mathematics, English or the Greek language. The following quotes are typical:

"Digital literacy is taught for 2-3 hours per week for both the first and second year students. Sessions take place in the computer lab where I introduce them in using ICT. For example, I start from the very basic and then I go to more elaborate stuff, like Power Point, E-mail, Excel, Internet, etc. It's an absolutely practical session and learners have to follow me and do what I do on my PC. Basically, the digital literacy course is performed in the lab, where ICT competence tasks and activities take place. These are addressed to students of both stages aiming at developing further their ICT technical skills and competence on using computers and general purpose software ..."

Educator 1

"There is a general framework based on the SCS Curriculum. Everyday practices are mainly determined by adults' interests and motivation... I place emphasis on the social aspects of ICT. How ICT is connected to their everyday life and labour world ..."

Educator 5

"Interdisciplinary teaching concerned the joint teaching of two literacies in one class. It involved the connection of two subjects. For example, this year, at the second stage, I taught digital literacy in collaboration with my colleague who teaches social literacy. The topic was about the most important agencies of the EU policy on the Internet. I was showing them how to trace the information on the web, and then my colleague was analysing the information regarding the social aspect of it".

Educator 1

However, as far as the case of ICT courses is concerned research data point out that cross-thematic teaching was implemented to a small extent. The difficulties to develop cross-thematic teaching practices recognized by the educators in the sample were originated by:

- the lack of relevant in-service training focused on how to design and implement cross-thematic practices;
- their former experiences and practices from the typical secondary school;
- the lack of motivation and willingness on behalf of them to try a new and unknown pedagogical approach;
- the difficulties faced when collaborating with their colleagues.

Some of the above factors are summarised in the following words of an inexperienced adult ICT educator how argued:

"I embarked on interdisciplinary teaching to a very small extent, and it wasn't easy for me to

complete it…the experiences that we, as educators, carry from the typical school prevent us from doing so… it's difficult to adjust to the philosophy of the SCSs programme. In addition, the in-service training I undertook has not helped me to understand effectively how interdisciplinary teaching works. It's also an issue of having to work with other colleagues… in the typical school I got used to organise the sessions by myself".

Educator 7

"… I also put in place ICT-based projects. These are cross-thematic assignments on various topics that students of both stages are involved from the beginning of the academic year. For example, a project assigned this year concerned the use of Internet and the evaluation of the sources coming from Internet. In doing this, my students had to work in depth so that they would get the information, access it, report it and present the evaluation…"

Educator 4

"Iindividualised teaching is implemented once per week and involves supporting the weakest of the students. The latter would come to the lab for about an hour before the beginning of the main course to get some extra time, help and support in using the PC…"

Educator 3

It's worth pointing out that individual instruction sessions were not implemented at one of the SCSs in the study due to the unavailability of the computer lab out of scheduled hours. This SCS is hosted by a typical school and, as a result, the computer lab was not free and available all the time for the learners.

As can be seen from the description of the teaching practices and approaches above, these are not clearly defined as being separate; they are either interrelated and there is no clear-cut distinction between them. The above is a common place in the interviews with almost all the educators. The latter also argued that practices and approaches were designed on the basis of problem areas and activities identified by the adult learners. They were also adjusted to the sources available (e.g., material infrastructure, classrooms, PCs available), the competences of the educators and their willingness to experiment and put in practice instructional approaches that they had never used before either in the typical school, where they use to teach, or in other contexts.

To sum up, an open and flexible view for the digital literacy sessions was implemented, while teaching practices and approaches were under continuous change and adjustment. The findings identify that ICT courses varied in all four schools and not all the educators designed sessions of the same content and by using the same activities, paradigms and examples.

Learning Barriers

The second theme explored in the study focused on the barriers educators faced while teaching digital literacy. They reported a wide range of interrelated factors that inhibit a) their professional work in the digital literacy classroom, and b) their participants' performance and development in ICT skills and digital literacy. From the analysis of the experiences and perceptions of the adult educators, four categories of factors emerged that shape the context of digital literacy in SCS in Greece; *a) adult personal factors, b) adult learning factors, c) pedagogical factors, and d) school factors.* Table 3 incorporates a brief presentation of the factors determining the learning barriers that educators and learners faced in the course of the digital literacy lesson in SCS. (See Table 3)

a. Adult Personal Factors

A considerable number of adult learners are coming to SCS having negative attitudes toward ICT, lack of confidence in using computers and fear towards ICT and the Internet. Moreover, adults' personal characteristics, such as age, social income, physical condition (e.g., luck of sight, hearing, fatigue) constitute important factors for their performance with ICT. Most of the adults in the sample have time restrictions and lack of significant usage opportunities in their social environment. They lack their own computer and Internet connection at home, having thus restricted opportunities to practice and develop their ICT competence and skills. Many adults have serious difficulties in reading and writing in Greek and in English as well. These difficulties constitute a critical factor for their competence in using various software and ICT applications.

The above are clearly present in the following transcript:

"One of the major difficulties was the fact that some of the learners were negative towards ICT. They used to call the PC 'devils' machine'. They were just negative and refused to change their disposition to learning...another barrier was illiteracy; some of the learners could hardly spell their name and didn't know numeracy and English, thus had problems with Word and Excel... the most important barrier is related to the false knowledge and misconceptions that adults had of the PC, etc. This is very difficult to change since it is deeply rooted. On the contrary, those of the students who started from scratch and exhibit a positive disposition to learning had a great progress. It's easier and more efficient to teach someone who knows nothing, than someone who knows a few things in the wrong way, especially when teaching digital literacy".

Educator 4

b. Adult Learning Factors

Most of the adult learners' difficulties in learning ICT are totally different to those encountered by young pupils. Adults do not easily construct effectual representations and notions about the various computational systems and their operation. Moreover, they have built an integrated view and approach concerning the impact of ICT in our modern society and the usefulness of ICT in everyday life.

Adult learners come into the classroom with various beliefs and habits about teaching and learning, as well as beliefs about literacy. For example, a problem, identified by both adult educators and learners in the study, regarding project work, was the lack of collaborative skills and spirit among the learners, presumably originating from their lack of previous supportive experiences.

Illustrative of the adult learning factors that constitute barriers to learning is the following quote from the interview with an educator:

«They (learners) have difficulties, and sometimes they are even unwilling, to understand technical concepts and knowledge about computers and computational systems. It is hard for them to understand basic technical terms. They are not able to react in the above and this is discouraging..... They are much better in learning technical skills about the use of computers and general purpose software. They are also interested in learning about the social dimension of ICT »

Educator 8

c. Pedagogical Factors

ICT educators in SCS are greatly influenced in their teaching by their previous experiences and practices at typical secondary schools. Their *prior* instructional routines and pedagogical approaches, with whom they are familiar with, could not be effective when instructing or supporting adult learners in ICT.

The ICT adult educators participated in the study identified their own difficulty or lack of collaborative culture to work with other colleagues in the SCS, so that they could design and promote interdisciplinary and multi-literacy lessons, and ICT-based projects.

The educators in the study had limited training about adults' education and the basic principles of andragogy (Knowles, 1990). They lack the appropriate skills to apply in practice the andragogical philosophy of instruction. For example, ICT educators are not effectively prepared to identify adults' learning habits and beliefs and, even more, to pay attention to them when designing ICT learning events and activities.

The following quote is characteristic:

"There are horrendous learning difficulties on behalf of the adult learners as far as the digital literacy course is concerned, since the subject is 'new'. This is quite discouraging and up to some point it's humiliating for me as an educator. There are learners who at the end of the academic year don't know how to use the mouse…for some of them it takes lots of time to comprehend new things and this prevents you (educator) from saying lots".

Educator 5

d. School Factors

The model followed in SCS for ICT infrastructure is the computer laboratory. This model induces various technical and space drawbacks (e.g., in most cases a small room is transformed to a computer lab; there is not always a PC available for every adult to practice during the school hours, etc.). There is also another problem attached to this model, namely the lack of computers available in every classroom. In some of the SCSs in the study the imperative was reported for further development of ICT infrastructure (particularly new generation PCs and computer networks, broadband connections to the Internet, updated versions of the main software used, appropriate educational software, etc.).

CONCLUSION

The analysis presented in this article adds considerable amount of knowledge on the factors that shape the instruction framework of digital literacy in SCS in Greece. As findings indicate, the complexity and interrelationship between the various factors that affect ICT learning in SCS (e.g., adults' needs, beliefs and learning habits, life experiences, the institutional context of SCS, socio-cultural factors, etc.), reveal the imperative need for adult educators to perceive and identify their teaching as a process that creates learning opportunities for all. In this, adults' active engagement and educators' guiding and supportive role are seen as the key success factors. The role of the ICT educator in identifying adults' needs, interests and difficulties, as well as in designing proper learning-teaching events that promote adults' engagement, lies with their ability to be critical. The ICT adult educator rather than trying to apply the particular teaching methods in a general and strict way should preferably put effort in understanding how learning opportunities and learning outcomes could emerge in particular contexts. Many of the principles elucidated by Knowles (1990) remain relevant and important in establishing successful digital literacy programs in SCS:

- *problem-based* and *activity-centred* rather that subject-centred learning
- adults' engagement through *active and self-directed learning*
- the *social context* of ICT and digital literacy learning.

Though most of the educators in the sample were supposed to be aware of the basic principles related to adults' learning (andragogy), in contrast to childrens' learning, (pedagogy), this study has identified a number of serious difficulties that educators faced while they tried to put into practice the andragogical principles. It seems that their *prior* habits and experiences as high school teachers constitute a major difficulty factor. Only well-trained and motivated adult educators can improve the learning conditions offered to adult learners in SCS. Hence future adult educators' training and professional development programmes might be focused on three main directions aiming at preparing them to:

- be able to identify adults' prior ICT knowledge and skills, as well as their needs, intentions and learning styles.
- be able to design successful teaching-learning events aiming at adults' ICT competence and digital literacy development.
- develop a routine of effective teaching and supporting initiatives in digital literacy classroom that could promote adults' engagement and competence.

Summarizing, the results of this study emphasized that adult learners consist a population with special characteristics and traits regarding the teaching and learning of ICT. There are still a lot of parameters to be identified regarding the way adult learners perceive digital literacy, their difficulties when using computers and solving problems with ICT, as well as the appropriate ways that should be used by the educators to support and encourage adults when learning about and with ICT. Our further research is directed at developing an integrated framework describing best practices and critical success factors for adult digital literacy and ICT integration in the SCS.

REFERENCES

Bickel, W. E., & Hattrup, R. A. (1995). Teachers and researchers in collaboration: reflections on the process. *American Educational Research Journal*, *32*(1), 35–62.

Bogdan, R. C., & Biklen, S. K. (1982). *Qualitative research for education: An introduction to theory and methods.* Boston: Allyn & Bacon.

Bromley, D. B. (1986). *The case - study method in psychology and related disciplines.* Chichester, UK: John Wiley & Sons.

Brookfield, S. (1986). *Understanding and facilitating adult learning: A comprehensive analysis of principles and effective practices.* Milton Keynes, UK: Open University Press.

Chua, S. L., Chen, D., & Wong, A. F. L. (1999). Computer anxiety and its correlates: A meta-analysis. *Computers in Human Behavior*, *15*, 609–623. doi:10.1016/S0747-5632(99)00039-4

Deem, R. (2002). *The knowledge worker and the divided university* (inaugural lecture). Bristol, UK: Graduate School of Education, University of Bristol.

DfES. (2003). *21st century skills: Realising our potential*. Retrieved May 25, 2009, from http://www.dcsf.gov.uk/skillsstrategy/uploads/documents/21st%20Century%20Skills.pdf

Efstratoglou, A., Nikolopoulou, V., & Pauli-Korre, M. (2006). *Basic dimensions of illiteracy in Greece*. Athens, Greece: Hellenic Association of Adult Education.

European Commission [EC]. (1997). *Second chance schools: Combating exclusion through education and training*. Brussels, Belgium: Education Training Youth.

European Commission [EC]. (2000a). *A memorandum on lifelong learning*. Brussels, Belgium: Author.

European Commission [EC]. (2000b). *eEurope 2002: An information society for all action plan*. Brussels, Belgium: Author.

European Commission [EC]. (2001). *Making a European area of lifelong learning a reality*. Brussels, Belgium: Author.

European Commission [EC]. (2003). *Implementing lifelong learning strategies in Europe: Progress report on the follow-up to the 2002 council resolution*. Brussels, Belgium: Author.

Evans, L. (2002). *Reflective practice in educational research*. London: Continuum.

General Secretariat for Adult Education [GSAE]. (2003). *A new chance: Second chance schools*. Athens, Greece: Ministry of Education.

Gorard, S., Selwyn, N., & Madden, L. (2003). Logged on to learning assessing the impact of technology on participation in lifelong learning. *International Journal of Lifelong Education*, *22*(3), 281–296. doi:10.1080/02601370304845

Goulding, A. (2001). Information poverty or overload? *Journal of Librarianship and Information Science*, *33*(3), 109–111. doi:10.1177/096100060103300301

Gravani, M. N. (2007). Unveiling professional learning: Shifting from the delivery of courses to an understanding of the processes. *Teaching and Teacher Education*, *23*, 688–704. doi:10.1016/j.tate.2006.03.011

Gravani, M. N., & John, P. D. (2005). 'Them and us': Teachers' and tutors' perceptions of a 'new'professional development course in Greece. *Compare*, *35*(3), 305–321. doi:10.1080/03057920500212597

Gravani, M. N., & Marmarinos, I. (2008). Current trends in lifelong education in Greece: The case of the General Secretariat for Adult Education (GSAE). *Adult Education*, *15*, 26–31.

Hitchcock, G., & Hughes, D. (1989). *Research and the teacher.* London: Routledge.

Jarvis, P. (2006). Teaching styles and teaching methods. In P. Jarvis (Ed.), *The theory and practice of teaching* (pp. 28-38). Abingdon, UK: Routledge.

Jimoyiannis, A. (2008). Factors determining teachers' beliefs and perceptions of ICT in education. In A. Cartelli & M. Palma (Eds.), *Encyclopedia of information communication technology* (pp. 321-334). Hershey, PA: IGI Global.

Jimoyiannis, A., & Gravani, M. (2008). Digital literacy in second chance schools: An investigation of educators' beliefs and experiences. In V. Komis (Ed.), *Proceedings of the 4th Panhellenic Conference on 'Didactics of Informatics'*, Patra, Greece (pp. 405-414).

Jimoyiannis, A., & Komis, V. (2006). Exploring secondary education teachers' attitudes and beliefs towards ICT adoption in education. *Themes in Education*, *7*(2), 181–204.

Jimoyiannis, A., & Komis, V. (2007). Examining teachers' beliefs about ICT in education: implications of a teacher preparation programme. *Teacher Development*, *11*(2), 181–204. doi:10.1080/13664530701414779

Kambouri, M., Mellar, H., & Logan, K. (2006). Adult learners and ICT: An intervention study in the UK. In W. Nejdl & K. Tochtermann (Eds.), *1st European Conference on Technology Enhanced Learning* (pp. 213-226). Berlin-Heidelberg, Germany: Springer.

Knezek, G., & Christensen, R. (2002). Impact of new information technologies on teachers and students. *Education and Information Technologies*, *7*(4), 369–376. doi:10.1023/A:1020921807131

Knowles, M. S. (1990). *The adult learner: A neglected species*. Houston, TX: Gulf.

Lawson, K. (2005). Using eclectic digital resources to enhance instructional methods for adult learners. *OCLC Systems & Services*, *21*(1), 49–60. doi:10.1108/10650750510578154

Levine, T., & Donitsa-Schmidt, S. (1998). Computer use, confidence, attitudes, and knowledge: a causal analysis. *Computers in Human Behavior*, *14*, 125–146. doi:10.1016/S0747-5632(97)00036-8

Locke, K. D. (2001). *Grounded theory in management research*. Thousand Oaks, CA: Sage.

Mason, R. (2006). Learning technologies for adult continuing education. *Studies in Continuing Education*, *28*(2), 121–133. doi:10.1080/01580370600751039

Miles, M. B., & Huberman, A. M. (1994). *Qualitative data analysis: An expanded sourcebook*. London: Sage.

NIACE. (2005). *ICT skill for life* (Action Research Project, Rep. to DfES). Retrieved May 25, 2009, from http://archive.niace.org.uk/Research/ICT/ICT-SfL-Action-Research-Project.pdf

Selwyn, N. (2004). Reconsidering political and popular understandings of the digital divide. *New Media & Society*, *6*(3), 341–362. doi:10.1177/1461444804042519

Sugar, W., Crawley, F., & Fine, B. (2004). Examining teachers' decisions to adopt new technology. *Educational Technology and Society*, *7*(4), 201–213.

Van Deursen, A. J. A. M., & Van Dijk, J. A. G. M. (2009). Improving digital skills for the use of online public information and services. *Government Information Quarterly*, *26*, 333–340. doi:10.1016/j.giq.2008.11.002

Van Dijk, J. (2006). Digital divide research, achievements and shortcomings. *Poetics*, *34*, 221–235. doi:10.1016/j.poetic.2006.05.004

Van Dijk, J., & Hacker, K. (2003). The digital divide as a complex and dynamic phenomenon. *The Information Society*, *19*, 315–327. doi:10.1080/01972240309487

Vecris, L., & Hodolidou, E. (Eds.). (2003). *Educational guidelines for the second chance schools*. Athens, Greece: IDEKE.

Wilfong, J. D. (2006). Computer anxiety and anger: The impact of computer use, computer experience, and self-efficacy beliefs. *Computers in Human Behavior*, *22*, 1001–1011. doi:10.1016/j.chb.2004.03.020

Yin, R. (1984). *Case study research: Design and methods*. Newbury Park, CA: Sage.

ENDNOTES

1. Spain, France, Finland, Italy, Germany, Portugal, Greece, The Nederlands, Denmark, United Kingdom, Sweden, Belgium
2. Bilbao, Barcelona, Marseille, Hämeenlinna, Catania, Köln, Halle, Seixal, Athens, Heerlen, Ribe, Leeds, Norrköping, Brussels.
3. SCSs in Greece are not addressed only to young people, as in the other European Countries, but mainly to the illiterate adults (GSAE, 2003). As stated by Efstratoglou, Nikolopoulou & Pauli-Korre (2006), their number reached up to 646 677 in 2004.

This work was previously published in International Journal of Digital Literacy and Digital Competence, Volume 1, Issue 1, edited by Antonio Cartelli, pp. 40-60, copyright 2010 by IGI Publishing (an imprint of IGI Global).

Chapter 11
Information Communication Technologies for the Lifelong Learning:
The Multimedia Documentation of Best Practices in Education

Laura Corazza
University of Bologna, Italy

ABSTRACT

In today's knowledge society, better identified as a learning society, the opportunities for self-instruction and lifelong learning are playing an increasing role due to Information Communication Technologies. Old and new communication technologies offer possibilities for learning, as long as the worker is capable of learning in autonomy. Training has a central role as an educational activity, which aims at promoting and updating knowledge. Knowledge society does not only require citizens and workers to have basic skills; it asks for a life-long learning. Documentation is a form of communication that allows tacit, unexpressed, informal knowledge to emerge. It provides knowledge of the individual experiences of teachers and educators that can be widely shared. In knowledge management, audiovisual and multimedia documentation has proved to be a useful and efficient means of recording the experiences that are to be shared.

BACKGROUND: CYBERSPACE AND CYBERCULTURE

For Lévy, what is interesting about cyber-culture is the unification of all differences and heterogeneity (Lévy, 1997). He believes in the ability of cyberspace to bring out the best of human intelligence in every person through communicative relationships which create a collective intelligence and a cyber-culture,. In this sense we can assert that cyber-culture is both a trans-culture and an inter-culture, since it is universal without being oppressively uniform.

If we take cyberspace as the *location*, then communication is the *mean* that permits the

DOI: 10.4018/978-1-4666-0903-7.ch011

creation of this collective intelligence and cyber-culture. Computer users can communicate with each other in a novel way on the internet since they can be more than mere passive users and isolated consumers like today's television viewers. In cyber-culture communication is not limited to "one to one" exchange; it is reciprocal, interactive and communitarian. Moreover it is universal as anyone can be an active communicator. The expansion of interconnections shows that there is only one general humanity. This is what Levy means by "universal": the idea of universality in the enlightenment sense of the word, where our goal is the unity of human kind and the affirmation of universal principles such as the rights of man. All human beings can virtually come into reciprocal contact and can collectively become conscious of their existence. The more we add links, the more diverse and heterogenic material circulates on the net.

Morin has highlighted the problem of the inadequacy of knowledge (which is *divided* by the boundaries between disciplines while the reality of the world is increasingly global and interconnected) and the challenge of complexity (Morin, 1985). Complexity is a method and a form of knowledge which requires a dialogical approach.

Gregory Bateson also spent his life demonstrating the interdependence between elements and the interconnections between different worlds and disciplines. He theorises about the ecology of ideas, an ecosystem in which there is a plurality of levels of application of ideas, using a systematic approach which, from the point of view of learning, means giving importance to contexts, relationships and functions (Bateson, 1972).

So the new idea of knowledge does not only refer to concepts that are to be *transmitted* but, above all, to the itineraries and the network of individual and collective experiences which are in a state of perpetual change.

This is the challenge that the individual can take up, notwithstanding the risks of cognitive standardisation on one hand, and fragmentation or individualism on the other. Morin's "*tête bien faite*" requires the full use of intelligence in the organisation of ideas, in the search for links, routes and new itineraries, knowing full well that it is not possible to attain totality but that we must put into *practice* collective and individual cognitive *practices* at the same time because they exploit the power of connectivity. "If a document is put on the World Wide Web you are doing two things at the same time: first, you are increasing the amount of information that is available, but second, you are doing another thing with the links between your document and the others: you offer the surfer who finds your document your point of view. So you are not merely offering information but a point of view in a collection of information. The World Wide Web is not only an enormous mass of information; it is the expression of thousands of different points of view. It should be viewed from this aspect" (Levy, 1995). There is space for every diversity and every point of view on the Web, if you allow yourself to become enchanted by hyper-textual logic, by the links and maps and if you allow yourself to feel part of a whole, a collective intelligence and a universal culture.

SHARING THE EXPERIENCE OF LIFELONG LEARNING

In today's *knowledge society*, which might be defined more accurately as *the learning society,* the opportunities for self-instruction and lifelong learning are taking on an increasingly important role with the use of Information Communication Technologies (Corazza, 2008)

There are new contexts where the production of knowledge takes place in relation to the development of scientific knowledge and new technological products that require a high degree of specialisation, creativity and autonomy on the part of those who use them. This creates an enormous gap between those who simply know how to use something and those who can interpret, evaluate, chose and reinvent. Instruction and training therefore have a fundamental role. As the European commission stated in the 1995 "the ultimate use of training is that of developing autonomy in people; and their professional skills make it the privileged element in adaptation and evolution".

In this globalised society a veritable revolution has affected the activities of men and women: the way they organise their lives, their relationships, their ways of reasoning and conceiving society and politics. Among the various consequences of this technological revolution and the progressive dematerialisation of work we have seen the emergence of the *knowledge worker* and the need for lifelong training. (Alberici, 2002)

Industry is in a state of constant change, continually transforming itself, reconstructing itself on new foundations and effecting changes. The knowledge worker is expected to have the ability to produce original thought (the new added value) whilst at the same time being skilled at problem solving, cooperation and renewal.

Training and learning have taken on the role once held by raw materials and the emphasis has moved from initial training to lifelong learning. The initial training, which provides the minimum knowledge necessary to start a job, is still important, however the maintenance and development of knowledge throughout working life has emerged as the key strategic dimension.

Aureliana Alberici sees "knowledge society "or "learning society" as metaphors, which emphasise the pervasiveness and functionality of knowledge and competencies, and therefore of learning in all the dimensions of a person, both in working and social life. Just like all metaphors they have a symbolic value that highlights complexities and interrelationships on the interpretative level. One possible reading is the suggestive image of a new human condition in a society where knowledge itself, in addition to information, plays a structural role in economic and social development (Alberici, 2002).

Another way of interpreting the metaphor of the *knowledge society* is through the educational and learning dimension and the related question of how skills and knowledge are acquired. In order for members of a modern society to play a full, conscious and responsible role in the economic and social order, they require access to opportunities for acquiring, revising, and developing knowledge. (Alberici, 2004). Individuals must know how to learn and use their knowledge and skills to pursue wealth and improved living conditions in this global and multicultural Information Society.

From this interpretative viewpoint the concept of the *knowledge society* is still "under construction" and needs the learning paradigm to be fully developed. Training takes on a central role as educational activity, which aims at promoting and updating knowledge and applications for this knowledge. The overall goal is the cultural, social, professional and personal development of individuals through an inextricable link between learning and change which leads to the acquisition of competencies (Quaglino, 1985). Knowledge society not only requires citizens and workers to possess basic skills but above all the ability to learn throughout the entire span of their lives.

The current European context is that of the Lisbon Summit in March 2000: the development of an information society based on the challenges of globalisation in which people, with their knowledge and skills, are the key resource. The European Parliament considers lifelong learning fundamental for achieving personal fulfillment, active citizenship, social cohesion and employability in a knowledge society.

BEST EDUCATIONAL PRACTICES AND MULTIMEDIA DOCUMENTATION

Why is it important to document best practices in education?

In some ways documentation can be compared to a story told by more than one narrator. In all stories there is a central thread which allows those who have not followed the story from the beginning to retrace the step in the story and understand the meaning of events. The significance of documentation lies in providing the possibility to see who are the actors and giving them the opportunity to tell their tale. (Biondi, 2000)

Documentation is a form of communication that allows tacit, unexpressed, informal knowledge to emerge. It provides knowledge of the individual experiences of teachers and educators that can be widely shared.

The goal of documentation is not merely to report the outcome of work. It has to describe the route that was taken, the various stages, the problems that arose along the way and the solutions used to overcome them, the network of human relationships involved and the contributions made.

A consideration of the entire experience is useful for all the participants in a teaching project (Canevaro, 2000). In particular:

- It helps those who planned the project to avoid the underestimation or forgetting the experience and to return to it with a critical eye;
- It allows those who participated (whether they be adults, teenagers or children) to retrace their steps and revisit the experience;
- It allows for critical evaluation of the project;
- It permits other teachers and educators to learn from the best practices employed and even make suggestions and comments to improve on the original work.

In knowledge management, audiovisual documentation has proved to be a useful and efficient instrument for recording the experiences that are to be shared. It goes beyond the textual limits of the paper and captures social/affective elements as well as stimulates the attention of the interlocutor.

The object of communication is the learning situation. The protagonists are the setting and the group, collective work, human relationships, affective displays, sharing and mutual help.

An Example: The Turismo Siamo Tutti (1) Project

The project *"Turismo siamo tutti"* ("all together as tourists") was carried out during the year 2007-2008, at the "G. Carducci" Primary School in Bologna.

This project was based on an idea of Claudio Quintano and Franco Garbaccio who developed the project ""Turismo somos todos y es area de todos", which was aimed at increasing awareness of the importance of Tourism (Garbaccio & Quintano, 2005).

The project set out to get the children to find out data and information about their own city, since they knew very little about the town they lived in, apart from the route they took from home to school.

The project began with a trip on the *GIRO-TOUR*, a bus tour which takes tourists around Bologna with a guide speaking in English. Once back in class, the children were asked which of the monuments they would like to adopt. They were also asked to write a description of the monument in English, which involved the application of some structures they learnt so far, and the finding of more information about the monument.

The descriptions were sent by the students to their pen-friends in the Primary School in Madonna di Lonigo (Vicenza), an Italian town far more than 200 Km from Bologna, who were doing a similar project. Having enjoyed themselves discovering their own city, the pupils decided to create a DVD and a journal to show other children just how beautiful their city was and how much it has to offer.

With the help of the University of Bologna, and especially of the MELA Laboratory, the children made the DVD at the Asinelli tower (one of the well known monuments in the town), before moving on to the *Collezioni Comunali* (Museums), where they found out a lot of material on the history of Bologna.

To finish off, they visited a hand-made pasta shop, where they filmed how to prepare typical Bologna food: *sfoglia* and *tortellini*. Back in class, the children started putting together all the materials they had collected into a journal to have a written record of their experience. It included photos they had taken, pieces that had been written and syntheses from books they read together.

This project has had many positive results. First of all, it has enabled the students to get to know their city better, and pass this experience on to other children. It is something prepared by children for children, consequently it is far more appropriate for them than materials written by adults. Secondly, this project has encouraged awareness of the city's buildings and traditions and it has helped the children to be proud of their city.

Thirdly, it has been an interesting learning/teaching experience as both children and their families have worked together on this project and have brought about a pleasant community spirit. It has also been an opportunity to work in two languages, Italian and English. The project was awarded in the 2008 Competition organised by the *Agenzia Nazionale Italiana per lo Sviluppo dell'Autonomia Scolastica* Italian Agency for the Development of School Autonomy (2).

In order to prepare all the materials the school got the assistance of the MELA laboratory (*Media Education E-learning Laboratory*) in the University of Bologna. The laboratory records, documents and promotes best teaching practices; it also shares these documents as well as with the students' families and other interested parties. The documents have also been sent to the *Prendiville College* in Perth, Australia, as part of a knowledge sharing agreement as well as to schools in the Campania region in Italy, which have carried out a similar project.

All the film clips have been published on MELA's site (3) so that Internet and cyberspace became an occasion and a space to share experience and knowledge.

FUTURE DEVELOPMENTS

Knowledge workers are bearers of a new professionalism that involves the ability to use various competencies and knowledge in permanent learning. Old and new communication technologies can offer possibility for learning, as long as the worker is capable of learning in autonomy. At the same time the use of technology requires planning with clear specific educational objectives.

We therefore need to consider on one hand, how educational agencies can train people to have the necessary skills for lifelong learning and, on another hand, how the same people can make a valid use of technology in education.

REFERENCES

Bateson, G. (1972). *Steps to an Ecology of Mind*. Chicago, IL: University of Chicago Press.

Biondi, G. (2000). *La società dell'informazione e la scuola: la documentazione educativa*. Azzano San Paolo: Junior

Calvani, A. (2001). *Educazione, comunicazione e nuovi media. Sfide pedagogiche e cyberspazio*. Torino, Italy: Utet.

Calvani, A., & Rotta, M. (2000). *Fare formazione in Internet. Manuale di didattica online*. Trento, Italy: Erickson.

Canevaro, A. (2000). Alcuni punti per collegare scrittura e impegno creativo. In Canevaro, A. (Ed.), *Scrivere di educazione* (pp. 6–32). Roma, Italy: Carocci.

Castells, M. (1996). *The rise of the network society*. Oxford, UK: Blackwell.

Castells, M. (2001). *The Internet Galaxy*. Oxford, UK: Oxford University Press.

Corazza, L. (2008). ICT and Interculture Opportunities offered by the Web. In *Encyclopedia of Information and Communication Technology* (*Vol. 1*, pp. 357–364). Hershey, PA: IGI Global.

Corazza, L. (2008). *Internet e la società conoscitiva*. Trento, Italy: Erickson.

Dewey, J. (1899). *The School and the Society*. Chicago, IL: The University of Chicago Press.

Dewey, J. (1916). *Democracy and education: an introduction to the philosophy of education*. New York: Macmillan.

European Commission. (1995). *White Paper on Education and Training. Teaching and Learning. Towards the Learning Society*.

Garbaccio, F., & Quintano, C. (2005). *Turismo siamo tutti*. Napoli, Italy: Denaro Libri.

Kelly, K. (1999). *New Rules for the New Economy*. New York: Penguin Books.

Lévy, P. (1995, September 4). *L'intelligenza collettiva, intervista a "Mediamente."* Parigi: European IT Forum. Retrieved from http://www.mediamente.rai.it/HOME/bibliote/intervis/l/levy.htm

Lévy, P. (1997). *Cyberculture*. Paris: Jacob.

McLuhan, H. M. (1998). *Media e nuova educazione. Il metodo della domanda nel villaggio globale*. Roma, Italy: Armando.

Morin, E. (1985). Le vie della complessità. In Bocchi, G., & Cerruti, M. (Eds.), *La sfida della complessità* (pp. 49–60). Milano, Italy: Feltrinelli.

Morin, E. (1999). *Une tête bien faite*. Paris: Seuil.

Quintano, C. (2008). La ridefinizione della nozione di turismo e la ricerca di un nuovo "abito mentale". In Quintano, C., & Garbaccio, F. (Eds.), *Turismosiamotutti atto secondo* (pp. 39–48). Napoli, Italy: Denaro Libri.

Willinsky, J. (2002). Democracy and education: the missing link may be ours. *Harvard Educational Review*, *72*(3), 25–43.

Willinsky, J. (2005). Scientific research in a democratic culture: or what's a social science for? *Teachers College Record*, *107*(1), 38–51. doi:10.1111/j.1467-9620.2005.00455.x

ENDNOTE

1 The project was organised and carried out by Maria Carmen Triola, primary school teacher and teaching practice supervisor at the faculty of Educational Science Università di Bologna. It took place at the Carducci Primary School in Bologna, with the collaboration of Daniela Turci and the teachers Annamaria Billi, Rossella Naldi, Francesca Nappi.

2 The site of the Italian agency for the development of School autonomy http://gold.indire.it/nazionale/

3 The sites of the laboratory for Media education and e-learning: http://www.mela.scedu.unibo.it and http://diplin.scedu.unibo.it/melawiki/index.php/TUrismo_siamo_tutti

This work was previously published in International Journal of Digital Literacy and Digital Competence, Volume 1, Issue 2, edited by Antonio Cartelli, pp. 22-27, copyright 2010 by IGI Publishing (an imprint of IGI Global).

Chapter 12
E-Skills and ICT Certification in Greek Cultural and Travel Agencies:
An Exploratory Study

Fotis Lazarinis
University of Ioannina, Greece

Dimitris Kanellopoulos
University of Patras, Greece

ABSTRACT

ICT skills are fundamental for the further enhancement and development of productivity and knowledge-intensive products and services. The long-term-demand for professionals with ICT skills still exceeds the supply, particularly in user industries such as the travel industry. This paper presents the results of a study aimed at analysing the impact of ICT certification for people working in cultural and travel agencies in Greece. The authors consider if the e-skills acquired during training for an ICT certification are of practical value while presenting the opinions of the survey participants, statistics about the required e-skills, and the correlation between these skills and the syllabus of the ECDL ICT certification. It is claimed that the ECDL ICT certification plays a crucial role in cultural and travel agencies as their employees being technologically skilful can offer better services to their customers.

INTRODUCTION

In the Lisbon summit held in the year 2000, the European governments agreed that "Businesses and citizens must have access to an inexpensive, world-class communications infrastructure and a wide range of services. Every citizen must be equipped with the skills needed to live and work in this new information society" (Bulletin EU 3, 2000).

Therefore, the task of equipping every citizen with the skills necessary to live in the information society is very challenging. The importance of

DOI: 10.4018/978-1-4666-0903-7.ch012

e-skills is globally recognized (e-Europe, 2002; Curley, 2003) and several programmes have been launched towards this direction in European countries. One initiative was the establishment of a certification related to basic ICT (Information and Communication Technologies) skills, called Computer Driving Licence (CDL) (Haarala-Muhonen & Sokura, 2000). CDL, presently named ECDL (European CDL), is globally recognized as the certification which holds the larger market share (CEPIS, 2004). A few other private organizations and Universities followed the ECDL paradigm issuing analogous ICT certifications. Calzarossa et al. (2007) presented the results of a monitoring exercise aimed at analyzing the impact of the ECDL programme in the Italian Universities. In (Cole & Kesley, 2004), the ECDL programme is used as a reference standard to define basic skills of nurses and nursing staff.

ICT certifications are nowadays considered quite important for most people. According to the eSkills Certification Consortium (eSCC, 2004) and CEPIS, ICT certifications are important primarily because employees stay current with information technologies and because they help them to find a job. This is verified by independent academic studies as well (Sokura, 2005). The key-benefit of ICT certifications is that candidates need to follow a well-organized ICT seminar in order to obtain the certification.

ICT skills are essential in the travel industry as the travel and cultural promotion agencies greatly rely on ICT to attract more visitors and buyers. In particular, over the years the nature and development of the travel industry have undergone major changes. For attracting and serving tourists and visitors, new practices were applied, which are heavily dependent on ICTs (Buhalis, 1998; Sigala, 2002). Most of the people working in these types of agencies need to be computer literate in order to efficiently serve their customers. However, many of them have only partial knowledge of the various IT tools used in their every day duties or they have to face a lot of difficulties when utilizing them.

Based on the previous discussion, the main aims of the survey reported in the current paper are:

i. To record the e-skills required by people working in Greek travel and cultural agencies,
ii. To identify the importance of proper training, and
iii. To measure the correlation between the syllabus of the international ECDL certification and the required e-skills of the employers of the cultural and travel agencies.

The remainder of the paper is organized as follows. In the next section we focus on the e-skills required by employees of the travel and cultural agencies. Soon after we briefly present the structure of the ECDL certification. Then we present the findings of the study and, finally, the conclusions and future developments are outlined.

REQUIRED E-SKILLS IN TRAVEL AND CULTURAL AGENCIES

The Internet is expected to change the role of tourism promotion agencies as information providers. There are arguments for and against the disintermediation of travel agents (Buhalis, 1998, p. 416). The most extreme opinion suggests the end of travel agencies in the near future. As the power of the Internet grows and empowers customers to develop and buy their own itineraries, the very existence of the travel agents will be threatened.

On the other hand, the role of the travel agencies is expected to grow in importance, since their greatest ability is "to collate, organize and interpret large amount of data in a way that delivers the best value and the most exciting travel experiences for the customer" (O'Connor, 1999, p. 114). It is claimed that travel agencies provide not only information, but also advice. Therefore, as long as they strengthen their advice-giving capacity, they will remain secure in the chain of distribution. ICTs are having the effect of changing mainly:

- The ways by which travel agencies utilize their information management systems, such as computer reservation systems (CRS) and electronic point of sales (EPOS). CRS are computerized systems used to store and retrieve information and conduct transactions related to travel. CRS were extended to travel agents as a sales channel; major CRS operations are also known as Global Distribution Systems (GDS). Airlines have divested most of their direct holdings to dedicated GDS companies, and many systems are now accessible to consumers through Internet gateways for hotel, rental cars, and other services as well as airline tickets. GDS provide travel information services, such as real-time availability and price information for flights, hotels and car rental companies (French, 1998). Currently four systems, namely SABRE (www.sabretravelnetwork.com), GALILEO (www.galileo.gr), AMADEUS (www.amadeus.gr), and WORLDSPAN (www.worldspan.com) dominate the global market. GDS's efficiency and reliability enable principals to distribute and manage their reservations globally, by bridging consumer needs with the tourism supply. The employers of the travel agencies have to know the operation of the dominant GDS;
- The ways travel agencies communicate; how customers look for information and purchase travel goods and services (Smith & Jenner, 1998, p. 77).

ICTs enhance a number of intra-travel agencies processes, by supporting a certain level of integration between various functions within travel agencies; typically the 'front' and 'back' office. Typical examples include integrated points of sales systems; inventory control for tour operators; accounting and payroll systems etc. The aim is to increase the strategic and operational management of the travel agency. Intranet technology facilitates an internal network by deploying the same technology and presentation tools as the Internet, but restricting access to authorized personnel only. The personnel of a travel agency must be familiar with future e-platforms such as mobile devices, portable communication devices, interactive TV, and new Web technologies (e.g., semantic web services) applied to the travel industry. Similar skills are required by people working in cultural promotion agencies in order to manage and serve the e-visitors and the online museum presentations.

In cultural heritage agencies, ICTs play an important role in the digitization and presentation of cultural objects (Go et al., 2003). Personnel of museums or related agencies need to utilize computer or other hi-tech devices on a constant basis for inserting data or searching for information (Amin et al., 2008). As more innovative applications emerge, there is an inherent need for employees to have at least basic computer handling abilities.

Based on the above discussion, we felt important to get a clearer picture of the required e-skills in the mentioned sectors.

THE ECDL PROGRAMME

The ECDL programme was initially introduced in Finland and then promoted at a European level (Carpenter et al., 2000) by CEPIS (Council of European Professional Informatics Societies http://www.cepis.org), a federation of 17 national ICT professional associations. CEPIS introduced the ECDL programme in the year 1995 with the support of some EU funding. Currently, the governing body of the programme is the European Computer Driving Licence Foundation (ECDL-F http://www.ecdl.com), a not-for-profit organization established by the national ICT professional societies of more than 40 countries. The ECDL programme in Greece is governed by the Greek ECDL organization and previously by the Greek

Computer Society with the contribution of CEPIS (Council of European Professional Informatics Societies http://www.cepis.org). The main features of the ECDL programme can be summarized as follows:

- *Internationality:* after the initial experimentation in the European Union, 137 countries worldwide have adopted the programme; the certification exam – based on the so-called QTB (Question and Test Base) – is available in 32 languages;
- *Integration between academia and industry*: the programme is supported by the national professional societies that integrate professional and academic competences;
- *Technological neutrality*: the programme defines ICT skills independently of hardware and software vendors. In particular, it is possible to obtain the certificate using only open source non-proprietary technologies.

The ECDL certificate proves that its recipient has some basic skills in using a computer, such as editing a document with a word processor, preparing a table using a spreadsheet, querying a database, browsing the Web. The ECDL syllabus version 4 consists of seven modules:

1. Basic concepts of information technology;
2. Using the computer and managing files;
3. Word processing;
4. Spreadsheets;
5. Database;
6. Presentation;

7a. Information and communication (WWW)

7b. Information and communication (E-mail)

There are two types of certificate: (1) a START license (obtained after passing four exams out of the seven ECDL modules) and (2) a FULL license (obtained after passing the exams of all seven ECDL modules). Each module describes in detail every concept and ability that the candidate should understand and develop to get the examination. ECDL is designed to cover all the potential operations performed using Microsoft Office tools, even the rare ones, e.g. change the default uses of Microsoft Word. The first module aims at providing candidates with all the concepts needed to understand most of the common Information Society terms. The last module is further divided into Internet Explorer and Outlook Express. The six latter ECDL units match the Microsoft products.

METHODOLOGY AND RESULTS OF THE STUDY

The Survey

The first phase of the research concentrated on the recognition of the e-skills required in the Greek agencies. To identify and systematically record the e-tasks involved in everyday activities, 197 employees working in various travel agencies were interviewed. We selected travel agencies by the Greek Travel Pages (GTP), which includes a record of about 3,000 tourism promotion agencies around Greece. GTP is considered to be the most comprehensive directory of Greek tourism and is widely used by the industry. The museums and their employees were randomly selected based on a selection of linked resources found at http://www.greece-museums.com/. The research was conducted by means of an electronic questionnaire mailed to the travel and museum organizations. The questionnaire was completed into three phases spanning a period from summer 2005 to spring of 2008. It was very difficult to find participants to voluntarily complete the questionnaire. Therefore, we had to contact more than once some agencies in order to get a satisfactory number of responses. Some initial results of a small sample of the survey are already reported in (Lazarinis, 2006).

Our survey subjects were occupied in the travel and cultural heritage promotion industry for a period varying from 3 to 12 years. They were all high school graduates and 102 of them were college graduates. All the survey participants were office personnel, interacting with computers in various ways. This distribution of our sample ensures that the results of our survey will be valid according to the objectives set.

Then, we compared these e-tasks with the syllabus of ECDL. Our main intention was to realize whether the e-skills acquired during formal training for the ECDL certification, would be of real value to the employees. Also, we asked the participants to evaluate whether official ICT transcripts are important in job hunting.

Hereafter, we present the queries asked to the participants, statistics about the ICT tasks involved in their professions, and the overlay factor between acquired knowledge and the required e-skills. Also, we recorded the additional difficulties of the employees, which lacked official training of the basic ICT tools utilized. The main conclusion of our work is that the acquisition of ECDL (or of another similar ICT) certification is significant because job applicants can prove their knowledge to the prospective employers. Most importantly, job applicants follow a structured and complete course in order to obtain their certification, and thus they become more productive.

Utilization of Information Tools

The participants were initially asked to identify the software tools utilized in their daily activities. The subjects of the survey had to inform us which tools they used and in which ways they depend on them. The main software categories identified in the questionnaire were:

1. Windows (or another similar flavour of a Windows based system)
2. Word processing
3. Spreadsheets
4. Databases
5. Presentations
6. Internet
7. Email
8. Specialized tools

As reported in Figure 1, all participants heavily depend on computers with Windows and on tools such as WinWord, Excel, Internet Explorer and Outlook. Two noticeable points are the minimum usage of presentation software and database software. For example, the employees participating in the study rarely make presentations to clients, so they do not use MS PowerPoint. Specific software covers most of the functionality offered by tools such as MS Access.

The participants had also to describe in more detail the various ways they use the previously mentioned tools. For example, we asked them to describe which operations they usually perform in Windows. The purpose of this demand was twofold. On the one hand, we wanted to see how heavily they rely on these tools. On the other hand, we wanted to be able to measure the correlation between the actual e-skills required and the ECDL syllabus.

After inspecting the usage details, we realized that although all the personnel uses Windows, most of them simply use the system in order to start other tools. This means that they do not use advanced operations such as folder creation and navigation, file searching, and file copying. They solely start up or shut down other applications. Another conclusion is that most of the people working in travel agencies do not develop databases, not even simple ones. Basically, they make use of ready database applications developed by the technically team or other external software agencies.

The participants were then asked to identify the vendor of the software tools used in their everyday duties. As already anticipated most of the employees (more than 70%) use Microsoft products to perform their tasks. Some travel agen-

Figure 1. Utilization of different information tools

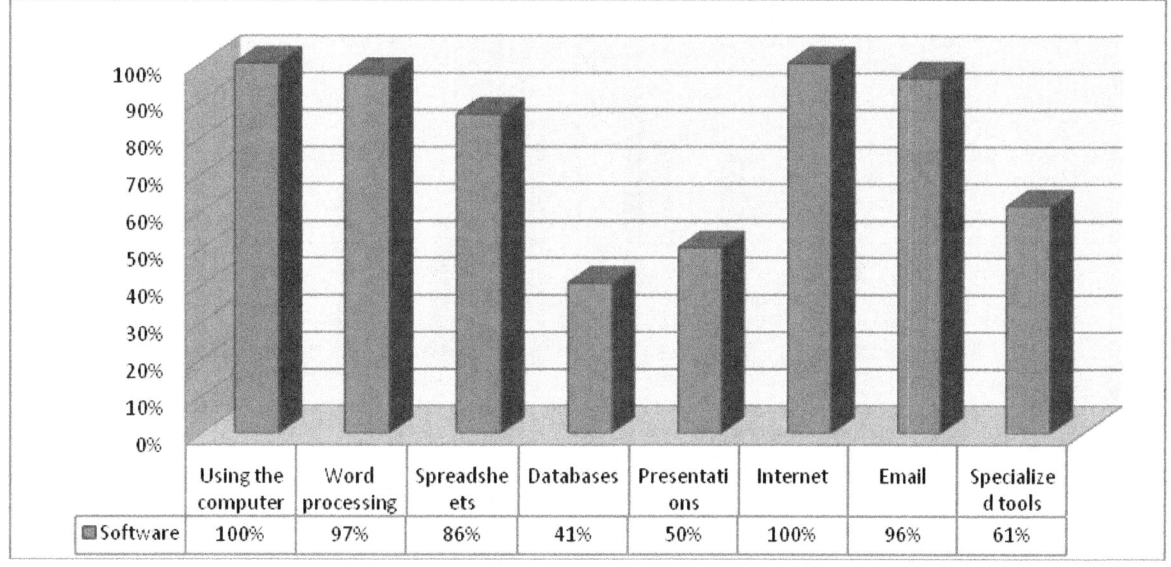

cies use other freeware programs, such as Open Office, Mozilla Firefox for Web navigation and Web mailers. This observation is important, as most ICT assessments rely on Microsoft Office, which obviously is a barrier to those candidates who are accustomed with other products.

e-Tasks and ECDL Syllabus

From the detailed descriptions of the personnel's e-tasks, a list of the various actions performed per tool was constructed. This list contains the union of actions of every employee. For example, some employees do not need to create folders, whereas some others have to organize their documents in a continuously expanding folder hierarchy. In this case, we recorded the folder creation in the list of actions for the "Using the Computer and Managing Files" module. We constructed seven such indexes corresponding to the seven modules of the ECDL.

For measuring the correlation between the e-skills of the employees and the first ECDL module, we devised another technique, since the concepts of this unit are theoretical rather than practical. In this case, we showed the participants a list of terms resulting from the respective ECDL module and we asked them to mark the terms they were familiar with. Following this request, we were able to form a list of the concepts that were better known.

After the construction of the indexes, we were able to compare the e-tasks performed by the employees occupied in the tourism agencies professions with the ECDL syllabus. Figure 2 depicts the results of this analysis. More specifically, it shows the percentage of the concepts and skills of the ECDL modules needed and applied by the travel agencies' staff.

Some interesting points arise from Figure 2. Only half of the concepts of the information technology module (module 1) are recognized by the participants. Also, almost 36% of the functions described in module 2 of the ECDL syllabus do not appear to be useful to the employees. This observation is even more noticeable in the database unit (module 5), where less than half of the tasks described in the programme of the study is utilized.

With respect to the other modules, Figure 2 illustrates a high overlay factor between the tasks

Figure 2. Correlation of e-tasks and ECDL

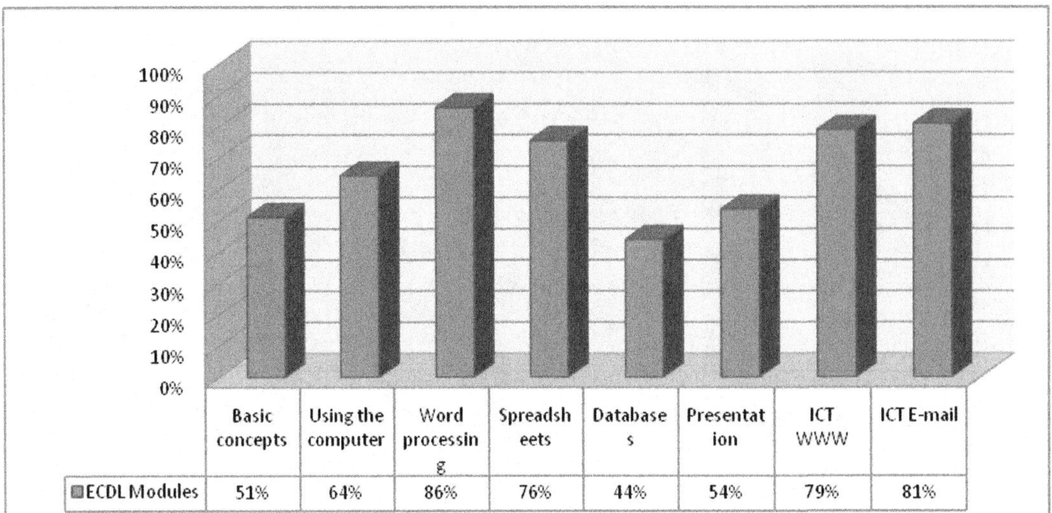

performed by the staff and the tasks described in the ECDL modules. Clearly, word processing, spreadsheets, Web navigation, and e-mail software are among the most common functions performed daily in an office environment.

Another outcome of this analysis is that all the tasks performed by the employees are a subset of the tasks described in the certification's syllabus. This is an important conclusion as it proves that the ICT certification under inspection is designed so as to cover a wide range of e-tasks that will comply with the requirements of several ICT dependent professions.

A final point that was not officially measured, but it was deduced by sporadic discussions with members of our sample, was that some of the concepts described in the programme of study of the ICT certification were unknown to our contributors. This led us to assume that whether they were aware of the additional features and capabilities of the tools they would have exploited them. Proper training is one of the potential solutions to this problem.

Questions to the Employees

In the second phase of the study, the participants had to fill out a short questionnaire. The main goal was to realize if proper training for an ICT certification would be of real value to the trainees with respect to their everyday e-duties.

Problems from the Utilization of the Software

The first question asked to the participants related with the difficulties that they face when they use one of the software tools mentioned previously. They were asked to indicate the tool or tools, which they find more difficult to use and on which they meet several problems.

Figure 3 shows that the tools causing the major difficulties are spreadsheets and databases. These specific tools require a good understanding of their functions in order to operate them properly. A few participants have problems with other tools as well, with the less trouble causing tools being the Internet tools.

Possession of a Certification

The next question aimed at counting the persons who already held ECDL or another similar certification. 119 (60.40%) of the participants held an ICT certification. We then compared the answers

Figure 3. Problems per software tool

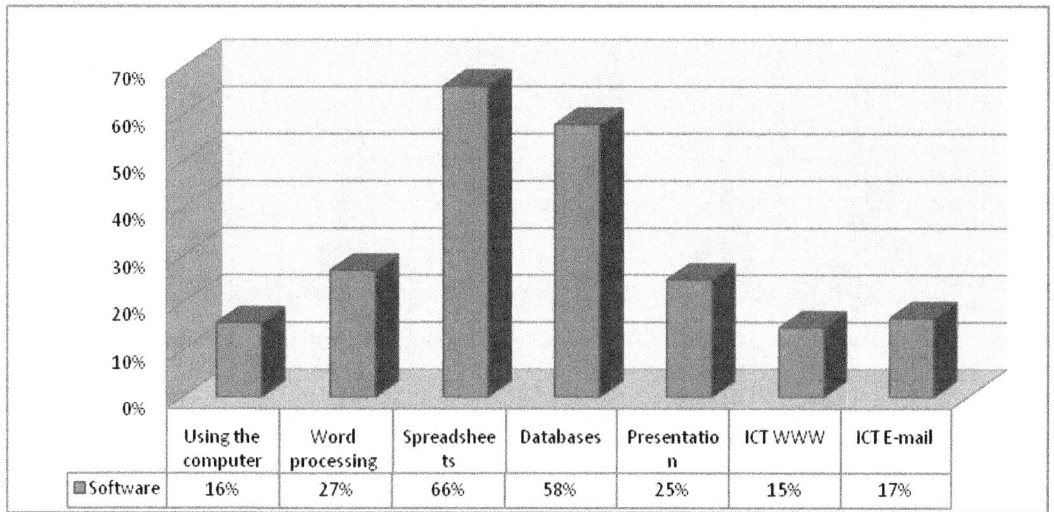

they gave to the previous question and realized that the difficulties they are experienced with are less relevant, when compared to those of the other participants to the survey. However, it is difficult to reach a quantitative result in this field.

ICT Training

Next, the participants were asked to identify the educational methods used so as to be trained in the use of necessary software tools. The participants could select one among the following five alternatives: *i.* seminar, *ii.* college/university, *iii.* school, *iv.* self-study, *v.* online lessons.

As reported in Figure 4, most of the subjects have attended an adult training program to acquire the necessary e-skills. A few obtained the e-skills through secondary or higher education, and only a very small percentage become skilled through self-study or online lessons. Comparing the results to this question with those to the former one, one could expect that the problems people had to face in the use of the different tools was less than indicated in Figure 3. However, as brought up by some of the participants, many seminars are too broad, meaning that they cover a lot of subjects with minimum practical value, while they overlook some e-tasks, which are considered very useful. Additionally, some of the adults training programs are too brief so they tend to cover the concepts only epigrammatically. At last, seminars without ending examinations for the attendees tend to be less effective then the others.

Importance of ICT Certification

We then asked the people who filled the questionnaires the following question:

Do you believe that an adult training program which aims at covering the study programme of an ICT certification, with a final examination at the end of it, would help you more than other general purpose ICT seminars?

All of them replied positively to this question and to support their answers they stated that the goal of the seminar would be well defined and the programme of the ICT certifications would fit their needs. In addition, they mentioned that everyone in the seminar would have been more careful, and more pedagogical effectiveness would have been detected.

Figure 4. Training methods for acquiring the e-skills

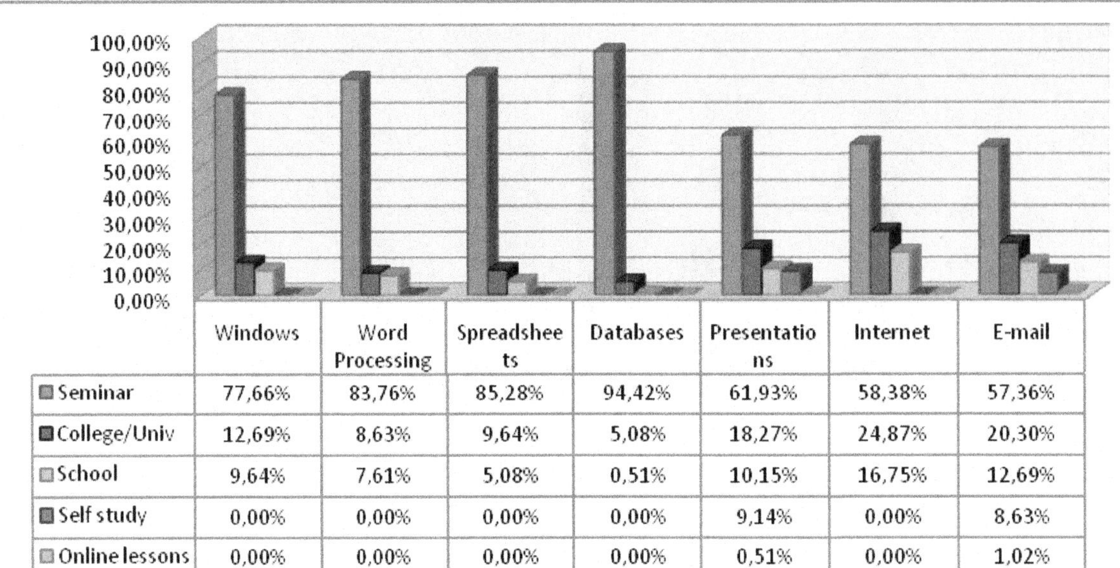

	Windows	Word Processing	Spreadsheets	Databases	Presentations	Internet	E-mail
Seminar	77,66%	83,76%	85,28%	94,42%	61,93%	58,38%	57,36%
College/Univ	12,69%	8,63%	9,64%	5,08%	18,27%	24,87%	20,30%
School	9,64%	7,61%	5,08%	0,51%	10,15%	16,75%	12,69%
Self study	0,00%	0,00%	0,00%	0,00%	9,14%	0,00%	8,63%
Online lessons	0,00%	0,00%	0,00%	0,00%	0,51%	0,00%	1,02%

Although the proportions vary at some points between the two continents, it can be agreed that finding a job or increase the productivity and credibility are some of the most significant reasons for the individuals to increase productivity (see Table 1).

With Table 1 as a starting point, we asked the participants to specify their primary reason for potential certification pursuing. As reported in Figure 5, the vast majority of the people wants to increase its productivity or fulfill the requirements of their current or a new job position. From the answers it can be inferred that in the travel and cultural heritage promotion sector the employees are very concerned with their performance and productivity as they constantly serve customers. Therefore, being technologically skillful is essential so as to offer better services to their customers.

Table 1. Why individuals pursue certification [source: eSCC, 2004]

Reasons	*North America*	*Europe*
Increase productivity	11%	12%
Prepare for new position	7%	15%
Help find a job	19%	6%
Increase compensation	8%	8%
Increase credibility	16%	19%
Fulfil job requirement	11%	11%
Assess knowledge	10%	19%
Stay current with new technology	19%	8%

CONCLUSION AND FURTHER WORK

The results of the survey focusing on the correlation between the e-tasks of personnel in cultural and travel agencies and the syllabus of the ECDL certification can be summarized as follows:

- Most part of employers' everyday e-tasks are included in the syllabus of the certification and concern word processing, spreadsheet use and Internet access. The other modules (computer usage, databases, presentations) include much more topics than the required ones and they are less used than former ones,

Figure 5. Reasons Greek employees pursue certification

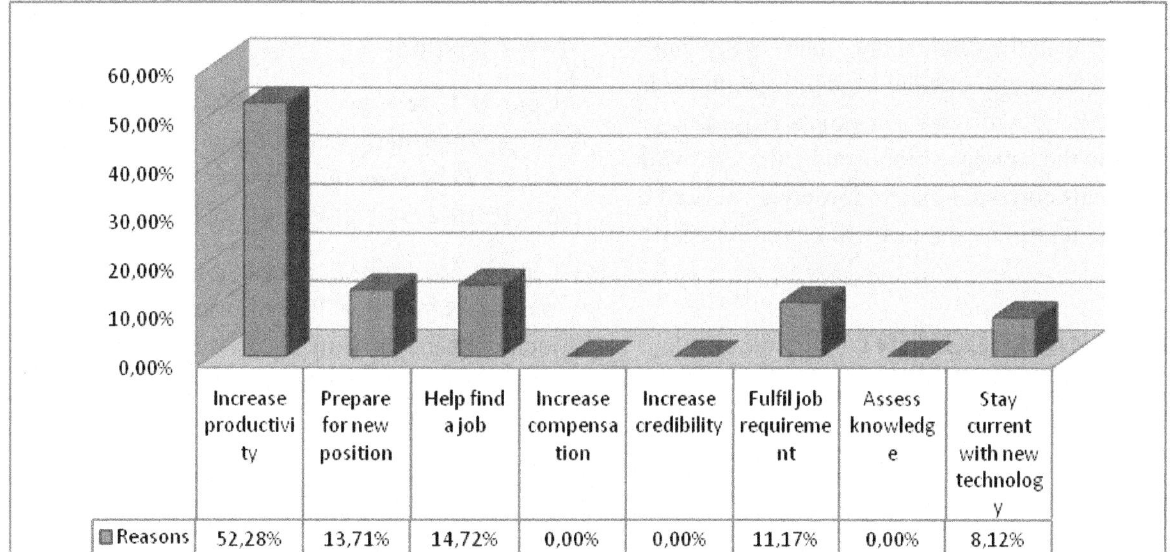

- Most part of the 197 participants stated that the role of well structured training programs which could lead to an ICT certification is very important. ICT certifications can play an important role in cultural and tourism promotion agencies. Through well designed, specialized and of appropriate length adult training programs, employees can be more productive and acquire an extra formal qualification. The programme of study of the available ICT certifications covers most the abilities and concepts required in employers' work. However, there are a few potential improvements or points that worth attention. First, since some agencies use non-Microsoft tools and it would be appropriate to offer the possibility to assess workers' knowledge by using alternative freeware software such as Open Office. Second, although ECDL consists of seven assessment modules, a selection of fewer modules, based on individual needs, would be a welcome option. Furthermore the "Concepts of Information Technology" and some tasks of the "Database" modules should be either removed or made optional, as they are very specialized technical topics.

As a concluding remark it can be argued that the ECDL initiative and the current ICT certifications play an important role in the discussed businesses, as in other professions as well, and it should be expected more and more people to take such certifications in the future.

In the near future, we will apply the Correspondence Analysis (CA) (Greenacre, 1993) to identify profiles that characterize the management of ICT certification programmes in Greek travel agencies. The CA technique is used to study the relationships between modalities (or categories) of two or more discrete variables (usually qualitative). The aim of CA is to highlight the structure of the associations among these variables (or characters) whose modalities and frequencies are reorganised into contingency tables that often have a complex structure and tend to distort – or even hide – essential relationships. Variables under consideration could be the geographic zone of the travel agencies and the type of agency (large, medium or small size). CA will allow the visualization of these relationships in terms of points in a space that is smaller than the original one, thus greatly facilitating their interpretation. Modalities with strong associations will represent points close to each other in the subspace produced by the CA, while the points corresponding to loosely associated or non-associated modalities will be further apart.

ACKNOWLEDGMENT

We would like to thank the employees of the various Greek travel and cultural agencies, who participated in the exploratory study.

REFERENCES

Amin, A., van Ossenbruggen, J., Hardman, L., & van Nispen, A. (2008). Understanding cultural heritage experts' information seeking needs. In *Proceedings of the 8th ACM/IEEE-CS Joint Conference on Digital Libraries (JCDL '08)* (pp. 39-47). New York: ACM. Retrieved from http://doi.acm.org/10.1145/1378889.1378897

Buhalis, D. (1998). Strategic use of information technologies in the tourism Industry. *Tourism Management*, *19*(5), 409–421. doi:10.1016/S0261-5177(98)00038-7

Bulletin, E. U. 3. (2000). *Preparing the transition to a competitive, dynamic and knowledge-based economy*. Retrieved from http://europa.eu.int/abc/doc/off/bull/en/200003/i1006.htm

Calzarossa, M. C., Ciancarini, P., Maresca, P., Mich, L., & Scarabottolo, N. (2007). The ECDL programme in Italian Universities. *Computers & Education*, *49*(2), 514–529. doi:10.1016/j.compedu.2005.10.008

Carpenter, D., Dolan, D., Leahy, D., & Sherwood-Smith, M. (2000). ECDL/ICDL: A global computer literacy initiative. In *Proceedings of IFIP ICEUT2000*.

CEPIS. (2004). *ICT-Skills Certification in Europe* (CedepofProgram Report). Retrieved from http://www.cepis.org

Cole, I. J., & Kesley, A. (2004). Computer and information literacy in post-qualifying education. *Nurse Education in Practice*, *4*(3), 190–199. doi:10.1016/S1471-5953(03)00065-9

Curley, M. (2003). *Addressing the ICT skills shortage in Europe*. Paper presented at the Early identification of skill needs in Europe Conference. Retrieved from http://www.cedefop.eu.int/mtconference/mtconf1.html

e-Europe. (2002). *E-Business and ICT skills in Europe* (ICT skills Monitoring Group Final Report). Retrieved from http://europa.eu.int/comm/enterprise/ict/policy/ict-skills/es-br.pdf

eSCC. (2004). *The situation and the role of e-skills industry certification in Europe*. Paper presented at the European e-Skills 2004 Conference. Retrieved from http://www.e-scc.org/

French, T. (1998). The future of global distribution systems. *Travel and Tourism Analyst*, *3*, 1–17.

Go, F., Lee, R., & Russoe, A. (2003). E-heritage in the globalizing society: enabling cross-cultural engagement through ICT. *Information Technology & Tourism*, *6*(1), 55–68. doi:10.3727/109830503108751225

Greenacre, M. J. (1993). *Correspondence analysis in practice*. New York: Academic Press.

Haarala-Muhonen, A., & Sokura, B. (2000). *Computer driving licence – a forerunner of skills tests, Innovations in Higher Education*. Retrieved from http://www.helsinki.fi/inno2000/

Lazarinis, F. (2006). The importance of ICT Certification in Tourism and Cultural Professions. In *Proceedings of the Critical Issues in Leisure & Tourism Education*, Buckinghamshire, UK (pp. 165-173).

O'Connor, P. (1999). *Electronic information distribution in tourism and hospitality*. New York: CAB International.

Sigala, M. (2002). The evolution of Internet pedagogy: Benefits for tourism and hospitality education. *Journal of Hospitality, Leisure, Sport & Tourism Education*, *1*(2), 29–45.

Smith, C., & Jenner, P. (1998). Tourism and the Internet. *Travel & Tourism Analyst*, *1*, 62–81.

Sokura, B. (2005). *ICT Certification and its Effects on the Intellectual Capital of an Organization.* Retrieved from http://www.ifipwg82.org/Oasis2005/Bertta Sokura.pdf

This work was previously published in International Journal of Digital Literacy and Digital Competence, Volume 1, Issue 2, edited by Antonio Cartelli, pp. 28-38, copyright 2010 by IGI Publishing (an imprint of IGI Global).

Chapter 13
Digital Literacy for Health:
The Promise of Health 2.0

Ela Klecun
London School of Economics and Political Science, UK

ABSTRACT

This paper outlines and challenges expectations and promises regarding the potential of the internet and Web 2.0 for empowering patients and citizens. It focuses on literacies required to make a meaningful (to the individual) use of these technologies for health and health care related purposes. The author briefly discusses how these should be taught and concludes that these literacies, including digital literacy and health literacy, are complex and challenging to many while the empowering claims are over-stated. Traditional sources of information and advice will remain essential to maintaining quality of health care.

INTRODUCTION

The changes that developed societies have experienced in recent decades have been given many descriptions, each emphasising a particular aspect or aspects of the 'new' order. For some, the developments in information and communications technology (ICT) are seen as pivotal to the process of shaping our society (Miles, 1996; Webster, 1995). The term 'information society' has permeated academic and policy publications, as well as popular media, and the Internet is seen as central to production and consumption of information.

Others focus on cultural changes, proposing that we live in a world in which there is no overall 'truth' but there are many 'truths' and where we construct own meanings, history and lifestyles (Baudrillard, 1988; Bauman, 2000). We are also told that 'liquid' is an apt description of our societies (Bauman, 2000). Many people have nomadic lifestyles, or at least have no permanent attachment to a particular geographical place or a job. Old traditional loyalties, customary rights and obligations have been melted down, giving

DOI: 10.4018/978-1-4666-0903-7.ch013

the individual freedom to choose and to act (at least to a greater extent than before). Respect for professionals, including medics, has been undermined and the knowledge they represent has been challenged.

But freedom is a mixed blessing. Individualisation and empowerment place demands on us, to choose, to construct our own destinies, to cope with consequences of our choices and external events (Bauman, 2000). There is an obligation of care of self (e.g. to have a healthy lifestyle). We are now increasingly encouraged (and sometimes forced) to make choices with regard to diagnosis, treatments and providers (some of the choices being between traditional medicine and scientific medicine, private and public health care, and within each of those categories, of particular type of treatments and providers).

For some time now, the Internet has been seen as playing an important role in patient/consumer empowerment. Health related and lifestyle management sites have mushroomed on the Internet, and they vary in purpose, quality, content, interactivity and scope for collaboration. More recently the use of the Web, and in particular Web 2.0, is seen as potentially altering how citizens/patients engage with health care services. Web 2.0 is hailed as exciting new set of technologies for collaboration and social interaction in many domains including health care. The applications include blogs, wikis, Wikipedia, podcasts, social networking sites and mash-ups. Examples of their use in health domain include Web-based personal health records, on-line appointment scheduling, doctor-patient e-mail, health/disease or patient group focused blogs and social networking sites and HealthMap, which combines data from different people, RSS feeds and Google Earth to aggregate the information in order to examine outbreaks of different conditions.

A new term 'Health 2.0' is being used to denote the application of these new technologies in the area of health care. However, some see it as a paradigm-like shift in the way health care is delivered and experienced. Members of International Medical Informatics Association (IMIA) Web 2.0 Exploratory Taskforce suggest that: "Health 2.0 may go far beyond just the pervasive social networking technology of Web 2.0 to support a complete reinvention in the way that health care is delivered." (Murray et al., 2008, p. 47). Patient empowerment, and in particular communication and collaboration between patients, their caregivers, citizens and health care professionals are seen by them as key to such a re-invention of health care delivery.

The notion of patient empowerment is central to the European Union (EU) and many national and local governments' policies, and new ICT and services they facilitate (often referred to as e-health) are seen as playing an important role in achieving this goal. The EU e-health action plan (EU, 2004) includes a section on "Empowering health consumers: patients and healthy citizens". The plan stresses the importance of personal health education and disease prevention. The role of e-health services is defined as supporting managing people's own diseases, risks and lifestyles by providing timely information tailored to individuals in need. The examples of e-health services include health information networks, electronic health records, telemedicine services, wearable and portable monitoring systems and health portals.

In the UK, the government is promoting a patient-centred model of health care. This includes a vision of patients or rather consumers of health care, as we are now often referred to, having access to information on medical conditions, treatments, prevention and lifestyles, as well as data on availability of different services, performance of health care providers (e.g. through published hospital league tables, including statistics on different health specialists, e.g. surgeons). Furthermore, patients/citizens are increasingly envisaged in the policies not only as knowledgeable consumers of health information and health care services but also as co-authors of their care programmes involved in shaping health and social care services (DOH 1999, 2001).

These aspirations evident in policy rhetoric are reflected in some of the changes to the way health care is structured and delivered (e.g. through offering (limited) choices of where and by whom one is treated, e.g. in which hospital). ICT and in particular different Internet applications are seen as an important medium facilitating the journey from passive patients to informed consumers and co-authors of health plans. To that effect the UK government has sponsored different applications, for example Map of Medicine[1], NHS Direct Online (online health advice service) or HealthSpace (on-line personal health organiser/record). However, there are numerous problems with (technology deterministic) visions of patient empowerment enabled by ICT (Henwood et al., 2003).

The following section outlines and challenges the claims made in the literature for the empowering potential of the Internet and in particular Health 2.0 applications. This paper then considers the skills required by citizens/patients to take on the role of knowledgeable 'consumers' and co-authors of health care services. It focuses on digital literacies required to make a meaningful (to the individual) use of these applications for health and health care related purposes and briefly discusses how these should be taught. The main points of the paper are summarised in the conclusion.

PROMISES, REALITIES AND CHALLENGES OF ICT FACILITATED PATIENT/CITIZEN EMPOWERMENT

Promises

Literature often makes claims as to the empowering potential of the Internet, and in particular of its facility to transform passive patients into informed consumers of health care services (Murray, 2008). Frost and Massagli (2008) also suggest that finding other individuals with similar experiences facilitates communication, allows sharing specific health knowledge, enables peer-support and is a source of motivation for behavioural change.

One of the main reasons for searching the Internet is to obtain health and health care related information. According to surveys conducted by Pew Internet & American Life Project 61% of American adults look online for health information (Fox & Jones, 2009). In Britain, Oxford Internet Institute Survey found that the search for health information is the fourth most popular activity being done on the web (after information seeking related to travel plans, local events information and news) (Dutton et al., 2009). Importantly, online health inquiries have an impact on decisions or actions (Fox & Jones, 2009; Meric et al., 2002). Some people seek information on their disease, available treatments and join Internet-based support groups. Although pensioners use the Internet less than younger people, they search the Internet more to find health information than those in the 18-24 age group according to an IBM study reported by British Computer Society (BCS, 2009)

Blogs, discussion groups and online communities centred on patients and their diseases, such as PatientsLikeMe, are becoming increasingly popular. Health-related groups are forming on large social networking sites like Facebook and MySpace. A group discussing depression has one of the largest memberships on MySpace. Such groups aim to provide support for particular patients groups or caregivers or to bring people together to raise awareness on particular issues.

In virtual social communities, e.g. Second Life, people can visit Health Info Island to obtain information from real medical professionals on their condition. Health professionals are also developing a medical wiki, Ganfyd.org, which is a collaborative medical reference that can be read by everyone but updated only by medical professionals and invited non-medical experts (BCS, 2009).

Some providers enable patients to see their doctors in person and / or to contact them through e-mails, texts, instant-messages or video-chats. They might also offer patients their own online patient health records (PHR). The proponents of such services proclaim that better and more communication via these networks will have various benefits, including allowing for richer engagement and deeper doctor-patient relationships resulting in better care for patients, as well as making it easier to spread innovation in health care (Hawn, 2008).

In addition, PHR are seen as empowering patients by giving them control over the management of and responsibility for their health. This is seen as having many benefits, including health promotion and prevention (NCVHS, 2006). Recently Microsoft and Google have entered the PHR market with Microsoft HealthVault and Google Health. Both companies provide patients with a single locus to aggregate health data from various providers as well as a gateway to external health websites. Google Health promises access to customised services, depending on the degree of personal information that is shared with them.

There are also more specialised telemedicine and telecare applications which, for example, support living with chronic illnesses, through the provision of information, monitoring of vital signs and decision support tools. Their potential benefits and barriers to adoption are well documented (Wootton et al., 2006), although there is less literature on their actual benefits.

Challenges

There is a growing body of literature highlighting problems with the notion of ICT-enabled patients' empowerment (Henwood et al., 2002; Henwood et al., 2003; Hirji, 2004; Klecun, 2008; Theofanos & Mulligan, 2004). As Henwood et al. (2002) point out, just because the potential for empowerment exists, it does necessarily occur. For example, searching health related websites poses problems of equity of services and validity of information and related risks of acting upon incorrect information. Being able to use the Internet from home does not mean equal ability to investigate online health care data. Hirji (2004) points out that many consumers are not trained in information retrieval skills, a fact that is similarly overlooked by many website designers and health care providers placing information online. The author quotes studies, which seem to indicate that people may overestimate their own ability to evaluate online material. Birru et al. (2004) assert that Web health information requires a reading level that prohibits optimal access by some low-literacy adults. Sponsored websites seem to be easier to use, look more attractive and thus seem to attract low-literacy users. They also note that it is of concern that participants in the study did not seem to differentiate between the information from non-sponsored and sponsored web sites. Although based on a very small sample of 8, the findings seem to indicate that that health searches may present unique challenges to a low-literacy population that makes it difficult for them to find accurate, trustworthy health information. This is supported by a study of IT use and literacy, which found that nearly one in two US adults have difficulty in understanding information necessary to make basic health decisions (Institute of Medicine, 2004).

Furthermore, a UK study found that very few participants seemed aware of the sources of information available on the Internet, and some considered the Internet in general as a trustworthy source. Furthermore, despite that NHS Direct Online has been widely publicised not all participants were aware of it (Henwood et al., 2002). It is not clear how many people and to what extent are able to use the information found to negotiate their care plans with health care providers.

Moreover, research has shown that for various reasons, including implementation/adoption problems, technical challenges, interoperability of data, privacy, security, lack of access and limited health literacy, electronic PHR are not widely used (Kaelber et al., 2008; Vascellaro & Bulkeley, 2009). For example, in the US the adoption of electronic PHRs is less than 3% (Connecting for Health, 2008), although there are some success stories e.g. Kaiser Permanente My Health Manager or the Department of Veterans Affairs MyHealththeVet (Detmer et al., 2008). A survey results indicate that that 9 in 10 Americans believe that electronic PHR could improve their health and nearly half indicate some interest in using online records (Connecting for Health, 2008). The vision for such records extends beyond allowing users to access, manage and control data collected from multiple sources, towards 'personal health management systems' that allow seamless connection to workflows of both providers and payers (e.g. in the US), programmatic access to the data to create new tools and for people to search and share relevant health information (Neupert & Mundie, 2009). This vision assumes that that the users of such systems have a sophisticated set of skills (including ability to program) and pays little attention to organisational problems posed by those systems.

Thus we argue that the idea of 'patient empowered health care' based on patients having the information they need to be able to make rational health care decisions (e.g. as presented by Murray et al. (2008)) is based on leaps of faith, as to the accessibility and quality of information but more importantly as to the ability of patients to make 'rational' decisions and negotiate their ideas with health care providers, insurers and payers. At the very least information must be relevant to people's needs, delivered in an appropriate form (accurate, timely, and easy to understand), people must be willing and have the ability to engage with it and act upon it. To put it differently, information must relate to people's self understanding and personal understanding of the world and to be coherent with their personal narratives. However, personal narratives are often re-written due to increasing occurrence of life turning moments in liquid societies (Gaviria & Bluemelhuber, 2010). Hence different information will appeal to us at different moments of our lives. Furthermore, different activities (searching for health related information, blogging, using social networking sites, podcasting, etc.) require overlapping but not identical sets of skills, which we need, acquire and loose at different times in our lives.

The following section discusses skills needed for utilising the Internet, including Web 2.0 applications, for health and wellness purposes.

DIGITAL LITERACIES FOR HEALTH

This section is based on the literatures on digital literacy (or e-literacy), media literacy and health literacy, as well as findings from a research project (PENCEIL)[2] exploring people's needs and aspirations regarding the use of ICT, e-literacies they acquired and needed, and the way e-literacy should be taught.

There is a broad agreement on what skills and competencies might be needed to make meaningful use of different ICTs and services they enable, although they might be categorised and labelled in different ways, e.g. as digital literacy, media literacy or e-literacy. For example, Livingstone (2003) proposes that media literacy or more generally literacy is the ability: "To access, analyse, evaluate and communicate messages in a variety of forms" (p. 6), as well as to create content. While Ofcom (2005) defines media literacy "as the ability to access, understand and create communications in a variety of contexts. At its simplest level it is the ability to use a range of media and be able to understand the information received. At a more advanced level it moves from recognising and understanding the information to critical thinking skills such as questioning, analysing, appreciating and evaluating that information." Bradbrook and Fisher (2004) provide the following breakdown of literacies:

Information Literacy

- *Information literacy* explains the critical analytical skills that allow the user to seek out, access and evaluate the usefulness of information resources.

Technology-Related Literacies

- *ICT literacy* explains the user's ability to acquire and then transfer skills to new/changing technologies.
- *Net/Web literacies* describe competencies required to use online tools and work within values/rules developed for electronic interactions, such as netiquette.

Composite Literacies

- *E-learning literacy* describes the competencies required to utilise the tools, support and resources necessary for technology-supported learning.
- *E-citizenship literacy* describes the use of the appropriate tools, support and resources to meet citizenship (social) goals with the use of technology. This also requires an understanding of the rights and responsibilities associated with active citizenship.

Focusing on eHealth, i.e. the use of ICT, especially the Internet, to improve or enable health and health care, Norman & Skinner (2006) define eHealth literacy as "the ability to seek, find, understand, and appraise health information from electronic sources and apply the knowledge gained to addressing or solving a health problem". They outline a set of six fundamental eHealth skills (or literacies): traditional literacy, health literacy, information literacy, scientific literacy, media literacy, and computer literacy.

Essential skills for assessing web-based information are identified by Edgar et al. (2002) as the ability to conduct a search and find the 'right' sites; the ability to judge the quality of information; and the ability to synthesize that information into a useful context for personal/individual health. How can the quality of evidence be judged? The literature advocates looking at the source of information, date published and updated, and the site sponsor. A reflective user must then evaluate the content, taking into account if the evidence presented is convincing (e.g. how well it is supported, how the research was conducted). Ideally, the user might cross-check the information found against other sources. Evaluating information is difficult even for people skilled in critical analysis. Hence, existing literature often suggests that information seekers should use portals sponsored by governments or other non-profit organizations, follow checklists created by professionals or health educators, and /or download special toolbars, all of which will assist them in finding and evaluation information on the web (Adams & de Bont, 2007). However, using 'approved' portals means that the information is pre-selected and this selection includes certain biases (Adams & de Bont, 2007). Moreover, even findings published in established, peer–review journals might be based on questionable research, as the case of the study of side effects of MMR vaccine demonstrates. The worrying trend is that as people's trust in established authorities (e.g. medical professionals and governmental bodies) rapidly declines, media-fuelled 'scare' stories grip people's imagination. Once the story takes hold of the public's imagination it is difficult to correct it. Hence, people need to be willing to continuously evaluate the evidence and to re-evaluate their own opinions as new information comes to light.

Likewise, the advice gained through participating in online support groups might be misleading or not appropriate to someone else's circumstances. Therefore understanding and evaluating the information in the context of one's situation is needed, and the following questions should be asked. What does it mean for me? To what extent does it reflect my circumstances? And - what should I do next?

Finally, being a content creator, e.g. through blogging or using wikis, requires different skills. Although Web 2.0 applications are increasingly designed so their users require only basic computing skills, these skills still have to be learnt. Beyond computing skills content creation requires high literacy skills, creativity and self-confidence. People must be interested in those activities and have time to pursue them. Furthermore, they should have awareness of their security and privacy implications.

It seems that only a minority of Internet users create content. The emerging rule of thumb suggests that for each 100 people online, one will create content, 10 will 'interact' with it (e.g. offer comments) and 89 will just view (Murray et al., 2008). This perhaps is not surprising, or even something to be unduly concerned about. After all, just because the technology exists it does not mean we all have to use it in the same way. However, ideally, decisions about use or non-use should be a result of an informed choice rather than lack of awareness or opportunities. Eng & Gustafson (1999) quoted in Adams & de Bont (2007) argue that one of the skills needed is the ability to decide which of the existing tools works best for the individual. "Only in finding the right tool can s/he implement a personal evaluative framework and learn how to be an educated consumer" (Adams & de Bont, 2007, p. 279).

Such understood digital literacy requires an approach to teaching based on development of critical skills through discussion, sharing and mutual support rather than purely individual work 'at the screen'. For example, a course developed during the PENCEIL project to teach digital literacy to adult learners placed emphasis on discussing different ways and reasons for using ICT, analysing and evaluating sources of information and their content, as well as communication and content creation and discussing related issues of privacy and security (Cushman & Klecun, 2005). Students were asked to produce a project (portfolio) based on their interests and skills. Such an approach reflected our belief that moving away from following worksheets and discrete tasks better prepares learners to evaluate, and when appropriate utilize, ever-changing technologies and applications. To address people's fears and every day problems with computers the course also covered the key aspects of managing computers at home. Furthermore, it also introduced other technologies, such as digital cameras and MP3 players. As Web 2.0 is not only about computers, but about a host of other digital technologies teaching should include how these could be integrated, e.g. to provide content.

The findings from the PENCEIL project support a view that digital literacy needs to be considered as a set of competencies for achieving individually directed tasks rather than a set defined from outside or above. Competencies sit within an individual's interaction with and appropriation of technologies and not in abstract form. Teaching should be seen as a process that creates learning opportunities for all. This requires adults' active engagement and educators' guidance and support (Jimoyiannis & Gravani, 2010). Furthermore, acquiring digital literacy for health should be seen as a continuous learning experience.

CONCLUSION

Studies have shown that there is scope for improvement in the way health web sites are designed and information presented, in order to help all of us, but in particular those with disabilities and low literacy levels, to search for and understand the information (Theofanos & Mulligan, 2004). Government or non-for profit organizations' health portals are seen as helping the users to avoid unreliable sources and directing them to approved information. Although this is a helpful approach, it has its limitations, including the impossibility of monitoring all of the health information online. Thus, it remains important to foster people's ability to critically analyse the data they find (Hirji, 2004).

The digital skills required to utilise the Internet, and in particular Web 2.0 applications, for health and wellness are complex and challenging to many. They include the ability to access, analyse, evaluate the (digital) information, to communicate effectively and to create content. All of these pre-suppose traditional literacy, health literacy and communication skills. Technology-related literacies are also necessary and these need to be constantly updated. Deciding which existing tools work best requires the ability to 'keep up' with the technology and the ability to evaluate it.

More generally, people need to acquire meta-cognitive and meta-design skills needed to respond to challenges of living in a liquid society and to create their own destiny (Giovannella & Graf, 2010).

However, people have their own, legitimate reasons for not using the Internet or other ICT. Activities like searching the web, or blogging might not be a part of their daily life, and hence they might not see a reason to invest time, emotional effort and money in learning new skills they require. It is acknowledged in the academic literature that people must have a 'compelling proposition' and that learning ICT skills must be a purposeful activity (Selwyn, 2003).

Moreover, not everyone will have the ability master digital literacy or health literacy. Hence, many people need a 'warm expert', a person who would facilitate access and to help to make sense of complex medical knowledge and its relevance to one's situation (Wyatt et al., 2003). PENCEIL research has shown the importance of social networks (neighbours, friends and sometimes children) in facilitating on-going utilization of ICT. Nevertheless, when providing health care we need to cater for the needs of those unwilling or unable to utilize online applications for their health care needs. It is vital that the personal ('off-line') avenue to access to health care and relevant information must be maintained.

So, will Health 2.0 applications facilitate patients and citizens empowerment? They may well do, but only to a certain extent and for some. Claims made for Health 2.0 should be understood in the context of wider societal trends and people's personal narratives.

REFERENCES

Adams, S., & de Bont, A. (2007). Information Rx: Prescribing good consumerism and responsible citizenship. *Health Care Analysis*, *15*, 273–290. doi:10.1007/s10728-007-0061-9

Baudrillard, J. (1988). *The ecstasy of communication*. Semiotext(e): New York.

Bauman, Z. (2000). *Liquid modernity*. Cambridge: Polity Press.

BCS. (2009). *British Computer Society report, Web 2.0 woven into health information's future*. Retrieved March 10, 2010, from www.bcs.org/tld/hif09

Birru, M. S., & Steinman, R. A. (2004). Online Health Information and Low-Literacy African Americans. *Journal of Medical Internet Research*, *6*(3). doi:10.2196/jmir.6.3.e26

Bradbrook, G., & Fisher, J. (2004, March). *Digital equality: Reviewing digital inclusion activity and mapping the way forwards.* Retrieved from http://www.citizensonline.org.uk/site/media/documents/2190_DigitalEquality_(2004).pdf.

Connecting for Health. (2008). *Americans Overwhelmingly Believe Electronic Personal Health Records Could Improve Their Health, a survey report.* Retrieved March 15, 2010, from http://www.connectingforhealth.org/resources/ResearchBrief-200806.pdf

Cushman, M., & Klecun, E. (2005). Non-users of computers in south London: their experiences and aspirations for use. In *Proceedings of the IRFD World Forum on Information Society: Digital Divide, Global Development and the Information Society,* Tunis, Tunisia. Retrieved from http://penceil.lse.ac.uk/documents/06_WFIS.pdf

Detmer, D., Bloomrosen, M., Raymond, B., & Tang, P. (2008). Integrated personal health records: transformative tools for consumer-centric care. *BMC Medical Informatics and Decision Making*, *8*, 45. doi:10.1186/1472-6947-8-45

DOH. (1999). *Saving Lives: Our Healthier Nation*. London: Department of Health, HMSO.

DOH. (2001). *The expert patient a new approach to chronic disease management for the 21st century*. London: Department of Health, HMSO.

Edgar, L., Greenberg, A., & Remmer, J. (2002). Providing Internet lessons to oncology patients and family members: A shared project. *Psycho-Oncology*, *11*, 439–446. doi:10.1002/pon.590

Eng, T. R., & Gustafson, D. H. (Eds.). (1999). *Wired for health and well-being. From the science panel on interactive communication and health*. Washington, DC: U.S. Department of Health and Human Services, U.S. Government Printing Office.

EU. (2004). *Communication from the Commission to the Council, the European Parliament, the European Economic and Social Committee and the Committee of the Regions - e-Health - making health care better for European citizens: an action plan for a European e-Health Area*. Retrieved March 3, 2010, from http://eur-lex.europa.eu/LexUriServ/LexUriServ.do?uri=CELEX:52004DC0356:EN:NOT

Fox, S., & Jones, S. (2009).*The social life of health information*. Retrieved February 21, 2010, from http://www.pewinternet.org/~/media//Files/Reports/2009/PIP_Health_2009.pdf

Frost, J. H., & Massagli, M. P. (2008). Social uses of personal health information within PatientsLikeMe, an online patient community: what can happen when patients have access to one another's data. *Journal of Medical Internet Research*, *10*(3), e15. doi:10.2196/jmir.1053

Gaviria, P. R., & Bluemelhuber, C. (2010). Consumers' transformations in a liquid society: introducing the concepts of autobiographical-concern and desire-assemblage. *Journal of Consumer Behaviour*, *9*(2), 126–138. doi:10.1002/cb.309

Giovannella, C., & Graf, S. (2010). Challenging technologies, rethinking pedagogy, being design-inspired: The grand challenge of this century. *eLearn Magazine*. Retrieved April 18, 2010, from http://www.elearnmag.org/subpage.cfm?section=articles&article=114-1

Hawn, C. (2009). Take Two Aspirin And Tweet Me In The Morning: How Twitter, Facebook, And Other Social Media Are Reshaping Health Care. *Health Affairs*, *28*(2), 361–368. doi:10.1377/hlthaff.28.2.361

Henwood, F., Wyatt, S., Hart, A., & Smith, J. (2002). Turned on or turned off? Accessing health information on the Internet. *Scandinavian Journal of Information Systems*, *14*(2), 79–90.

Henwood, F., Wyatt, S., Hart, A., & Smith, J. (2003). Ignorance is bliss sometimes: constraints on the emergence of the 'informed patient' in the changing landscapes of health information. *Sociology of Health & Illness*, *25*(6), 589–607. doi:10.1111/1467-9566.00360

Hirji, J. (2004). Freedom or folly? Canadians and the consumption of online health information. *Information Communication and Society*, *7*(4), 445–465. doi:10.1080/1369118042000305593

Institute of Medicine. (2004). *Health Literacy: A Prescription to End Confusion*. Washington, DC: National Academies Press. Retrieved February 2, 2010, from http://www.iom.edu/Reports/2004/Health-Literacy-A-Prescription-to-End-Confusion.aspx

Jimoyiannis, A., & Gravani, M. (2010). Digital Literacy in a Lifelong Learning Programme for Adults: Educators' Experiences and Perceptions on Teaching Practices. *International Journal of Digital Literacy and Digital Competence*, *1*(1), 40–60.

Kaelber, D. C., Jha, A. K., Johnston, D., Middleton, B., & Bates, D. W. (2008). A research agenda for personal health records (PHRs). *Journal of the American Medical Informatics Association, 15*(6), 729–736. doi:10.1197/jamia.M2547

Klecun, E. (2008). Bringing lost sheep into the fold: questioning the discourse of digital divide. *Information Technology & People, 21*(3), 267–282. doi:10.1108/09593840810896028

Livingstone, S. (2003). *The changing nature and uses of media literacy* (MEDIA@LSE Electronic Working Papers). London: London School of Economics and Political Science.

Meric, F., Bernstam, E. V., & Mirza, N. Q. (2002). Breast cancer on the World Wide Web: cross sectional survey of quality of information and popularity of Websites. *British Medical Journal, 324*, 577–581. doi:10.1136/bmj.324.7337.577

Miles, I. (1996). The Information Society: competing perspectives on the social and economic implications of information and communication technologies. In Dutton Oxford, W. H., & Peltu, M. (Eds.), *Information and communication technologies: visions and realities* (pp. 37–52). Oxford, UK: Oxford University Press.

Murray, P., Cabrer, M., Hansen, M., Paton, C., Elkin, P., & Erdley, W. (2008). Towards addressing the opportunities and challenges of Web 2.0 for health and informatics. *Yearbook of Medical Informatics*, 44–51.

NCVHS. (2006). *Personal Health Records and Personal Health Record Systems, A report and recommendations from the National Committee on Vital and Health Statistics*. Retrieved October 11, 2009, from http://www.ncvhs.hhs.gov/0602nhiirpt.pdf

Neupert, P., & Mundie, C. (2009). Personal Health Management Systems: Applying the Full Power of Software to Improve the Quality and Efficiency of Care. *Health Affairs, 28*(2), 390–392. doi:10.1377/hlthaff.28.2.390

Norman, C., & Skinner, H. (2006). eHealth literacy: Essential skills for consumer health in a networked world. *Journal of Medical Internet Research, 8*(2), e9. doi:10.2196/jmir.8.2.e9

Ofcom. (2005). Introduction to the bulletin. *Media Literacy Bulletin, September*(3).

Selwyn, N. (2003). Apart from technology: understanding people's non-use of information and communication technologies in everyday life. *Technology in Society, 25*, 99–116. doi:10.1016/S0160-791X(02)00062-3

Theofanos, M., & Mulligan, C. (2004). Empowering Patients through Access to Information. *Information Communication and Society, 7*(4), 466–490. doi:10.1080/1369118042000305601

Vascellaro, J. E., & Bulkeley, W. M. (2009, February 5). Google, IBM Promote OHRs. *Wall Street Journal.*

Webster, F. (1995). *Theories of the information society*. London: Routledge.

Wootton, R., Craig, J., & Patterson, V. (2006). *Introduction to telemedicine* (2nd ed.). London: The Royal Society of Medicine Press Ltd.

Wyatt, J., Allison, S., Donoghue, D., Horton, P., & Kearney, K. (2003). *Evaluation of CMF Funded UK online Centres*. DfES.

ENDNOTES

1. Map of Medicine visually represents a patients' journey through the health care system to allow easy allocation of relevant information. Its initial aim was for specialist knowledge to be made available to all clinicians to improve the quality of referrals. However, it is now envisaged to be more than that - as a tool to mediate a dialogue between care settings. It can also be accessed by patients to familiarise themselves with

care pathways relevant to their condition and the locality, i.e. to find out recommended treatments and use it as a starting point of discussion with their health and social care providers. Map of Medicine provides a link to National Library for Health, which can be searched.

2 The Penceil Project, "How People ENCounter E-ILiteracy" run between 2004-2006 and was funded by the UK Economic and Social Research Council under grant RES-341-25-0036 as part of its e-society program (http://penceil.lse.ac.uk/). The project partners were the London School of Economics and the National Institute of Adult and Continuing Education.

This work was previously published in International Journal of Digital Literacy and Digital Competence, Volume 1, Issue 3, edited by Antonio Cartelli, pp. 48-56, copyright 2010 by IGI Publishing (an imprint of IGI Global).

Section 4
Digital Literacy in Organizations

Chapter 14
Framework for the Experiences in Digital Literacy in the Spanish Market

C. De Pablos Heredero
Rey Juan Carlos University, Spain

ABSTRACT

The information society must be considered, above all, a society composed by people. For that reason, a social priority for the information society development should be centered in the acquisition of knowledge. To be included in the digital literacy means to have the technological capabilities that allow a person surviving in the information society. We try to offer real examples for the development of digital literacy in a variety of areas of application: education, social inclusion and firms. For that reason we describe and analyze the contribution of digital literacy to the following Spanish projects: Educared, which promotes the spread of Internet for innovation and pedagogical training amongst teachers, parents and students in primary and secondary schools; the Dana Project, which identifies good practices to reduce the digital gap based in gender; and Competic, a program offers good practices for the promotion of information and communication technologies in small and medium size firms.

INTRODUCTION

Digital literacy can be defined as "the capacity to understand and use sources of information when they are offered by a computer" (Gilster, 1997). Gutierrez Martin (2003) explains that digital literacy has more to do with the domain of ideas than with computers itself. The literacy must be considered as the ability for surviving that improves the quality of life of everyone, no matter sex, race, religion and origin (Gilster, 1997).

DOI: 10.4018/978-1-4666-0903-7.ch014

Information and communication networks (ICN) promote a more interactive civil society and this also creates new models of inequalities or divisions in the way we communicate each other (Frederick, 1993). Although the access to the information is today more universal, we can find more sophisticated systems that prohibit some accesses (Tascón, 2006). We can still find main barriers for the access to Internet: technological infrastructure,

Internet segmentation, etc., but the most important one is the lack of education. So the creation of digital literacy policies is crucial to create a more democratic society. The information society is composed by people, so the emphasis must be put on them. The information society in different countries must promote social integration and make of people active and critic users of information and communication networks. We must build a culture centered in the relationships between users. In our society users must be the information builders apart from consumers (Casacuberta, 2003).

In this paper we try to offer real examples of digital literacy in a variety of areas of application: education, social inclusion, and firms. For that reason we describe the contribution of digital literacy to the following Spanish projects, Educared, a program for promoting digital literacy in education, the Dana Project, a program for promoting a decrease in the digital divide based in genres, Competic, it is a Program that tries to offer good practices for the promotion of information and communication technologies for small and medium size firms. We have chosen two different industries that have been a priority for the development of the Spanish Information Society from the end of the nineties, education and small and medium size firms.

THE EFFECTS OF DIGITAL LITERACY IN THE SOCIETY

Literacy in a wide sense is a basic principle of any educational system. Today, the most important areas to perform literacy are the family, the school and the communication media. Digital literacy is just a part of the general literacy. As long as training actions are taking place for the development of literacy, they should also be considered for digital literacy. In this sense we define digital literacy as a group of training actions driven to the development of technical, social and ethical abilities related to the use of information and communication technologies, organized by Institutions, Associations, NGOs, and so forth (Travieso & Planella, 2008, p. 3).

The digital literacy requires of a degree of organization and systematization that is assumed by the educational Institutions, specially the school. However it should be also provided in an informal way by the family and by the communication media. As we have mentioned before, it is just a part of the general literacy in its multiple aspects.

Digital literacy must not only be provided by technologists since literacy is not only provided by linguistics, writers or book editors. In this sense, two kind of basic actions should be provided,

- Teachers working on the compulsory education in the first years of life should be trained in the possibilities and use of information and communication technologies
- Older persons should be permanently trained in information and communication technologies.

The Public Administrations are promoting the use of electronic services for improving their daily relationships with citizens and firms. In this sense they are offering a great opportunity for citizens to increase their computer abilities. The local portals are becoming each time more a key source of information.

Electronic government apart from using ICT services for improving citizen relationships, should position customers in the heart of all we do and build the access to services (Kavan et al., 1999; Evangelidis, 2005).

Some of the initial studies in digital literacy have been focused in e-governance (Marche and McNiven, 2003), critical success factors (Siau & Long, 2004; Ke & Wei, 2004) and Balanced Scorecard (Gueorguiev et al., 2005). Although there might be many factors of risk affecting the projects (Evangelidis, 2005), there are lots of benefits derived from the initiatives of electronic governance by including an increase in the efficiency of manual tasks, fast online responses and increases in organizational competitiveness in the public sector. The electronic government helps to create and reinforce the trust of citizens in new information and communication technologies (OECD, 2003).

THE NEED OF INFORMATION POLICIES IN THE NEW GLOBAL SOCIETY

Hill (1995) explains how the information policies must control the capacity and freedom to acquire, keep, use and transmit the information. This author takes into account the economic, social and cultural contexts implied in the planning and development of these policies.

Other authors support that the main role of an information policy is providing the legal and institutional framework where the interchange of information can be possible. Daniel (2000) thinks that an information policy is the group of formal and informal rules that restrict and promote flows of information. For this author, an information policy includes: literacy, privacy in the distribution of the information, freedom for the access to information and protection of the personal privacy and intellectual rights.

There are not good or bad policies, it depends on the compromise assumed by the different interests independently of the way they are defined. The use and access to information are key aspects in the new globalised society. The universal character of the information has driven to different countries to cooperate in this issue. Many countries have created groups of experts to analyze the situation and propose strategies aimed to increase the information society degree. This is the trend followed by the European Union where different Information Society plans, projects and actions are promoted. Spain has prioritized for the building of the information society two sectors, education and small and medium size firms.

The difference between poor and rich countries, developed and underdeveloped ones has been stressed by the availability and use of information and communication technologies. This way we can speak of info-rich and info-poor countries. The political profile of the information is each time more intensive, so we can define geographic areas according their informative capacity.

To avoid these differences a group of alternatives have emerged in disperse geographical areas. For example, in Europe the eEurope initiative: an information society for everyone was created in 1999 with the approval of the European Commission. The objective of this initiative was to accelerate the implementation of new digital technologies in Europe to warranty that all the Europeans can have the needed abilities (new literacy) to use them. The main motive to promote this initiative was the belief that the application of ICT is a main factor for the sustainable development of a "new economy" or an "electronic economy" in Europe. The Spanish government following the European trend has designed a similar information policy firstly named INFOXXI, an Information Society for everyone. Today it is the AVANZA Plan.

SPANISH PROJECTS FOR DIGITAL LITERACY

The Educared Project

Educared is a program promoted by the Telefónica Foundation and a great number of educative organizations.

Educared was created 10 years ago and it tries to generalize Internet as a tool for innovation and pedagogical training amongst teachers, parents and students at Primary and High degree Schools. 12.000 Spanish educational centers take part in the network. They held each two years a conference.(See Figure 1)

Educared, as a place for the analysis of the implications of the use of information and communication technologies at school, promotes the research in this field by using different thematic workgroups.

Figure 1. Educared web page (retrieved June 6, 2009, from http://www.educared.es)

- The role of the parents in the new educational environment
- Profession and teaching: the new profile of the professor
- New challenges for the management of the centers
- Contents, methodologies and tools for the network in the school

The areas of work in the net where created in 2003 as a formula to promote the debate on the new opportunities that information and communication technologies offer to identify strategies that allow the program to accomplish its mission: to offer to the educational community ideas, formulas and resources to help them in the task of implementing ICT in the classes.

For example the first group, the role of the parents in the new educational environment, counts on with the collaboration of experts that have prepared an interactive guide to enable the feedback of the parents worried about the presence of a computer in house and the use that students can make of it.

The main objectives of this group are:

- To stress the importance that the ICT have acquired in the education of children and youngsters in the last years.
- To make families know about the dangers of Internet
- To concern about the importance to prevent risks in Internet
- To offer proper tools to educate in Internet
- To promote responsible attitudes in the screen
- To facilitate the debate on the relationship between values and Internet.

By using a group of tools, role playing, screens, etc. the group tries to be focused in the following facts and concepts and uses the adequate procedures to promote attitudes, values and rules (See Table 1).

Four work dynamics are offered to achieve the main objectives of the group in this concrete issue. We show some of them as example:

Table 1. Tools for promoting digital literacy

Facts and concepts	Procedures	Attitudes, values and rules
✓ Internet as a source of danger ✓ Internet as a source of knowledge ✓ Internet as a community metaphor	✓ Capacity of analysis ✓ The promotion of the critic point of view ✓ Effectiveness and proper use of the network	✓ Values and misconceptions in the network ✓ To educate in the mutual respect and tolerance ✓ To consider the rights and duties of the "small size users" in the network

Dynamic one: behind the screen (20 minutes)

The main objectives of this dynamic are,

- To know the basic technical aspects required to enter and move in the chat
- To offer some risks of the Internet
- To persuade families of the need to educate in the responsibility and use of Internet
- To see Internet as a source of knowledge and find interesting contacts

Dynamic two: under the skin (20 minutes)

The main objectives of the dynamic are,

- To have a view of the relationship between own feelings and emotions with the network
- To be aware of the consequences of our acts in other persons taking part in the virtual community
- To promote responsibilities amongst people in Internet
- To promote empathy in a virtual society

Dynamic three: reasons of weight (30 minutes)

The main objectives of this dynamic are,

- To make people understand Internet from different points of view
- To motivate for the critic reflection
- To promote the reflection about the use of the network at home from the own reality, further theoretical or stereotyped visions

Dynamic four: without time and barriers, but with values and emotional intelligence

We are social animals, by nature. We have always lived in community and Internet is another way of keeping in touch and share experiences in the global community.

The idea is to offer a global debate in the following questions,

- If we do not allow children go on their own at school, why do they go on their own to a chat?
- If we want to meet their friends at school, why do we not try to know their virtual friends?
- If we offer them some values and ethical contents in the "real live", why do we not offer them concrete examples via Internet?
- Can we educate for the respect, tolerance and solidarity in Internet?
- Do I dedicate enough time to my children?
- In case I do not count on with too much time, how can be my time of quality?

The idea is to offer knowledge, expert points of view or own experiences on these issues.

This dynamic is based in a group of guided questions and spontaneous answers. Each participant must offer his or her own experience to the group and his/her feelings facing the rest of the people that he or she is interacting with, and they must search inside them information about the education and values we should transmit to our children to avoid the risks and promote the richness of the Internet.

The person in charge of the activity offers the following questions, what have you felt?

What do you think other people have felt?

Once all the members of the group have taken part, it is important to offer a debate on the implications that at an emotional level can cause a good or bad experience in the chart, specially in the childhood and adolescence

Educared is divided in the following areas of work

- Educational resources, where we can find services for professors, innovative experiences to share, and suggestions on how to interact with Internet for teaching-learning purposes, free software resources to use in educative contexts, etc.
- Activities, events to perform (for example conferences where the results of the network are presented, etc).
- Education in values, where we can find some recommendations for promoting good and health habits in education.
- Virtual community, a space of the interchange of information amongst parents and professors
- Tools and services, where some resources for educational purposes are offered, work tools, web mail, etc.
- Training, where some tools and special recommendations for training in a virtual context are shown, innovative experiences, teaching to learn (for example a school for learning how to make the best of new technologies, etc).
- News, where updated information is offered (for example, information in educational laws, prices, press bulletins, etc).

Eucared has recently developed an important study about the profile of the teacher in the XXI century and his/her relationship with information and communication technologies (Educared, 2008).

For that objective a questionnaire realized in 389 primary and secondary schools in Spain, distributed in all the geography has been applied. The main objectives of the study were the following ones,

- To analyze the profile of the teacher using ICT for teaching-learning objectives
- To find out the knowledge and capabilities of teachers in ICT
- To know about the use that teachers make of ICT
- To know about the ICT competences of the teachers

Amongst the main results offered by the study, we can stress, that that profile of the participant teachers are mainly females. There are still 7% of teachers that do not have an Internet connection at home,

1. Knowledge and training of the teachers in ICT tools

They have doubled the use of other services as chat and email lists (57.5%) in comparison with the results obtained in 2005 (27.7%).More than half of the surveyed recognize to have ICT knowledge at a level of user. A 28.3% recognize to have a very good level in ICT, 12.7% consider they have a low level of knowledge and a 5.8% consider themselves experts. Only a 2.1% of teachers consider they do not need to be trained in ICT

2. Use of ICT by teachers

The most typical use is for searching information in Internet (96.2%) and email services (90.6%). They use Internet for the performance of activities (37.1%), access to the forums (34%), publication of contents (33%), web design (25%), simulations (15.1%) or chat (12.8%).

The subjects using more Internet are mathematics (27.2%), knowledge of the environment (21.6%), languages (20.8%) and computing (20.8%).

3. ICT competences of the teachers

Three out of four teachers (78.7%) access to the sources of information and resources in ICT support. A 63.9% integrates ICT resources in the training programs in their centre. A 56.7% of teachers identify ICT resources applied to their subject and designs didactic explanations applied to classes. A 50.6% of teachers teach students basic notions about the use of ICT

A 49.4% promotes strategies for self-learning in students. A 39% of teachers offer students the performance of collaborative projects in ICT support by using Internet sources of information and with the help of distance communication channels. 35.7% uses basic applications of programs for the edition and publishing of web pages to realize didactic applications based in the use of web pages.

The Dana Project

The Dana project started in 2006. It is about the inequality of possibilities for men and women when they access to information. The digital divide based in genre seems to stress the existence of inequalities when accessing to some professions and employments. In the same way, the differences in the use of information and communication technologies contributes to make wider the professional differences between both sexes and their consequences in terms of salaries, labor stability, possibilities of promotion and equal opportunities. (See Figure 2)

Spain is one of the European countries that present a higher distance percentage between men and women in the use of Internet. However amongst the Spanish Internet users under 30 years, the percentage of women is higher than the men, according to the last General Study on Internet (GSI). The digital genre divide has the logical negative social implications. Women present lower rates of activity and employment, her salaries are lower too and this makes it difficult to acquire computer equipments and the budgeting to Internet access. The biggest part of women work in less computerized environments (education, health and social services).

Some of the implications of the digital divide based in genre are the following ones,

Figure 2. The Dana project web page (retrieved June 6, 2009, from http://www.danaproject.es)

1. The differences of professional and labor profiles between men and women in general and its consequences in terms of salaries, employment stability, promotion and equal opportunities.
2. A lack of use of the ICT to correct the genre problems. As for example, the telework practices at home in maternity times, advanced communications, responses to specific problems (genre violence, training, and so on.).
3. A delay in the development of the electronic commerce.

The SIGIS3 Report in 2004, offers four reasons explaining why women must be motivated to participate in the information and communication technologies sector,

- Justice, women must not be excluded of an opportunity to contribute and influence in a growing technology for all the society environments
- The equality of opportunities. Women have the right to benefit from the opportunities offered by the ICT market
- Lost of talents, it we do not consider women capabilities we miss their contribution.
- Labor market, the women can contribute to the employment by being trained in the use of ICT.

The main objective of the Dana project consists of identifying good practices, strategies and policies of regional authorities driven to the reduction of the digital divide based in genre.

In the Dana project a group of experts is working in the identification of a series of indexes that measure the impact of the strategies and regional policies directed to the reduction of the digital divide based in genre. In this sense, three different methods for measuring are being identified,

4. The quantitative method, in this category the identification and description of surveys or quantitative studies on ICT that have been used to measure de access and the use of ICT by women.
5. The qualitative method, by trying to identify different actions that offer us information about the state of the art of the digital divide (expert systems, forums, etc.)
6. Evaluation of policies and initiatives of e-inclusion/information society dedicated to evaluate the equality in genre. The main objective consists of identifying the efforts dedicated to the evaluation of policies related to the reduction of the digital divide based in genre. Besides, we can find evaluations related with the industry policies that are important from the inclusion point of view, for example, e-government, e-learning, e-health.

The Competic Project

The Competic project (Competing by using information and communication technologies) helps small and medium size firms to take advantage of the use of information and communication technologies. The program started 10 years ago and 4.560 SMEs have benefit today from it.

The Competic project has been selected by the European Union as an example of good practices in the area of digital literacy and promotion of the use of information and communication technologies in Small and Medium Size firms. Competic is known in Europe in the framework of other three projects FOCUS, I-AFIEL and SPREAD. FOCUS

FOCUS is a project in the EU that tries to interchange good practices in the field of information and communication technologies by small and medium size firms. FOCUS enables the interchange of good practices in the policies developed in the area of ICT. The Competic program has been presented by FOCUS as an example to follow in the promotion of information and communication technologies in small and medium size firms. The program offers to firms the access to free services, training, consulting services, financial support for connectivity and the promotion of electronic commerce in the European Union.

The main objective of the project is to increase the productivity and competitiveness of small and medium size firms in Spain. It has been elected the "project of the month" in the September number of the e-learning portal in Europe, the European Commission portal that promotes the use of ICT for permanent learning.

i-AFIEL

This project is co-ordinated by the Barcelona Generalitat through the General Direction of the Public Administrations and co-funded by the e-learning project in the European Union. There are a group of partners collaborating in this project amongst others, Spain, Italy and the United Kingdom.

This project is centered on the analysis of innovative methods for the inclusion of anyone interested in electronic learning.

The main product of the project is a guide of the best practices that show the experience of the partners in the project in digital literacy, specially centered in a group of people and organizations presenting more risk in the digital divide.

SPREAD

SPREAD is a strategic guide showing different initiatives of digital literacy in Europe. It is a guide of excellence in the planning and managing of sustainable actions in digital literacy at a great scale. It is offered to all the national, regional and international institutions that finance, initiate or co-ordinate projects to consolidate the digital literacy and enables the platform and specific support to evaluate, plan and manage digital programs at great scale.

In the framework of this program, the network is shared with managers of all Europe.

The Spread Guide has been elaborated by using open source tools as the wiki, creating a collaborative environment of work and showing how the Public Administration can be an example for the modernization of firms.

This project also offers the vision of the e-learning program in the European Commission that attempts to mobilize to the economic and social actors with the main objective to make it possible the Information Society designed in the Lisbon strategy.

The main objective of Competic is to improve the competitiveness of the Spanish firms, by using in a clever way the opportunities offered by information and communication technologies. (See Figure 3)

For this purpose it tries,

- to generate a climate for the application and absorption of the knowledge and innovation in ICT in firms in Spain
- to promote the development of the human capital in Spanish firms by paying attention to the training based in a continuum learning of the possibilities that information and communication technologies offer
- to avoid the "digital divide" in industries and firms in Spain
- to make the presence of Internet possible in our firms so that they can improve their marketing efforts and offer new products or services

CONCLUSION

Information and communication technologies allow information be distributed everywhere. This makes possible a change in the relationships of power and, therefore it offers an opportunity to improve the position of those in a first situation of disadvantage.

Figure 3. The Competic Project main page (retrieved June 6, 2009 from http://www.danaproject.es)

The life long learning is already a pre-requisite in the information society. The training in information and communication technologies is part of the needed permanent training for any person, which due to professional or personal reasons, for working or leisure time needs to manipulate interactive multimedia documents in digital formats. Maybe we should demystify a little the idea that the digital literacy is something new and revolutionary. It just means the needed training to live, work, enjoy, understand and express oneself in the information society. This training apart of being a part of the informal education nowadays, it must be acquired during the formal education and in the activities that are part of the non-formal education.

The digital literacy actions can remove social exclusion (Finquelievich, 2002; Warschauer, 2003). Information and communication technologies can promote the creation of networks that improve the collaborative work and the social development.

In general, it is easier to find quantitative data about the information society development in different regions that qualitative information. Real cases can offer us a more objective view on habits and social transformation in digital literacy terms. Analyzing different cases and projects performed for increasing digital literacy in various areas, can offer us a solid base to extrapolate the main drivers and motivators for explaining benefits and social welfare.

For that reason in the present article we have offered a description of different experiences carried up to now on digital literacy in the Spanish market. We have chosen those areas that have mainly been prioritized in the Spanish information society policies from the nineties, education, social inclusion and small and medium size firms since they mean a 90% of the firms operating in the Spanish market (COTEC, 2008).

Following this idea we have described the contribution of digital literacy to the following Spanish projects.

Educared, a program sponsored by the Spanish Telefonica Foundation, and the most important associations taking part in educational actions. It tries to promote the spread of Internet as the main tool for innovation and pedagogical training amongst teachers, parents and students in primary and secondary schools. 12.000 Spanish Centers take part in this program.

The Dana Project tries to identify good practices and extrapolate a group of common indicators to measure the impact of the strategies and policies of regional authorities to reduce the digital gap based in gender. Some actions and programs that motivate the participation of women in the Information Society are put into action.

Competic, it is a Program that tries to offer good practices and the promotion of information and communication technologies for small and medium size firms. It is subdivided in three main projects, awarded by the European Commission. Amongst them, we find the Focus project that makes possible the interchange of good practices in policies realized in the EBSN (European Network for the promotion of electronic commerce in Small and Medium Size firms)

From the three experiences shown, we can conclude that digital literacy efforts must not only be focused on the achievement of a group of basic skills for manipulating software and communication networks. The examples we have offered here are equally centered on:

- Providing the knowledge on the languages that are part of the interactive multimedia documents and the way they are integrated.
- Offering a way to use the most common tools and techniques for the processing of information
- Promoting the evaluation and the social and cultural implications of the new multimedia technologies
- Enabling a responsible attitude for spreading information in democratic communication contexts

Most countries in the European Union have emulated different initiatives first shown in the Global Information Infrastructure performed by the Clinton government in the United States at the end of the eighties. All of them try to perform the human right to the information. If the technology and the information do not reach everyone, the globalization offers a risk to increase the inequalities. For these reasons it is important to reinforce new policies to achieve a democratic spirit

REFERENCES

Bangemann Report. (1994). *Europe and the global information society. Recommendations to the European Council, Brussels*. Retrieved October 14, 2001, from http://www2.echo.lu/eudocs/en/bangemann.html

Casacubierta, D. (2003). *Collective creation*. Barcelona, Spain: Gedisa.

Daniel, E. (2000). *Information policy*. Chapell Hill, NC: University of North Carolina, School of Information and Library Science. Retrieved June 25, 2000, from http://ils.unc.edu/daniel/infopolicy.html

Delors. (2003). *White paper on growth, competitiveness and employment: the challenges and ways forward into the 21st century*. Retrieved November 17, 2003, from http://europa.eu.int/en/record/white/c93700/contents.html

Educared. (2008). *The profile of the teachers using ICT for teaching-learning processes*. Retrieved October 25, 2008, from http://www.educared.net

Evangelidis, A. (2005). FRAMES – a risk assessment framework for e-services. *Electronic Journal of E-Government, 3*(1).

Finquelievich, S. (2002). *Global actions for the social inclusion in the information society: From consumers to citizens*. Retrieved November 26, 2007, from http://www.links.org.ar/infoteca/accionesglobales paralainclusión.rtf

Frederick, H. (1993). *Computer networks and the emergence of global civil society: The case of the Association for Progressive Communications (APC)*. Retrieved 02 January 2, 2008, from http://w2.eff.org/Activism/global_civil_soc_networks.paper

Gilster, P. (1997). *Digital literacy*. New York: Wiley.

Gueorguiev, I., Dimitrova, S., Komitsha, M., Traykor, H., & Spassov, K. (2005). Balance Scorecard based management information system – a potential for public monitoring and good governance advancement. *Electronic Journal of E-Government*, *3*(1).

Gutierrez Martín, A. (2003). *Digital literacy: Some more than computers*. Barcelona, Spain: Gedisa.

Hill, M. (1995). Information policies: Premonitions and prospects. *Journal of Information Science*, *21*(4), 279. doi:10.1177/016555159502100403

InfoXXI. (2000). *The information society for everyone*. Special Commission for the Development of the Information Society in Spain. Retrieved March 15, 2004, from http://infoxxi.min.es/Documentos/infoxxi.pdf

Kavan, B., O'Hara, M., Patterson, E., & Bostrom, R. (1999). Excellence in client/server information system implementations: Understanding the STS Connection. *Management Decision*, *37*(3), 295–301. doi:10.1108/00251749910264532

Ke, W., & Wei, K. (2004). Succesful e-government in Singapore. *Communications of the ACM*, *47*(6), 95–99. doi:10.1145/990680.990687

Marche, S., & McNiven, J. (2003). E-government and e-governance: The future isn't what it used to be. *Canadian Journal of Administrative Sciences*, *20*(1), 74–86.

Ministry of Education, Spain. (n.d.). *IDOC Plan, a framework for acting from a national perspective, 1984-86*. Madrid, Spain: Author.

Moore, N. (1993). Information policy and strategic development. *Aslib Proceedings*, *45*(11/12), 281–285. doi:10.1108/eb051334

Report, C. O. T. E. C. (2008). *The situation of innovation in Spanish firms*. Madrid, Spain: COTEC Foundation.

Siau, K., & Long, Y. (2004). *Factors impacting e-government development*. Paper presented at the Twenty-Fifth International Conference on Information Systems, ICIS, Poland.

Tascón, M. (2006). Development of a place for the information society. In R. Casado (Ed.), *Keys for digital literacy. Seminar on digital literacy* (pp. 187-194). Madrid, Spain: Telefónica Foundation. Retrieved December 18, 2006, from http://sociedaddelainformación.telefónica.es/documentos/articulos/clavesdelaalfabetizacióndigital.pdf

Travieso, J. L., & Planellá, J. (2008). Digital literacy as a factor for social inclusion: A critical view. *Review on the Knowledge Society*, *6*, 1–7.

UNESCO. (2000). *Creating a new UNESCO Programme for a just and free information society with universal benefits*. Retrieved November 23, 2002, from http://www.unesco.org/webworld/future/index.shtml

Warschauer, M. (2003). *Technology and social inclusion: Rethinking the digital divide*. Cambridge, MA: MIT Press.

This work was previously published in International Journal of Digital Literacy and Digital Competence, Volume 1, Issue 1, edited by Antonio Cartelli, pp. 61-76, copyright 2010 by IGI Publishing (an imprint of IGI Global).

Chapter 15
Frameworks for the Benchmarking of Digital and Knowledge Management Best Practice in SME and Organizations

Antonio Cartelli
University of Cassino, Italy

ABSTRACT

The paper discusses the impact of IT/ICT on society by analyzing the effects it has on subjects and organizations. The recent proposal of frameworks for digital competence assessment and the construction of suitable instruments helping students in the acquisition of this competence are the main reason for the transfer to Small and Medium Enterprises (SMEs). In this paper, the author compares knowledge phenomena in subjects with the strategies of knowledge management in the organizations. A framework for benchmarking best practices in SME and organizations is also given on the basis of the results obtained in virtual campuses. The author presents instruments for the acquisition of further information from all stakeholders, and possible interventions toward the improvement of digital processes in SMEs and organizations are discussed.

INTRODUCTION

It is well known that the spreading of computing, computer networks and especially the Internet have produced a revolution in our way of living during the last forty years; they have also deeply transformed our intrapersonal and interpersonal relations and have highly influenced the structure and management of processes in corporate and organizations.

As regards mankind it is today evident the need for a new literacy, named digital literacy, letting people be the citizens of the knowledge society. Its most accepted definition is as follows: "Digital Literacy is the awareness, attitude and ability of individuals to appropriately use digital

DOI: 10.4018/978-1-4666-0903-7.ch015

tools and facilities to identify, access, manage, integrate, evaluate, analyse and synthesize digital resources, construct new knowledge, create media expressions, and communicate with others, in the context of specific life situations, in order to enable constructive social action; and to reflect upon this process" (Martin, 2005).

In the meanwhile the attention of research and institutions has focused on how people use digital resources and processes, more than on what they must know and be able to do with technologies. This new approach to the analysis of the impact of new technologies on mankind led to concentrate on the concept of competence and on the active involvement of the subjects in their interaction with digital equipments, without forgetting their representations of reality, their knowledge and skills (Le Boterf, 1990).

On this side the European Commission issued in 2005 the Recommendation on key competences for lifelong learning and stated the features of the digital competence, the fourth among them (Commission of the European Parliament, 2005). For the European Commission the digital competence is based on the confident and critical use of Information Society Technology (IST) for work, leisure and communication and is underpinned by basic skills in ICT: that is the use of computers to retrieve, assess, store, produce, present and exchange information, and to communicate and participate in collaborative networks via the Internet.

The above issues led to the definition of suitable strategies to help students develop sound digital competence. Among them the proposal of a framework for digital competence assessment must be remarked (Cartelli et al., 2010); although all the features of the framework reported in Figure 1 still need to be defined in its details, the results obtained until now from the answers to the questionnaire built under the guidelines of the framework confirm the hypothesized model.

Evolutionary phenomena for the description of the impact of digital equipments on human beings and activities can be easily detected also in corporate and organizations; it is well known in fact that computers, networks and the Internet deeply modified production and organization processes.

On the above bases, starting from the '90s, the main ideas of knowledge management were given (Wiig, 1993) and they aimed at storing, describing, retrieving and communicating data and information. In this first phase, called first generation knowledge management, the information technology was the key factor for the success of a firm, due to its ability in the capture, management and communication of organizational knowledge.

The second phase of knowledge management has focused on the sharing, within the organization, of the professional knowledge that each subject builds up, and on the construction of communities (i.e., especially to communities of practices). They are considered the key factor for organizational growth and corporate/organization success.

The main problem with the planning and use of knowledge management strategies is the relevant amount of funds and resources which limit their presence and use to big industries and organizations.

It is well known, on the contrary, that most part of work force and human capital can be found in small and medium corporate and organizations (i.e., Small and Medium Enterprises, with a number of employees between 25 and 500 persons, as reported in the *Recommendation 2003/361/EC: SME Definition*).

As a consequence the following questions ask for an answer:

Is it possible to define strategies to be shared among SME to let them access the knowledge management resources needed in the global marked and in today society?

Is there any connection between the problem of digital competence assessment in students, and more generally in individuals, and the SME and organizations "competence" in the

Figure 1. The digital competence assessment framework for students

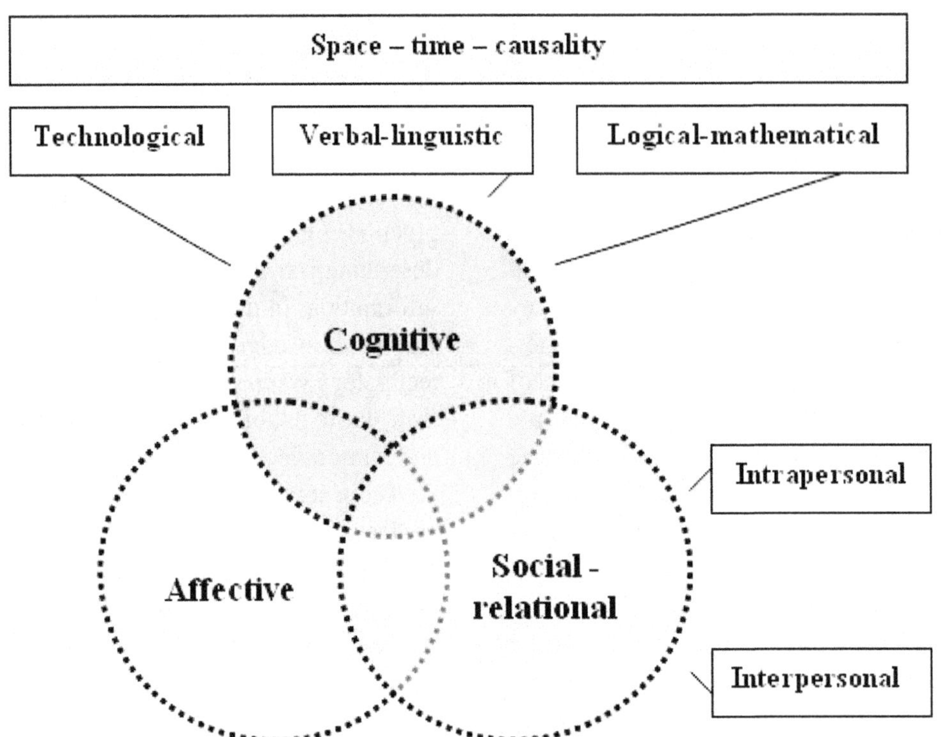

access and use of knowledge management strategies?

Is there any theoretical principle which can explain the presence of common bases in both the above phenomena?

In the next sections a first attempt of giving an answer the above questions will be made.

TOOLS FOR KNOWLEDGE MANAGEMENT IN SME AND THE PROBLEM OF THE "COMPETENCES"

First of all the third question reported at the end of the former section will be analyzed. An answer for it can be found in the author's hypothesis on the tri-partition of knowledge construction phenomena. By following this idea subjects, communities and the whole society, autonomously develop their knowledge and use different instruments and methods to do it. They also interact one another to exchange and communicate their knowledge and share it, as reported in figure 2 (Cartelli, 2008a).

The above ideas follow the tradition of studies on learning organizations, started from Nonaka and Takeuchi (1995), and consider the transformation of the people's tacit knowledge in explicit knowledge and its capture and acquisition in the knowledge capital of the organization.

Main ideas underlying the schema in Figure 2 are:

- A multi-level structure for knowledge construction and evolution can be hypothesized;
- Mankind knowledge comes from three different contributions: the individual, the community and the society; ICT acts at

Figure 2. Scheme for the analysis of knowledge construction phenomena

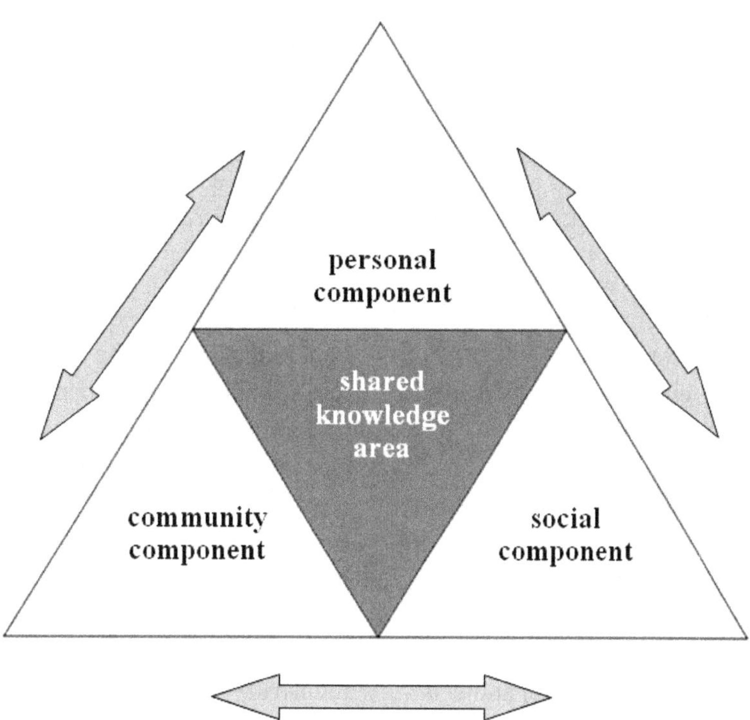

all three levels while modifying the ways knowledge is built up (Cartelli, 2008a),

- Management Information Systems (MISs) can be used for data management and processes' implementation at all levels and are good instruments for corporate knowledge management and personal knowledge management (Cartelli, 2009),
- MISs can help both corporate and people in the development of strategies helping them in overcoming difficulties; this phenomenon is quite obvious for corporate and organizations but can be easily understood also for subjects, when they work on themselves to the development of personal strategic thinking (Cartelli, 2009).

The last two statements can be seen as the result of the application of a new pedagogical paradigm, called "implementation of practices by means of IT/ICT", which is based on the use of online information systems for the creation of communities of learning and practice; these systems implement the processes used by scholars and professionals in analyzing phenomena and collecting information; they also let students, and more generally people, learn to work in a similar way (Cartelli 2008b).

The features that the new paradigm has in common with other well known methods are reported in the table below:

The differences between the new method and the others can be summarized as follow:

a) As regards cognitive apprenticeship, now no coach or tutor is needed; otherwise stated no one has a more relevant role in the community with respect to other people,
b) With respect to peer learning, now the cognitive experience is the result of two different interaction: - with the system implementing the practice of the scientific/professional

Table 1. Features the paradigm "the implementation of practices with the IT/ICT" has in common with other paradigms

Paradigm	Common feature
Cognitive apprenticeship	The guided approach to experience
Peer learning	Both are based on the subjects in the community
Simulation in virtual environments	The proposal of a virtual context within which experiences can be carried out

community, - with other people working on the same information system,

c) At last no virtual environment physically reproducing the context is made up.

Otherwise stated, notwithstanding the similarities, this method is different from classical and modern educational methods and can be included among the new approaches to ICT use in education.

It is important to remark here that the above method is a knowledge method for the subjects involved in the use of the MISs, but it is also an instrument for the development of knowledge in the corporate or the organization within which the MIS works.

The main conclusion from the above remarks is the answer we can give to the last question in the introduction:

a) Knowledge phenomena in subjects, communities and organizations are based on different instruments and methods but interact with each other and are today deeply based on the IT/ICT use,
b) MISs, among new technological instruments, have a relevant role in the management of knowledge processes because they work both on personal and organizational sides.

If MISs are the elements connecting subject and organization knowledge phenomena, what is playing the role of the competences of the subjects in the organizations? Is there the need of talking of assessment?

The experience of recent years shows that benchmarking is the process of comparing one's business/organizational processes and performance metrics to corporate bests and/or best practices from other corporate. Dimensions typically measured are quality, time, and cost. Improvements from learning mean doing things better, faster, and cheaper.

Benchmarking involves management identifying the best firms in their industry, or any other industry where similar processes exist, and comparing the results and processes of those studied (the "targets") to one's own results and processes to learn how well the targets perform and, more importantly, how they do it.

The application of the above considerations led the author to the development of a framework for benchmarking digital best practices in virtual campuses. This model was first made up within the European funded project "Promoting Best Practices in Virtual Campuses (PBP-VC)" which came after different European virtual university/campus initiatives. They were hindered by much of the hype and unrealistic expectations that plagued eLearning and virtual campus initiatives in the mid-late 90s. It was clear in fact that after the failure of a number of high profile experiences across the world (e.g. California Virtual University, Danish Virtual University), the sustainability of eLearning and virtual campus initiatives needed that stakeholders understood how new models of teaching and learning could transform the institution and how they could be used to enhance knowledge construction, flexibility and inclusiveness.

The PBP-VC project aimed at the understanding of the key issues and critical success factors underlying the implementation of virtual campuses. It produced a practical framework to help guide the creation of best practice in virtual campuses and collected examples of best practice, case studies and use case scenarios. Among its most important results there were:

a) Raised awareness of the issues and approaches to successful and sustainable virtual campuses;
b) Raised awareness of the institutional transformation induced by the development and application of new models of teaching and learning (Cartelli et al., 2008).

On the basis of the above results and considering the similarity of Virtual Campuses with SME and organizations the author decided to apply that framework to the new case of SME and organizations, and in next section the way it has been performed is explained.

THE FRAMEWORK FOR BENCHMARKING DIGITAL BEST PRACTICES IN SME (SMALL MEDIUM ENTERPRISES) AND ORGANIZATIONS

In this section the model developed within the European project Promoting Best Practices in Virtual Campuses (PBP-VC) is used to create a new framework for the more general situation of benchmarking digital best practices in Small and Medium Enterprises (SME) and organizations.

First of all the model aims at:

- A better understanding of the key issues and critical success factors underlying the implementation of digital and knowledge management processes in SME and organizations;
- The construction of a practical framework to help guide the process of creating best practice in SME and organization;
- Publishing the examples of best practice, case studies and use case scenarios;
- Raising the awareness of the issues and approaches to creating successful and sustainable digital processes and knowledge management in SME and organizations;
- Raising the awareness of how digital transformation can be brought about by the development and application of models of digital processes and knowledge management in SME and organizations;
- Raising the awareness of how the successful implementation of digital processes and knowledge management can contribute to the success of the SME and organization and to the increase in the quality of their products.

The elements which are translated from the old model (PBP-VC) into the new model concern the organizational issues, the technological issues, the financial issues and the consolidation issues. With respect to the Pedagogical issues reported in the former model now the Knowledge management issues are introduced.

The new framework for SME and organizations is reported in Figure 3 below.

The tentative model comprises five main areas that can be viewed as being interrelated:

1. ***Organizational Issues***
   These appear to play an important role in success and underpinning best practice and in many ways can be the most difficult issues to address since they comprise largely human/'soft' elements. Such issues include bureaucracy and administration that can differ markedly among corporate partners and cause significant problems in attempting to provide seamless, coherent experiences and exit awards, particularly when a

given project is delivered between numerous partners across international boundaries. Also related to this issue is differing government, political and legal systems which can affect important concerns such as copyright in terms of ownership of materials and equipments that have been planned and developed. The problem of language and culture can emerge from the use of English which could be the second or third language of some of the staff. In addition, certain areas may have a cultural resistance to the use of knowledge management instruments and methods, which may lead to problems in the uptake and successful completion of supply chain and production. Also included within organizational issues are the problems relating to effective teamwork and agreeing on roles and responsibilities and ensuring that all partners work well together in achieving the same outcomes.

2. ***Technological Issues***

This issue can be problematical in situations where it might be difficult for the partners to initially agree on the adoption of common platforms and software. This can also cause problems in the integration of other functions such as data record and accounting systems. Also identified as being an important issue is the need to frequently evaluate and monitor the use of the digital systems and knowledge management platforms to ensure that staff are using them in the most effective way.

3. ***Knowledge Management Issues***

The choice of appropriate knowledge management strategies underpinning SME and organizations is of great importance since it has a big impact on the progress and experience of the work force. Therefore, it is vital that the knowledge management underpinning a SME and an organization supports and enhances the workers' externalization/internalization of knowledge in all subject area. Providing proper guidance to workers can be an important factor in underpinning success and inclusion, with some SME identifying peer support among workers being part of good practice. Also supporting knowledge management issues is ensuring the quality of the project and evaluating it on a regular basis.

4. ***Financial Issues***

If digital and knowledge management processes in SME and organization must run and be sustainable by themselves, appropriate costing methods and effective cost/benefit analysis are vital for the corporate surviving. Very little work has been conducted into determining the true costs and benefits of providing digital and knowledge management strategies and processes and whether they can be self funding and financially sustainable. Much work is needed to analyze the creation of shared MIS which can have a smaller impact on the budget of the organization.

5. ***Consolidation Issues***

It is important that the benefits achieved from the development and running of digital and knowledge management processes are not lost once the experimental period has elapsed. Therefore, consolidation issues reflect the kind of activities that can help achieve this such as developing adequate marketing and dissemination plans in order to promote the benefits of a particular project at targeted groups of key stakeholders. Furthermore the accreditation from professional bodies can determine the goodness of a project and how much its transport to other realities can be useful.

Figure 3. Framework of issues underpinning best practice in SME and organizations

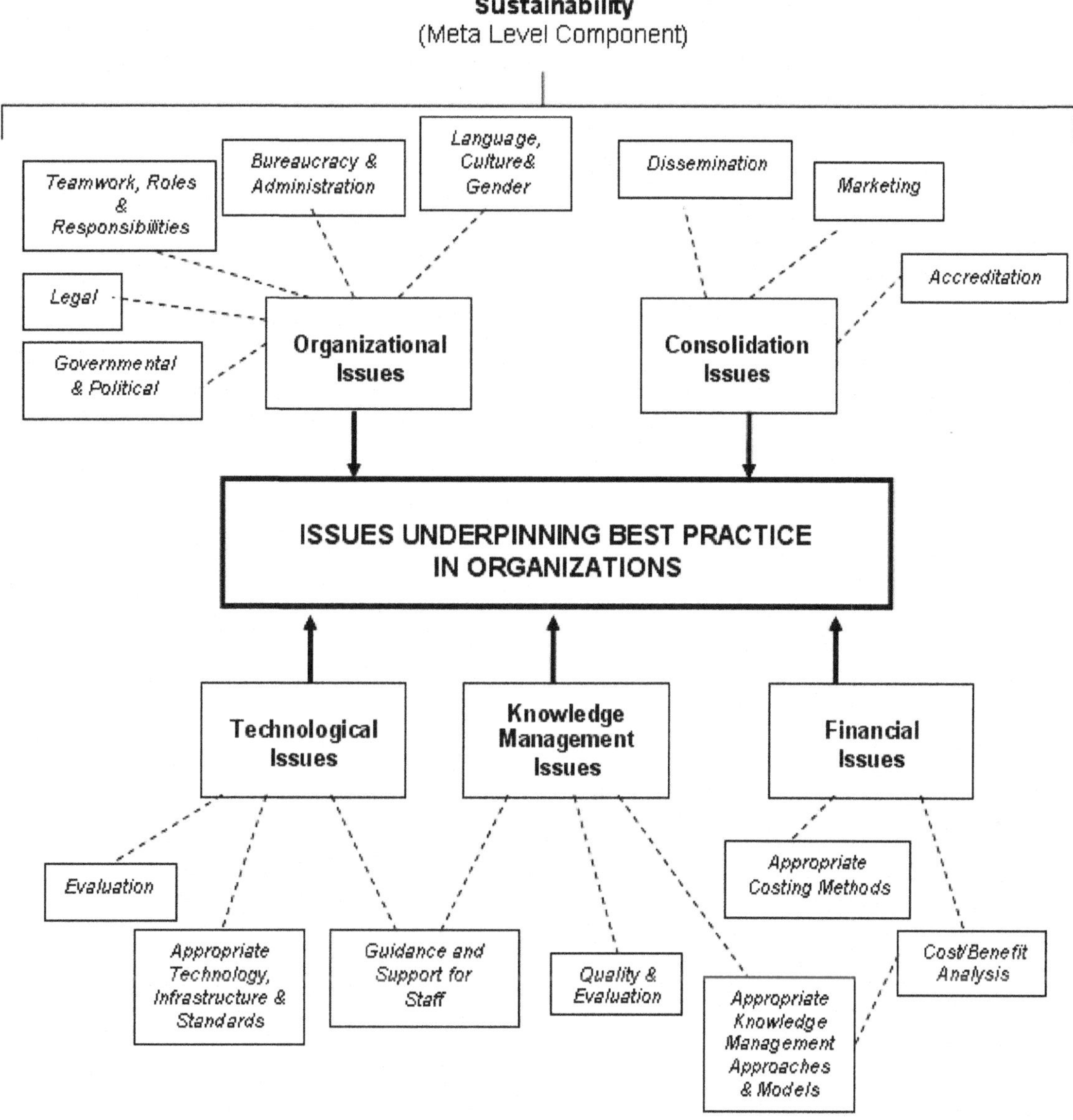

Within Figure 3, sustainability is shown as a meta-level component since it appears to overarch all of the issues rather than being a separate issue on its own. It could be argued that for a SME or organization to exhibit best practice then the concept of sustainability should run throughout all the aspects of the adoption of knowledge management strategies (i.e. organizational, technological, knowledge management, financial and consolidation).

At last it has to be noted that the tentative model in Figure 3 is far from being complete since it merely illustrates the main issues that have been identified so far from an initial investigation and application of former ideas. This reinforces the need for promoting cooperation and exchange of strategic experiences between all stakeholders within the area of use of digital resources and knowledge management systems in SME and organizations.

CONCLUSION AND FUTURE STUDIES

While remarking that the framework reported in Figure 3 needs to be improved, different experiences can be reported that show the level of interest for the introduction of information and communication technologies in SME and organizations. The COMPETIC project in Spain (Competing by using information and communication technologies), described by C. De Pablos (2010) is an example of good practice in this area.

The next step needed for the carrying out of the study is the proposal of a suitable questionnaire to a given target of SME and organizations to analyze the areas of interest and the suitability of the framework.

The questionnaire looks now the best instrument for the following reasons:

a) Its immediateness,
b) Its adaptability and portability to different situations and groups of corporate,
c) Its ease of use both on paper and electronically (due to the opportunity of being easily reviewed and modified),
d) The acquisition of feed-back information from the analysis of first answers, which can lead to the development of suitable instruments, helping SME and organizations to better understand phenomena and to overcome the difficulties they can meet in the global market.

REFERENCES

Cartelli, A. (2008a). Towards a new model for knowledge construction and evolution. In Cartelli, A., & Palma, M. (Eds.), *Encyclopedia of Information Communication Technology* (pp. 767–774). Hershey, PA: Information Science Reference.

Cartelli, A. (2008b). Is the implementation of practices with the ICT a new teaching-learning paradigm? In Cartelli, A., & Palma, M. (Eds.), *Encyclopedia of Information Communication Technology* (pp. 413–418). Hershey, PA: Information Science Reference.

Cartelli, A. (2008c, November 6-8). E-Learning and E-Citizenship Between PKM and PST. In D. Remenyi (Ed.), *Proceedings of the 7th European Conference on E-Learning (ECEL 2008)*, Agia Napa, Cyprus (Vol. 1, pp. 169-177) Reading, UK: Academic Publishing.

Cartelli, A., Dagiene, V., & Futschek, G. (2010). Bebras Contest and Digital Competence Assessment: Analysis of Frameworks. *International Journal of Digital Literacy and Digital Competence*, *1*(1), 24–39.

Cartelli, A., Stansfield, M., Connolly, T., Jimoyiannis, A., Magalhães, H., & Maillet, K. (2008). Towards the development of a New Model for Best Practice and Knowledge Construction in Virtual Campuses. *Journal of Information Technology Education*, *7*, 121–134.

De Pablos, C. (2010). Framework for the Experiences in Digital Literacy in the Spanish Market. *International Journal of Digital Literacy and Digital Competence*, 61–76.

European Parliament and Council. (2005). *Recommendation on key competences for lifelong learning*. Retrieved from http://ec.europa.eu/education/policies/2010/doc/keyrec_en.pdf

Le Boterf, G. (1990). *De la compétence: Essai sur un attracteur étrange*. Paris: Les Ed. de l'Organisation.

Martin, A. (2005). DigEuLit – a European Framework for Digital Literacy: a Progress Report. *JeLit, Journal of eLiteracy, 2*(2).

Nonaka, I., & Takeuchi, H. (1995). *The knowledge-creating company: how Japanese companies create the dynamics of innovation*. New York: Oxford University Press.

Wiig, K. (1993). *Knowledge Management Foundations: Thinking about Thinking – How People and Organizations Create, Represent, and Use Knowledge*. Arlington, TX: Schema Press.

This work was previously published in International Journal of Digital Literacy and Digital Competence, Volume 1, Issue 2, edited by Antonio Cartelli, pp. 39-47, copyright 2010 by IGI Publishing (an imprint of IGI Global).

Chapter 16
Free Software Implementation Experiences for the Promotion of the Liquid Society

C. De Pablos Heredero
Universidad Rey Juan Carlos, Spain

D. López Berzosa
Universidad de León, Spain

ABSTRACT

Information and communication technologies have changed the way in which citizens interact with Public Administrations. Digital literacy is key for the development of the Liquid Society, and Public Administrations must take the lead in promoting more efficient, universal, and user oriented public services. The migration to open source standards allows Public Administration to offer more democratic, universal, and efficient channels for establishing relationships with citizens. In this article, the authors present international experiences that show how certain Public Administrations have migrated to open source software to promote digital literacy in the contexts they are operating. The final results depend on contextual and organizational factors, including the need to change, the political support and the existence of available technological resources, the organizational climate, motivation levels of human resources, and the kind of leadership for the project or the organizational complexity. Change efforts have strategic and organizational impacts that the organization must evaluate beforehand.

INTRODUCTION

Information and communication technologies allow us the establishment of new ways of relationships never thought before. Institutions seem to be trapped in a universe where they do not clearly understand the control mechanisms (Giddens, 2002), yet they know it is going to offer them new and more efficient ways for promoting digital literacy in the "liquid society". Bauman (2004) analyses the state of the art in today's societies and establish the term "liquid modernity". It refers to the way societies adapt today to new contexts. Time and space are more relative and

DOI: 10.4018/978-1-4666-0903-7.ch016

allow us to shape new social scenarios, new ways to interrelate and to organize ourselves. Information and communication technologies allow us new possibilities to de-integrate the traditional ways we relate each other and integrate them in a different way. Liquid society is in permanent change. Institutions, Public Administrations, firms have transformed themselves and demand new ways of interaction. Public Administrations make use of ICT to promote digital literacy as "the capacity to understand and use sources of information when they are shown via a computer" (Gilster, 1997) in the liquid society. Public Administrations must make the best to implement ICT in order to improve the quality of life of everyone by removing technological and operational barriers.

Related to liquid society is the concept of Social Computing as an emergent paradigm characterized by user-centric, collaborative knowledge sharing, community-building activities using the Internet EU (2009). Social computing as an important phenomenon is now mainstream among citizenship and therefore should not be ignored by policy makers. Social computing creates new opportunities for user empowerment but also represents new threats such as digital divide or privacy concerns.

Although access to information is quite universal today, there are still some barriers either technical, cognitive (Tascón, 2006) or administrative.

A revealing case of existing administrative barriers hindering complete access to existing information is the measure that the Obama administration adopted in its early days calling for more transparent, participatory and collaborative government, USA (2009).

From a technical point of view, traditional business models of software development are failing to deliver the flexibility that modern society and electronic services require. At this point free software paradigm, as an alternative business model based on co-creation, can be an opportunity for surpassing these limits.

OPEN SOURCE AS ENABLER OF LIQUID SOCIETIES

Open source migration (F/OSS) was first applied in the sixties. In the nineties it becomes a quite consolidated business alternative. Since then, free software implementation has been studied from both, a technical point of view (Raymond, 1999; Hunter, 2006; Rossi, 2006; Berry, 2008) as well as an economic emergent possibility in the market (Lerner y Tirole, 2002; Lerner y Tirole, 2005; Riehle, 2007).

Free software migration means an efficient solution in terms of costs, specially for the public industry and in contexts demanding great technological resources as it is the case of education (Lerner & Tirole, 2002; Riehle, 2007; Lakhan y Jhunjhunwala, 2008). The implementation of free software tools promotes the innovation and the development in Public Administrations worldwide (David y Steinmueller, 1994; Shiff, 2002; Hippern y Krogh, 2003; Bitzer, 2005; Osterloh y Rota, 2007). Most experiences have just been started in the twenties and they are still in progress (Ahmed, 2005; UOC Report, 2009).

We must build a culture centered in the relationships between users. In our information society users must be the builders apart from consumers (Casacuberta, 2003). Free software developments can offer an opportunity to this fact.

We posit that open source development model can promote the development of liquid societies. Open source fosters a culture of sharing and collaboration in which users take a prominent role therefore leading innovation and technology adoption (Von Hippel, 2005).

Despite the benefits provided by free software to organizations, there are still some barriers for its use. In a recent Report published last April 2009 (EOI Report, 2009) amongst the positive effects of open source software, we find,

- It is an opportunity for firms and Public Administrations, since it implies a global technological option.

- It promotes public participation
- It decreases computing costs
- It increases possibilities to choose and optimize hardware and software products
- It offers possibilities for increasing the development of the information society

In this research we try to present real experiences on open source migration in Public Administrations worldwide. From our perspective the results can help policy makers to define public polices to promote the adoption of free software tools since it allows the maximization of the services that are offered to the final customer. This paper shows some of the results obtained in 2009 in the project "Migrafloss, migration to open source software" financed by CENATIC, A Spanish National Centre of Reference for Information and Communication Technologies".

THE EMPIRICAL ANALYSIS

The grounded theory is a qualitative method of research that tries to build theories from data collected in real scenarios (Myers, 2009). It is an inductive method that allows the production of emergent theories where some knowledge gaps are identified.

This methodology specially applies for descriptions centered in a context where organizational phenomena appear (Myers, 2007). The grounded theory has first been applied to psychology (Glaser y Strauss, 1967; Strauss y Corbin, 1990) and later in the information systems area (Orlikowski, 1991, 1993) including our area of interest, the research in open source software (Dedrick y West, 2005).

Some researchers that have studied processes for technology adoption (Venkatesh et al., 2003; Sameh e Izak, 2009) have stressed the importance for modeling user's behavior. For this present work a wider perspective is required. The adoption of free software and the upper migration to different firm's processes is going to have impacts in wide business areas and many different stakeholders can benefit from it, amongst others the final customers. Therefore, for our analysis an organizational approach is required. This approach demands not only quantitative approaches (Gonzalez-Barahona, 1991, 2004; Wheeler, 2007) but also positive ones since we lack of hypothesis around free software implementations. Contrary to traditional, hypothesis-based, research methods theory is being built as data is being processed.

We believe that a dual approach at a firm's level and macro level provides the right perspective to explain the progressive adoption of free software at firms. In total eight Public Administrations have been analyzed, please refer to Table 1.

Following Glaser and Strauss technique (1967) of theoretical sampling, the projects have been selected according to criteria of maximum variability in terms of context, size, main objective and degree of use of ICT amongst others. If we consider that there are many factors that can intervene at different levels, it is important to define concepts, categories and relationships that allow us design and emergent theory as Strauss and Corbin mention (1990).

Theoretical sampling is cumulative due to the fact that future experiences in migration add value to the existent knowledge suggesting new concepts that can be relevant for open source migration initiatives. We posit that adopting an evolutionary approach for theory building moderates the obsolescence that technical migration guides can present when disruptive technologies or new standards emerge.

Table 1. The cases analyzed

1. Munich Town Hall Germany
2. Postal Service, USA
3. Birmingham Town Hall, Great Britain
4. Zaragoza Town Hall, Spain
5. Bucarest Meteorology Service, Rumania
6. Finnish Justice Ministry, Finland
7. Brasil Education Ministry, Brasil
8. Arles Town Hall, France

Figure 1. Free software migration lifecycle

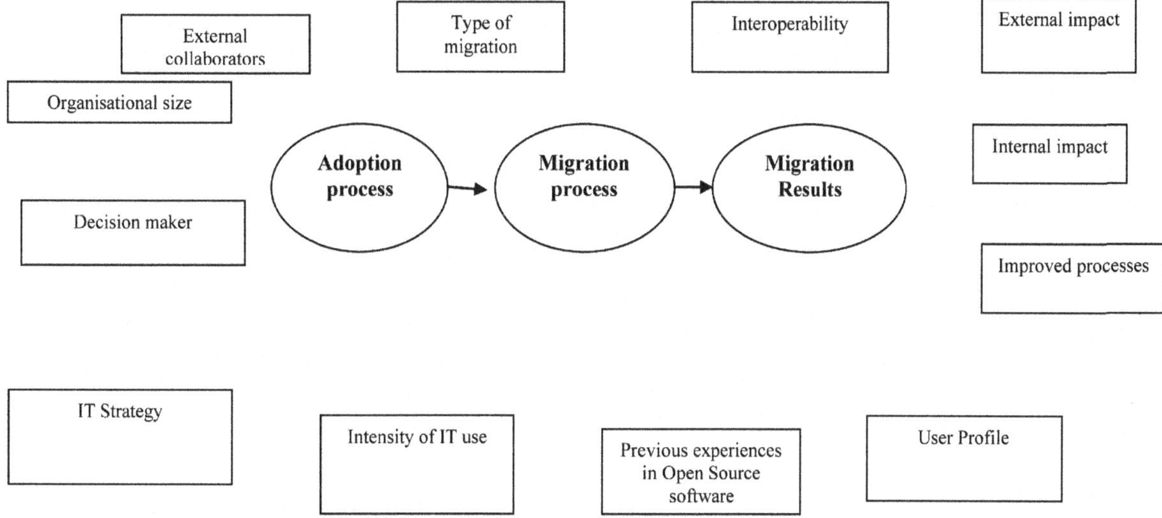

The experiences come from Public Administrations of eight different countries (Germany, USA, Great Britain, Spain, Rumania, Finland, Brasil and France). For each of them we have considered the following aspects,

1. Main objectives for the migration
2. Time estimated for the migration
3. Kind of software and migrated service
4. Cost for the migration
5. Critical success factors in the migration
6. Critical failure factors in the migration
7. The obtained results
8. The perceived benefits

The collection of data based in the grounded theory has been developed in an iterative way (Glaser & Strauss, 1967) starting by an exploratory perspective and searching afterwards for approaches more centered in the relevant aspects and structured interviews. Extensive information regarding considered experiences can be retrieved at: http://cenatic.interoperabilidad.org:8080/web/guest/administraciones-publicas

The inductive analysis searches for relevant concepts and relations amongst them. Initially the existent data are analyzed by grouping them in open coding categories (Strauss y Corbin, 1990). In a second phase, an axial coding is developed, initial categories are grouped into sub-categories that answer to questions such as: when, how, why, where and what for.

Having an intra firm perspective in mind, software migration projects are considered as internal processes for change. We believe that this approach centered on processes offers a view of real organizational structures therefore promoting its adoption by business units.

As it is shown in Figure 1, open source migration projects present three stages: the process of adoption, the migration process and the evaluation of obtained results. Each stage, or main category according to the grounded theory, entails a series of secondary categories that intervene in the migration process.

Secondary categories further refine in a progressive way the context under which the project takes place: the existence of external collaborators, the size of the firm or the existence of strategic plans

In a similar way, concepts as the interoperability (defined as the compatibility with the software running in the organization), previous experiences or internal ICT competencies moderate the following main categories: migration process and results.

THE RESULTS OF THE ANALYSIS

From our analysis we have got three different ways for the adoption of free software in Public Administrations: organizations that strive for vendor independence and therefore consider free software as a strategic asset.

Public Administrations that consider open source software as a better option than proprietary software in terms of results and new options. And last, organizations that have budgetary restrictions, and see in free software an interesting option in a typical cost analysis benefit in terms of licenses and hardware obsolescence.

First Group: Strategic Movers

In this group, the organizations have faced forced migrations due to different motives, as for example the end of the maintaining service of the previous software option or the need to decrease the costs of information and communication technologies. For this group, the removal of the barriers imposed by the provider of private software become a priority for the managers that define the strategic plans where the evolution to open source software is a priority.

These organizations tend to be big in human resources and in ICT budget. Besides they maintain specific personal dedicated to the development and support of ICT services.

Although they are intensive ICT users, they face interoperability problems amongst the working services and the resistance of users to the change in the established routines and procedures. They adopt a gradual approach in the migration of software that often includes calendars that determine years in finishing the migration. Besides, these calendars move according to the found scenarios (resistance to the change, interoperability problems, development of additional functionalities amongst others).

The migration processes in this case require of external collaborators with the technical experience and further experience in similar developments, especially in the case that the organization lacks of previous experiences or faces scenarios that challenge non interoperable ICT.

The result of the migration initiatives in these cases is positive in general in terms of improvement in the internal processes. Besides, normally positive externalities are created in other business units. The nature at a great extent of this initiatives are often reflected in the general society providing new services or improved software that is available in a public way. Clear examples in this group are the Munich Town Hall, the USA Postal Service and the Education Ministry in Brazil. Table 2 shows the typical characteristics of this group.

Second Group. Feature Seekers

In this category we often find medium and big size organizations that use in an intensive way ICT in their business processes searching for new opportunities to improve the ICT capabilities available, as for example, embedded systems, supercomputing. Examples of this group are the Birmingham Town Hall in Great Britain, The Ministry of Justice in Finland and the Zaragoza Town Hall in Spain.

The migration projects are started by internal experts that consider the advantages that can offer the new developments in software and hardware. An IT expert working in a financial Institution states "There are no fans in open source software; we search for the best solution in a context plenty of different possibilities".

Table 2. Group A. Strategic movers

Adoption process	
Organisation size	Normally big
Decisión makers	Top management
ICT strategy	Independence from provider, flexibility to specific requirements
The personal experience	High, normally there are specific units in ICT
The intensity in ICT	Great intensity, good equipment in hardware and software
External collaborators. Degree of autonomy	Often they count on them depending on their experiences and internal capabilities
Previous analysis	yes, cost and technical analysis
Migration process	
Kind of migration	Structural or key services
Previous experiences in OSS	No normally
External collaborators. Implementation	The vast majority of cases
Barriers to inter-operability	Normally high barriers due to the existent applications
The management of change	Emphasis in educational programs, gradual approaches
Business process reengineering	High, especially when there are pre-established procedures
Users base	Big
Time horizon	Years
Migration results	
Re-trials for migration	They often do not stop the started tendency
Impact in other units	Practically always
Impact in external organisations	Quite often
Objectives reached	Often reached, sometimes a re-planning of the Project is required
Improved processes	Almost always

Instead of having the technical expertise, normally they collaborate with external agents to get the specific experience.

Due to the lack of strategic nature of the affected services, the interoperability does not play an essential role. At the same time, taking into account that the final users are not experts, there is not great resistance to change.

As different from the previous category, the deadlines in the migration are maintained during months with the processes defined beforehand. The success criteria are clearly determined.

The results in this initiative are not normally transformed in the sense of producing impacts exclusively in the internal services. Table 3 shows the most frequent characteristics for this group.

Third Group. Budget Optimizers

Small and medium size Public Administrations often adopts open source software as the best option in terms of cost-benefit analysis. Normally they implement new services that are no key, by using open source software as a less cost alternative.

The typical profile is a local administrator that operates in a small and medium size organization in a market that it is not intensive in the use of ICT. Examples of this group can be the Arles Town Hall or the Bucarest Meteorology Service. Table 4 shows the most important characteristics for this group.

Table 3. Group B. Seekers for functional opportunities

Adoption process	
Firm size	Médium of big
Decision makers	Normally internal staff or technical units
The ICT strategy	Oriented to business support or new opportunities
Employee experiencies	High, normally there are specific ICT units
ICT intensity of use	Great intensity, good equipment in hardware and software
External collaborators. Degree of autonomy	Sometimes
Previous analysis	Sometimes
The Migration process	
Kind of migration	in no key services
Previous experience in OSS	Not necessarily
External collaborators. Implementation	Almost always
Barriers to interoperability	Normally it is not relevant except in applications that requires it from the legal point of view
The management of change	Procedures to make sure the lowest impact in the operations
Business process reengineering	Mínimum
Users base	Minimum
Time horizon for the migration	Months
Migration results	
Re-trials for migration	Yes, always that it is needed
Impact in other units	Minimum
Impact in external organisations	Often
Objectives reached	Yes
Improved processes	Yes, additional services

IMPLICATIONS OF THE MIGRATION PROCESSES TO OPEN SOURCE SOFTWARE IN THE LIQUID SOCIETY

As general practice it is convenient to search for interoperable technologies in software developments to make sure the independence of the software provider and the flexibility to get adapted to new user's requirements. Public Administrations must not impose to their final customers any specific technology or software in order to provide efficient and flexible means to practice e-practices in the liquid society they are living in.

The legal systems of the different countries we have shown here try to adapt their Acts to the technological possibilities to promote a more democratic and accessible Public Administration for all. As examples we find in Spain, the Spanish Acts RD 3/2010 y RD 4/2010, known as the Framework for Interoperability Security, constitute an advance in this sense. They define a set of good practices that help to eliminate potential situations in which administrations face vendor lock-in.

Some companies adopt a migration strategy by being centered in previous experiences and they try to proof new prototypes that can be adapted to their own circumstances according to the feedback they have received. We consider this a very appropriate approach since it assures the continuity of the business and it makes users to be participants at the same time. It reinforces the

Table 4. Group C. Budget optimizers

Adoption process	
Firm size	Usually small or medium size firm
Decision makers	Internal staff normally
The ICT strategy	Oriented to main business support and cost minimization
Employee experiencies	Medium or low
ICT intensity of use	Medium or low
External collaborators. Degree of autonomy	Sometimes
Previous analysis	Minimum
The Migration process	
Kind of migration	In no key services
Previous experience in OSS	Medium or minimum
External collaborators. Implementation	Sometimes
Barriers to interoperability	They do not exist normally
The management of change	It is not required normally
Business process reengineering	It is not required normally
Users base	Frequent
Time horizon for the migration	Months
Migration results	
Re-trials for migration	Yes, always a cost decrease is justified
Impact in other units	Few times
Impact in external organisations	Few times
Objectives reached	Yes
Improved processes	Yes, new proceses

idea that software migration initiatives require of business process reengineering efforts from the technical and organizational perspectives.

According to the results obtained in this research, most of the time big size Administrations hires the services of external organizations that offer them the technical knowledge or their own migration experience.

Independently of the way of adoption: strategic, functional or optimizer, initially the open source software is considered as an alternative in specific areas and it is later extended in a gradual way to other business areas. This behavior based in the experienced trust agrees with other models for technology acceptance at different organizational levels (Venkatesh et al., 2003).

In open source projects we need to consider four different promoters: managerial support, clear procedures that promote the change efforts, an effective management of the project and the implication of the agents that take part in the project and final users in the implementation process.

Managerial support: Finney and Corbett (2007) support the importance of this aspect. They develop a whole analysis of the literature review where they stress the importance of the support of managers in ICT projects. Besides according to our recent interviews with people responsible of open source migration processes in different countries, the managerial support is mentioned as one of the most important aspects for the final success of the projects. Managerial support provides leadership and trust in the long term. The leadership styles we have observed in the Public Administrations match with relevant changes in the organization promoted by ICT implementation (Kotter, 1995; UOC Report, 2009).

Clear paths for the process redesign: the existence of clear procedures when facing business process redesigns in the organizations is related in the literature review with the search of positive results in ICT implementations and with the management of the needed cultural change in the organization (Al-Mashari et al., 2003, Fui-Hoon et al., 2003; Finney y Corbett, 2007).

The migration to new systems requires of the redesign of previous processes in the organization. Often new implementations fail because firms underestimate the reach of the processes of change. Firms must be prepared for radical changes (Motwani et al., 2002).

The observation in software migration processes in large Organizations takes time and gradual executions. This idea fits with the need of inducing incremental change processes (Garvin, 1998).

Effective management of processes. The plans for the management of processes coordinate and control the complex activities of the industrial and commercial projects. The implementation of a new system means working in a variety of activities, all immersed in different functionalities and demanding of a global vision in the long term (Falwoski et al., 1998; Holland y Light, 1999; Rosario, 2000; Mabert, 2003).

Always the migration to open source software tries to integrate information at different organizational levels, is important to get the required support in the functional areas of the organization. Everyone is responsible of the whole system and key users in different areas must be clear on their needs in the implementation of the projects.

When a new implementation takes place, a methodology must be followed, where in a clear way the steps in the project must be established and the involvement of each key user and the consultancy team that takes part in the Project.

A reliable external support is related with the selection of tools (Sommers & Nelson, 2003; Al Mashari et al., 2003), and the relationship between the firm and the external services.

It is of great importance for both the Organization that decides to migrate to a new system and the providers, to align the implementation of the services with the objectives established for the project. The objectives must be defined in the design document elaborated once that the collect of information and analysis of requirements have finished. The design document must include the situation of the processes before the implementation and offer information on the future desired situation.

CONCLUSION

The results of this research confirm a group of hypotheses, as for example that the open source software is a real alternative to the private one; it offers a solution for unsatisfied segments, reduces the dependence in the software provider, provides a more democratic access to public services and optimizes hardware at a certain time.

Information and communication technologies are changing the way citizens get in touch with the Public Administration. The modification of ancient process rules makes it possible a new ideal way of what it has been called disorganized Organizations with the following characteristics,

- The information is warehoused in electronic means

- The communication between people is fully electronic
- There is lack of formal structure but information flows to the desired agents
- Networks allow the removal of the physical limits

The adoption of free software offers great opportunities to reach efficiency, flexibility and security in the organizational processes but it also offers some challenges. The answer of users to the changes in technologies has been explained by the technology acceptance models (TAM models) that consider software as a social actor in the organization. IT is capable of interacting with users at different levels in the organization (Samez et Izak, 2009). We think that future research areas can deliver interesting results since they can complement these models with other constructs at firms.

The political support for the use of open source software is also providing some help in organizations. The two mentioned Acts RD 3/2010 y RD 4/2010 make it possible a proper context to enable interactions with this kind of software. In each migration project there is always an internal sponsor or a group of persons leading the initiative. Forthcoming research in the leadership styles can help to identify better scenarios to influence the success in the adoption of this kind of software.

Having in mind that Public Administrations are intensive consumers of ICT and clear promoters of the liquid society generating frequent relationships with many agents, their political positions towards the use of open source applications can promote innovation and reuse of software promoting the final optimization of resources.

We have observed for all the analyzed cases that, the open source software does not necessarily imply savings in the budget. It is more dependant in other dimensions amongst we can cite, the own user experiences, the removal of the provider dependence, security issues, the reuse of hardware elements, etc.

We can perceive today a positive consensus on the importance of ICT in the educational systems and in the development of the economies in general. The Berkman Report (2009) shows that a 10% of the increase in the penetration of bandwidth increases a 1.2 per cent the NGP in the developed economies. If we consider that the open source software is able to offer technological resources at better costs, government incentives could be established for the promotion of digital literacy based in the paradigm of open source. Today it is useful to document the success initiatives performed up to now.

REFERENCES

Ahmed, O. (2005). *Migrating from proprietary to Open Source: Learning Content Management Systems*. Unpublished doctoral dissertation, Department of Systems and Computer Engineering, Carleton University, Ottawa, Ontario, Canada.

Al-Mashari, M., Al-Mudimigh, A., & Zairi, M. (2003). Enterprise Resource Planning: a taxonomy of critical factors. *European Journal of Operational Research, 146*, 352–364. doi:10.1016/S0377-2217(02)00554-4

Bauman, Z. (2004). *Modernidad Líquida*. Buenos Aires, Argentina: Fondo de Cultura Económica.

Berkman Center. (2009). *Berkman Center for Internet and Society Broadband Study for FCC, Report*. Cambridge, MA: Berkman Center.

Berry, D. M. (2008). *Copy, rip, Burn: the Politics of Copyleft and Open Source*. London: Pluto Press.

Bitzer, J. (2005). The impact of entry and competition by Open Source Software on Innovation Activity, Industrial Organization 051201, EconWPA.

Casacubierta, D. (2003). *Collective creation*. Barcelona, Spain: Gedisa.

Casado. (n.d.). *Keys for digital literacy. Seminar on Digital Literacy* (pp. 187-194). Madrid, Spain: Telefónica Foundation. Retrieved from http://sociedaddelainformación.telefónica.es/documentos/articulos/clavesdelaalfabetizacióndigital.pdf

David, P., & Steinmueller, E. (1994). Information Economics and Policy. *The Economics of Standards, 6*(3-4).

Dedrick, J., & West, J. (2005). *Why firms adopt Open Source Platforms: A grounded Theory of Innovation and Standards Adoption*. MIS Quarterly.

EOI. (2009). *The opportunities of free software: capacities, rights and innovation* (EOI Report). Eoi.

EU. (2009). *The Impact of Social Computing on the EU Information Society and Economy (JCR Scientific and Tech. Rep.)*. European Commission.

Falkowski, G., Pedigo, P., Smith, B., & Swamson, D. (1998). A recipe for ERP success. Beyond Computing. *International Journal of Human-Computer Interaction, 16*(1), 5–22.

Finney, S., & Corbett, M. (2007). ERP implementation: a compilation and analysis of critical success factors. *Business Process Management Journal, 13*(3), 329–347. doi:10.1108/14637150710752272

Fui-Hoon, F., Zuckweiler, K. M., & Lee-Shang, J. (2003). ERP implementation: Chief Information Officers' Perceptions on Critical Success Factors. *International Journal of Human-Computer Interaction, 16*(1), 5–22. doi:10.1207/S15327590IJHC1601_2

Garvin, D. A. (1998). The processes of Organization and Management. *Sloan Management Review, 39*(4), 33–50.

Giddens, A. (2002). *Consequences of modernity*. Madrid, Spain: Alianza.

Gilster, P. (1997). *Digital literacy*. New York: Wiley.

Glaser, G., & Strauss, A. (1967). *The discovery of Grounded Theory: Strategies for qualitative research*. New York: Aldine Publishing Company.

Gonzalez-Barahona, J. (2001). Counting Potatoes: the Size of Debian 2.2. *The European Online Magazine for the IT Professional, 2*(6).

Gonzalez-Barahona, J. (2004). *About free software*. Madrid, Spain: Rey Juan Carlos University.

Hammer, M. (2000). Reengineering Work: Do not Automate, Obliterate. *Harvard Business Review*, 37–46.

Hippern, L., & Krogh, S. (2003). Open source software and the private-collective innovation model: Issues for organization science. *Organization Science, 14*(2), 241–248.

Holland, C. P., & Light, B. (1999). A critical success factors model for ERP implementation. *IEEE Software*, 30–36. doi:10.1109/52.765784

Hunter, H. (2006). *Open Source Data Base Driven Web Development*. Oxford, UK: Chandos.

Kotter, J. P. (1995). Leading change: Why transformation effort Fail. *Harvard Business Review*, 42–56.

Lakhan, R., & Jhunjhunwala, V. (2008). Open Source in Education. *EDUCAUSE Quarterly, 31*(2), 32–40.

Lerner, J., & Tirole, J. (2002). The simple economics of Open Source. *The Journal of Industrial Economics, 50*(2), 197–234. doi:10.1111/1467-6451.00174

Lerner, J., & Tirole, J. (2005). The Economics of Technology Sharing: Open Source and Beyond. *The Journal of Economic Perspectives, 19*(2), 99–120. doi:10.1257/0895330054048678

Mabert, V., Soni, A., & Venkatamara, M. (2003). Enterprise Resource Planning: managing implementation process. *European Journal of Operational Research, 146*(2), 302–314. doi:10.1016/S0377-2217(02)00551-9

Motwani, J., Mirchandani, M., & Gunasekaran, A. (2002). Successful implementation of ERP Projects: evidence from two case studies. *International Journal of Production Economics, 75*, 83–96. doi:10.1016/S0925-5273(01)00183-9

Myers, M. D. (1997). Qualitative Research in information systems. *Management Information Systems Quarterly*, 209–223.

Myers, M. D. (2009). *Qualitative Research in Business and Management*. London: Sage.

Obama, B. (2009). Memorandum for the heads of executive departments and agencies. Subject: Transparency and Open Government. Retrieved from http://www.whitehouse.gov/the_press_office/Transparency_and_Open_Government/

Orlikowski, W. (1991). Information Technology and the Structuring of Organizations. *Information Systems Research*, 27–38.

Orlikowski, W. (1993). CASE Tools as Organizational Change: Investigating Incremental and Radical Changes in Systems Development. *Management Information Systems Quarterly*, 209–223.

Osterloh, M., & Rota, D. (2007). Open source software development, just another case of collective invention. *Research Policy*, *36*(2), 157–171. doi:10.1016/j.respol.2006.10.004

Raymond, E. (1999). The Cathedral and the bazaar. *Knowledge, Technology and Policy*, *12*(3), 23–49. doi:10.1007/s12130-999-1026-0

Riehle, D. (2007). The Economic Motivation of Open Source: Stakeholder Perspectives. *IEEE Computer*, *40*(4), 25–32.

Rosario, J. G. (2000). On the leading edge: critical success factors in ERP implementation projects. *Business World*, 21-27.

Rossi, D. (2006). Decoding the green open source software puzzle: A survey of theoretical and empirical contributions. In *Proceedings of the Economics of Open Source Software Development, 22nd IEEE International Parallel and Distributed Processing Symposium*, New York.

Sameh, B., & Izak, J. (2009). The Adoption and Use of IT Artifacts: A New Interaction Centric Model for the Study of User-Artifact Relationships. *Journal of the Association for Information Systems*, *10*(9), 661–685.

Shiff, T. (2002). The Economics of Open Source Software: a survey of the early literature. *Review of Network Economics*, *1*(1), 66–74.

Sommers, G., & Nelson, C. (2003). A taxonomy of players and activities across the ERP project life cycle. *Information & Management*, *41*(3), 257–278. doi:10.1016/S0378-7206(03)00023-5

Strauss, A., & Corbin, J. (1990). *Basics of Qualitative Research: Grounded theory, Procedures and Techniques*. London: Sage.

Tascón, M. (2006). Development of a place for the information society. In R. Casado (Ed.), *Keys for digital literacy. Seminar on Digital Literacy* (pp. 187-194). Madrid, Spain: Telefónica Foundation. Retrieved from http://sociedaddelainformación.telefónica.es/documentos/articulos/clavesdelaalfabetizacióndigital.pdf

UOC. (2009). *The use of open source in Public Administrations in Spain (UOC Rep.)*. Universitat Oberta de Calalunya.

Venkatesh, V., & Brown, S. A. (2003). User acceptance of information technology: Toward a unified view. *Management Information Systems Quarterly*, *27*(3), 425–478.

Von Hippel, E. (2005). *Democratizing Innovation*. Cambridge, MA: MIT Press.

Wheeler, D. (2007). *Why Open Source Software. Look at the Numbers*. Retrieved January 30, 2010, from dwheeler.com/oss_ls_why_html

This work was previously published in International Journal of Digital Literacy and Digital Competence, Volume 1, Issue 3, edited by Antonio Cartelli, pp. 36-47, copyright 2010 by IGI Publishing (an imprint of IGI Global).

Section 5

Digital Technologies at Large:

Learning and Ethics

Chapter 17
Cooperative Learning through Communities of Practice

Emilio Lastrucci
University of Basilicata, Italy

Angela Pascale
University of Basilicata, Italy

ABSTRACT

A community made up of a group of individuals becomes a "community of practice" when a mutual engagement is established between its members. The mutual engagement unites the participants in the carrying out of a common task (Wenger, 1998). The main aim of a community of practice is to find the solution to a problem by sharing experiences (Midoro, 2002). This paper examines the definition, characteristics, management and effectiveness of communities of practice. They are understood as being communities of self-managed learning where professional development is not based on a pre-set training course but on sharing experiences, identifying best practices and helping each other face the daily problems encountered in one's profession (Trentin, 2000). Such communities are useful in particular working environments as an opportunity to improve digital competences. In communities of practice, it is possible to encourage ways of co-building knowledge through teaching methods such as cooperative learning. Until now cooperative learning has been limited to traditional training contexts, but it can be realised via Web technologies.

INTERACTION, AN ESSENTIAL PREMISE TO STARTING UP A COMMUNITY OF PRACTICE

A virtual community is generally understood to be a place, a space on the Web that helps the real community to exist and survive. The difference between a real community and a virtual one is the way in which the members interact: the participants in a Web community communicate with each other with the aid of a computer (*Computer Mediated Communication*). To be part of a virtual community it is necessary to become an active member by participating in the life and growth of its members and of the space of the community, by establishing meaningful relationships with the participants and trying to be an integral part of the group. If we consider the educational implica-

DOI: 10.4018/978-1-4666-0903-7.ch017

tions of virtual communities, at least three types of groups can be identified:

1. Discussion groups or spontaneous communities;
2. Learning communities;
3. Communities of practice.

In spontaneous communities the participants are united by one or more topics which are connected to their personal interests and they do not always have specific aims. The members often do not use well settled computer platforms to interact, they mostly use simple interpersonal communication tools such as forums and above all mailing lists. Within these communities there are great differences regarding the participants' level of commitment and participation.

Learning communities and communities of practice, on the other hand, have specific aims. Learning communities are more focused on developing knowledge and skills in a teaching course, communities of practice deal with solving common problems or sharing experiences and cases that are useful in particular working environments or serve as a refresher opportunity for the professional development of adults at work. All the components of these communities should be helped in giving their contribution to the community: their participation should therefore be equal.

The starting up and the development of different ways of interaction and of intense social relationships, that can give life to communities (of special interests, of learning and of practice), can be traced back to the key concept of *social interaction*, which on Internet is usually defined as *communicative interaction* (Rivoltella, 2003). To explore the possibilities of developing this new sense of community, brought about by the Web, means to study the communicative exchanges among the members of the different communities. In the case of a community of practice, the activities can be carried out on line using specific computer platforms. The setting-up of these platforms must take into consideration the different types of exchanges of knowledge that can occur on them. Generally speaking, a computer platform should provide a public section, to be accessed by anonymous users, which gives them a general description of the community of practice's activities. There should also be a private section, where access is reserved only to authorized people so that they can actively participate in the community. *Peer tutoring* and *reciprocal teaching* are fostered within these contexts because the interaction and exchanges between the participants become mechanisms which can encourage and stimulate learning through interaction and sharing tools. All the means that allow both synchronous and asynchronous communication on the Web are interacting and sharing tools: email, chat-rooms and "teaching forums." They are virtual spaces where each participant makes his own contribution available to the whole group, thus creating the necessary conditions to "share" knowledge (Pascale, 2002). Within these areas the contributions are organised in a discussion *thread* sequence, the contents are more visible, there is more freedom as to when to use them, it is possible to trace back the communication, different points of view can be collected and the group can directly experience the ability to build knowledge. As regards this latter issue, the role of the *tutor,* who supports the distance-education teacher, is fundamental. His job is to help the users with the communication tools (technological function), to manage the exchanges and group dynamics (moderation function) and to encourage and support the participation (relational function) (Pascale, 2005).

A community of practice is a self-directed and self-organised group in which the mechanisms of sharing tacit knowledge and of enriching one's personal and professional identity are possible only if the participation is spontaneous and voluntary. There are various differences in on-line platforms compared to traditional communities of practice:

- They guarantee continuity in the communication between the members when it is not possible for them to physically meet up;

- They give more visibility to people and let quicker and better circulate internal information;
- They allow the setting up of a community that is spread over a wider geographical area and can include a large number of participants, including people who do not know each other;
- During the on line interaction, the users are not able to communicate face-to-face but can communicate only via technology which privileges explicit and verbal aspects above other factors.

This latter point reflects the dynamics of the interaction of the members of the community, and experts are divided on the possibility or not of creating true on line communities of practice. To automatically have a virtual community of practice it is not sufficient to create a community on the Web, it is needed that people share the same interests and profession. The existence of a community of practice is associated with factors that go beyond the use of technology because it requires the activation of processes and elements that distinguish it from its traditional form. According to Trentin (2004), a virtual community of practice must be founded on a "real" community of practice, built on the fact that people "physically" and "personally" know each other, and there must be reciprocal respect and trust together with the possibility of identifying oneself within the community.

DEFINITIONS AND CHARACTERISTICS OF A COMMUNITY OF PRACTICE

The development and sharing of knowledge, tacit or implicit they are, constitutes an innovative tool for personal and professional growth. It is advantageous not only to the individuals but also to the companies they work for. It is for this reason that companies, starting with the experience of the multinational Xerox Corporation in the 1980s, are increasingly interested in promoting the exchange of knowledge, especially implicit, through the setting up of communities of practice activated by technological means (Giglioli, 2005). Generally speaking, certain operations are foreseen when promoting a community of practice:

- Identifying the potential community of practice; that is, identifying the subjects who are able to increase the company or group's strategic capacities, or those who have special skills, experience or talent in solving problems of organisational or technical nature;
- Providing the community of practice with a technological infrastructure that allows the members apply their competences;
- Using non traditional methods to evaluate the importance of the community of practice for the company (understanding the complex relationship between the activity, knowledge and performance), and whether its setting up is a real asset for the company as well as for the individual.

One of the most well known examples of a community of practice is the one that was set up in the previously mentioned company Xerox Corporation. The problems that the Xerox technicians encountered whilst carrying out the repair of the photocopiers and the solutions suggested to solve the problems were made available to highly specialised colleagues via a Network. This group of technicians, who were spontaneously interested in their colleagues' problems, directly contributed in the providing of solutions, and consequently improved the efficiency and effectiveness of the repairs (diagnosis methods, intervention techniques, materials etc.). In this way there were notable improvements in the time and quality of the repairs on the Xerox photocopiers. The Xerox technicians' community of practice, largely made up of voluntary workers who wanted to share their reciprocal work experience, was set up informally and outside of any company "programme". Its impact, however, on *customer satisfaction* and on Xerox's business, has reached an inestimable value over the last few years.

The term "community of practice", introduced by Lave and Wenger (1991), is used to include all of the situations where groups of people, who have a professional interest in common, work together and learn from one another in an interaction where they are all on the same level and have the common perception that each member needs to know what the others know (Brown & Duguid, 1991). Within a community of practice, collaborative and interactive dynamics are activated in order to *negotiate meaning*. Each member not only negotiates how he performs a professional task, how he faces and solves a problem, what he identifies and defines as a problem, but he also negotiates his role within the community, his way of participating and, at last, he behaves both as a person and a professional.

Wenger (1998) identifies the following elements in a dialectical relationship, which determines the *mutual engagement* and its main characteristics:

1. *Cooperative Work*, is the carrying out of an activity to pursuit a product or a service; from solving a problem, in general, to performing a task or accomplishing a function, of any nature.
2. *Diversity and Partiality*, is the subdivision of roles and functions in the carrying out of cooperative work. The work of each member of the group requires the work of the other members and it is part of a complex organisation depending on the nature of the task. While a job is carried out, the members of the community need to have different competences (*diversity*), which are necessary to perform the segments (*partiality*) of each individual job.
3. *Mutual Relations,* are the consequence of the mutual engagement, which is accomplished by a series of functional relations, often not only functional, between the members of the community. The carrying out of a task lets the community members develop mutual engagement, thus reinforcing their functional relations and leading to the increase in the individuals' competences.

The community uses a shared *repertoire*, consisting of objects and procedures to carry out a task. Furthermore, what keeps a community of practice together and polarises the activity is the carrying out of a *common enterprise*. Whichever way we look at it, the common enterprise, according to Wenger (1998), has the following main characteristics:

- Each member negotiates, within the community, his role and how to perform it (*negotiated common enterprise*);
- The successful carrying out of a task requires the individuals to feel involved in the common enterprise (*involvement in the common enterprise*);
- Each community member realises that every other members' work is relevant in carrying out the common enterprise (*mutual relevance*).

More specifically, according to Wenger (1998), the carrying out of a task by a community involves three main activities called "reification", "participation" and "negotiation of meaning".

Wenger (1998) also maintains that the model and learning processes found in a virtual learning environment are the same as those that regulate the development of the individuals' identity in a community of practice. He describes the different characteristics of the learning that takes place in such a context and, more generally, of the interaction with the world, as follows:

- *Learning as the creation of meaning.* Learning is a continuous process and an integral part of our life by which we give a meaning to our experiences of life and of the world;
- *Learning as the development of identity.* Learning is a process that transforms our ability to take part in the world by changing who we are, our practices and our belonging to communities;
- *Learning as belonging to a community.* Learning is a process through which we are able to belong to a community. Learning as belonging is concerned with our ability to be part of a community, a community in which our participation is recognised as a competence;
- *Learning as the result of performing a task within a community.* Learning can be defined as the re-alignment of experience and competences. There is an imbalance when these two factors are too distant or too near each other to produce the necessary generative tension.

COMMUNITIES OF PRACTICE AS SOCIAL LEARNING SYSTEMS

Wenger (1998) highlights the concept of the learners' participation (and of their motivation) as being the driving force of the process of knowledge. More specifically, as regards adults who are already in the working world, learning is fundamentally an experiential and social process, which requires a continual dialectic between experience and competence. An essential component of learning is therefore the social interaction, not just with the teachers but also with the other learners. Taking these factors into consideration, the *cooperative learning* approach is developed (this will be discussed in further detail later) in the case of distance education. This type of education is understood to be a training experience where the technological means include not so much ways of providing the contents but the creation of active learning communities. In this training context, the roles of the teacher/tutor/trainer are redefined and are placed on the same level as the learner. In professional learning communities of practice, the user is not a passive subject of the training process, because he recognises and requires an active approach which is constituted both by knowledge and the management of the processes.

With this cooperative approach to on line training the student does not just assimilate the contents, he activates a meta-cognitive process that leads him to acquire his own personal way of learning. On line learning, in its "cooperative" form, is therefore carried out in such a way that learners are brought all together and not isolated one each other. More specifically "peer classes" are made up of learners who have the same training needs and personal and professional interests. These classes could not be established in a formal context for the presence of geographical and organisational barriers; on-line learning communities (i.e., training place, information and interaction) are based on the participants' sharing of knowledge (Pascale, 2002), more than on the materials that hierarchically and linearly represent the discipline structure and are given to the students.

The key figures in the management of a community of practice are: the designer, the scientific head, the coordinator and the leader of the community. The coordinator is the facilitator/tutor within the community. His/her profile is very similar to that of any on-line tutor (i.e., he is engaged with organisation, management, technical and content support), but he/she is different from the coordinator of a learning community because he must "motivate" the community (Pascale, 2005). He/she has to maintain a positive attitude in order to stimulate the dialogue and discussion about the topics of the course. He/she must also identify the interest areas of the learners and find any need for training or information which did not emerge during the planning stage. On one hand, he/she is the mediator between the scientific head and the community; on the other hand he is actively engaged in the interaction and communication, from the planning of the provision of the contents to the definition of the graphical layout of the interface (together with the software developers). If a community of practice is a learning structure that is fuelled from the bottom, the community coordinator must nourish this drive without dominating it. He should also:

- Know the main characteristics of distance education;
- Have previous experience as a user of a "cooperative" on line course;
- Know and be able to deal with the main interactive relations when managing a community of practice.

As a consequence, communities of practice function as real social learning systems, where learning is not limited to acquiring knowledge (*learning about*), nor extends to knowing how to adequately perform a specific task, but it is a process of structuring and restructuring one's professional identity, beginning form own experiences and negotiating meaning within the group (*learning-to-be*) (Wenger, 1998).

More specifically, the sharing of tacit knowledge and the creation of new knowledge is possible by means of the continuous transformation of knowledge from tacit to explicit and vice versa. Tacit knowledge is the knowledge that a subject has, but finds difficult to define or put into words. It cannot immediately be expressed in manuals or reports. From a certain point of view it is more relevant than explicit knowledge because it is based on the individual's personal experience. In the professional field, if we take into consideration two workers who have the same explicit knowledge (due to training and refresher courses etc.), the more experienced and competent of the two is the one with more tacit knowledge. To let tacit knowledge be transmitted and exchanged between subjects there have to be "self-organising" teams (Nonaka, 1994) and a reciprocal *trust* among the components of the group. In communities of practice it is especially true for the construction of knowledge because people recognise themselves in the other members of the community.

According to Midoro (2002), a community of practice is an entity that starts up and evolves in a spontaneous way. It has its own rules for growth and development but, above all, it is also a learning environment. The members of a learning community must be "mutually engaged", like those in a community of practice. To hit this target the conditions of mutual dependence must be created. It can be obtained by taking into consideration the characteristics of the mutual engagement in a community of practice:

- *Cooperative Work.* During the whole training course the members of the community are involved in carrying out a common task and this task induces the mutual engagement: the members share the tasks in order to create something new or different, by means of a deliberate and structured process. They decide what goals and common values must be adopted, they put together the individuals' competences for the group's advantage, they choose independently who to work with and organise the group in a flexible way.
- *Diversity and Partiality.* Carrying out cooperative work necessarily means that there is a subdivision of roles and functions. A learning community is typically made up of the participants in a course and of the course's staff. The staff are involved in the management of the course. Each person, who has his own role, works within the community and makes only part of the work. All the members of the community should constantly have an overall view of how the work is developing.

- *Mutual Relations.* Within a community, there is a complex weave of relationships. The tutors' job is to put forward activities and to coordinate and facilitate them; the experts suggest solutions, materials and the procedures to follow when carrying out a task; the technical staffs solves any technical problems and the participants perform the task. Different types of relationships are created between the participants depending on the task and the subject of the cooperative work they are focusing on.
- *Shared Repertoire.* This regards the objects and procedures used in the course. The objects are of two types:
    1. Study *material*, based on different technology (printed material, video, internet websites etc) and supporting the use of technology. This also includes all the products made by the participants during the course;
    2. *Technology supporting the course.* In the case of a Web course, the system of *computer mediated conferencing* (CMC) and the way it is used, are good examples of this kind.
- *Common Enterprise.* The common enterprise in a learning community usually consists of cooperatively making a product or a service, collectively finding the solution to a problem or carrying out a task within the course. Also in this case, the common enterprise has its main features that must be respected:
    1. It is important that each participant on the course negotiates his role and how to perform it within the community. This step could be carried out at the beginning of the course during a socialisation stage (*negotiated common enterprise*);
    2. In order to effectively carry out an activity, the individuals have to feel involved in the common enterprise. In a learning community this is concerned with motivation. It is also important that the participants are able to organise themselves to carry out the common enterprise (*involvement in the common enterprise*);
    3. Within a learning community the cooperative work has to be organised in such a way that each member's work is necessary to carry out the common task (*mutual relevance*).
- *Practice.* In a learning community "reification" can be viewed as the cooperative activity necessary for obtaining the common enterprise (product). The objects produced can be texts, hypertexts and websites but also projects and programmes etc. The objects produced depend on the course content domain. Theoretical elaborations, solutions to problems and definitions of principles can also be considered as objects. In such a case, they are conceptual objects. "Participation" to a course has to do with the continuity with which each member carries out the course. It has to do with the systematic reading and writing of messages, the constant involvement in the activities and the participation in the meetings. "Negotiation of meaning" happens when individual knowledge is developed and gains the sense that it must have in the content domain.

Furthermore, like in online courses, the shared repertoire is enriched and the common enterprise is modified, so that there is a growth of the participants' identity (Midoro, 2002).

COOPERATIVE LEARNING

Cooperative learning is a special teaching method by which the students learn in small groups; they help one each other and feel co-responsible for their learning. This method is different from both competitive learning and individual learning and, unlike them, can be applied to any task, subject or curriculum. The teacher takes on the role of facilitator and organiser of the activities; he/she gives a structure to "learning areas", where the students transform each learning activity into a process of "group problem solving" with the help of a positive atmosphere. The students achieve the planned goals after having developed given skills and social competences, within the small learning groups. These are interpersonal and small group skills that are fundamental for developing and maintaining a high quality level of cooperation.

Group work is not new in training environments; however students can work together without any benefit. It can happen that they work together but have no interest or satisfaction in doing so. In cooperative learning groups, on the contrary, the students enjoy working on the activity and actively take part in all the stages of the work, from the planning to the evaluation, while teacher is above all the facilitator and organiser of the learning activity.

According to Ellerani and Pavan (2003), *cooperative learning*, compared to the traditional way of teaching, has the following advantages:

- *Better results*: the learners work more and obtain better results. There is thus an increase in their intrinsic motivation and they develop higher skills of reasoning and critical thinking;
- *Positive relationship between the students*: the students are aware of the importance of everybody's contribution to the task thus developing reciprocal respect and the spirit of team work;
- *More psychological well-being*: the learners develop a higher sense of self-respect and of being able to work more effectively, which helps them bear difficulties.

Ellerani and Pavan (2003) also state that there are five factors that make cooperation effective:

1. *Positive interdependence*: the students work hard to improve each member's output because it is not possible to be individually successful without collective success;
2. *Individual and group responsibility*: the group is responsible for reaching the goals and each member is responsible for his own contribution;
3. *Constructive interaction*: the learners have to work together, encouraging and supporting each member's efforts and praising each other for the successes they obtain;
4. *The activation of specific and necessary social skills for the interpersonal relationships in small groups*: the students work in the various roles required for them by the task and create an atmosphere of collaboration and trust. They handle conflicts and, more generally, social competences are of particular importance.
5. *Group evaluation*: the group evaluates its results and its way of working. It also sets out goals for growth and development.

Within this general draft the different interpretations of interdependence and the more meaningful variables regarding learning (interaction, motivation to learn, the teacher's task and role) have led to the development of different *cooperative learning*. There are currently various research areas, the most relevant ones being those of D. Johnson and R. Johnson of the University of Minnesota in Minneapolis, Slavin at the Johns Hopkins University in Baltimore and Sharan at the Tel Aviv University. Some aspects of *cooperative learning* are still under discussion and research: the situation concerning the gifted students, the inclusion of the seriously handicapped, different types of specific transversal objectives and the possibility of developing new strategies by means of new technologies.

A summary is given by Danielson (2002), who sees *cooperative learning* as a highly stimulating approach for teachers. When they adopt cooperative learning in their classes they are forced to carefully plan their work. This helps students to work together and to challenge one each other within the group thus maintaining their motivation at a high level. The learners are therefore encouraged to appreciate the different competences and experience of their peers and to learn from them.

A cooperative classroom, as seen from Baloche (1998), is made of small groups of students, relatively permanent and heterogeneously put together by the teacher, who is united in accomplishing a task and producing projects and products. Individual responsibility is required from each member of the group to acquire the right competences to achieve the planned goal.

As regards online cooperative teaching, Slavin (1990) highlights the factors that must be present, and among them notices the following:

- The awareness of the existence of a network of individuals before the technological one;
- A group of learners who have a task in common but cannot physically work together;
- A specific task which requires active and meaningful participation on behalf of the student;
- The access to a reliable computer network;
- The responsibility towards the group and the tasks;
- A strong leadership in the group and the ways to assess the final evaluation;
- Decisions to be shared when forming group projects;
- Active and visible collaboration;
- Highly structured group work;
- Reciprocal commitment on behalf of the students and teachers.

The Web can therefore facilitate models of knowledge and of learning through group work, research activity, sharing experiences and goals. Innovative projects, based on the communication between peers, have a profound influence both on the interpersonal relationships as well as on the participants' roles. The teacher, who is the undisputed reference point for the group-class in the traditional classroom, in these situations is a member of the community who works together with the others (Pascale, 2006).

According to Wenger's model (Wenger, McDermott, & Snyder, 2002), the distinctive characteristics of the community of practice, made through cooperative learning, are the following:

- *Specific domain.* A community of practice is not just a friends' club or a network of people. It has its own identity, defined by a shared domain of interest. Membership, therefore, implies a commitment to that domain and a shared competence that distinguishes its members from other people. The domain is not necessarily something which is recognised as an "expert competence", outside of the community. The members evaluate their collective competences and learn from one another, even if a few people outside the group recognise their "expert competence";
- *Community.* In order to pursue their interest in the domain, the members are engaged in the internal activities and discussions of the community, helping each other and sharing information. They build up relationships that allow them to learn from the others. To have the same job and the same position does not mean for people that they belong to a community of practice. Furthermore, the members of a community of practice not necessarily work together in the same place;
- *Practice.* A community of practice is not just a community of interest. The members of this kind of community are practitioners and develop a shared repertoire of resourc-

es: experiences, stories, and recurrent ways to face and solve problems (i.e., a shared practice). This requires time, continuous interaction and conscious practice. Web technologies can help the setting-up of the community by expanding the times of the communication and letting people cultivate the idea of a community of practice.

As stated by Midoro (2002, p. 10), "if it is true that cooperative learning is just one of the infinite ways of learning and training on the web, it is just one of the possible ways for distance education; furthermore, it is true that cooperative learning produces deep changes in the identities of those who are involved in it, and the on-line systems, based on cooperative learning, have opened up new frontiers in the world of distance education".

CONCLUSION

Adults are free to manage their own learning paths, making their choices in order to achieve specific goals. They decide how to act by judging from the experiences they have made and on the relevance they attribute to each activity. They establish their motivation for learning in a different way in order to create social relationships. They also take into consideration the obstacles to learning such as family and work commitments, the lack of time, organisational difficulties and the lack of interest in the topics to be learnt (Knowles, 1984).

For adults to be trained, all the above factors must be considered, to find valid alternatives to formal education. Communities of practice constitute a valid model to refer to for creating alternative paths. The type of learning that develops within a community of practice is based on social theories of learning, whereby it is assumed that "knowledge" also includes participating in carrying out a task. The teaching methods used with a community of practice, find in the web the sub-layer necessary for their existence and development; the web is a virtual meeting space as well as a physical space for supporting communication (Wenger, McDermott, & Snyder, 2002).

Reciprocal and situated learning is based on elementary but extremely effective concepts:

- If you have a problem you can try asking your colleagues for help;
- When the solution is suggested, the problem is solved and at the same time new knowledge is acquired;
- If nobody knows the answer, and someone else is experiencing a similar problem or is interested in its solution, it can be useful to cooperate with one's peers (Trentin, 2000).

As a conclusion, one of the greatest advantages of an on line community of practice is that it remains even when the course finishes, and it is possible to continue on its activity. In fact, if a community is alive it will continue to exist even after the formal contents have been delivered, due to the participants' interest and motivation. They recognise that the exchange of information, which started off during the community experience, is an ongoing informal training support which can increase both the member's personal and professional growth.

REFERENCES

Baloche, L. (1998). *The cooperative classroom. Empowering learning*. Upper Saddle River, NJ: Prentice-Hall.

Brown, J. S., & Duguid, P. (1991). Organizational Learning and Communities-of-practice: Toward a Unified View of Working, Learning and Innovation. *Organization Science*, *2*(1). doi:10.1287/orsc.2.1.40

Danielson, C. (2002). *Enhancing student achievement: a framework for school improvement*. Alexandria, VA: ASCD.

Ellerani, P., & Pavan, D. (2003). *Il cooperative learning: una proposta per l'orientamento formativo*. Napoli, Italy: Tecnodid.

Giglioli, A. (2005). Le Comunità di Pratica Apprendistato in FVG. In Frignani, P., Galliani, L., Giacomantonio, M., & Poletti, G. (Eds.), *E-learning: protagonista dello sviluppo della società della conoscenza – Atti del convegno Expo e-learning 2005*. Ferrara, Italy: Omniacom Editore.

Knowles, M. (1984). *Andragogy in Action*. San Francisco, CA: Jossey-Bass.

Lave, J., & Wenger, E. (1991). *Situated Learning: legitimate peripheral participation*. New York: Cambridge University Press.

Midoro, V. (1998). Per una definizione di apprendimento cooperativo. In Midoro, V. (Ed.), *Argomenti di Tecnologie Didattiche* (pp. 169–198). Ortona, Italy: Ed. Menabò.

Midoro, V. (2002). Dalle comunità di pratica alle comunità di apprendimento virtuali. *Tecnologie Didattiche*, *1*, 3–10.

Nonaka, I. (1994). Come un'organizzazione crea conoscenza. *Economia&Management*, *3*, 31–48.

Pascale, A. (2002). E-learning: produrre conoscenza comunicando in rete. *Rinnovare la scuola, 18,* 5-18.

Pascale, A. (2005). Le figure professionali nell'e-learning: il tutor on line. *Rinnovare la scuola, 28,* 6-28.

Pascale, A. (2006). *Professione docente e nuove tecnologie. Indagine quali-quantitativa sull'impatto delle TIC sull'identità professionale degli insegnanti*. Roma, Italy: Edizioni A.N.S.I.

Rivoltella, P. C. (2003). *Costruttivismo e pragmatica della comunicazione on line*. Trento, Italy: Erickson.

Slavin, R. E. (1990). *Cooperative Learning: Theory, Research and Practice*. Upper Saddle River, NJ: Prentice Hall.

Trentin, G. (2000). Dalla formazione a distanza alle comunità di pratica attraverso l'apprendimento in rete. *Tecnologie Didattiche, 20*, 21–29.

Trentin, G. (2004). *Apprendimento in rete e condivisione delle conoscenze*. Milano, Italy: Franco Angeli.

Wenger, E. (1998). *Community of practice*. Cambridge, UK: Cambridge University press.

Wenger, E., McDermott, R., & Snyder, W. M. (2002). *Cultivating Communities of Practice. A guide to managing knowledge*. Boston: Harvard Business School Press.

This work was previously published in International Journal of Digital Literacy and Digital Competence, Volume 1, Issue 2, edited by Antonio Cartelli, pp. 11-21, copyright 2010 by IGI Publishing (an imprint of IGI Global).

Chapter 18
Levels of Self-Efficacy among Harassed Teachers

Isabel Cantón
University of León, Spain

Consuelo Morán
University of León, Spain

ABSTRACT

The aim of this study was to examine the differences among harassed teachers and un-harassed ones, regarding coping strategies, self-efficacy, and locus of control. Participants were 255 teachers (163 women and 92 men) who completed a set of three questionnaires, the Mobbing Perceived Questionnaire, a battery of control expectancies, and the Brief COPE to assess, respectively, mobbing perceived at work, self-efficacy, locus of control, and cooping strategies. The results showed differences in self-efficacy, locus of control, and use of coping strategies depending on the teachers' degree of mobbing perceived. The authors believe that the efforts for preventing mobbing made by educational organizations must be intensified, as they not only affect teachers' quality of life but also the quality of the educational system, furthermore new technologies can have a relevant role on this side by making available all information on those phenomena.

INTRODUCTION

Since the beginning of the 21st century, the European educational system has had to take up the challenge of changes in the student population, which has increased in both numbers and diversity. Education professionals have been trying to adapt to the needs of students who speak different languages and who come from different backgrounds, some of whom are at risk of becoming excluded from the educational system, and many with special needs (Wertheim & Leyser, 2002).

In Spain, in the last twenty years, we have had seven mutually contradictory educational laws. None of which has been completely developed against the backdrop of the old dichotomy of two

DOI: 10.4018/978-1-4666-0903-7.ch018

cultures, or philosophical-ideological substratum upholding the idea of education based on legislation. Rules and regulations and different practices which are mutually incompatible if not integrated: *educare* for students who are *tabula rasa* and *educere* for those who already have knowledge and need it to be brought out: reproduce or transform, liberate or repress, rousseauists or scholastics: pedagogical optimists or pessimists (Cantón & Perisset, 2009).

The rational-positivist or technical rationality intellectual current is based on reason and on a degree of pedagogical pessimism, and proposes stable teaching routines that are difficult to change, based on expert language, on effort and on the instilling of traditional, compact and safe moral values, with some eschewing of pedagogy. In teaching centres, it takes the form of a dense, highly structured curriculum, drilling, knowledgeable teachers perhaps lacking in pedagogical competence, and high levels of strict discipline, where the consequences of violence are noticed early on and nipped in the bud.

Opposed to this is practical rationality, typical of the nineties, based on facts, on pedagogical optimism taken to the extreme, on play learning and impregnation, upheld by the theories of German Romanticism of the 19th century and the Rousseau's concept of the *Noble Savage*. Children are naturally good, it is society, and the school itself that pervert them with their teachings, so the important thing is change, innovation – education cannot be systemized. With it, there appeared what has come to be called specific pedagogical language, the curriculum has to be negotiated with the students and adapted to their interests, with greater stress on lay values and large doses of moral relativism (Ayuso, 2005). In schools, it appears as permissiveness, a variable curriculum, negotiation, teacher-mediators, multicultural and pluralist values that are unstable, diffuse, and contingent; criticism and social examination of the values of the teachers; students with low or no discipline and difficulties in tackling disruptive conduct. An example of this tendency may be seen in the final provisions of the Spanish Education Act of March 2006: *"collective decisions made by students in the third year of compulsory secondary education and above regarding class attendance shall not be considered as irregular conduct and shall not be punished...."*

Classroom violence is the direct result of the adoption by governments and society of practical rationalism as guidelines for a sort of relativist overregulation of education, at both school and social level. But it is also the fruit of society's upholding and applauding such practices, which translate into confrontations between two sectors that in theory are working to the same end: teachers and parents, the former adopting a threatening posture towards the latter regarding permissiveness towards their children and the latter giving up the battle as lost and seeking release from teaching into administration or retirement. A third sector, in which we find ourselves, also has a great deal of responsibility in this topic: the experts, who, ensconced in their academic ghettos, take no part in, have no relationship with and contribute no solutions from their research to current social affairs, which they do not get involved in but merely contemplate from their ivory towers. Violent students must obviously take their part of the blame for clinging onto social, legal, and educational extremes.

In this context of change, the study of a teacher's efficiency becomes relevant in psycho-educational research.

From Bandura's Social Cognitive theory (1977, 1997), a teacher's perceived efficacy may be defined as their consideration of their capability of integrating social, cognitive and behavioural skills in order to organize and carry out the actions necessary to achieve the desired results. Perceived self-efficacy affects thoughts, emotions and behaviour, stimulating people to make substantial efforts to achieve their aims, persisting in the face of adversity and always seeking to keep control over the relevant events affecting their lives.

(Bandura, 1997; Milner, 2002; Tschannen-Moran & Woolfolk-Hoy, 2001). Therefore, as far as teachers are concerned, perceived self-efficacy may affect different aspects of their thinking, regarding both decision-making and behaviour. If teachers consider that their actions are going to have little influence on their students' academic attainment, then they will probably make less effort to apply new techniques that would improve students' yield. Nevertheless, teachers with a high perception of their self-efficacy will always use a wide range of new educational activities in order to gain back those students with poorer academic results and behaviour problems (Emmer & Hickman, 1991; Ghaith & Yaghi, 1997; Tschannen-Moran et al., 1998; Wertheim & Leyser, 2002).

Originally, the concept of a teacher's self-efficacy went hand in hand with that of locus of control that is the extent to which teachers believe themselves to be in control of reinforcement of their actions, that is whether control over what happens to them depends on internal factors. Teachers who perceive external factors as having more effect than their own abilities to influence their students firmly believe that learning is out of their control and depends on external factors. On the other hand, those with more faith in their teaching abilities, when faced with unmotivated students and those with learning disabilities, believe that they have an internal control over the reinforcement of their teaching activities (Tschannen-Moran & Woolfolk Hoy, 2001).

This research is based on the premise that psychological harassment at work reduces teachers' perceived self-efficacy and is also concerned with the locus of control of reinforcements, and therefore alters the efforts and results of harassed teachers.

We consider that psychological harassment in the workplace (mobbing) is a serious problem for many people in Europe (Einarsen, Hoel, Zapt, & Cooper, 2003), and for labour organizations. According to Schuster (1996), it is one of the most devastating experiences that a human being can be subjected to in western society. It means feeling excluded and actively rejected by one's own social grouping. It also questions one's professional competence, while threatening one with unemployment and the consequent loss of resources. It very frequently occurs for arbitrary, inexplicable and irrational reasons with nothing to do with the professional competence or personal value of the person in question.

We have defined mobbing (Morán, 2002) as the persistent, deliberate and systematic mistreatment by several members of an organization of another member in order to annihilate them psychologically and socially and force them to leave the organization.

The characteristics of psychological harassment (Leymann, 1996) are intimidation, abusive behaviour or psychological violence during a period of over six months, and systematically applied (once a week), manifested as repeated actions (up to 45 times) consisting in attacks on the victim's organization of work, social relationships, private life, attitudes and all this through physical, verbal or psychological violence.

According to the Third European Survey on Working Conditions published by the International Labour Organization in 2000, the 9% of European workers (13 million persons) have been victims of bullying, with a social cost of over 90 million euros for sick leave or professional invalidity, according to the same survey.

Mobbing can take different forms ranging from direct attacks such as acts of aggression, which make it difficult for victims to do their work, to less obvious actions like spreading rumours, defamation, insults or sexual harassment. According to Hansen, Hogh, Persson, Karlson, Garde, and Ørbæk (2006), indirect harassment also occurs when a victim is cut off and not given the information necessary for carrying out their work. Occasionally it is the superiors who instigate harassment, while on other occasions it is the victim's colleagues, who, for some reason, are stronger than the victim. Sometimes subordinates gang up on a superior.

We have sought to ascertain whether there are differences in the ways of coping with the stressful problems among people who feel harassed in the workplace and those who do not. Lazarus and Folkman (1986) defined coping as the cognitive and behavioural efforts used to manage demands assessed as situations surpassing or overburdening a person's resources. In the same line, Carver, Sheier, and Weintraub (1989) proposed the COPE inventory for assessing coping strategies. Later, Carver (1997) adapted the questionnaire proposing the BriefCOPE, which assesses the following 14 ways of coping: self-distraction, active coping, denial, substance use, emotional support, instrumental support, disengagement, venting, positive reframing, planning, humour, acceptance, religion, and self-blame.

Personality studies performed with the Costa & McCrae's Five-Factors Model show no significant differences among mobbing victims for any personality factors (Morán, 2005). For this reason, we sought to ascertain whether any other variables such as expected situational control, including the locus of control of reinforcement (Rotter, 1966) and perceived self-efficacy (Bandura, 1977) might decide which teachers may of may not become the targets of mobbing. We studied these beliefs of situational control with the BEEGC-20 questionnaire (*Batería de Escalas de Espectativas Generales de Control*, = Battery of Scales of General Control Expectancies) drawn up by Palenzuela, Prieto, Barros, and Almeida (1997).

In this study, we set out with the primary aim of ascertaining, using a sample of Spanish teachers, the differences in self-efficacy, locus of control and ways of coping of harassed and un-harassed teachers in the workplace.

METHOD

Participants

In the study, 255 teachers from all levels of education: including primary, secondary, and university, 92 men (36%). The average age was 38 and the range from 21 to 65 years (Standard deviation was 10.09). They had been working for an average of 13 years, periods in service ranging from 1 to 37 years.

Measures

The Mobbing Perceived Questionnaire (Moran, Gonzalez, & Landero, 2009) measures, with 15 items, different behaviours and feelings of harassment in the workplace. Examples of items are: *7, I don't feel that I can trust my colleagues*; *9, It's difficult to feel safe: there's always somewhere they can attack you from* and *13, I feel that I'm being harassed in the workplace*. Participants score the frequency with which they are experiencing the feeling in each item on a scale of 5, where 1 = never and 5 = always, with intermediate scores. The questionnaire was drawn up to assess psychological harassment in the workplace. The confidence index by internal consistency was 0.92 for this study.

Batería de Expectativas Generales de Control- BEEGC ("Battery of General Expectancies of Control") (BEEGC-20). Drawn up by David L. Palenzuela, it includes 20 items and measures three perceptions of control: (1) locus of control, (2) self-efficacy, and (3) expectancies of success (which we did not study). The perception of locus of control is multidimensional, its three dimensions being internal locus of control, helplessness and belief in luck. The others are one-dimensional. Each dimension is assessed with four items on a Likert scale with nine response options, where 9 = totally agree and 1 = totally disagree, with middle scores. The psychometric properties of this *Battery* are available in Palenzuela, Almeida, and Barros (1992).

BriefCOPE (Carver, 1997). This is a shortened version of the COPE (Carver, Scheier, & Weintraub, 1989), with 28 items to measure different behaviours and cognitive activities commonly used to cope problems with stress. Participants answered each item with a score of up to 4, where 1 = "I haven't been doing this at all" and 4 = "I've been doing this a lot", with intermediate scores, to indicate how much they generally use each strategy to solve stressful problems in the workplace.

Procedure

The questionnaires were administered by people trained in running psychological tests. Teachers completed there in their workplace. Participation was voluntary and anonymous, although many were nor concerned with anonymity and wrote down their names.

Statistical treatment was carried out with SPSS, version 13.0 for Windows.

RESULTS

Differences in Subjects with High and Low Perceptions of Harassment

Are there any differences between those subjected to high levels of mobbing and those who are not in the way they cope with stressful problems?

We divided our sample into three groups according to the mobbing questionnaire scores. The low mobbing group included 42 individuals scoring below 17 (the lowest score was 15); the high mobbing group of 30 scored over 40, with a maximum of 65. The middle group, comprising 183 was omitted from the analyses. Our classification was based on the statistics showed in studies like Piñuel's (2001), according to which 15% of Spanish workers may be harassed in the workplace (30 individuals is 12%). The t test for comparing averages gives the following results: teachers who do not feel harassed make greater use of such coping strategies as planning, the low-rated mobbing group being greater planners than the high-rated group (t = 1.981; p = .05), while the high group made less use of positive reframing (t = 2.691; p = .009). Moreover, the high-rated group scored higher on emotion-centred strategies such as denial (t = -2.347; p = .022), self-distraction (t = -2.676; p = .011) or venting (t = -2.215; p = .032), and lower on acceptance of responsibility (t = 2.497; p = 0.15). The results are shown in Table 1.

The results show that harassed teachers are using more dysfunctional coping strategies, while those who do not feel harassed tend to use more functional ones when they have to solve stressful problems.

What differences are there, according to perceptions of situational control between the low- and high-rated groups?

By the BEEGC-20 questionnaire (Palenzuela et al., 1997), we assessed three general control expectancies: internal locus of control, external locus of control and self-efficacy. Table 2 shows the differences revealed by the t test between the individuals in the high- and low-rated groups for these general perceptions. Those with a high feeling perception of harassment scored significantly higher for the external locus of control (t = .3.299; p = .002). Likewise, lower scores for the internal locus of control are scored by the high-rated group, as is born out by the t = 3.147; p = .002. There is also a significant difference in self-efficacy, which is lower among the more harassed (t = 2.802; p = .007).

These results show a greater external locus of control and a lesser internal one among teachers who feel harassed in the workplace. Harassed teachers perceive a considerably lower level of self-efficacy than un-harassed ones.

DISCUSSION AND CONCLUSIONS

One of our aims was to determine the differences between subjects who did not feel harassed and those who did regarding both coping strategies and their beliefs concerning situation control (locus of control of reinforcement and self-efficacy) (Jordan, 2007). The results show a greater use among the un-harassed of such strategies as planning when

Table 1. Differences between harassed and non-harassed for the 14 coping strategies

	Mobbing Groups	N	mean	*t*	Sig.
Active coping	Low	42	6.60	1.599	.114
	High	30	5.73		
Planning	**Low**	**42**	**6.45**	**1.981**	**.050**
	High	**30**	**5.33**		
Emotional support	Low	42	5.69	1.506	.137
	High	30	4.63		
Use of instrumental support	Low	42	4.88	.502	.617
	High	30	4.53		
Religion	Low	42	1.98	-.500	.618
	High	30	2.30		
Positive reframing	**Low**	**42**	**6.07**	**2.691**	**.009**
	High	**30**	**4.10**		
Acceptance of responsibility	**Low**	**42**	**5.19**	**2.497**	**.015**
	High	**30**	**4.00**		
Denial	**Low**	**42**	**.76**	**-2.345**	**.022**
	High	**30**	**1.67**		
Humour	Low	42	3.05	.264	.793
	High	30	2.87		
Self-distraction	**Low**	**42**	**2.10**	**-2.676**	**.011**
	High	**30**	**3.35**		
Self blame	Low	42	2.14	-1.251	.218
	High	30	2.78		
Behavioural disengagement	Low	42	.24	-1.111	.273
	High	30	.48		
Venting	**Low**	**42**	**1.86**	**-2.215**	**.032**
	High	**30**	**2.96**		
Substance use	Low	42	.19	-1.712	.094
	High	30	.78		

it came to solving stressful problems and of positive reframing (assessing the problem in terms of what might be positive about it and what it might entail in terms of self improvement). These strategies are considered functional (Carver, Scheier, & Weintraub, 1989). Nevertheless, harassed teachers make greater use of dysfunctional (emotionally centred) coping strategies. These strategies, according to Lazarus and Folkman (1986) are suitable only when the problem has no solution and include self-distraction and denial. Although they minimize stress, in the long term, they lead to those affected not using strategies suitable for dealing with the problem. For this reason, such strategies are considered dysfunctional in most laboratory studies (Carver, Scheier, & Weintraub, 1989) and are linked with increased stress levels. In another study, Morán (2005b) found that the coping strategies present in the resilient personality are those focussing on the problem, like active coping (attempting the causes or the people behind the problem), planning – i.e., the planned search for solutions and putting the most suitable ones in practice – and positive reframing.

Teachers who feel they to be the victims of mobbing have a lower self-efficacy that is they generally believe that they are not competent to carry out their work. Nevertheless, this is an effect of being harassed in the workplace; at least we believe this to be the case (Reid, Monsen, & Rivers, 2004). Psychological harassment is aimed basically at reducing the victim's professional worth and their self-esteem. In this case, the mobbers have

Table 2. Descriptive statistics and t test for the groups rated high and low according to the Mobbing Questionnaire

	Mobbing Groups	N	Mean	*t*	Sig.
Internal control	Low	42	31.55	3.147	.002
	High	30	28.53		
External control	Low	42	12.69	-3.299	.002
	High	30	17.77		
Self-efficacy	Low	42	28.69	2.802	.007
	High	30	25.57		

achieved their aim, for the harassed teachers consider themselves less able to do what they have to do to get results than teachers who are not harassed. Harassed teachers feel less efficient in their work.

Harassment victims are usually selected at random, which may be a reason why the victims think that strange forces are controlling their lives. That they have lost control, which may explain why they have a lower internal control (a greater locus of external control), although we are not sure whether it is a consequence of harassment or is a difference between victims and non-victims. More studies are needed in this regard.

The results of this study are not conclusive, further studies are needed to determinate why the victims fail to cope with certain workplace situations such as bullying at work. We are motivate to continue researching in this field, with the hope of shedding some light on the reason why victims do not defend themselves, or do not do so effectively.

Furthermore, suitable instruments based on the use of IT/ICT and on information systems can be planned and carried out to help teachers recognize and monitor harassment and bullying (Lannon, 2010). The use of such systems will make available rigorous documentation and will record usable and actionable information so that everyone can become directly involved in awareness building and debate about the contrast to those hurting phenomena.

REFERENCES

Ayuso, J. A. (2005). Profesión docente y estrés laboral: Una aproximación a los conceptos de estrés laboral y burnout. *Revista Iberoamericana de Educación, 39*(3), 1-15. Retrieved from http://www.rieoei.org/1341.htm.

Bandura, A. (1993). Perceived self-efficacy in cognitive development and functioning. *Educational Psychologist, 28*(2), 117–148. doi:10.1207/s15326985ep2802_3

Bandura, A. (1997). *Self-efficacy. The exercise of control*. New York: Freeman.

Cantón, I. (2004). *Intervención organizativa en la sociedad del Conocimiento*. Granada, Spain: GEU.

Cantón, I. (2004). *Planes de mejora en centros educativos*. Málaga, Spain: Aljibe.

Cantón, I., & Perisset, P. A. (2009). Expectativas y actividades de los profesores con alumnos desfavorecidos socialmente. *Revista de Ciencias de la Educación, 218*, 197–220.

Carver, C. (1997). You want to measure coping but your protocol's too long: consider the Brief COPE. *International Journal of Behavioral Medicine, 4*(1), 92–100. doi:10.1207/s15327558ijbm0401_6

Carver, C., Scheier, M., & Weintraub, J. K. (1989). Assessing coping strategies: A theoretically based approach. *Journal of Personality and Social Psychology, 56*, 267–283. doi:10.1037/0022-3514.56.2.267

Einarsen, S. (2005): The nature, causes and consequences of bullying at work: The Norwegian experience. *Pistes, 7*(3), 1-14. Retrieved from http://www.pistes,uqam.ca/v7n3/articles/v7n3a1en.htm

Einarsen, S., Hoel, H., Zapf, D., & Cooper, C. L. (2003). The concept of bullying at work. The European tradition . In Einarsen, S., Hoel, H., Zapf, D., & Cooper, C. L. (Eds.), *Bullying and emotional abuse in the workplace. International perspectives in research and practice* (pp. 3–30). London: Taylor & Francis.

Einarsen, S., Hoel, H., Zapt, D., & Cooper, C. (2003). *Bullying and emotional abuse in the workplace: International perspectives in research and practice*. New York: Taylor & Francis.

Einarsen, S., & Nielsen, M. B. (Eds.). (2004, April 20). *The Fourth International Conference on Bullying and Harassment in the Workplace*. Retrieved from http://www.bullying.no/content/bbrg/Book%20of%20abstract%20FICBHWP

Hames, J., & Harvey, M. (2006). Workplace bullying: a cross-level assessment. *Management Decision*, *44*(9), 1214–1230. doi:10.1108/00251740610707695

Hansen, Ä. M., Hogh, A., Persson, R., Karlson, B., Garde, A. H., & Ørbæk, P. (2006). Bullying at work, health outcomes, and physiological stress response. *Journal of Psychosomatic Research*, *60*, 63–72. doi:10.1016/j.jpsychores.2005.06.078

Hansen, Ä. M., Hogh, A., Persson, R., Karlson, B., Garde, A. H., & Ørbæk, P. (2006). Bullying at work, health outcomes, and physiological stress response. *Journal of Psychosomatic Research*, *60*, 63–72. doi:10.1016/j.jpsychores.2005.06.078

Hoel, H., Zapf, D., & Cooper, C. L. (2002). Workplace bullying and stress. *Historical and Current Perspectives on Stress and Health*, *2*, 293–333. doi:10.1016/S1479-3555(02)02008-5

Jordan, J. G. (2007, January 1). *Factors that influence teacher responses to bullying situations* (Tech. Rep. No. AAI3290009). Detroit, MI: Wayne State University. Retrieved from http://digitalcommons.wayne.edu/dissertations/AAI3290009

Kyriacou, C. (2001). Teacher stress: directions for future research. *Educational Review*, *53*(1), 27–35. doi:10.1080/00131910120033628

Lannon, J. (2010). The Role of Information and Communication Technologies in Human Rights Monitoring and Advocacy. In Martin, J., & Hawkins, L. (Eds.), *Information Communication Technologies for Human Services Education and Delivery: Concepts and Cases*. Hershey, PA: IGI Global.

Lazarus, R. S., & Folkman, S. (1986). *Estrés y procesos cognitivos*. Barcelona, Spain: Martínez Roca.

Leymann, H. (1996a). *Mobbing: La persécution au travail*. París: Seuil.

Leymann, H. (1996b). The content and development of mobbing at work. *European Journal of Work and Organizational Psychology*, *5*(2), 165–184. doi:10.1080/13594329608414853

Leymann, H., & Gustafsson, A. (1996). Mobbing at work and the development of Post-traumatic Stress Disorders. *European Journal of Work and Organizational Psychology*, *5*(2), 251–275. doi:10.1080/13594329608414858

Malinauskiene, V. (2004). Bullying among teachers in Kaunas, Lithuania. In S. Einarsen & M. B. Nielsen (Eds.), *The Fourth International Conference on Bullying and Harassment in the Workplace*. Retrieved from http://www.bullying.no/content/bbrg/Book%20of%20abstract%20FICBHWP

Mikkelsen, E. G. (2004). Coping with exposure to bullying at work – results from an interview study. In S. Einarsen & M. B. Nielsen (Eds.), *The Fourth International Conference on Bullying and Harassment in the Workplace*. Retrieved from http://www.bullying.no/content/bbrg/Book%20of%20abstract%20FICBHWP

Mikkelsen, G. E., & Einarsen, S. (2001). Bullying in Danish work-life: Prevalence and health correlates. *European Journal of Work and Organizational Psychology*, *10*, 393–413. doi:10.1080/13594320143000816

Milner, H. R. (2002). A case study of an experienced English teachers' self-efficacy and persistence through "crisis" situations: Theoretical and practical considerations. *High School Journal*, *86*(1), 28–35. doi:10.1353/hsj.2002.0020

Morán, C. (2002). Mobbing: Persecución o psicoterror en el trabajo. *Capital Humano*, *151*, 44–48.

Morán, C. (2005). Personalidad, afrontamiento y burnout en profesionales de atención a personas con discapacidad intelectual. *Siglo Cero*, *31*(213), 30–39.

Morán, C. (2006). El cansancio emocional en servicios humanos: Asociación con acoso psicológico, personalidad y afrontamiento (Emotional exhaustion in social services: Its relations to mobbing, personality, and coping). *Revista de Psicología del Trabajo y de las Organizaciones*, *22*(2), 227–239.

Morán, C., González, M. T., & Landero, R. (2009). Valoración Psicométrica del Cuestionario de Acoso Psicológico Percibido. Psychometric Evaluation of the Perceived Mobbing Questionnaire. *Revista de Psicología del Trabajo y de las Organizaciones*, *25*(1), 7–16.

Morán, C., González, M. T., & Landero, R. (2009). El Cuestionario de Acoso Psicológico Percibido-CAPP: Un instrumento para evaluar el mobbing. *Infocoponline*. Retrieved from http://www.infocop.es/view_article.asp?id=2496

Palenzuela, D. L. (1994). *BEEGC. Batería de Escalas de Expectativas Generalizadas de Control*. Salamanca, Spain: Universidad de Salamanca.

Pehkonen, H. (2004). Workplace bullying and coping strategies. A longitudinal study. In S. Einarsen & M. B. Nielsen (Eds.), *The Fourth International Conference on Bullying and Harassment in the Workplace*. Retrieved from http://www.bullying.no/content/bbrg/Book%20of%20abstract%20FICBHWP

Piñuel, I. (2005). La identificación, medida y prevención del mobbing en la organización. *Capital Humano*, *188*, 96–102.

Reid, P., Monsen, J., & Rivers, I. (2004). Psychology's contribution to understanding and managing bullying within schools. *Educational Psychology in Practice*, *20*(3), 241–258. doi:10.1080/0266736042000251817

Rotter, J. B. (1966). Generalized expectancies for internal versus external control of reinforcement. *Psychological Monographs: General and Applied*, *80*, 609.

Schuster, (1996). Rejection, exclusion, and harassment at work and in schools. *European Psychologist*, *1*, 293-309.

Tschannen-Moran, M., & Woolfolk-Hoy, A. (2001). Teacher efficacy: Capturing an elusive construct. *Teaching and Teacher Education*, *17*, 783–805. doi:10.1016/S0742-051X(01)00036-1

Wertheim, C., & Leyser, Y. (2002). Efficacy beliefs, background variables, and differentiated instruction of Israeli prospective teachers. *The Journal of Educational Research*, *96*(1), 54–64. doi:10.1080/00220670209598791

This work was previously published in International Journal of Digital Literacy and Digital Competence, Volume 1, Issue 2, edited by Antonio Cartelli, pp. 48-56, copyright 2010 by IGI Publishing (an imprint of IGI Global).

Chapter 19
Employee Monitoring and Ethics:
Can They Co-Exist?

Angelina I. T. Kiser
University of the Incarnate Word, USA

Timothy Porter
University of the Incarnate Word, USA

David Vequist
University of the Incarnate Word, USA

ABSTRACT

More advanced technologies that make it possible to monitor employees in the workplace have led to controversies on both legal and ethical grounds. Employers can now easily monitor emails, Internet usage and sites visited, and keystrokes, as well as use GPS systems to track employees' movements throughout the day. At one end of the spectrum is the employer who claims that monitoring not only improves productivity but is a legal necessity that assists in keeping the company from becoming legally liable for employees' misuse of technology. Employees, on the other hand, want their privacy protected, and many believe that it is more a matter of them not being trusted. In this paper, an examination is presented that describes various forms of workplace surveillance and monitoring, viewpoints of both employers and employees, policies that companies have implemented, and the ethical and legal implications of such policies.

INTRODUCTION

Employee monitoring has always occurred in business as supervisors oversaw the activities of their employees. Employees were, and are still, subjected to such measures as random bag checks to ensure that no company property was being stolen, punching time clocks to ensure the employee is at work at the specified times, and secured entrances that only allow certain employees to access restricted areas. Eventually, employee monitoring moved to employers recording phone conversations between customers and employees or using video surveillance to stay

DOI: 10.4018/978-1-4666-0903-7.ch019

abreast of employee productivity and activities. Today, with the emergence of the Internet and other digital technologies, employers now have numerous options with which to monitor their employees – not just what they do, but when and where they do it. Computer software used by companies is being utilized to record computer key strokes, monitor websites visited, and even "spy" on employees in real-time (Turri, Maniam, & Hynes, 2008). According to the American Management Association (2007), 45% of employers track Internet content, keystrokes, and time spent on the keyboard, 43% store and review computer files, 12% monitor the blogosphere, and 10% monitor social networking sites.

Electronic monitoring has brought with it a barrage of controversies as employers insist that it is necessary and employees claim that it is an invasion of their privacy. According to Wakefield (2004), employers use monitoring and surveillance of their employees to: 1) protect the rights of employees, 2) create a safe work environment, 3) protect sensitive corporate information and assets, and 4) comply with federal laws. Corporations and other organizations gather and store sensitive information, and they are required to safeguard that information. Employee surveillance is simply one more safeguard to ensure that the information is secure. Employers also cite improved productivity as a reason for making use of employee monitoring and surveillance. Snapshotspy.com reported that 50% of employees use the Internet for personal use during a normal workday, which negatively affects productivity, customer service, network resources, and may even render a company vulnerable to legal liability (Young, 2010).

On the other end of the spectrum are the employees who feel that their privacy is being invaded and that their employers simply do not trust them or want to monitor every minute of their workday. Some employees have challenged the legal aspects of employee monitoring based on the concept of invasion of privacy (Hornung, 2005). Employers should be conscious of the employees' desire for some privacy and attempt to avoid unnecessary intrusions that lead to a proliferation of monitoring and surveillance (Nord, McCubbins, & Nord, 2006).

EMPLOYEE CONCERNS

People have an expectation of privacy, and they value that privacy in their personal lives. However, how much privacy should a person expect to have within the employment context? How invasive should an organization be in monitoring its employees? It appears that technology has outpaced the once traditional expectations of privacy. In the past, employees saw the manager watching them, or they were well aware of video and phone surveillance. Today, employees are "watched" through their use of their work computers via email and Internet usage. Companies can monitor what employees are doing during the entire workday with at least 40 million U.S. workers being subject to electronic monitoring (Alder & Ambrose, 2005).

In a study conducted by Hoffman, Hartman, and Rowe (2003), they cite several reasons for limiting employee monitoring:

- Monitoring may create a suspicious and hostile work environment.
- The lack of privacy may constrain work flow.
- It may be important for employees to conduct some personal business from the workplace.
- Workplace stress and press are increased.
- Freedom of expression and autonomy are hindered.
- Monitoring is intrusive upon one's right to privacy of thought.

Should workers feel excessively stressed in the workplace because of a negative work environment, productivity may actually decrease (Everett,

Wong, & Paynter, 2004), which would counteract one of the purposes of employee monitoring. High levels of negative stress in employees can then lead to indirect costs to an organization, such as low morale, dissatisfaction, breakdowns in communication, and disruption of working relationships (Nelson & Quick, 2009). Therefore, it is important for employers to effectively communicate the reasons for electronic monitoring and find a balance between the need for the monitoring and the privacy of the employees.

EMPLOYER CONCERNS

Employers monitor their employees for a multitude of reasons, including: 1) minimize security risks, 2) ensure stable productivity, 3) protect stakeholder interests, 4) protect against potential liability, 5) ensure legislative compliance, and 6) performance evaluation and feedback (Star Workforce Solutions, Inc., 2009). The growing improper use of company resources with respect to Internet use and company email continues to grow, and companies face exposure to significant liability (Arnesen & Weis, 2007).

A major concern of employers is the lack of productivity if employees are spending valuable work time using the Internet and checking personal emails. Most employers accept that employees will spend some personal time using the computer; however, monitoring is in place to ensure that it does not begin to negatively affect productivity and customer relations. An employee monitoring program with the aim of risk management can help companies manage the risks of lost productivity (Latto, 2007).

Companies also have a legal and ethical obligation to protect against employee misuse of the Internet and email as well as other employee actions that might infringe on stakeholder privacy. Employers monitor to make certain that employees are not leaking information such as trade secrets or intellectual property. For example, employees from Coca-Cola were caught trying to sell trade secrets to Pepsi (Associated Press, 2006). Pepsi reported the information to the FBI, and email monitoring led to the employees who had attempted to divulge the information.

CYBERLOAFING

The term cyberloafing refers to using email and the Internet for personal use while at work. Cyberloafing comes in various forms including, but not limited to: 1) sending and receiving personal emails, 2) checking news headlines, 3) shopping online 4) banking online, 5) downloading music, and 6) surfing adult sites. These forms of cyberloafing bring varying levels of concern for organizations. A survey conducted with 221 employed Masters of Business Administration (MBA) students at a Southwestern university revealed cyberloafing behaviors by the participants (Blanchard & Henle, 2008) (see Table 1).

Employers are being forced to monitor and regulate Internet use because of cyberloafing (Young, 2010). If employees take part in illegal

Table 1. Cyberloafing behaviors

Percentage (%) Engaging in this Behavior at Work	
Behavior	Percentage (%)
Checking non-work email	90
Visiting news sites	90
Visiting stock sites	65
Visiting financial sites	83
Visiting sports sites	50
Shopping online	68
Booking vacation/travel	50
Job hunting	46
Downloading music	11
Visiting adult sites	5
Visiting personals	10
Gambling online	3

activities online such as downloading music or visiting adult sites, the company could be open to legal ramifications (Lichtash, 2004), whereas other forms of cyberloafing might not have a negative legal effect on the organization. However, negative effects of cyberloafing do not only come in the form of legal issues. According to a whitepaper report by Symantec Hosted Services (2008), when employees are cyberloafing instead of working, there are these non-legal implications:

- Reduced productivity – employees spend time on the Internet instead of working. More time on the Internet translates to poor customer service and an inability to meet deadlines (Young, 2010).
- Security problems – infected websites create Malware issues.
- Wasted bandwidth – Internet connections are slowed due to non-work related web traffic. System responsiveness is slower when employees are using bandwidth for personal use causing more wait time for customers (Young, 2010).
- Reputation risk – employees can leak confidential information or spread detrimental rumors online

A reduction in employee productivity ultimately results in lost revenues. United States employees spend roughly six hours per week using the Internet for non-work related activities, resulting in a suggested productivity loss of $5.3 billion (Glover, 2002). A more recent study by Klein (2007) reported that employees spend over 81 minutes per day on non-work related computer activities.

The Internet has created valuable tools for businesses and led to improved communication and productivity. However, there have also been negative effects, and organizations are faced with the task of controlling problems caused by cyberloafing. The proliferation of employee misuse of company property, the Internet, company vehicles and phones, etc., has led to a greater degree of electronic monitoring in order to curb potential legal implications and lost revenues due to a decrease in productivity. Many companies now have electronic monitoring policies in place that include guidelines for employees as well as possible punishments should they not abide by the rules.

ELECTRONIC MONITORING POLICIES

While employers may well be able to justify the use of employee monitoring, they should consider a balanced policy that takes into account the various stakeholders – owners, managers, and employees - in order to help with employee acceptance of the policy (Friedman & Reed, 2007). A formal written policy regarding electronic monitoring polices should be provided to employees and should include information regarding the amount of monitoring that will occur, the exact rules and regulations, and the consequences for breaking the rules or regulations (Turri, Maniam, & Hynes, 2008; Young, 2010).

The Electronic Communications Privacy Act (ECPA) gives employers the legal right to protect themselves through electronic monitoring activities (Wen, Schwieger, & Gershuny, 2007). According to Latto (2007), companies can take two approaches to electronic monitoring of their employees, absolute monitoring or a flexible approach. An absolute monitoring policy prohibits any personal use of company computers while a more flexible approach allows for a reasonable amount of personal use as long as it is not at the expense of productivity (Latto, 2007).

But should employers always inform employees about electronic monitoring? Some employers believe the keeping the monitoring a secret will actually increase its effectiveness while others believe that misconduct will be deterred just by the mere fact that employees are aware of the electronic monitoring (Nelson & Tyson, 2010). Disclosing the policies surrounding electronic monitoring is the better alternative from a legal perspective since it removes the expectation of privacy, which employees often use as a reason for invasion of privacy lawsuits (Nelson & Tyson, 2010).

Punishments

If an electronic monitoring policy is put in place to deal with misuse of company equipment (i.e. Internet, email, phone, vehicles, etc.), it should address the consequences for breaking the regulations. Organizations must decide how best to respond to employees breaking Internet usage policies. A framework for managing employees Internet usage should include practices relating to hiring, prevention, enforcement, and termination or rehabilitation (Young, 2010). However, not all companies inform their employees that they are being electronically monitored. In point of fact, secret monitoring of employees is actually widespread (Adler, Ambrose, & Noel, 2006), and only four states – California, Connecticut, Delaware, and Massachusetts – have legislation that required employers to disclose the existence of workplace monitoring (Nelson & Tyson, 2010).

Whether companies are informing their employees about electronic monitoring or not, more of them are firing employees who do not adhere to their monitoring policies and guidelines. A survey conducted by the American Management Association and The ePolicy Institute, which included 304 U.S. companies, found that more than a quarter of employers had fired workers for misusing email, and one third had fired employees for misusing the Internet on the job (Gohring, 2008). Companies fire employees for various reasons; one major concern is the legal liability that the company takes on when it does not take action if an employee is conducting illegal activities via email, the Internet, etc. Additionally, some employees harass other employees through the use of the company's Internet or email system. When the company has an electronic monitoring system in place, it becomes much easier for the employer to investigate and not simply rely on people's statements.

Legal Issues

Employers themselves can be held liable for their employees who misuse company email and Internet. In April, 2006, the U.S. Supreme Court approved amendments that now require companies to provide information regarding electronic discovery (Ward, Purwin, Sipior, & Volonino, 2009). For example, companies have been sued because employees sexually harass other employees using the company's email system. Chevron paid $2.2 million because of a sexual harassment suit brought about by four female employees who sued the company after claiming pornographic pictures were sent using the company's email system. The company was required to turn over the electronic communications, and the plaintiff's claims were found to be true (Arnesen & Weis, 2007). Cases of companies being sued for racial harassment via their Internet systems include Curtis v. Dimaio, 1999, Daniels v. WorldCom Corp., 1998, and Owens v. Morgan Stanley & Co., Inc., 1997. In the case of Owens v. Morgan Stanley & Co., Inc., the courts allowed plaintiffs to proceed with a $60 million lawsuit because of a racist joke sent over the company's email system (Arnesen & Weis, 2007).

METHODS OF ELECTRONIC MONITORING

Monitoring Internet Usage

Internet abuse in the workplace has been on the rise for years. With the inception of DSL, Cable and Fiber Optics, speed has allowed employees to multi-task at their job without being detected. For decades, employers have been monitoring employee Internet usage, but in recent years organizations have made drastic changes like installing sniffers and firewalls. Smartphones, tablets, and laptops connected to an organization's Wi-Fi network pose concerns for employers too. Recent on-line industry studies show that web usages in the workplace can cost U.S. organizations approximately $1 billion annually in terms of lost productivity, not to mention other potential legal liabilities, such as libel, defamation, and harassment lawsuits (Mahatanankoon, Anandarajan, & Igbaria, 2004).

The U.S. Treasury Department found that non-work-related computing (NWRC),such as online shopping, checking personal finances, answering personal emails, and using chat rooms, accounted for 51% of an employee's time online (Davis, 2001). Urbaczewski and Jessup (2002) refer to the lost productivity that takes place directly after granting employees Internet access as a "productivity vacuum," where the easy access to non-work-related activities is too tempting for employees to resist (Ugrin & Pearson, 2008).

An employer's technique for monitoring Internet usage covers a broad spectrum. Internet consumption in the workplace falls into several categories. The computer-based monitoring technology table in Table 2 shows many classifications of monitoring (Wen & Gershuny, 2005).

According to the American Management Association's 2001 Electronic Monitoring and Surveillance Survey, 46% of organizations sur-

Table 2. Computer-based monitoring technology

Keystroke monitoring	• Maintains a record of keystrokes along with the window they are typed in and time stamped.
	• Tracks computer idle time.
	• Recreates "deleted" documents because the keystrokes are logged and stored even if deleted.
Emails sent and received	• Monitors and logs all emails sent and received by users of all company owned computers.
	• Screens emails for potentially offensive or inappropriate messages.
	• Scans employee emails for questionable keywords pre-determined by the employer.
Events timeline logging	• Logs all events users performed and views them in an organized chronologically ordered listing.
	• Views what events the user performed, in the order they did them.
	• Logs program starts/stops, website visits, document viewings and printings.
Application usage	• Monitors and logs all applications run by users.
	• Logs when the application was started, stopped, and how long it was actually used.
	• Records application installations performed by users.
	• Logs software name, installation path, and time of installation is logged.
Window activity	• Records documents and files opened and viewed by users.
	• Logs all windows in which the user directly interacts on the desktop.
	• Monitors and logs all Internet sessions and all chat conversations made on the PC.
	• Records documents and files that are printed by users.
	• Logs all passwords used during monitoring sessions via its keystrokes recorder.
Remote desktop viewing	• Takes snapshots of every desktop at set intervals of time, allowing managers to visually see what is happening.
	• Views a listing of various system information for the remote PC, including processor type, system directory.
	• Views a list of the current Internet connections on the PC.
	• Views a list of the recent documents users have opened.
	• Remotely views what the user is doing in real-time.

veyed monitored email use, and that number rose to 52% in 2003 (e-policy institute) and 55% in 2005(Snyder, 2010). The reasons for the growth in monitoring are noted in Table 2. The percentages in monitoring will continue to soar because of ease of access to the Internet in the workplace. When we take into account that employees spend the vast amount of their day working, employers should have a reasonable expectation that Internet usage will always be present.

Two recent moments in history are variables in Internet usage in the workplace. Variables like these will continue to provide problems in the workplace. President Barack Obama's inauguration was a global moment, not just in terms of history and politics but also web participation (Gannes, 2009). Akamai Technologies, which powers many sites including CNN, said it had its largest single day on record of concurrent live viewership, with 7 million active simultaneous streams (the majority of them live) at about 12:15 p.m. ET on inauguration day. Akamai said it also saw its largest-ever amount of Flash streams, with more than 800 Gbps of Flash streaming served (Young & Faris, 2009).

According to Paul (2009), one of the first trusted news sources to verify Michael Jackson's death, reported nearly 2.3 million page views in just one hour -- the highest traffic the newspaper had experienced in such a short time. That page view record beats any hour during the Times' highest traffic day of all time -- November 5, 2008, the day after Barack Obama was elected President. These moments in history occurred while millions of Americans were working.

Keystrokes-Hardware and Software

We all know technologies are advancing every single day as we hear about new inventions. Employers are also seeking new technologies in order to keep their workforce moving forward, and company leaders have become more technology savvy as they have to innovate considerably faster. One approach more employers have become accustomed to is the ability to monitor employees' computer usage by means of hardware and software keystrokes. A keystroke is the action of pressing a key on a keyboard. If you press 15 keys you would have a total of 15 keystrokes. There are numerous keylogging methods, ranging from hardware and software-based approaches to electromagnetic and acoustic analysis (Software Informer, 2010).

Technology companies have made money integrating keystrokes with software and hardware platforms calling them software and hardware keyloggers. Software keyloggers are software surveillance programs or tools installed on computers and servers where the goal is to obtain keystrokes. The data obtained is then stored and can be easily retrieved through a web browser as an employee is making the keystrokes. Information Technology personnel hired by the employer remotely install and configure the software keylogger to send keystrokes to one or multiple supervisors. Below are software programs designed to work on the target computer's operating system. From a technical perspective there are five categories:

- Hypervisor-based: The keylogger can theoretically reside in a malware hypervisor running underneath the operating system, which remains untouched. It effectively becomes a virtual machine. Blue Pill is a conceptual example.
- Kernel based: This method is difficult both to write and to combat. Such keyloggers reside at the kernel level and are thus difficult to detect, especially for user-mode applications. They are frequently implemented as rootkits that subvert the operating system kernel and gain unauthorized access to the hardware, making them very powerful. A keylogger using this method can act as a keyboard driver for example, and thus gain access to any information typed on the keyboard as it goes to the operating system.

- API-based: These keyloggers hook keyboard APIs, the operating system then notifies the keylogger each time a key is pressed, and the keylogger simply records it. APIs such as GetAsyncKeyState(), GetForegroundWindow(), etc. are used to poll the state of the keyboard or to subscribe to keyboard events. These types of keyloggers are the easiest to write, but where constant polling of each key is required, they can cause a noticeable increase in CPU usage, and can also miss the occasional key. A more recent example simply polls the BIOS for preboot authentication PINs that have not been cleared from memory.
- Form Grabber based: Form Grabber-based keyloggers log web form submissions by recording the web browsing onSubmit event functions. This records form data before it is passed over the Internet and bypasses httpsencryption.
- Packet analyzers: This involves capturing network traffic associated with HTTP POST events to retrieve unencrypted passwords (Software Informer, 2010).

Hardware keyloggers are hardware devices like U.S.B drives, PS2 keyboard connecters and wireless connectors. Employers have adjusted to wireless connectors as their workforce becomes more aware of an organization's monitoring techniques. Hardware keyloggers are not easily detected because they are installed mainly after hours and hidden to the naked eye. Below are several types of hardware keyloggers:

- A Regular Hardware Keylogger is used for keystroke logging by means of a hardware circuit that is attached somewhere in between the computer keyboard and the computer. It logs all keyboard activity to its internal memory which can be accessed by typing in a series of pre-defined characters. A hardware keylogger has an advantage over a software solution because it is not dependent on the computer's operating system, and it will not interfere with any program running on the target machine making it undetectable by any software. They are typically designed to have an innocuous appearance that blends in with the rest of the cabling or hardware, such as appearing to be an EMC Balun. They can also be installed inside a keyboard itself (as a circuit attachment or modification), or the keyboard could be manufactured with this "feature". They are designed to work with legacy PS/2 keyboards, or more recently, with U.S.B keyboards. Some variants, known as wireless hardware keyloggers, have the ability to be controlled and monitored remotely by means of a wireless communication standard.
- Wireless Keylogger sniffers - Collect packets of data being transferred from a wireless keyboard and its receiver and then attempt to crack the encryption key being used to secure wireless communications between the two devices.
- Firmware - A computer's BIOS, which is typically responsible for handling keyboard events, can be reprogrammed so that it records keystrokes as it processes them.
- Keyboard overlays - a bogus keypad is placed over the real one so that any keys pressed are registered by both the eavesdropping device as well as the legitimate one that the customer is using (Software Informer, 2010).

All of these devices help companies monitor web traffic to minimize network bandwidth. "Employers are not prepared to tolerate misuse of the Internet generally but especially in the current climate," said Mark Hatfield, employment law partner at Mace & Jones. "Staff who idle away on the Internet are wasting valuable time which should be being deployed to maintain company efficiency and productivity (My Business, 2009).

Email Monitoring

Email is the most common and widely used electronic communication in all organizations today. The trend of companies monitoring employees' email and phone usage is continuing, according to the results of the most recent annual Electronic Monitoring and Surveillance Survey conducted by the American Management Association (AMA) and the ePolicy Institute. The data shows that more than one-quarter of employers have fired employees for misusing email. Likewise, almost one-third have fired workers for misusing the Internet (Nancherla, 2008). We have all received emails from friends, family and coworkers pertaining to non-related work functions like birthdays, movies, weekend events, and etc. We receive and reply to these emails with the assurance that no one is monitoring or reading our messages. In addition to email, Facebook and Twitter can be integrated into email clients tempting us once more to bend the rule of productivity. We do this forgetting about the computing use policy we signed in Human Resources that states all electronic communications are the property of the employer.

Email monitoring involves employers storing records of employee emails that are transferred through company servers and using keyword searches or natural language processing to locate and flag suspicious text (Spitzmüller, & Stanton, 2006). We have heard of cases involving misuse or abuse of email and improper use of social networking sites where employers are struggling to provide a clear and up-to-date computing policy to address these issues. Vault.com conducted a survey in 1999 with 1,244 respondents, and found that 84% of employees sent non-work related emails and almost 90% surfed the Internet for non-work related purposes during office hours. Accordingly, many companies scrambled to get policies and guidelines in place to deal with the effects of non-work related computing (Gee-Woo & Ling, 2009). Companies have become stricter on abusers during this economy because productivity is vital to an organization's survival.

The present day state of email monitoring by employers sends a strong message that efficiency and productivity are priorities. Termination as a result of improper email usage was broken down into violation of any company policy (64%), use of inappropriate or offensive language (62%), and breach of confidentiality (22%). Misuse of the Internet included viewing, downloading, or uploading inappropriate or offensive content (84%), violation of company policy (48%), and excessive personal use (34%). Email monitoring was done by 43% of companies, with almost all of them tracking external emails. In contrast, only slightly more than one-half monitored internal emails, which often become evidence in litigation (Nancherla, 2008).

There seems to be a zero tolerance for abusers using company resources for non-work related activities while being monitored. The question everyone must ask is, "Will current laws be updated to adapt to the ever changing technology era and will employees ever have a right to privacy in the workplace?". The Ninth Circuit's recent decision in Quon v. Arch Wireless, the Idaho Supreme Court's recent decision in Cowles Publishing Co. v. Kootenai County Board of County Commissioners, and the Southern District of New York's decision in Pure Power Fitness Bootcamp v. Warrior Fitness Boot Camp provide cases with four key practice points that all employers, including law offices, should follow:

- Ensure that your policy is updated to account for all types of electronic hardware and software in use within your office;
- Ensure that no informal policies, practices, or customs have arisen outside the parameters of your written policy;
- Update, and obtain signatures acknowledging and consenting to, electronic usage policies from all employees using mobile electronics; and

- For government attorneys and employees, be fully aware of the public nature of the use of electronics and the limitations on employer access (Kane, 2009).

It is essential that employers and their attorneys revisit these policies on a regular basis to insure they are clear, up to date, and consistent with current case law (Kane, 2009).

SOCIAL NETWORKING – THE NEW TECHNOLOGY

Are social networking sites the newest tool employers will begin to monitor? Facebook, MySpace, Twitter and LinkedIn are examples of social networking sites that have been introduced in the workplace with major concerns. Forty-five percent of employers reported in a recent CareerBuilder survey (CareerBuilder, 2009) that they use social networking sites to research job candidates, a big jump from 22% last year. Another 11% plan to start using social networking sites for screening. More than 2,600 hiring managers participated in the survey, which was completed in June 2009. Of those who conduct online searches/background checks of job candidates, 29% use Facebook, 26% use LinkedIn and 21% use MySpace. One-in-ten (11%) search blogs while 7% follow candidates on Twitter.

So what are social networking sites? We define social networking sites as web-based services that allow individuals to (1) construct a public or semi-public profile within a bounded system, (2) articulate a list of other users with whom they share a connection, and (3) view and traverse their list of connections and those made by others within the system. The nature and nomenclature of these connections may vary from site to site (Boyd & Ellison, 2007). Social networking web sites are a relatively new format that allows people to post personal information to be viewed by "private" friends and the public as well. Managers may wish to access these sites, with or without permission, and use that information in hiring and retention decisions. Managers may, in fact, be required to monitor employees' social networking sites to defend against the possibility of negligent hiring and retention lawsuits being filed against their companies (Elzweig & Peeples, 2009).

Social networking sites such as Facebook, Linkedin, and Twitter have become additional avenues of monitoring employees during the hiring process and after becoming employed. While many people use social networking sites as a way to reconnect and communicate with friends and family, employers are using them to conduct background checks on job applicants or to monitor employees' actions. The amount and type of information a person places on his/her Facebook page can definitely have an impact when it comes to employment.

According to a 2007 survey by Vault.com, 44% percent of employers used social networking sites to research a potential employee, and 39% researched a current employee (Oleniczak, Pike, Mishra, & Mishra, 2010). When companies use Facebook in considering an applicant, they become vulnerable to lawsuits in which the applicants may claim discrimination based on the information found on the Facebook page. While there are no specific guidelines for how Facebook can be used in the applicant screening process, more "failure to hire" lawsuits are expected as applicants file claims of discrimination based on a number of factors (Oleniczak et al., 2010).

When an employer decides not to hire a job applicant based on information found on a social networking site, they do not typically inform the applicant of the information they found and that it was used in the decision making process (Clark & Roberts, 2010). Therefore, applicants receive the typical "thank you for applying" letter and never really know the reason(s) they were not hired. A law student in the U.S. had a job offer rescinded when the law firm discovered that the student was affiliated with a website that posted negative comments about female law students. Although the student had not actually posted any negative comments, his job offer was rescinded (Samborn, 2007).

In other instances, employees are coming under the scrutiny of their employers who become aware of information on their employees' social networking sites. In the case of Dan Leone, his Facebook account affected him not prior to employment, but after he had been employed for several years. Leone was employed by the Philadelphia Eagles football franchise and was in charge of the front gate of the stadium. After posting on his Facebook page that he was unhappy about the team's decision to move, he was fired (Oleniczak, 2010). In Varian Medical Systems, Inc. v. Delfino, two former employees left derogatory remarks on Internet bulletin boards. While the two employees claimed that the information on the bulletin board would not be taken seriously, the courts disagreed and agreed that the comments and accusations were libelous (Wise, 2009).

Employers, employees, and applicants should become aware of the potential risks of social networking sites when it comes to hiring and firing. Employers should be cautious of viewing the sites of potential applicants as this may lead to accessing protected information such as age, marital status, race, or religious affiliation. Potential employees and current employees should also be aware that information they post on social networking sites will not necessarily be private, and while they may feel they have a case of discrimination, the case may be very difficult, if not impossible, to prove. We have already learned so much from a short period of time from these sites. Many organizations have blocked the use of these new tools during business hours while others have fired employees for using them while at work. Organizations are struggling to reform their computing policy to relate to these technologies. So why the sudden and drastic change in business processes due to social networks? Some interesting findings are:

- According to Ipsos Insight's (2007) latest "Face of the Web" study, social networking is becoming the dominant online behavior. The study found that 24% of American adults have visited a social networking web site, with two thirds visiting within the 30 days previous to the polling. This usage is even higher in other countries such as South Korea, where 49% of adults had visited a social networking site at least once (Ipsos Insight, 2007).
- The two most popular social networking sites are MySpace and Facebook.com (Facebook) (Hitwise, 2008).
- In May of 2008, Facebook had 123.9 million unique visitors and MySpace had 114.6 million (McCarthy, 2008).
- The fastest growing demographic on Facebook is those who are 25 years old and older (ComScore, 2007).
- More than half of its users are over age 35 (Comscore, 2006; Elzweig & Peeples, 2009).

ETHICS AND EMPLOYEE MONITORING

Ethical Dilemma

We use Williams' (2011) definition of ethics as a "set of moral principles or values that defines right and wrong for a person or group." The dilemma here is whether employee monitoring equates to ethical or unethical behavior. Is it simply that employers want to know what their employees are doing at all times during the workday? Employers justify their behavior for numerous legal and productivity reasons. Is the monitoring really unethical if employees know that they are being monitored or is the monitoring itself unethical regardless of who has knowledge of it? On the other side of the spectrum are the ethical dilemmas with regards to the organizations' stakeholders. Does a company have an ethical obligation to monitor its employees in order to protect its customers, investors, and other stakeholders? If a company is ethically bound to protect its stakeholders, then it reasons that employee monitoring is an obligation of the company. Therefore, the quandary lies in balancing employee rights with stakeholder rights.

Ethical Decision Making

When considering an electronic monitoring policy and the punishment for violation of a company's policy, in this case misuse of the email system and/or Internet, the intensity of the violation may contribute to the ethical decision the manager ultimately makes (Williams, 2011):

- magnitude of the consequence – total harm or benefit derived from the ethical decision. The magnitude is greater with respect to the number of people harmed.
- social consensus – agreement as to whether the behavior is good or bad.
- probability of effect – the chance that some harm will result to others as a result of the event.
- temporal immediacy – time between the act the consequences it produces.
- proximity of effect – the social, psychological, cultural, or physical distance of the decision maker to those affected by the decision.
- concentration of effect – how much an act affects the average person.

When establishing a company electronic monitoring policy, companies should consider how to make ethical decisions that address the intensity of the violation. For example, if an employee checks personal email on company time, the punishment should not be as severe as for an employee who use email in an attempt to steal proprietary secrets, as in the aforementioned case of the Coca-Cola employees. Employees are more likely to regard a reasonable policy as ethical as opposed to an invasion of their privacy.

Employee Ethics

Would there be a need for electronic monitoring if employees themselves behaved ethically? Is it reasonable to expect each and every employee of a company to make ethical decisions, and if so, who determines what is ethical? Ethical dilemmas occur because of a conflict between competing goals of the employee and employer, and ethics in an electronic age continue to develop (Baltzan & Phillips, 2008). The reality is that not every employee will behave ethically all the time. That has been shown in case after case of employee misuse of company resources.

Therefore, if employees behave unethically, then they should expect that employers would have an ethical obligation to monitor them. Since employers can be held liable for the conduct of their employees, employers actually have an ethical obligation to monitor. If they do not, then the employers could face negative legal consequences as well as harm the reputation of the company. Employees could also view electronic monitoring as a way to protect themselves. If an employee were harassing another employee via email, if the company is monitoring the email, the complaint is much easier to justify and prove. Consequently, the employee with the complaint could justify the ethical nature of the electronic monitoring. If it is ethical in a case of employee harassment toward another employee, it stands to reason that the monitoring is ethical in other cases.

Ethical Theories in Business

The following two ethical theories will be evaluated in relation to electronic monitoring of employees: 1) utilitarianism and 2) formalist. Each will be discussed and applied with regards to both employers and employees. Do these ethical theories justify electronic monitoring of employees? Do employees have a better argument when it comes to the ethics of employee monitoring?

Companies are duty bound to make certain that their employees conduct themselves in an ethical manner and meet their responsibilities (Halpern, Reville, & Grunewald, 2008). The utilitarianism approach to ethical decision making is concerned with the consequences of an act that have the greatest good for the greatest number of people (Ferrell, Fraedrich, & Ferrell, 2011). In the case of businesses, the greatest number of people refers to the company stakeholders. The stakeholders include employees, customers, investors, vendors, and other companies. Therefore, using the utilitarianism approach to business ethics, employers must consider the consequences of an act as having the most benefit to its stakeholders. Electronic monitoring is seen as an act that controls productivity and limits legal liability to the company and its stakeholders and is therefore ethical. If companies do nothing to stop activities that are negatively affecting productivity, then those actions could be detrimental to the stakeholders (Halpern et al., 2008), which is contractor to the utilitarianism approach to ethics.

On the other hand, the formalist approach considers not on the consequences of an act, but rather it considers a set of rules or principles for guiding behavior (Alder, Schminke, & Noel, 2007). Kant, a German philosopher, developed formalism, and connected it to his theory of Categorical Imperative (Mujtaba, 2003). Making a decision using the Categorical Imperative, one would define the act and determine if the act could justly be applied universally. If not, then the act would be deemed unethical regardless of the consequences.

Therefore, managers considering an electronic monitoring policy and the rules to put in place should employees break those rules should consider if the policy could ethically be administered universally. In the case of employee monitoring, the following questions need to be answered: Is it good to monitor employees? Is it good to apply this to everyone? The benefit of others should be the end goal when using the Categorical Imperative. Using this logic, companies could argue that applying an employee monitoring policy to everyone is good and as long as it is applied to everyone, and in the end, it is actually to the benefit of others. However, it should be noted that the end result, or consequence, should not be the driving factor in using the formalist ethics approach. The acts themselves are the primary considerations. If a company enacts an electronic monitoring policy for employees, then under this formalist theory, everyone in the company would be under the policy, not just employees at particular levels of the organization. If this situation is the case, then companies can argue that it is ethical because it is a good policy and applied to all employees at all levels.

CONCLUSION

Employee monitoring has become widespread as companies want to maintain a specific level of productivity as well as avoid potential lawsuits. Employers and employees are faced with the ethical implications of this monitoring. Employees want their privacy, and employers have obligations to their stakeholders to protect the company and continue to reap a profit. While some degree of cyberloafing by employees may be tolerated, it is the responsibility of the organization not to allow this activity to interfere with the mission and goals of the company.

A culture of ethical behavior is vital to the success of a company, and if a company opts to implement an employee monitoring policy, it should be clearly written and communicated to all employees. There should be a balance between employee rights and the responsibilities of the organization. Therefore, if companies construct a well-written monitoring policy and explain the importance of that policy to the employees, it is more likely that employees will understand

and not feel that their privacy is being violated. Managers should explain the purpose of monitoring and how the policy protects them as well as the company.

Using the utilitarianism and formalist approaches to ethics, a company can definitely defend an electronic monitoring policy. A well-crafted policy protects both the company and the employees, making it good for all stakeholders. The act of creating the policy can be seen as good as well as the consequences of having the policy. In fact, companies actually have an ethical and legal obligation to protect its employees, assets, and interests of its stakeholders. Therefore, an electronic monitoring policy does fall within ethical boundaries, and companies should have one in place.

REFERENCES

Alder, G. S., & Ambrose, M. L. (2005). An examination of the effect of computerized performance monitoring feedback on monitoring fairness, performance, and satisfaction. *Organizational Behavior and Human Decision Processes*, *97*, 161–177. doi:10.1016/j.obhdp.2005.03.003

Alder, G. S., Ambrose, M. L., & Noel, T. W. (2006). The effect of formal advance otice and justification on internet monitoring fairness: Much about nothing? *Journal of Leadership & Organizational Studies*, *13*(1), 93–108. doi:10.1177/10717919070130011101

Alder, G. S., Schminke, M., & Noel, T. W. (2007). The impact of individual ethics on reactions to potentially invasive HR practices. *Journal of Business Ethics*, *75*(2), 201–214. doi:10.1007/s10551-006-9247-6

American Management Association. (2007). *2007 electronic monitoring and surveillance survey.* Retrieved November 5, 2010, from http://www.amanet.org/news/177.aspx

Arnesen, D., & Weis, W. (2007). Developing an effective company policy for employee internet and email use. *Journal of Organizational Culture. Communication and Conflict*, *11*(2), 53–65.

Associated Press. (2006). *Three arrested for allegedly stealing, plotting to sell Coca-Cola recipes.* Retrieved October 30, 2010 from http://www.foxnews.com/printer_friendly_story/0,3566,202235,00.html

Baltzan, P., & Phillips, A. (2008). *Business driven information systems*. New York: McGraw-Hill Irwin.

Blanchard, A. L., & Henle, C. A. (2008). Correlates of different forms of cyberloafing: The role of norms and external locus of control. *Computers in Human Behavior*, *24*, 1067–1084. doi:10.1016/j.chb.2007.03.008

Boyd, D., & Ellison, N. (2007). Social network sites: Definition, history, and scholarship. *Journal of Computer-Mediated Communication*, *13*(1), 210–230. doi:10.1111/j.1083-6101.2007.00393.x

CareerBuilder. (2009). *Forty-five percent of employers use social networking sites to research job candidates, CareerBuilder survey finds*. Retrieved November 12, 2010, from http://uncw.edu/stuaff/career/documents/employersusingsocialnetworkingsites.pdf

Clark, L. A., & Roberts, S. J. (2010). Employer's use of social networking sites: A socially irresponsible practice. *Journal of Business Ethics*, *95*, 507–525. doi:10.1007/s10551-010-0436-y

Elzweig, B., & Peeples, D. (2009). Using social networking web sites in hiring and retention decisions. *SAM Advanced Management Journal*, *74*(4), 27–35.

Everett, A. M., Wong, Y., & Payner, J. (2004). Balancing employee and employer rights: An international comparison of e-mail privacy in the workplace. *Journal of Individual Employment Rights*, *11*(4), 291–310.

Ferrell, O. C., Fraedrich, J., & Ferrell, L. (2011). *Business Ethics*. Mason, OH: South-Western Cengage Learning.

Friedman, F., & Reed, L. J. (2007). Workplace privacy: Employee relations and legal implications of monitoring employee e-mail use. *Employee Responsibilities and Rights Journal, 19*(2), 75–83. doi:10.1007/s10672-007-9035-1

Gannes, L. (2009). *The Obama inauguration live stream stats*. Retrieved November 13, 2010, from http://gigaom.com/video/the-obama-inauguration-live-stream-stats/

Gee-Woo, B., & Swee Ling, H. (2009). Non-work related computing (NWRC). *Communications of the ACM, 52*(4), 124–128. doi:10.1145/1498765.1498799

Glover, R. (2002). Privacy in the workplace – complex issues for employers. *Metropolitan Corporate Counsel, 10*(6), 1-2, 9-10.

Gohring, N. (2008). Over 50% of companies have fired workers for e-mail, Net abuse. *Computerworld.* Retrieved November 2, 2010, from http://www.computerworld.com/s/article/9065659/Over_50_of_companies_have_fired_workers_for_e_mail_Net_abuse

Halpern, D., Reville, P. J., & Gruenwald, D. (2008). Management and legal issues regarding electronic surveillance of employees in the workplace. *Journal of Business Ethics, 80*, 175–180. doi:10.1007/s10551-007-9449-6

Hoffman, W. M., Hartman, L. P., & Rowe, M. (2003). You've got mail...and the boss knows: A survey by the center for business ethics of companies' email and internet monitoring. *Business and Society Review, 108*(3), 285–307. doi:10.1111/1467-8594.00166

Hornung, M. S. (2005). Think before you type: A look at email privacy in the workplace. *Fordham Journal of Corporate and Financial Law, 11*, 115–160.

Kane, B. (2009). It's not your blackberry: The courts remind employers to update their workplace electronics policies. *Computer & Internet Lawyer, 26*(3), 35–38.

Klein, K. E. (2007). Setting a realistic web-use policy. *Business Week Online, 18*.

Latto, A. (2007). Managing risk from within: monitoring employees the right way. *Risk Management, 54*(4), 30–34.

Lichtash, A. E. (2004). Inappropriate use of e-mail and the Internet in the workplace: The arbitration picture. *Dispute Resolution Journal, 59*, 26–36.

Mahatanankoon, P., Anandarajan, M., & Igbaria, M. (2004). Development of a measure of personal web usage in the workplace. *Cyberpsychology & Behavior, 7*(1), 93–104. doi:10.1089/109493104322820165

Mujtaba, B. G. (2003). Ethical implications of employee monitoring: what leaders should consider. *Journal of Applied Management and Entrepreneurship, 8*(3), 22–43.

My Business. (2009). *Employers should limit staff net use*. Retrieved November 13, 2010, from http://www.mybusiness.co.uk/YSy1ncE.html

Nancherla, A. (2008). SURVEILLANCE: Increases in workplace. *T+D, 62*(5), 12.

Nelson, C. H., & Tyson, L. (2010). HR undercover: Factor in privacy rights before rolling out surveillance programs. *HR Magazine.* Retrieved November 1, 2010, from http://www.thefreelibrary.com/HR+undercover%3a+factor+in+privacy+rights+before+rolling+out...-a0240605411

Nelson, D. L., & Quick, J. C. (2011). *ORGB*. Mason, OH: South-Western Cengage Learning.

Nord, G. D., McCubbins, T. F., & Nord, J. H. (2006). E-monitoring in the workplace: Privacy, legislation, and surveillance software. *Communications of the ACM, 49*(8), 73–77.

Oleniczak, M., Pike, C., Jitendra, M., & Bharat, M. (2010). Employers use Facebook too, for hiring. *Advances in Management, 3*(1), 13–17.

Paul, I. (2009). *Jackson's death a blow to the internet.* Retrieved November 13, 2010, from http://www.pcworld.com/article/167435/jacksons_death_a_blow_to_the_internet.html

Samborn, H. V. (2007). Go google yourself. *ABA Journal, 93*(8), 56–57.

Snyder, J. (2010). E-mail privacy in the workplace: A boundary regulation perspective. *Journal of Business Communication, 47*(3), 266–294. doi:10.1177/0021943610369783

Software Informer. (2010). *Anti-keylogger wiki.* Retrieved November 13, 2010, from http://anti-keylogger2.software.informer.com/wiki/

Spitzmüller, C., & Stanton, J. (2006). Examining employee compliance with organizational surveillance and monitoring. *Journal of Occupational and Organizational Psychology, 79*(2), 245–272. doi:10.1348/096317905X52607

Star Workforce Solutions, Inc. (2009). *Underperformance in the workplace: How much is it costing? And What are the solutions?* Retrieved October 20, 2010, from http://www.starworkforce.com

Symantex Hosted Services. (2008). *Employee web use and misuse: Companies, their employees and the internet.* Retrieved November 1, 2010, from http://whitepapers.zdnet.com/abstract.aspx?docid=397147

Turri, A. M., Maniam, B., & Hynes, G. E. (2008). Are they watching? Corporate surveillance of employees' technology use. *The Business Review, Cambridge, 11*(2), 126–130.

Ugrin, J., & Pearson, J. (2008). Exploring internet abuse in the workplace: How can we maximize deterrence efforts? *Review of Business, 28*(2), 29–40.

Wakefield, R. L. (2004). Computer monitoring and surveillance. *The CPA Journal, 74*(7), 52–55.

Ward, B. T., Purwin, C., Sipior, J. C., & Volonino, L. (2009). Recognizing the impact of e-discovery amendments on electronic records management. *Information Systems Management, 26*(4), 350–356. doi:10.1080/10580530903245721

Wen, H., & Gershuny, P. (2005). Computer-based monitoring in the American workplace: Surveillance technologies and legal challenges. *Human Systems Management, 24*(2), 165–173.

Wen, H. J., Schwieger, D., & Gershung, P. (2007). Internet usage monitoring in the workplace: Its legal challenges and implementation strategies. *Information Systems Management, 24*(2), 185–196. doi:10.1080/10580530701221072

Williams, C. (2011). *MGMT.* Mason, OH: South-Western Cengage Learning.

Wise, P. A. (2009). Tweet, tweet, you're fired. *Employment & Labor Relations Law, 7*(4), 7–12.

Young, J., & Faris, N. (2009). *Akamai delivers record streaming and web content during historic presidential inauguration.* Retrieved November 1, 2010, from http://www.akamai.com/html/about/press/releases/2009/press_012009.html

Young, K. (2010). Killer surf issues: Crafting an organizational model to combat employee internet abuse. *Information Management Journal, 44*(1), 34–38.

This work was previously published in International Journal of Digital Literacy and Digital Competence, Volume 1, Issue 4, edited by Antonio Cartelli, pp. 30-45, copyright 2010 by IGI Publishing (an imprint of IGI Global).

Compilation of References

Adams, S., & de Bont, A. (2007). Information Rx: Prescribing good consumerism and responsible citizenship. *Health Care Analysis*, *15*, 273–290. doi:10.1007/s10728-007-0061-9

Aguaded Gómez, J. I. (Ed.). (2007). Media Education in Europe. *Comunicar, 28*.

Ahmed, O. (2005). *Migrating from proprietary to Open Source: Learning Content Management Systems*. Unpublished doctoral dissertation, Department of Systems and Computer Engineering, Carleton University, Ottawa, Ontario, Canada.

Alder, G. S., & Ambrose, M. L. (2005). An examination of the effect of computerized performance monitoring feedback on monitoring fairness, performance, and satisfaction. *Organizational Behavior and Human Decision Processes*, *97*, 161–177. doi:10.1016/j.obhdp.2005.03.003

Alder, G. S., Ambrose, M. L., & Noel, T. W. (2006). The effect of formal advance otice and justification on internet monitoring fairness: Much about nothing? *Journal of Leadership & Organizational Studies*, *13*(1), 93–108. doi:10.1177/107179190701300111101

Alder, G. S., Schminke, M., & Noel, T. W. (2007). The impact of individual ethics on reactions to potentially invasive HR practices. *Journal of Business Ethics*, *75*(2), 201–214. doi:10.1007/s10551-006-9247-6

Al-Mashari, M., Al-Mudimigh, A., & Zairi, M. (2003). Enterprise Resource Planning: a taxonomy of critical factors. *European Journal of Operational Research*, *146*, 352–364. doi:10.1016/S0377-2217(02)00554-4

American Management Association. (2007). *2007 electronic monitoring and surveillance survey.* Retrieved November 5, 2010, from http://www.amanet.org/news/177.aspx

Amin, A., van Ossenbruggen, J., Hardman, L., & van Nispen, A. (2008). Understanding cultural heritage experts' information seeking needs. In *Proceedings of the 8th ACM/IEEE-CS Joint Conference on Digital Libraries (JCDL '08)* (pp. 39-47). New York: ACM. Retrieved from http://doi.acm.org/10.1145/1378889.1378897

Anderson, K. J. (2001). Internet use among college students: an exploratory study. *Journal of American College Health*, *50*(1), 21–26. doi:10.1080/07448480109595707

Anderson, L. W., & Krathwohl, D. (Eds.). (2001). *A Taxonomy for Learning, Teaching and Assessing: a Revision of Bloom's Taxonomy of Educational Objectives*. New York: Longman.

Appadurai, A. (1996). *Modernity at large: Cultural dimension of globalization.* Minneapolis, MN: University of Minnesota Press.

Aptech, E. (2001). Minimizing the digital divide and the intergeneration gap. *Ubiquity*. Retrieved June 12, 2009, from http://www.acm.org/ubiquity/

Arnesen, D., & Weis, W. (2007). Developing an effective company policy for employee internet and email use. *Journal of Organizational Culture . Communication and Conflict*, *11*(2), 53–65.

Associated Press. (2006). *Three arrested for allegedly stealing, plotting to sell Coca-Cola recipes.* Retrieved October 30, 2010 from http://www.foxnews.com/printer_friendly_story/0,3566,202235,00.html

Augé, M. (1992). *Non-lieux. Introduction à une anthropologie de la surmodernité*. Paris: Le Seuil.

Ausubel, D. P. (1968). *Education psychology: A cognitive view*. New York: Holt, Rinehart & Winston.

Ayuso, J. A. (2005). Profesión docente y estrés laboral: Una aproximación a los conceptos de estrés laboral y burnout. *Revista Iberoamericana de Educación, 39*(3), 1-15. Retrieved from http://www.rieoei.org/1341.htm.

Baloche, L. (1998). *The cooperative classroom. Empowering learning*. Upper Saddle River, NJ: Prentice-Hall.

Baltzan, P., & Phillips, A. (2008). *Business driven information systems*. New York: McGraw-Hill Irwin.

Bandura, A. (1993). Perceived self-efficacy in cognitive development and functioning. *Educational Psychologist, 28*(2), 117–148. doi:10.1207/s15326985ep2802_3

Bandura, A. (1997). *Self-efficacy. The exercise of control*. New York: Freeman.

Bangemann Report. (1994). *Europe and the global information society. Recommendations to the European Council, Brussels*. Retrieved October 14, 2001, from http://www2.echo.lu/eudocs/en/bangemann.html

Bateson, G. (1972). *Steps to an Ecology of Mind*. Chicago, IL: University of Chicago Press.

Bateson, G. (1984). *Verso una ecologia della mente* (p. 207). Rome, Italy: Adelphi.

Baudrillard, J. (1988). *The ecstasy of communication*. Semiotext(e): New York.

Bauman, Z. (2000). *Liquid Modernity*. Cambridge, UK: Polity.

BBC Monitoring International Reports. (2002). *Coverage: April 2001 to date*. Retrieved July 15, 2009, from http://ds.datastarweb.com/ds/products/datastar/sheets/bbcm.htm

BCS. (2009). *British Computer Society report, Web 2.0 woven into health information's future*. Retrieved March 10, 2010, from www.bcs.org/tld/hif09

Beck, U. (1998). *Was ist Globalisierung? Irrtümer des Globalismus, Antworten auf Globalisierung*. Frankfurt am Main: Suhrkamp.

Bennett, S., Maton, K., & Kervin, L. (2008). The 'digital natives' debate: A critical review of the evidence. *British Journal of Educational Technology, 39*(5), 775–786. doi:10.1111/j.1467-8535.2007.00793.x

Benyon, D., Turner, P., & Turner, S. (2005). *Design Interactive Systems*. Harlow, UK: Pearson Education.

Bereiter, C., & Scardamalia, M. (2005). *Technology and Literacies: From Print Literacy to Dialogic Literacy. Ontario Institute for Studies in Education of the University of Toronto* (p. 10). http://www.oise.utoronto.ca/projects/impactonpolicy/pdfs/bereiter_edited_Feb_20_04.pdf

Berkman Center. (2009). *Berkman Center for Internet and Society Broadband Study for FCC, Report*. Cambridge, MA: Berkman Center.

Berry, D. M. (2008). *Copy, rip, Burn: the Politics of Copyleft and Open Source*. London: Pluto Press.

Bers, M. U., New, R. S., & Boudreau, L. (2004). Teaching and learning when no one is expert: Children and parents explore technology. *Journal of Early Childhood Research and Practice, 6*(2), 60–75.

Bickel, W. E., & Hattrup, R. A. (1995). Teachers and researchers in collaboration: reflections on the process. *American Educational Research Journal, 32*(1), 35–62.

Bindé, J., Cotbett, J., & Verity, B. (2005). *21st- century talks: Towards knowledge society*. Paris: UNESCO.

Biondi, G. (2000). *La società dell'informazione e la scuola: la documentazione educativa*. Azzano San Paolo: Junior

Birru, M. S., & Steinman, R. A. (2004). Online Health Information and Low-Literacy African Americans. *Journal of Medical Internet Research, 6*(3). doi:10.2196/jmir.6.3.e26

Bitzer, J. (2005). The impact of entry and competition by Open Source Software on Innovation Activity, Industrial Organization 051201, EconWPA.

Blanchard, A. L., & Henle, C. A. (2008). Correlates of different forms of cyberloafing: The role of norms and external locus of control. *Computers in Human Behavior, 24*, 1067–1084. doi:10.1016/j.chb.2007.03.008

Bloom, B. S. (1956). *Taxonomy of Educational Objectives, Handbook I: The Cognitive Domain*. New York: David McKay Co. Inc.

Bogdan, R. C., & Biklen, S. K. (1982). *Qualitative research for education: An introduction to theory and methods*. Boston: Allyn & Bacon.

Bolasco, S. (1999). *Analisi Multidimensionale dei dati*. Roma, Italy: Carocci.

Bolter, J. D., & Grusin, R. (1999). *Remediation. Understanding new media*. Cambridge, MA: MIT Press.

Bonomi, A. (1997). *Il capitalismo molecolare. La società al lavoro nel nord Italia*. Torino, Italy: Einaudi.

Bove, C. (2004). *Le idee degli adulti sui piccoli. Riflessioni e ricerche per una pedagogia culturale*. Bergamo, Italy: Edizioni Junior.

Boyd, D., & Ellison, N. B. (2007). Social network sites: Definition, history, and scholarship. *Journal of Computer-Mediated Communication, 13*(1). Retrieved October 28, 2009 from http://jcmc.indiana.edu/vol13/issue1/boyd.ellison.html

Boyd, D., & Ellison, N. (2007). Social network sites: Definition, history, and scholarship. *Journal of Computer-Mediated Communication, 13*(1), 210–230. doi:10.1111/j.1083-6101.2007.00393.x

Bradbrook, G., & Fisher, J. (2004, March). *Digital equality: Reviewing digital inclusion activity and mapping the way forwards*. Retrieved from http://www.citizensonline.org.uk/site/media/documents/2190_DigitalEquality_(2004).pdf.

Brandhorst, A. R. (1976). Toward a Taxonomy of Educational Objectives in the Relational Domain. In *Proceedings of the Annual Meeting of the National Council for Social Studies*, Washington, DC. Retrieved August 4, 2010, from http://www.eric.ed.gov/ERICWebPortal/search/detailmini.jsp?_nfpb=true&_&ERICExtSearch_SearchValue_0=ED134505&ERICExtSearch_SearchType_0=no&accno=ED134505

Bromley, D. B. (1986). *The case - study method in psychology and related disciplines*. Chichester, UK: John Wiley & Sons.

Brookfield, S. (1986). *Understanding and facilitating adult learning: A comprehensive analysis of principles and effective practices*. Milton Keynes, UK: Open University Press.

Brown, J. S. (2002). *Growing Up Digital: How the Web Changes Work, Education, and the Ways People Learn. United States Distance Learning Association*. Retrieved July 31, 2010, from http://www.usdla.org/html/ journal/FEB02_Issue/article0 1.html

Brown, A. L., & Campione, J. (1994). Guided discovery in a community of learners . In McGilly, K. (Ed.), *Classroom lesson: Integrating cognitive theory and classroom practice* (pp. 229–270). Cambridge, MA: MIT Press.

Brown, A. L., & Campione, J. (1996). Psychological theory and the design of innovative learning environments: On procedure, principles and systems . In Schaube, L., & Glaser, R. (Eds.), *Innovation in learning* (pp. 289–375). Mahwah, NJ: Lawrence Erlbaum.

Brown, J. S., & Duguid, P. (1991). Organizational Learning and Communities-of-practice: Toward a Unified View of Working, Learning and Innovation. *Organization Science, 2*(1). doi:10.1287/orsc.2.1.40

Bruner, J. (1966). *Towards a theory of instruction*. Cambridge, MA: Harvard University Press.

Bruner, J. (1996). *The culture of education*. New York: Harvard University Press.

Buckingham, D. (2005). *Media Education: literacy, learning and contemporary culture*. Cambridge, UK: Polity Press.

Buhalis, D. (1998). Strategic use of information technologies in the tourism Industry. *Tourism Management, 19*(5), 409–421. doi:10.1016/S0261-5177(98)00038-7

Bulletin, E. U. 3. (2000). *Preparing the transition to a competitive, dynamic and knowledge-based economy*. Retrieved from http://europa.eu.int/abc/doc/off/bull/en/200003/i1006.htm

Callis, (2009). Improving Wikipedia: educational opportunity and professional responsibility. *Trends in Ecology & Evolution, 24*(4), 177–179. doi:10.1016/j.tree.2009.01.003

Callois, R. (2001). *Man, Play and Games*. Champaign, IL: First Illinois. (Original work published 1958)

Calvani, A. (2001). *Educazione, comunicazione e nuovi media. Sfide pedagogiche e cyberspazio*. Torino, Italy: Utet.

Calvani, A., Cartelli, A., Fini, A., & Ranieri, M. (2008). Models and Instruments for Assessing Digital Competence at School. *Journal of E-learning and Knowledge Society, 4*(3), 183–193.

Calvani, A., & Rotta, M. (2000). *Fare formazione in Internet. Manuale di didattica online*. Trento, Italy: Erickson.

Calvert, S. L., Rideout, V. J., Woolard, J. L., Barr, R. F., & Strouse, G. A. (2004). Age, ethnicity, and socioeconomic patterns in early computer use: A national survey. *The American Behavioral Scientist*, *48*(5), 590–607. doi:10.1177/0002764204271508

Calzarossa, M. C., Ciancarini, P., Maresca, P., Mich, L., & Scarabottolo, N. (2007). The ECDL programme in Italian Universities. *Computers & Education*, *49*(2), 514–529. doi:10.1016/j.compedu.2005.10.008

Cambi, F. (2003). *Manuale di storia della pedagogia*. Rome, Italy: Editori Laterza.

Canevaro, A. (2000). Alcuni punti per collegare scrittura e impegno creativo . In Canevaro, A. (Ed.), *Scrivere di educazione* (pp. 6–32). Roma, Italy: Carocci.

Cantón, I. (2004). *Intervención organizativa en la sociedad del Conocimiento*. Granada, Spain: GEU.

Cantón, I. (2004). *Planes de mejora en centros educativos*. Málaga, Spain: Aljibe.

Cantón, I., & Perisset, P. A. (2009). Expectativas y actividades de los profesores con alumnos desfavorecidos socialmente. *Revista de Ciencias de la Educación*, *218*, 197–220.

CareerBuilder. (2009). *Forty-five percent of employers use social networking sites to research job candidates, CareerBuilder survey finds*. Retrieved November 12, 2010, from http://uncw.edu/stuaff/career/documents/employersusingsocialnetworkingsites.pdf

Caron, A. H., & Caronia, L. (2007). *Moving cltures. Mobile communication in everyday life*. Kingston, Ontario, Canada: McGill-Queen's University Press.

Carpenter, D., Dolan, D., Leahy, D., & Sherwood-Smith, M. (2000). ECDL/ICDL: A global computer literacy initiative. In *Proceedings of IFIP ICEUT 2000*.

Carroll, J. B. (1963). A model of school learning. *Teachers College Record*, *64*, 723–733.

Cartelli, A. (2008). *T.I.C. e alfabetizzazione digitale* (Issue no 3 of the Faculty Centre for ICT and online teaching). Cassino, Italy: Idea Stampa by Ivo Sambucci.

Cartelli, A. (2008c, November 6-8). E-Learning and E-Citizenship Between PKM and PST. In D. Remenyi (Ed.), *Proceedings of the 7th European Conference on E-Learning (ECEL 2008)*, Agia Napa, Cyprus (Vol. 1, pp. 169-177) Reading, UK: Academic Publishing.

Cartelli, A. (2010a). Frameworks for Digital Competence Assessment: Proposals, Instruments and Evaluation. In E. Cohen & E. Boyd (Eds.), *Proceedings of the Informing Science + Information Technology Education International Conference (InSITE 2010)* (pp. 561-574).

Cartelli, A. (2010b). Digital Competence Assessment and Teaching Strategies in the Knowledge Society. In *Proceedings of the 7th Pan-Hellenic Conference with International Participation (HCICTE 2010)*, Korinthos, Greece.

Cartelli, A. (2010c). Digital Competences in Online Classes. In *Proceedings of the European Conference on E-Learning (ECEL 2010)*, Porto, Portugal.

Cartelli, A. (in press). Frameworks for digital literacy and digital competence assessment. In *Proceedings of the European Conference on E-Learning (ECEL2009)*, Bari, Italy.

Cartelli, A. (2008a). Towards a new model for knowledge construction and evolution . In Cartelli, A., & Palma, M. (Eds.), *Encyclopedia of Information Communication Technology* (pp. 767–774). Hershey, PA: Information Science Reference.

Cartelli, A. (2008b). Is the implementation of practices with the ICT a new teaching-learning paradigm? In Cartelli, A., & Palma, M. (Eds.), *Encyclopedia of Information Communication Technology* (pp. 413–418). Hershey, PA: Information Science Reference.

Cartelli, A., Dagiene, V., & Futschek, G. (2010). Bebras Contest and Digital Competence Assessment: Analysis of Frameworks. *International Journal of Digital Literacy and Digital Competence*, *1*(1), 24–39.

Cartelli, A., Stansfield, M., Connolly, T., Jimoyiannis, A., Magalhães, H., & Maillet, K. (2008). Towards the development of a New Model for Best Practice and Knowledge Construction in Virtual Campuses. *Journal of Information Technology Education*, *7*, 121–134.

Carver, C. (1997). You want to measure coping but your protocol's too long: consider the Brief COPE. *International Journal of Behavioral Medicine*, *4*(1), 92–100. doi:10.1207/s15327558ijbm0401_6

Carver, C., Scheier, M., & Weintraub, J. K. (1989). Assessing coping strategies: A theoretically based approach. *Journal of Personality and Social Psychology*, *56*, 267–283. doi:10.1037/0022-3514.56.2.267

Casacubierta, D. (2003). *Collective creation*. Barcelona, Spain: Gedisa.

Casado. (n.d.). *Keys for digital literacy. Seminar on Digital Literacy* (pp. 187-194). Madrid, Spain: Telefónica Foundation. Retrieved from http://sociedaddelainformación.telefónica.es/documentos/articulos/clavesdelaalfabetizacióndigital.pdf

Casey, P. J. (1997). Computer programming: A medium for teaching problem solving. []. New York: The Haworth Press.]. *Computers in the Schools*, *XIII*, 41–51. doi:10.1300/J025v13n01_05

Castells, M. (1996). *The information age: Economy, society and culture. Vol. I: The rise of network society*. Malden, MA: Blackwell Publishers.

Castells, M. (1997). *The information age: Economy, society and culture. Vol. II: The power of identity*. Malden, MA: Blackwell Publishers.

Castells, M. (1999). Flows, networks, identities. In P. McLaren (Ed.), *Critical education in the new information age* (pp. 37- 64). New York: Rowman & Littlefield.

Castells, M. (2000). *The information age: Economy, society and culture. Vol. III: End of millennium*. Malden, MA: Blackwell Publishers.

Castells, M. (2001). *The Internet galaxy. Reflections on the Internet, business, and society*. New York: Oxford University Press.

Castells, M., & Himanen, P. (2002). *The information society and the welfare state. The Finnish Model*. Oxford, UK: SITRA.

Castells, M. (1996). *The rise of the network society*. Oxford, UK: Blackwell.

Castells, M. (2001). *The Internet Galaxy*. Oxford, UK: Oxford University Press.

CEPIS. (2004). *ICT-Skills Certification in Europe* (CedepofProgram Report). Retrieved from http://www.cepis.org

Cheung, C. (2000). Identity construction and self-presentation on personal homepages: Emancipatory potentials and reality constraints. In D. Guantlett & R. Horsley (Eds.), *Web studies* (pp. 53-68). London: Arnold.

Chomski, N. (1998, December). Finanza e silenzio. In *Le monde diplomatique*.

Chua, S. L., Chen, D., & Wong, A. F. L. (1999). Computer anxiety and its correlates: A meta-analysis. *Computers in Human Behavior*, *15*, 609–623. doi:10.1016/S0747-5632(99)00039-4

Churches, A. (2008). Bloom's Taxonomy Blooms Digitally. *Tech&Learning online Journal*. Retrieved August 4, 2010, from http://www.techlearning.com/article/8670

Clark, L. A., & Roberts, S. J. (2010). Employer's use of social networking sites: A socially irresponsible practice. *Journal of Business Ethics*, *95*, 507–525. doi:10.1007/s10551-010-0436-y

CLEMI/Academie De Bordeaux (Ed.). (2003). *Parcours médias au collège: approches disciplinaires et transdisciplinaires*. Aquitaine, France: Sceren-CRDP.

Codogno, M. (2009). Wikipedia, i Pokémon e la teoria della complessità nei sistemi emergenti. In *Proceedings of the conference "From Diderot to Wikipedia: an epistemological revolution"*? University of Padua, Italy.

Coffield, C., Mosely, D., Hall, E., & Ecclestone, K. (2004). *Learning styles and Pedagogy in Post-16 Learning* (Tech. Rep.). London: University of Newcastle upon Tyne, Learning and Skill Research Centre.

Cohen, N. (2007). A history department bans citing Wikipedia as a research source. *The New York Times*. Retrieved from http://www.nytimes.com

Cole, I. J., & Kesley, A. (2004). Computer and information literacy in post-qualifying education. *Nurse Education in Practice*, *4*(3), 190–199. doi:10.1016/S1471-5953(03)00065-9

Cole, M. (1996). *Cultural psychology. A once and future discipline*. Cambridge, MA: Belknap Press.

Connecting for Health. (2008). *Americans Overwhelmingly Believe Electronic Personal Health Records Could Improve Their Health, a survey report.* Retrieved March 15, 2010, from http://www.connectingforhealth.org/resources/ResearchBrief-200806.pdf

Corazza, L. (2008). ICT and Interculture Opportunities offered by the Web . In *Encyclopedia of Information and Communication Technology* (*Vol. 1*, pp. 357–364). Hershey, PA: IGI Global.

Corazza, L. (2008). *Internet e la società conoscitiva*. Trento, Italy: Erickson.

Cotten, R., & Jelenewicz, S. M. (2006). A disappearing digital divide among college students? *Social Science Computer Review*, *24*(4), 497–506. doi:10.1177/0894439306286852

Council of European Parliament. (2005). *Recommendation of the European Parliament and of the Council on key competences for lifelong learning*. Retrieved June 1, 2010, from http://ec.europa.eu/education/policies/2010/doc/keyrec_en.pdf

Curley, M. (2003). *Addressing the ICT skills shortage in Europe*. Paper presented at the Early identification of skill needs in Europe Conference. Retrieved from http://www.cedefop.eu.int/mtconference/mtconf1.html

Cushman, M., & Klecun, E. (2005). Non-users of computers in south London: their experiences and aspirations for use. In *Proceedings of the IRFD World Forum on Information Society: Digital Divide, Global Development and the Information Society,* Tunis, Tunisia. Retrieved from http://penceil.lse.ac.uk/documents/06_WFIS.pdf

D'Amato, M. (2006). *Le pubblicazioni del Centro nazionale*. Retrieved from http://www.minori.it/pubblicazioni/quaderni/pdf/quad_38.pdf

Dagiene, V., & Futschek, G. (2008). Bebras International Contest on Informatics and Computer Literacy: Criteria for good tasks. In *Informatics education – supporting computational thinking* (LNCS 5090, pp. 19-30).

Dagiene, V., & Skupiene, J. (2004). Learning by competitions: Olympiads in informatics as a tool for training high grade skills in programming. In T. Boyle, P. Oriogun, & A. Pakstas (Eds.), *2nd International Conference on Information Technology: Research and Education,* London (pp. 79-83). Washington, DC: IEEE Computer Society.

Dagiene, V. (2006). Information technology contests – introduction to computer science in a attractive way. *Informatics in Education*, *5*(1), 37–46.

Daniel, E. (2000). *Information policy*. Chapell Hill, NC: University of North Carolina, School of Information and Library Science. Retrieved June 25, 2000, from http://ils.unc.edu/daniel/infopolicy.html

Danielson, C. (2002). *Enhancing student achievement: a framework for school improvement*. Alexandria, VA: ASCD.

David, P., & Steinmueller, E. (1994). Information Economics and Policy. *The Economics of Standards, 6*(3-4).

De Chiara, R., Di Matteo, A., Manno, I., & Scarano, V. (2007, November). CoFFEE: Cooperative face2face educational environment. In *Proceedings of the 3rd International Conference in Collaborative Computing: Networking, Applications and Worksharing (CollaborateCom2007),* New York.

De Kerckhove, D. (1991). *Brainframes: Technology, mind and business*. Utrecht, The Netherlands: Bosch & Keuning.

De Kerckhove, D. (1995). *The skin of culture*. Toronto, Canada: Somerville House.

De Pablos, C. (2010). Framework for the Experiences in Digital Literacy in the Spanish Market. *International Journal of Digital Literacy and Digital Competence*, 61–76.

Dedrick, J., & West, J. (2005). *Why firms adopt Open Source Platforms: A grounded Theory of Innovation and Standards Adoption*. MIS Quarterly.

Deem, R. (2002). *The knowledge worker and the divided university* (inaugural lecture). Bristol, UK: Graduate School of Education, University of Bristol.

Delors. (2003). *White paper on growth, competitiveness and employment: the challenges and ways forward into the 21st century*. Retrieved November 17, 2003, from http://europa.eu.int/en/record/white/c93700/contents.html

Detmer, D., Bloomrosen, M., Raymond, B., & Tang, P. (2008). Integrated personal health records: transformative tools for consumer-centric care. *BMC Medical Informatics and Decision Making*, *8*, 45. doi:10.1186/1472-6947-8-45

Dewey, J. (1899). *The School and the Society*. Chicago, IL: The University of Chicago Press.

Dewey, J. (1916). *Democracy and education: an introduction to the philosophy of education*. New York: Macmillan.

DfES. (2003). *21st century skills: Realising our potential.* Retrieved May 25, 2009, from http://www.dcsf.gov.uk/skillsstrategy/uploads/documents/21st%20Century%20Skills.pdf

DOH. (1999). *Saving Lives: Our Healthier Nation.* London: Department of Health, HMSO.

DOH. (2001). *The expert patient a new approach to chronic disease management for the 21st century.* London: Department of Health, HMSO.

Dourish, P. (2004). *Where the Action is: The Foundation of Embodied Interaction.* Cambridge, MA: MIT Press.

Downes, S. (2007). *What Connectivism Is.* Retrieved August 18, 2010, from http://halfanhour.blogspot.com/2007/02/what-connectivism-is.html

Drotner, K. (2000). Difference and diversity: Trends in young Danes' media use. *Media Culture & Society, 22*(2), 149–166. doi:10.1177/016344300022002002

Duffy, T. M., & Jonassen, D. (Eds.). (1992). *Constructivism and the technology of instruction: A conversation.* Hillsdale, NJ: Lawrence Erlbaum Associates.

Duffy, T. M., Lowyck, J., & Jonassen, D. (Eds.). (1993). *Designing environments for constructivist learning.* Berlin: Springer-Verlag.

EAVI. (2004). *Advancing European Viewers Interests.* Brussels, Belgium: Author.

Eco, U. (1999). *Kant and the Platypus.* London: Secker and Warburg.

Edgar, L., Greenberg, A., & Remmer, J. (2002). Providing Internet lessons to oncology patients and family members: A shared project. *Psycho-Oncology, 11*, 439–446. doi:10.1002/pon.590

Educared. (2008). *The profile of the teachers using ICT for teaching-learning processes.* Retrieved October 25, 2008, from http://www.educared.net

e-Europe. (2002). *E-Business and ICT skills in Europe* (ICT skills Monitoring Group Final Report). Retrieved from http://europa.eu.int/comm/enterprise/ict/policy/ict-skills/es-br.pdf

Efstratoglou, A., Nikolopoulou, V., & Pauli-Korre, M. (2006). *Basic dimensions of illiteracy in Greece.* Athens, Greece: Hellenic Association of Adult Education.

Einarsen, S. (2005): The nature, causes and consequences of bullying at work: The Norwegian experience. *Pistes, 7*(3), 1-14. Retrieved from http://www.pistes,uqam.ca/v7n3/articles/v7n3a1en.htm

Einarsen, S., & Nielsen, M. B. (Eds.). (2004, April 20). *The Fourth International Conference on Bullying and Harassment in the Workplace.* Retrieved from http://www.bullying.no/content/bbrg/Book%20of%20abstract%20FICBHWP

Einarsen, S., Hoel, H., Zapf, D., & Cooper, C. L. (2003). The concept of bullying at work. The European tradition . In Einarsen, S., Hoel, H., Zapf, D., & Cooper, C. L. (Eds.), *Bullying and emotional abuse in the workplace. International perspectives in research and practice* (pp. 3–30). London: Taylor & Francis.

Einarsen, S., Hoel, H., Zapt, D., & Cooper, C. (2003). *Bullying and emotional abuse in the workplace: International perspectives in research and practice.* New York: Taylor & Francis.

Eisenberg, M. (2008, March). Information Literacy: Essential Skills for the Information Age. *DESIDOC Journal of Library & Information Technology, 28*(2), 39–47.

Ellerani, P., & Pavan, D. (2003). *Il cooperative learning: una proposta per l'orientamento formativo.* Napoli, Italy: Tecnodid.

Ellison, N. B., Steinfeld, C., & Lampe, C. (2007). The benefits of Facebook 'friends' Social capital and college students' user of online social network sites. *Journal of Computer-Mediated Communication, 12*(4). Retrieved October 28, 2009 from http://jcmc.indiana.edu/vol12/issue4/ ellison.html

Elzweig, B., & Peeples, D. (2009). Using social networking web sites in hiring and retention decisions. *SAM Advanced Management Journal, 74*(4), 27–35.

Eng, T. R., & Gustafson, D. H. (Eds.). (1999). *Wired for health and well-being. From the science panel on interactive communication and health.* Washington, DC: U.S. Department of Health and Human Services, U.S. Government Printing Office.

Enriquez, J., Ainsworth, S., Gelmini Hornsby, G., Buda, M., Crook, C., & O'Malley, C. (2008). Turn-taking and mode-switching in text-based communication in the classroom. In *Proceedings of the International Conference of the Learning Sciences*, Utrecht, The Netherlands.

EOI. (2009). *The opportunities of free software: capacities, rights and innovation* (EOI Report). Eoi.

eSCC. (2004). *The situation and the role of e-skills industry certification in Europe*. Paper presented at the European e-Skills 2004 Conference. Retrieved from http://www.e-scc.org/

EU. (2004). *Communication from the Commission to the Council, the European Parliament, the European Economic and Social Committee and the Committee of the Regions - e-Health - making health care better for European citizens: an action plan for a European e-Health Area*. Retrieved March 3, 2010, from http://eur-lex.europa.eu/LexUriServ/LexUriServ.do?uri=CELEX:52004DC0356:EN:NOT

EU. (2009). *The Impact of Social Computing on the EU Information Society and Economy (JCR Scientific and Tech. Rep.)*. European Commission.

European Commission [EC]. (1997). *Second chance schools: Combating exclusion through education and training*. Brussels, Belgium: Education Training Youth.

European Commission [EC]. (2000a). *A memorandum on lifelong learning*. Brussels, Belgium: Author.

European Commission [EC]. (2000b). *eEurope 2002: An information society for all action plan*. Brussels, Belgium: Author.

European Commission [EC]. (2001). *Making a European area of lifelong learning a reality*. Brussels, Belgium: Author.

European Commission [EC]. (2003). *Implementing lifelong learning strategies in Europe: Progress report on the follow-up to the 2002 council resolution*. Brussels, Belgium: Author.

European Commission. (1995). *White Paper on Education and Training. Teaching and Learning. Towards the Learning Society*.

European Parliament and Council. (2005). *Recommendation on key competences for lifelong learning*. Retrieved from http://ec.europa.eu/education/policies/2010/doc/keyrec_en.pdf

European Parliament Council. (2008). *Recommendation of the European Parliament and of the Council of 23 April 2008 on the establishment of the European Qualifications Framework for lifelong learning*. Retrieved from http://eur-lex.europa.eu/LexUriServ/LexUriServ.do?uri=OJ:C:2008:111:0001:0007:EN:PDF

Evangelidis, A. (2005). FRAMES – a risk assessment framework for e-services. *Electronic . Journal of E-Government*, *3*(1).

Evans, L. (2002). *Reflective practice in educational research*. London: Continuum.

Everett, A. M., Wong, Y., & Payner, J. (2004). Balancing employee and employer rights: An international comparison of e-mail privacy in the workplace. *Journal of Individual Employment Rights*, *11*(4), 291–310.

Falkowski, G., Pedigo, P., Smith, B., & Swamson, D. (1998). A recipe for ERP success. Beyond Computing. *International Journal of Human-Computer Interaction*, *16*(1), 5–22.

Fallis, D. (2008). Toward an Epistemology of Wikipedia. *Journal of the American Society for Information Science and Technology*, *59*(10), 1662–1674. doi:10.1002/asi.20870

Fantin, M. (2007). Alfabetização midiática na escola. In *Proceedings of the Anais do16 Congresso de Leitura do Brasil, COLE*. Campinas, Brazil: Unicamp.

Fantin, M. (2008). Os cenários culturais e as multiliteracies na escola. *Revista Comunicação e Sociedade, 13*.

Ferrell, O. C., Fraedrich, J., & Ferrell, L. (2011). *Business Ethics*. Mason, OH: South-Western Cengage Learning.

Ferri, P. (2004). *Fine dei Mass Media. Le nuove tecnologie della comunicazione e le trasformazioni dell'industria culturale*. Milano, Italy: Guerini & Associati.

Ferri, P. (2008). *La Scuola Digitale. Come le nuove tecnologie cambiano la formazione*. Milano, Italy: Bruno Mondadori.

Finney, S., & Corbett, M. (2007). ERP implementation: a compilation and analysis of critical success factors. *Business Process Management Journal*, *13*(3), 329–347. doi:10.1108/14637150710752272

Finquelievich, S. (2002). *Global actions for the social inclusion in the information society: From consumers to citizens*. Retrieved November 26, 2007, from http://www.links.org.ar/infoteca/accionesglobales paralainclusión.rtf

Flavell, J. H. (1985). *Cognitive development*. Englewood Cliffs, NJ: Prentice Hall.

Flyvbjerg, B. (2006). Five Misunderstandings about Case-Study Research. *Qualitative Inquiry*, *12*(2), 219–245. doi:10.1177/1077800405284363

Fox, S., & Jones, S. (2009).*The social life of health information*. Retrieved February 21, 2010, from http://www.pewinternet.org/~/media//Files/Reports/2009/PIP_Health_2009.pdf

Fox, C., Levitin, A., & Redman, T. (1994). The notion of data and its quality dimensions. *Information Processing & Management*, *30*, 9–19. doi:10.1016/0306-4573(94)90020-5

Frederick, H. (1993). *Computer networks and the emergence of global civil society: The case of the Association for Progressive Communications (APC)*. Retrieved 02 January 2, 2008, from http://w2.eff.org/Activism/global_civil_soc_networks.paper

Freire, P. (1971). *La pedagogia degli oppressi* (new ed.). Milan, Italy: Mondadori.

French, T. (1998). The future of global distribution systems. *Travel and Tourism Analyst*, *3*, 1–17.

Friedman, F., & Reed, L. J. (2007). Workplace privacy: Employee relations and legal implications of monitoring employee e-mail use. *Employee Responsibilities and Rights Journal*, *19*(2), 75–83. doi:10.1007/s10672-007-9035-1

Frost, J. H., & Massagli, M. P. (2008). Social uses of personal health information within PatientsLikeMe, an online patient community: what can happen when patients have access to one another's data. *Journal of Medical Internet Research*, *10*(3), e15. doi:10.2196/jmir.1053

Fui-Hoon, F., Zuckweiler, K. M., & Lee-Shang, J. (2003). ERP implementation: Chief Information Officers' Perceptions on Critical Success Factors. *International Journal of Human-Computer Interaction*, *16*(1), 5–22. doi:10.1207/S15327590IJHC1601_2

Futschek, G., & Dagiene, V. (2009). A contest on informatics and computer fluency attracts school students to learn basic technology concepts. In *Proceedings 9th WCCE 2009, Education and Technology for a Better World*, Bento Goncalves, Brazil (No. 120).

Gannes, L. (2009). *The Obama inauguration live stream stats*. Retrieved November 13, 2010, from http://gigaom.com/video/the-obama-inauguration-live-stream-stats/

Garbaccio, F., & Quintano, C. (2005). *Turismo siamo tutti*. Napoli, Italy: Denaro Libri.

Gardner, H. (1993). *Frames of mind: The theory of multiple intelligences*. New York: Basic Books.

Gardner, H. (1993). *Multiple Intelligences: The Theory in Practice*. New York: Basic Books.

Garvin, D. A. (1998). The processes of Organization and Management. *Sloan Management Review*, *39*(4), 33–50.

Garvoille, A., & Buckner, G. (2009). Writing Wikipedia Pages in the Constructivist Classroom. In *Proceedings of World Conference on Educational Multimedia, Hypermedia and Telecommunications 2009* (pp. 1600-1605). Chesapeake, VA: AACE.

Gaston, J. (2006). Reaching and teaching the digital natives. *Library Hi Tech News*, *23*(3), 12–13. doi:10.1108/07419050610668124

Gaviria, P. R., & Bluemelhuber, C. (2010). Consumers' transformations in a liquid society: introducing the concepts of autobiographical-concern and desire-assemblage. *Journal of Consumer Behaviour*, *9*(2), 126–138. doi:10.1002/cb.309

Gee-Woo, B., & Swee Ling, H. (2009). Non-work related computing (NWRC). *Communications of the ACM*, *52*(4), 124–128. doi:10.1145/1498765.1498799

General Secretariat for Adult Education [GSAE]. (2003). *A new chance: Second chance schools*. Athens, Greece: Ministry of Education.

Geser, H. (2007, June). From printed to "wikified" encyclopedias: Sociological Aspects of an incipient revolution. *Sociology in Switzerland: Towards Cybersociety and "Vireal" Social Relations*. Retrieved from http://socio.ch/intcom/t_hgeser16.pdf

Giddens, A. (2002). *Consequences of modernity*. Madrid, Spain: Alianza.

Giger, P. (2006). *Participation Literacy: Part I: Constructing the Web 2.0 Concept Series*. Karlskrona, Sweden: Blekinge Institute of Technology.

Giglioli, A. (2005). Le Comunità di Pratica Apprendistato in FVG . In Frignani, P., Galliani, L., Giacomantonio, M., & Poletti, G. (Eds.), *E-learning: protagonista dello sviluppo della società della conoscenza–Atti del convegno Expo e-learning 2005*. Ferrara, Italy: Omniacom Editore.

Giles, J. (2005). Internet Encyclopaedias Go Head to Head. *Nature, 438*, 900. IARD e IPRASE. (2009). *Insegnare in Trentino. Seconda indagine Istituto IARD e IPRASE sui docenti della scuola trentina*. Provincia Autonoma di Trento - IPRASE.

Gillani, B. B. (2003). *Learning Theories and the Design of E-learning Environments*. Lanham, MD: University Press of America.

Gilster, P. (1997). *Digital literacy*. New York: Wiley.

Gilster, P. (1997). *Digital literacy*. New York: Wiley.

Giovannella, C. (2007). An Organic Process for the Organic Era of the Interaction. In P. A. Silva, A. Dix, & J. Jorge (Eds.), *Proceedings of the HCI Educators 2007: creativity3: Experiencing to educate and design*, Aveiro, Portugal (pp. 129-133).

Giovannella, C. (2009). DULP: complessità, organicità, liquidità. *IxD&A, 7/8*, 11-15.

Giovannella, C., & Graf, S. (2010). Challenging Technologies, Rethinking Pedagogy, Being Design-Inspired. The Grand Challenge of this Century. *eLearn Magazine*. Retrieved from http://www.elearnmag.org/subpage.cfm?section=articles&article=114-1

Giovannella, C., Selva, P. E., & Fraioli, S. (2007). MapEvaluator in action: a comparative test on the efficiency of the quantitative concept map evaluation in a primary school. In *Proceedings of the ICALT2007, Distributed social and personal computing for learning and instruction* (pp. 566-569). Washington, DC: IEEE.

Giovannella, C. (2006). From 'Learning Space' to 'Design Place': transforming the present and challenging the future. *Metamorfosi, 62*, 62–65.

Giovannella, C. (2008a). L'uomo, la macchina e la comunicazione mediata: evoluzioni di paradigmi e design per le esperienze nell'era organica dell'interazione . In Graphics, B. A. (Ed.), *Machinae: tecniche arti e saperi del novecento* (pp. 471–490). Bari, Italy.

Giovannella, C. (2008b). 'Personal-in-place centered design' per formare gli attori dei 'Learning places' del futuro . In *E-learning tra formazione istituzionale e life-long learning*. Trento, Italy: Educare al.

Giovannella, C. (2008c). 2.0? In *E-learning tra formazione istituzionale e life-long learning*. Trento, Italy: Learning.

Giovannella, C., Camusi, A., & Spadavecchia, C. (2010a). From learning styles to experience styles. In [Washington, DC: IEEE.]. *Proceedings of the ICALT, 2010*, 732–733.

Giovannella, C., Spadavecchia, C., & Camusi, A. (2010b). Educational complexity: centrality of design and monitoring of the experience . In *Proceedings of UXFUL2010*. New York: Springer.

Giovannella, C., & Spinelli, A. (2009). Grand Challenge per il TEL: Design Inspired Learning . In Andronico, A., & Colazzo, L. (Eds.), *DIDAMATICA 2009*. Trento, Italy.

Glaser, G., & Strauss, A. (1967). *The discovery of Grounded Theory: Strategies for qualitative research*. New York: Aldine Publishing Company.

Glouberman, S. (2005, March 29). *Changing Conceptions of Health and Illness: Three Philosophical Ideas and Health*. Paper presented at the Workshop on Shaping the Future of Home Care, Toronto, ON, Canada.

Glover, R. (2002). Privacy in the workplace – complex issues for employers. *Metropolitan Corporate Counsel, 10*(6), 1-2, 9-10.

Go, F., Lee, R., & Russoe, A. (2003). E-heritage in the globalizing society: enabling cross-cultural engagement through ICT. *Information Technology & Tourism, 6*(1), 55–68. doi:10.3727/109830503108751225

Gohring, N. (2008). Over 50% of companies have fired workers for e-mail, Net abuse. *Computerworld*. Retrieved November 2, 2010, from http://www.computerworld.com/s/article/9065659/Over_50_of_companies_have_fired_workers_for_e_mail_Net_abuse

Gonzalez-Barahona, J. (2001). Counting Potatoes: the Size of Debian 2.2. *The European Online Magazine for the IT Professional, 2*(6).

Gonzalez-Barahona, J. (2004). *About free software*. Madrid, Spain: Rey Juan Carlos University.

Gorard, S., Selwyn, N., & Madden, L. (2003). Logged on to learning assessing the impact of technology on participation in lifelong learning. *International Journal of Lifelong Education, 22*(3), 281–296. doi:10.1080/02601370304845

Goulding, A. (2001). Information poverty or overload? *Journal of Librarianship and Information Science, 33*(3), 109–111. doi:10.1177/096100060103300301

Gravani, M. N. (2007). Unveiling professional learning: Shifting from the delivery of courses to an understanding of the processes. *Teaching and Teacher Education, 23*, 688–704. doi:10.1016/j.tate.2006.03.011

Gravani, M. N., & John, P. D. (2005). 'Them and us': Teachers' and tutors' perceptions of a 'new' professional development course in Greece. *Compare, 35*(3), 305–321. doi:10.1080/03057920500212597

Gravani, M. N., & Marmarinos, I. (2008). Current trends in lifelong education in Greece: The case of the General Secretariat for Adult Education (GSAE). *Adult Education, 15*, 26–31.

Gredler, M. E. (2001). *Learning and Instruction: Theory into Practice*. Upper Saddle River, NJ: Pearson Education.

Greenacre, M. J. (1993). *Correspondence analysis in practice*. New York: Academic Press.

Gueorguiev, I., Dimitrova, S., Komitsha, M., Traykor, H., & Spassov, K. (2005). Balance Scorecard based management information system – a potential for public monitoring and good governance advancement. *Electronic . Journal of E-Government, 3*(1).

Guidolin, U. (2005). *Pensare digitale. Teoria e tecniche dei nuovi media*. Milan, Italy: McGraw-Hill.

Gutierrez Martín, A. (2003). *Digital literacy: Some more than computers*. Barcelona, Spain: Gedisa.

Haarala-Muhonen, A., & Sokura, B. (2000). *Computer driving licence – a forerunner of skills tests, Innovations in Higher Education*. Retrieved from http://www.helsinki.fi/inno2000/

Halpern, D., Reville, P. J., & Gruenwald, D. (2008). Management and legal issues regarding electronic surveillance of employees in the workplace. *Journal of Business Ethics, 80*, 175–180. doi:10.1007/s10551-007-9449-6

Hames, J., & Harvey, M. (2006). Workplace bullying: a cross-level assessment. *Management Decision, 44*(9), 1214–1230. doi:10.1108/00251740610707695

Hammer, M. (2000). Reengineering Work: Do not Automate, Obliterate. *Harvard Business Review*, 37–46.

Hansen, Ä. M., Hogh, A., Persson, R., Karlson, B., Garde, A. H., & Ørbæk, P. (2006). Bullying at work, health outcomes, and physiological stress response. *Journal of Psychosomatic Research, 60*, 63–72. doi:10.1016/j.jpsychores.2005.06.078

Hawn, C. (2009). Take Two Aspirin And Tweet Me In The Morning: How Twitter, Facebook, And Other Social Media Are Reshaping Health Care. *Health Affairs, 28*(2), 361–368. doi:10.1377/hlthaff.28.2.361

Henwood, F., Wyatt, S., Hart, A., & Smith, J. (2002). Turned on or turned off? Accessing health information on the Internet. *Scandinavian Journal of Information Systems, 14*(2), 79–90.

Henwood, F., Wyatt, S., Hart, A., & Smith, J. (2003). Ignorance is bliss sometimes: constraints on the emergence of the 'informed patient' in the changing landscapes of health information. *Sociology of Health & Illness, 25*(6), 589–607. doi:10.1111/1467-9566.00360

Hill, M. (1995). Information policies: Premonitions and prospects. *Journal of Information Science, 21*(4), 279. doi:10.1177/016555159502100403

Hippern, L., & Krogh, S. (2003). Open source software and the private-collective innovation model: Issues for organization science. *Organization Science, 14*(2), 241–248.

Hirji, J. (2004). Freedom or folly? Canadians and the consumption of online health information. *Information Communication and Society, 7*(4), 445–465. doi:10.1080/1369118042000305593

Hitchcock, G., & Hughes, D. (1989). *Research and the teacher.* London: Routledge.

Hobbs, R. (1994). *Teaching Media Literacy – Yo! Are you Hip to This*? Retrieved December 16, 2007, from http://reneehobbs.org/renee's%20web%20site/Publications/Yo%20Are%20you %20 Hip.htm

Hobbs, R. (2003). *Lo que docents y estudiantes deben saber sobre los medios*. Retrieved November 10, 2007, from http://reneehobbs.org/renee's%20web%20site/Publications/lo_que_docentes_y_estudiantes_de.htm

Hoel, H., Zapf, D., & Cooper, C. L. (2002). Workplace bullying and stress. *Historical and Current Perspectives on Stress and Health, 2*, 293–333. doi:10.1016/S1479-3555(02)02008-5

Hoffman, W. M., Hartman, L. P., & Rowe, M. (2003). You've got mail…and the boss knows: A survey by the center for business ethics of companies' email and internet monitoring. *Business and Society Review*, *108*(3), 285–307. doi:10.1111/1467-8594.00166

Holland, C. P., & Light, B. (1999). A critical success factors model for ERP implementation. *IEEE Software*, 30–36. doi:10.1109/52.765784

Horkheimer, M., & Adorno, T. W. (1976). *The Culture Industry: Enlightenment as Mass Deception*. London: Continuum International Publishing Group.

Hornung, M. S. (2005). Think before you type: A look at email privacy in the workplace. *Fordham Journal of Corporate and Financial Law*, *11*, 115–160.

Hunter, H. (2006). *Open Source Data Base Driven Web Development*. Oxford, UK: Chandos.

InfoXXI. (2000). *The information society for everyone*. Special Commission for the Development of the Information Society in Spain. Retrieved March 15, 2004, from http://infoxxi.min.es/Documentos/infoxxi.pdf

Institute of Medicine. (2004). *Health Literacy: A Prescription to End Confusion*. Washington, DC: National Academies Press. Retrieved February 2, 2010, from http://www.iom.edu/Reports/2004/Health-Literacy-A-Prescription-to-End-Confusion.aspx

Jarvis, P. (2006). Teaching styles and teaching methods. In P. Jarvis (Ed.), *The theory and practice of teaching* (pp. 28-38). Abingdon, UK: Routledge.

Jenkins, H. (2006). *Convergence Culture: Where Old and New Media Collide*. New York: New York University Press.

Jimoyiannis, A. (2008). Factors determining teachers' beliefs and perceptions of ICT in education. In A. Cartelli & M. Palma (Eds.), *Encyclopedia of information communication technology* (pp. 321-334). Hershey, PA: IGI Global.

Jimoyiannis, A., & Gravani, M. (2008). Digital literacy in second chance schools: An investigation of educators' beliefs and experiences. In V. Komis (Ed.), *Proceedings of the 4th Panhellenic Conference on 'Didactics of Informatics'*, Patra, Greece (pp. 405-414).

Jimoyiannis, A., & Gravani, M. (2010). Digital Literacy in a Lifelong Learning Programme for Adults: Educators' Experiences and Perceptions on Teaching Practices. *International Journal of Digital Literacy and Digital Competence*, *1*(1), 40–60.

Jimoyiannis, A., & Komis, V. (2006). Exploring secondary education teachers' attitudes and beliefs towards ICT adoption in education. *Themes in Education*, *7*(2), 181–204.

Jimoyiannis, A., & Komis, V. (2007). Examining teachers' beliefs about ICT in education: implications of a teacher preparation programme. *Teacher Development*, *11*(2), 181–204. doi:10.1080/13664530701414779

Jonassen, D. H. (1999). *Computers as Mindtools for Schools: Engaging Critical Thinking*. Upper Saddle River, NJ: Prentice Hall.

Jones, S. (2002). The Internet goes to college: How students are living in the future with today's technology. *Pew Internet & American Life Project*. Retrieved October 28, 2009 from http://www.educause.edu/Resources/TheInternetGoestoCollegeHowStu/151825

Jones, S., Johnson-Yale, C., Millermaier, S., & Seoane Pérez, F. (2009). Everyday life, online: U.S. college students' use of the Internet. *First Monday, 14*(10). Retrieved October 28, 2009 from http://firstmonday.org/htbin/cgiwrap/bin/ojs/index.php/fm/article/viewArticle/2649/2301

Jones, J. C. (1980). *Design Methods* (2nd ed.). New York: Wiley.

Jordan, J. G. (2007, January 1). *Factors that influence teacher responses to bullying situations* (Tech. Rep. No. AAI3290009). Detroit, MI: Wayne State University. Retrieved from http://digitalcommons.wayne.edu/dissertations/AAI3290009

Kaelber, D. C., Jha, A. K., Johnston, D., Middleton, B., & Bates, D. W. (2008). A research agenda for personal health records (PHRs). *Journal of the American Medical Informatics Association*, *15*(6), 729–736. doi:10.1197/jamia.M2547

Kambouri, M., Mellar, H., & Logan, K. (2006). Adult learners and ICT: An intervention study in the UK. In W. Nejdl & K. Tochtermann (Eds.), *1st European Conference on Technology Enhanced Learning* (pp. 213-226). Berlin-Heidelberg, Germany: Springer.

Kane, B. (2009). It's not your blackberry: The courts remind employers to update their workplace electronics policies. *Computer & Internet Lawyer*, *26*(3), 35–38.

Kavan, B., O'Hara, M., Patterson, E., & Bostrom, R. (1999). Excellence in client/server information system implementations: Understanding the STS Connection. *Management Decision*, *37*(3), 295–301. doi:10.1108/00251749910264532

Kelly, K. (1999). *New Rules for the New Economy*. New York: Penguin Books.

Kennedy, G., Krause, K., Judd, T., Churchward, A., & Gray, K. (2006). *First year students' experiences with technology: are they really digital natives?* Melbourne, Australia: University of Melbourne. Retrieved October 28, 2009 from http://www.bmu.unimelb.edu.au/research/munatives/ natives_report2006.pdf

Ke, W., & Wei, K. (2004). Succesful e-government in Singapore. *Communications of the ACM*, *47*(6), 95–99. doi:10.1145/990680.990687

Klecun, E. (2008). Bringing lost sheep into the fold: questioning the discourse of digital divide. *Information Technology & People*, *21*(3), 267–282. doi:10.1108/09593840810896028

Klein, K. E. (2007). Setting a realistic web-use policy. *Business Week Online, 18*.

Knezek, G., & Christensen, R. (2002). Impact of new information technologies on teachers and students. *Education and Information Technologies*, *7*(4), 369–376. doi:10.1023/A:1020921807131

Knowles, M. S. (1990). *The adult learner: A neglected species*. Houston, TX: Gulf.

Knowles, M. (1984). *Andragogy in Action*. San Francisco, CA: Jossey-Bass.

Kohut, A., Keeter, S., Doherty, C., & Dimock, M. (2008). Social networking and online videos take off: Internet's broader role in campaign 2008. *Pew Research Center for the People and the Press*. Retrieved October 30, 2009 from http://people-press.org/reports/pdf/384.pdf

Kotter, J. P. (1995). Leading change: Why transformation effort Fail. *Harvard Business Review*, 42–56.

Krathwohl, D. R., Bloom, B. S., & Masia, B. B. (1973). *Taxonomy of educational objectives, the classification of educational goals. Handbook II: Affective domain*. New York: David McKay Co.

Krathwohl, D. R. (2002). A Revision of Bloom Taxonomy: an overview. [from http://www.unco.edu/cetl/sir/stating_outcome/documents/Krathwohl.pdf]. *Theory into Practice*, *41*(4), 212–218. Retrieved August 2, 2010. doi:10.1207/s15430421tip4104_2

Krathwohl, D. R., Bloom, B. S., & Masia, B. B. (1973). *Taxonomy of Educational Objectives, the Classification of Educational Goals. Handbook II: Affective Domain*. New York: David McKay Co. Inc.

Kvavik, R. B., Caruso, J. B., & Morgan, G. (2004). *ECAR study of students and information technology 2004: convenience, connection, and control*. Boulder, CO: EDUCAUSE Center for Applied Research. Retrieved October 31, 2009 from http://net.educause.edu/ir/library/pdf/ers 0405/rs/ers0405w.pdf

Kyriacou, C. (2001). Teacher stress: directions for future research. *Educational Review*, *53*(1), 27–35. doi:10.1080/00131910120033628

Laboratory of Comparative Human Cognition (LCHC). (1982). Culture and intelligence . In Sternberg, R. J. (Ed.), *Handbook of human intelligence*. Cambridge, MA: Cambridge University Press.

Lakhan, R., & Jhunjhunwala, V. (2008). Open Source in Education. *EDUCAUSE Quarterly*, *31*(2), 32–40.

Lannon, J. (2010). The Role of Information and Communication Technologies in Human Rights Monitoring and Advocacy . In Martin, J., & Hawkins, L. (Eds.), *Information Communication Technologies for Human Services Education and Delivery: Concepts and Cases*. Hershey, PA: IGI Global.

Latto, A. (2007). Managing risk from within: monitoring employees the right way. *Risk Management*, *54*(4), 30–34.

Lave, J., & Wenger, E. (1991). *Situated learning. Legitimate peripheral participation*. Cambridge, MA: Cambridge University Press.

Lawson, K. (2005). Using eclectic digital resources to enhance instructional methods for adult learners. *OCLC Systems & Services*, *21*(1), 49–60. doi:10.1108/10650750510578154

Lazarinis, F. (2006). The importance of ICT Certification in Tourism and Cultural Professions. In *Proceedings of the Critical Issues in Leisure & Tourism Education*, Buckinghamshire, UK (pp. 165-173).

Lazarus, R. S., & Folkman, S. (1986). *Estrés y procesos cognitivos*. Barcelona, Spain: Martínez Roca.

Le Boterf, G. (1990). *De la compétence: Essai sur un attracteur étrange*. Paris: Les Ed. de l'Organisation.

Lerner, J., & Tirole, J. (2002). The simple economics of Open Source. *The Journal of Industrial Economics*, *50*(2), 197–234. doi:10.1111/1467-6451.00174

Lerner, J., & Tirole, J. (2005). The Economics of Technology Sharing: Open Source and Beyond. *The Journal of Economic Perspectives*, *19*(2), 99–120. doi:10.1257/0895330054048678

Levine, T., & Donitsa-Schmidt, S. (1998). Computer use, confidence, attitudes, and knowledge: a causal analysis. *Computers in Human Behavior*, *14*, 125–146. doi:10.1016/S0747-5632(97)00036-8

Lévy, P. (1994). *L'intelligence collective: Pour une anthropologie du cyberspace*. Paris: La Découverte.

Lévy, P. (1997). *Cyberculture*. Paris: Jacob.

Ley Orgánica. (2006). *Disposiciones generales*. Retrieved from http://www.boe.es/boe/dias/2006/05/04/pdfs/A17158-17207.pdf

Leymann, H. (1996a). *Mobbing: La persécution au travail*. París: Seuil.

Leymann, H. (1996b). The content and development of mobbing at work. *European Journal of Work and Organizational Psychology*, *5*(2), 165–184. doi:10.1080/13594329608414853

Leymann, H., & Gustafsson, A. (1996). Mobbing at work and the development of Post-traumatic Stress Disorders. *European Journal of Work and Organizational Psychology*, *5*(2), 251–275. doi:10.1080/13594329608414858

Lichtash, A. E. (2004). Inappropriate use of e-mail and the Internet in the workplace: The arbitration picture. *Dispute Resolution Journal*, *59*, 26–36.

Licklider, J. C. R., & Taylor, R. W. (1968). Computer as communication device. In *Science and Technology* (pp. 61-87).

Lidwell, W., Holden, K., & Butler, J. (2003). *Universal Principles of Design*. Beverly, MA: Rockport.

Ligorio, M. B., Andriessen, J., Baker, M., Knoller, N., Klonyguy, M., & Tateo, L. (Eds.). (2009). *Talking over the computer: pedagogical scenarios to blend computers and face to face interaction*. Naples, Italy: Scriptaweb.

Lisbon European Council. (2000). *Presidency Conclusions*. Retrieved from http://www.europarl.europa.eu/summits/lis1_en.htm

Livingstone, S. (2003). *The changing nature and uses of media literacy* (MEDIA@LSE Electronic Working Papers). London: London School of Economics and Political Science.

Livingstone, S. (2003). *What is media literacy?* Retrieved November 10, 2007, from http://www.lse.ac.uk/collections/media@lse/pdf/What_is_media_literacy.doc

Livingstone, S. (2005). *Adult Media Literacy. A review of the research literature on behalf of Ofcom*. London: Department of Media and Communications, London School of Economics and Political Science. Retrieved October 14, 2010, from http://www.ofcom.org.uk/advice/media_literacy/medlitpub/medlitpubrss/aml.pdf

Livingstone, S., & Bovill, M. (2001). *Children and the changing media environmental, an European comparative study*. Mahwah, NJ: Lawrence Erlbaum Associates.

Locke, K. D. (2001). *Grounded theory in management research*. Thousand Oaks, CA: Sage.

Long, S. A. (2005). What's new in libraries? Digital natives: if you aren't one, get to know one. *New Library World*, *106*(3/4), 187. doi:10.1108/03074800510587381

Löwgren, J. (2006). Articulating the use qualities of digital designs. In *Proceedings of the Aesthetic computing* (pp. 383-403). Cambridge, MA: The MIT Press.

Lüders, M. (2008). Conceptualizing personal media. *New Media & Society*, *10*(5), 683–702. doi:10.1177/1461444808094352

Mabert, V., Soni, A., & Venkatamara, M. (2003). Enterprise Resource Planning: managing implementation process. *European Journal of Operational Research*, *146*(2), 302–314. doi:10.1016/S0377-2217(02)00551-9

Magnus, P. D. (2009). On trusting Wikipedia. *Episteme*, *6*, 74–90. doi:10.3366/E1742360008000555

Mahatanankoon, P., Anandarajan, M., & Igbaria, M. (2004). Development of a measure of personal web usage in the workplace. *Cyberpsychology & Behavior*, *7*(1), 93–104. doi:10.1089/109493104322820165

Malinauskiene, V. (2004). Bullying among teachers in Kaunas, Lithuania. In S. Einarsen & M. B. Nielsen (Eds.), *The Fourth International Conference on Bullying and Harassment in the Workplace*. Retrieved from http://www.bullying.no/content/bbrg/Book%20of%20 abstract%20FICBHWP

Manno, I., Belgiorno, F., De Chiara, R., Di Matteo, A., Erra, U., Malandrino, D., et al. (2007). Collaborative face2face educational environment (CoFFEE). In *Proceedings of the First International Conference on Eclipse Technologies (Eclipse-IT)*, Naples, Italy.

Mantovani, S., & Ferri, P. (2006). *Bambini e computer. Alla scoperta delle nuove tecnologie a scuola e in famiglia*. Milano, Italy: Etas.

Mantovani, S., & Ferri, P. (2008). *Digital kids. Come i bambini usano il computer e come potrebbero usarlo genitori e insegnanti*. Milano, Italy: Etas.

Mantovani, S., & Ferri, P. (2008). *Digital Kids*. Milan, Italy: Etas.

Marche, S., & McNiven, J. (2003). E-government and e-governance: The future isn't what it used to be . *Canadian Journal of Administrative Sciences*, *20*(1), 74–86.

Martin, A. (2005). DigEuLit – a European Framework for Digital Literacy: a Progress Report. *JeLit, Journal of eLiteracy*, *2*(2). Retrieved July 31, 2010, from http://www.jelit.org/65/01/JeLit_Paper_31.pdf

Mason, R. (2006). Learning technologies for adult continuing education. *Studies in Continuing Education*, *28*(2), 121–133. doi:10.1080/01580370600751039

McHale, T. (2005). Portrait of a digital native. *Technology and Learning*, *26*(2), 33–34.

McLuhan, H. M. (1998). *Media e nuova educazione. Il metodo della domanda nel villaggio globale*. Roma, Italy: Armando.

Mediappro. (2006). *The appropriation of new media by the youth*. Retrieved from http://www.mediappro.org/publications/finalreport.pdf

Mehra, B., Merkel, C., & Bishop, A. P. (2004). The internet for empowerment of minority and marginalized users. *New Media & Society*, *6*, 781–802. doi:10.1177/146144804047513

Menduni, E. (2000). *Educare alla multimedialità*. Florence, Italy: Giunti.

Meric, F., Bernstam, E. V., & Mirza, N. Q. (2002). Breast cancer on the World Wide Web: cross sectional survey of quality of information and popularity of Websites. *British Medical Journal*, *324*, 577–581. doi:10.1136/bmj.324.7337.577

Midoro, V. (1998). Per una definizione di apprendimento cooperativo . In Midoro, V. (Ed.), *Argomenti di Tecnologie Didattiche* (pp. 169–198). Ortona, Italy: Ed. Menabò.

Midoro, V. (2002). Dalle comunità di pratica alle comunità di apprendimento virtuali. *Tecnologie Didattiche*, *1*, 3–10.

Mikkelsen, E. G. (2004). Coping with exposure to bullying at work – results from an interview study. In S. Einarsen & M. B. Nielsen (Eds.), *The Fourth International Conference on Bullying and Harassment in the Workplace*. Retrieved from http://www.bullying.no/content/bbrg/Book%20of%20abstract%20FICBHWP

Mikkelsen, G. E., & Einarsen, S. (2001). Bullying in Danish work-life: Prevalence and health correlates. *European Journal of Work and Organizational Psychology*, *10*, 393–413. doi:10.1080/13594320143000816

Miles, M. B., & Huberman, A. M. (1994). *Qualitative data analysis: An expanded sourcebook*. London: Sage.

Miles, I. (1996). The Information Society: competing perspectives on the social and economic implications of information and communication technologies . In Dutton Oxford, W. H., & Peltu, M. (Eds.), *Information and communication technologies: visions and realities* (pp. 37–52). Oxford, UK: Oxford University Press.

Milner, H. R. (2002). A case study of an experienced English teachers' self-efficacy and persistence through "crisis" situations: Theoretical and practical considerations. *High School Journal*, *86*(1), 28–35. doi:10.1353/hsj.2002.0020

Ministry of Education, Spain. (n.d.). *IDOC Plan, a framework for acting from a national perspective, 1984-86*. Madrid, Spain: Author.

Moggridge, B. (2007). *Designing Interactions*. Cambridge, MA: The MIT Press.

Moore, N. (1993). Information policy and strategic development. *Aslib Proceedings*, *45*(11/12), 281–285. doi:10.1108/eb051334

Morán, C., González, M. T., & Landero, R. (2009). El Cuestionario de Acoso Psicológico Percibido-CAPP: Un instrumento para evaluar el mobbing. *Infocoponline*. Retrieved from http://www.infocop.es/view_article.asp?id=2496

Morán, C. (2002). Mobbing: Persecución o psicoterror en el trabajo. *Capital Humano*, *151*, 44–48.

Morán, C. (2005). Personalidad, afrontamiento y burnout en profesionales de atención a personas con discapacidad intelectual. *Siglo Cero*, *31*(213), 30–39.

Morán, C. (2006). El cansancio emocional en servicios humanos: Asociación con acoso psicológico, personalidad y afrontamiento (Emotional exhaustion in social services: Its relations to mobbing, personality, and coping). *Revista de Psicología del Trabajo y de las Organizaciones*, *22*(2), 227–239.

Morán, C., González, M. T., & Landero, R. (2009). Valoración Psicométrica del Cuestionario de Acoso Psicológico Percibido. Psychometric Evaluation of the Perceived Mobbing Questionnaire. *Revista de Psicología del Trabajo y de las Organizaciones*, *25*(1), 7–16.

Morin, E. (1985). Le vie della complessità . In Bocchi, G., & Cerruti, M. (Eds.), *La sfida della complessità* (pp. 49–60). Milano, Italy: Feltrinelli.

Morin, E. (1999). *Une tête bien faite*. Paris: Seuil.

Motwani, J., Mirchandani, M., & Gunasekaran, A. (2002). Successful implementation of ERP Projects: evidence from two case studies. *International Journal of Production Economics*, *75*, 83–96. doi:10.1016/S0925-5273(01)00183-9

Mujtaba, B. G. (2003). Ethical implications of employee monitoring: what leaders should consider. *Journal of Applied Management and Entrepreneurship*, *8*(3), 22–43.

Murray, P., Cabrer, M., Hansen, M., Paton, C., Elkin, P., & Erdley, W. (2008). Towards addressing the opportunities and challenges of Web 2.0 for health and informatics. *Yearbook of Medical Informatics*, 44–51.

My Business. (2009). *Employers should limit staff net use*. Retrieved November 13, 2010, from http://www.mybusiness.co.uk/YSy1ncE.html

Myers, M. D. (1997). Qualitative Research in information systems. *Management Information Systems Quarterly*, 209–223.

Myers, M. D. (2009). *Qualitative Research in Business and Management*. London: Sage.

Nancherla, A. (2008). SURVEILLANCE: Increases in workplace. *T+D*, *62*(5), 12.

NCVHS. (2006). *Personal Health Records and Personal Health Record Systems, A report and recommendations from the National Committee on Vital and Health Statistics*. Retrieved October 11, 2009, from http://www.ncvhs.hhs.gov/0602nhiirpt.pdf

Nelson, C. H., & Tyson, L. (2010). HR undercover: Factor in privacy rights before rolling out surveillance programs. *HR Magazine*. Retrieved November 1, 2010, from http://www.thefreelibrary.com/HR+undercover%3a+factor+in+privacy+rights+before+rolling+out...-a0240605411

Nelson, D. L., & Quick, J. C. (2011). *ORGB*. Mason, OH: South-Western Cengage Learning.

Neupert, P., & Mundie, C. (2009). Personal Health Management Systems: Applying the Full Power of Software to Improve the Quality and Efficiency of Care. *Health Affairs*, *28*(2), 390–392. doi:10.1377/hlthaff.28.2.390

NIACE. (2005). *ICT skill for life* (Action Research Project, Rep. to DfES). Retrieved May 25, 2009, from http://archive.niace.org.uk/Research/ICT/ICT-SfL-Action-Research-Project.pdf

Nonaka, I. (1994). Come un'organizzazione crea conoscenza. *Economia&Management*, *3*, 31–48.

Nonaka, I., & Takeuchi, H. (1995). *The knowledge-creating company: how Japanese companies create the dynamics of innovation*. New York: Oxford University Press.

Nord, G. D., McCubbins, T. F., & Nord, J. H. (2006). E-monitoring in the workplace: Privacy, legislation, and surveillance software. *Communications of the ACM*, *49*(8), 73–77.

Norman, C., & Skinner, H. (2006). eHealth literacy: Essential skills for consumer health in a networked world. *Journal of Medical Internet Research*, *8*(2), e9. doi:10.2196/jmir.8.2.e9

O'Connor, P. (1999). *Electronic information distribution in tourism and hospitality*. New York: CAB International.

O'Reilly, T. (2005). *What Is Web 2.0? Design Patterns and Business Models for the Next Generation of Software*. Retrieved October 28, 2009 from http://oreilly.com/web2/archive/what-is-web-20.html

Obama, B. (2009). Memorandum for the heads of executive departments and agencies. Subject: Transparency and Open Government. Retrieved from http://www.whitehouse.gov/the_press_office/Transparency_and_Open_Government/

OECD. (2009). *PISA 2006 Technical Report*. Retrieved June 1, 2010, from http://www.pisa.oecd.org/document/41/0,3343,en_32252351_32236191_42025897_1_1_1_1,00.html

Ofcom. (2005). Introduction to the bulletin. *Media Literacy Bulletin, September*(3).

Oleniczak, M., Pike, C., Jitendra, M., & Bharat, M. (2010). Employers use Facebook too, for hiring. *Advances in Management*, *3*(1), 13–17.

Oliver, B., & Goerke, V. (2007). Australian undergraduates' use and ownership of emerging technologies: implications and opportunities for creating engaging learning experiences for the Net generation. *Australasian Journal of Educational Technology*, *23*(2), 171-186. Retrieved October 28, 2009 from http://www.ascilite.org.au/ajet/ajet23/oliver.html

Olson, D. R., & Torrence, N. (1991). *Literacy and orality*. Cambridge, UK: Cambridge University Press.

Ong, W. J. (2002). *Orality and literacy: The technologizing of the word*. New York: Routledge.

Opmanis, M., Dagiene, V., & Truu, A. (2006). Task types at "beaver" contests standards. In V. Dagienė & R. Mittermeir (Eds.), *Proceedings of the 2nd Internatioanl Conference on Informatics in Secondary Schools: Evolution and Perspectives*, Vilnius (pp. 509-519).

Orlikowski, W. (1991). Information Technology and the Structuring of Organizations. *Information Systems Research*, 27–38.

Orlikowski, W. (1993). CASE Tools as Organizational Change: Investigating Incremental and Radical Changes in Systems Development. *Management Information Systems Quarterly*, 209–223.

Osterloh, M., & Rota, D. (2007). Open source software development, just another case of collective invention. *Research Policy*, *36*(2), 157–171. doi:10.1016/j.respol.2006.10.004

Palenzuela, D. L. (1994). *BEEGC. Batería de Escalas de Expectativas Generalizadas de Control*. Salamanca, Spain: Universidad de Salamanca.

Papert, S. (1996). *The connected family: Bridging the digital generation gap*. Atlanta, GA: Longstreet Press.

Papert, S. (1993). *The children's machine*. New York: Basic Books.

Pascale, A. (2002). E-learning: produrre conoscenza comunicando in rete. *Rinnovare la scuola, 18,* 5-18.

Pascale, A. (2005). Le figure professionali nell'e-learning: il tutor on line. *Rinnovare la scuola, 28,* 6-28.

Pascale, A. (2006). *Professione docente e nuove tecnologie. Indagine quali-quantitativa sull'impatto delle TIC sull'identità professionale degli insegnanti*. Roma, Italy: Edizioni A.N.S.I.

Paul, I. (2009). *Jackson's death a blow to the internet*. Retrieved November 13, 2010, from http://www.pcworld.com/article/167435/jacksons_death_a_blow_to_the_internet.html

Pedrò, F. (2006). *The new millennium learners, what do we know about the effectiveness of ICT in education and what we don't*. Retrieved July 15, 2009, from http://www.oecd.org/dataoecd/52/4/37172511.pdf

Pedrò, F. (2006). *The New Millennium Learners: Challenging our Views on ICT and Learning*. Paris: OECD. Retrieved October 28, 2009 from http://www.oecd.org/dataoecd/1/1/38358359.pdf

Pedrò, F. (2008). *The new millennium learner a project in progress*. Retrieved June 2006, from http://www.olis.oecd.org/olis/2008doc.nsf/ENGDATCORPLOOK/NT0000310E/$FILE/JT03245474.PDF

Pehkonen, H. (2004). Workplace bullying and coping strategies. A longitudinal study. In S. Einarsen & M. B. Nielsen (Eds.), *The Fourth International Conference on Bullying and Harassment in the Workplace*. Retrieved from http://www.bullying.no/content/bbrg/Book%20of%20abstract%20FICBHWP

Peluchette, J., & Karl, K. (2008). Social networking profiles: An examination of student attitudes regarding use and appropriateness of content. *Cyberpsychology & Behavior, 11*(1), 95–97. doi:10.1089/cpb.2007.9927

Pérez Tornero, J. M., & Celot, P. (2007). *Current trends and approaches to media literacy in Europe*. Retrieved from http://ec.europa.eu/culture/media/literacy/studies/index_en.htm

Pérez Tornero, J. M. (2005). *Media education in Spain*. Media Education Journal.

Pérez-Tornero, J. M. (2004). *Digital Literacy and Media Education: An Emerging Need.* Retrieved October 16, 2010, from http://www.elearningeuropa.info/directory/index.php?page= doc&docid =4935&doclng=6

Piaget, J. (1964) *Six études de psychologie*. Paris: Gonthier.

Piaget, J. (1967). *La construction du réel chez l'enfant*. Paris: Delachaux & Niestlé.

Piaget, J. (1952). *The origins of intelligence in children*. New York: International University Press. doi:10.1037/11494-000

Piaget, J. (1970). *Lo sviluppo mentale del bambino*. Turin, Italy: Einaudi.

Piñuel, I. (2005). La identificación, medida y prevención del mobbing en la organización. *Capital Humano, 188*, 96–102.

Pozzali, A., & Ferri, P. M. (2010). The Medial Diet of University Students in Italy: An Exploratory Research. *International Journal of Digital Literacy and Digital Competence, 1*(2), 1–10.

Prenksy, M. (2001a). Digital natives, digital immigrants. *Horizon, 9*(5), 1–6. doi:10.1108/10748120110424816

Prenksy, M. (2001b). Digital natives, digital immigrants, part II. Do they really think differently? *Horizon, 9*(6), 1–6. doi:10.1108/10748120110424843

Prensky, M. (2006). *Don't bother me mom—I'm learning*. Minneapolis, MN: Paragon House Publishers.

Quan-Haase, A. (2007). University students' local and distant social ties: Using and integrating modes of communication on campus. *Information Communication and Society, 10*(5), 671–693. doi:10.1080/13691180701658020

Quintano, C. (2008). La ridefinizione della nozione di turismo e la ricerca di un nuovo "abito mentale" . In Quintano, C., & Garbaccio, F. (Eds.), *Turismosiamotutti atto secondo* (pp. 39–48). Napoli, Italy: Denaro Libri.

Raymond, E. (1999). The Cathedral and the bazaar. *Knowledge . Technology and Policy, 12*(3), 23–49. doi:10.1007/s12130-999-1026-0

Reid, P., Monsen, J., & Rivers, I. (2004). Psychology's contribution to understanding and managing bullying within schools. *Educational Psychology in Practice, 20*(3), 241–258. doi:10.1080/0266736042000251817

Report, B. (2009). *Contribution's to the Rose Review*. Retrieved from http://publications.becta.org.uk/download.cfm?resID=40240

Report, C. O. T. E. C. (2008). *The situation of innovation in Spanish firms*. Madrid, Spain: COTEC Foundation.

Rideout, V. J., & Hammel, E. (2006). *The media family: Electronic media in the lives of infants, toddlers, preschoolers and their parents*. Menlo Park, CA: Henry J. Kaiser Family Foundation.

Riehle, D. (2007). The Economic Motivation of Open Source: Stakeholder Perspectives. *IEEE Computer*, *40*(4), 25–32.

Rifkin, J. (1995). *The end of work: The decline of the global labor force and the dawn of the post-market era*. New York: Putnam's Sons.

Rifkin, J. (2000). *The age of access: the new culture of hypercapitalism, where all of life is a paid-for experience*. New York: Tarcher/Putnam.

Rivoltella, P. C. (2008). From Media Education to Digital Literacy: A Paradigm Change? In *Digital literacy: Tools and Methodologies for Information Society* (pp. 217-29). Hershey, PA: IGI Publishing.

Rivoltella, P. C. (2003). *Costruttivismo e pragmatica della comunicazione on line*. Trento, Italy: Erickson.

Rivoltella, P. C. (2005). *Media education: fondamenti didattici e prospettive di ricerca*. Brescia, Italy: La Scuola.

Rivoltella, P. C. (2010). *Métodos e Técnicas da Pesquisa Educativa em Ambientes Digitais*. Florianópolis, Brazil: UFSC.

Rosario, J. G. (2000). On the leading edge: critical success factors in ERP implementation projects. *Business World*, 21-27.

Rose, J. (2009). *Primary Curriculum Review*. Retrieved from http://www.dcsf.gov.uk/primarycurriculumreview/

Rossi, D. (2006). Decoding the green open source software puzzle: A survey of theoretical and empirical contributions. In *Proceedings of the Economics of Open Source Software Development, 22nd IEEE International Parallel and Distributed Processing Symposium*, New York.

Rotter, J. B. (1966). Generalized expectancies for internal versus external control of reinforcement. *Psychological Monographs: General and Applied*, *80*, 609.

Samborn, H. V. (2007). Go google yourself. *ABA Journal*, *93*(8), 56–57.

Sameh, B., & Izak, J. (2009). The Adoption and Use of IT Artifacts: A New Interaction Centric Model for the Study of User-Artifact Relationships. *Journal of the Association for Information Systems*, *10*(9), 661–685.

Schön, D. A. (1983). *The Reflective Practitioner: How professionals think in action*. New York: Basic Books.

Schuster, (1996). Rejection, exclusion, and harassment at work and in schools. *European Psychologist*, *1*, 293-309.

Schwartz, D. (1999). *Ghost in the machine: Seymour Papert on how computers fundamentally change the way kids learn* (Interview with Seymour Papert by Dan Schwartz). Retrieved May 1, 2009, from http://www.papert.org/articles/GhostInTheMachine.html

Selwyn, N. (2003). Apart from technology: understanding people's non-use of information and communication technologies in everyday life. *Technology in Society*, *25*, 99–116. doi:10.1016/S0160-791X(02)00062-3

Selwyn, N. (2004). Reconsidering political and popular understandings of the digital divide. *New Media & Society*, *6*(3), 341–362. doi:10.1177/1461444804042519

Sen, A. K. (1999). *Development as freedom*. Oxford, UK: Oxford Oxford University Press.

Sharkey, J., & Brandt, D. S. (2008). Interating Technology Literacy and Information Literacy . In Rivoltella, P. C. (Ed.), *Digital literacy: Tools and Methodologies for Information Society* (pp. 85–97). Hershey, PA: IGI Publishing.

Shiff, T. (2002). The Economics of Open Source Software: a survey of the early literature. *Review of Network Economics*, *1*(1), 66–74.

Siau, K., & Long, Y. (2004). *Factors impacting e-government development*. Paper presented at the Twenty-Fifth International Conference on Information Systems, ICIS, Poland.

Siemens, G. (2005). Connectivism: A Learning Theory for the Digital Age. *Instructional Technology and Distance Learning*, *2*(1). Retrieved July 31, 2010, from http://www.itdl.org/Journal/Jan_05/article01.htm

Sigala, M. (2002). The evolution of Internet pedagogy: Benefits for tourism and hospitality education. *Journal of Hospitality, Leisure . Sport & Tourism Education*, *1*(2), 29–45.

Silverstone, R. (2005). *Por que estudar a mídia* (2nd ed.). São Paulo, Brazil: Loyola.

Skinner, B. F. (1953). *Science and human behaviour*. New York: Macmillan.

Slavin, R. E. (1990). *Cooperative Learning: Theory, Research and Practice*. Upper Saddle River, NJ: Prentice Hall.

Smith, C., & Jenner, P. (1998). Tourism and the Internet. *Travel & Tourism Analyst, 1*, 62–81.

Snyder, J. (2010). E-mail privacy in the workplace: A boundary regulation perspective. *Journal of Business Communication, 47*(3), 266–294. doi:10.1177/0021943610369783

Software Informer. (2010). *Anti-keylogger wiki*. Retrieved November 13, 2010, from http://anti-keylogger2.software.informer.com/wiki/

Sokura, B. (2005). *ICT Certification and its Effects on the Intellectual Capital of an Organization.* Retrieved from http://www.ifipwg82.org/Oasis2005/Bertta Sokura.pdf

Sommers, G., & Nelson, C. (2003). A taxonomy of players and activities across the ERP project life cycle. *Information & Management, 41*(3), 257–278. doi:10.1016/S0378-7206(03)00023-5

Spadavecchia, C., & Giovannella, C. (2010). Monitoring learning experiences and styles: the socio-emotional level. In [Washington, DC: IEEE.]. *Proceedings of the ICALT, 2010*, 445–449.

Spitzmüller, C., & Stanton, J. (2006). Examining employee compliance with organizational surveillance and monitoring. *Journal of Occupational and Organizational Psychology, 79*(2), 245–272. doi:10.1348/096317905X52607

Star Workforce Solutions, Inc. (2009). *Underperformance in the workplace: How much is it costing? And What are the solutions?* Retrieved October 20, 2010, from http://www.starworkforce.com

Star, S. L., & Griesemer, J. R. (1989). Institutional Ecology, 'Translations' and Boundary Objects: Amateurs and Professionals in Berkeley's Museum of Vertebrate Zoology, 1907-39. *Social Studies of Science, 19*(4), 387–420. doi:10.1177/030631289019003001

Strauss, A., & Corbin, J. (1990). *Basics of Qualitative Research: Grounded theory, Procedures and Techniques*. London: Sage.

Sugar, W., Crawley, F., & Fine, B. (2004). Examining teachers' decisions to adopt new technology. *Educational Technology and Society, 7*(4), 201–213.

Symantex Hosted Services. (2008). *Employee web use and misuse: Companies, their employees and the internet.* Retrieved November 1, 2010, from http://whitepapers.zdnet.com/abstract.aspx?docid=397147

Tapscott, D. (1998). *Growing up digital: the rise of the Net generation.* New York: McGraw-Hill.

Tapscott, D., & Williams, A. D. (2007). *Wikinomics. How Mass Collaborations Changes Everything*. London: Portfolio.

Tarallo, P. (2003). *Digital divide. La nuova frontiera dello sviluppo globale*. Milano, Italy: Franco Angeli.

Tascón, M. (2006). Development of a place for the information society. In R. Casado (Ed.), *Keys for digital literacy. Seminar on Digital Literacy* (pp. 187-194). Madrid, Spain: Telefónica Foundation. Retrieved from http://sociedaddelainformación.telefónica.es/documentos/articulos/clavesdelaalfabetizacióndigital.pdf

Theofanos, M., & Mulligan, C. (2004). Empowering Patients through Access to Information. *Information Communication and Society, 7*(4), 466–490. doi:10.1080/1369118042000305601

Tobin, J. J., Wu, D. Y. H., & Davidson, D. H. (1989). *Preschool in three cultures: Japan, China, and the United States*. New Haven, CT: Yale University Press.

Tornero, J. M. P. (2004). *Promoting digital literacy: Final report (EAC/76/03). Understanding digital literacy*. Barcelona, Spain: UAB. Retrieved September 25, 2009, from http://ec.europa.eu/education/archive/elearning/doc/studies/dig_lit_en.pdf

Tornero, J. M. P. (2004). *Promoting digital literacy: Under- standing digital literacy (Rep. No. EAC/76/03)*. Barcelona, Spain: UAB.

Travieso, J. L., & Planellá, J. (2008). Digital literacy as a factor for social inclusion: A critical view. *Review on the Knowledge Society, 6*, 1–7.

Trentin, G. (2000). Dalla formazione a distanza alle comunità di pratica attraverso l'apprendimento in rete. *Tecnologie Didattiche, 20*, 21–29.

Trentin, G. (2004). *Apprendimento in rete e condivisione delle conoscenze*. Milano, Italy: Franco Angeli.

Tschannen-Moran, M., & Woolfolk-Hoy, A. (2001). Teacher efficacy: Capturing an elusive construct. *Teaching and Teacher Education*, *17*, 783–805. doi:10.1016/S0742-051X(01)00036-1

Tuan, Y. (1977). *Space and Place. The Perspective of Experience*. Minneapolis, MN: University of Minnesota Press.

Turri, A. M., Maniam, B., & Hynes, G. E. (2008). Are they watching? Corporate surveillance of employees' technology use. *The Business Review, Cambridge*, *11*(2), 126–130.

Ugrin, J., & Pearson, J. (2008). Exploring internet abuse in the workplace: How can we maximize deterrence efforts? *Review of Business*, *28*(2), 29–40.

UNESCO. (2000). *Creating a new UNESCO Programme for a just and free information society with universal benefits*. Retrieved November 23, 2002, from http://www.unesco.org/webworld/future/index.shtml

UNO. (2001). *Making new technologies work for human development*. Retrieved July 15, 2009, from http://www.undp.org/hdr2001

UOC. (2009). *The use of open source in Public Administrations in Spain (UOC Rep.)*. Universitat Oberta de Calalunya.

Van Deursen, A. J. A. M., & Van Dijk, J. A. G. M. (2009). Improving digital skills for the use of online public information and services. *Government Information Quarterly*, *26*, 333–340. doi:10.1016/j.giq.2008.11.002

Van Dijk, J. (2006). Digital divide research, achievements and shortcomings. *Poetics*, *34*, 221–235. doi:10.1016/j.poetic.2006.05.004

Van Dijk, J., & Hacker, K. (2003). The digital divide as a complex and dynamic phenomenon. *The Information Society*, *19*, 315–327. doi:10.1080/01972240309487

Vascellaro, J. E., & Bulkeley, W. M. (2009, February 5). Google, IBM Promote OHRs. *Wall Street Journal*.

Vasilyeva, E. (2007). Towards personalized feedback in educational computer games for children. In *Proceedings of the Sixth IASTED International Conference on Web-Based Education*, Chamonix, France (Vol. 2, pp. 597-602). Anaheim, CA: ACTA Press.

Vecris, L., & Hodolidou, E. (Eds.). (2003). *Educational guidelines for the second chance schools*. Athens, Greece: IDEKE.

Veen, W. (2007). *Homo Zappiens and the need for new education systems*. Retrieved July 10, 2009, from http://www.oecd.org/dataoecd/0/5/38360892.pdf

Veen, W., & Vrakking, B. (2006). *Homo Zappiens, growing up in a digital age*. London: Network Continuum Education.

Venkatesh, V., & Brown, S. A. (2003). User acceptance of information technology: Toward a unified view. *Management Information Systems Quarterly*, *27*(3), 425–478.

Vieira, N. (2007, September). *As literacias e o uso responsável da Internet*. Paper presented at V Congresso SOPCOM.

Von Hippel, E. (2005). *Democratizing Innovation*. Cambridge, MA: MIT Press.

Vygotsky, L. S. (1978). *Mind in Society: The development of higher psychological processes*. Cambridge, MA: MIT Press.

Wakefield, R. L. (2004). Computer monitoring and surveillance. *The CPA Journal*, *74*(7), 52–55.

Wannemacher, K. (2009). Articles as assignments - Modalities and experiences of wikipedia use in university course. In M. Spaniol, Q. Li, R. Klamma, R. W. H. Lau (Eds.), *Proceedings of the Advances in Web Based Learning (ICWL 2009), 8th International Conference*, Aachen, Germany (pp. 434-443). Berlin: Springer.

Ward, B. T., Purwin, C., Sipior, J. C., & Volonino, L. (2009). Recognizing the impact of e-discovery amendments on electronic records management. *Information Systems Management*, *26*(4), 350–356. doi:10.1080/10580530903245721

Warschauer, M. (2003). *Technology and social inclusion: Rethinking the digital divide*. Cambridge, MA: MIT Press.

Wasserman, S., & Faust, K. (1994). *Social network analysis: methods and applications*. Cambridge, UK: Cambridge University Press.

Webster, F. (1995). *Theories of the information society*. London: Routledge.

Weiser, M. (1993). Some Computer Science Problems in Ubiquitous Computing. *Communications of the ACM*, *7*(36), 75–84. doi:10.1145/159544.159617

Wenger, E., McDermott, R., & Snyder, W. M. (2002). *Cultivating Communities of Practice*. Boston: HBS press.

Wenger, E. (1998). *Community of practice*. Cambridge, UK: Cambridge University press.

Wenger, E., McDermott, R., & Snyder, W. M. (2002). *Cultivating Communities of Practice. A guide to managing knowledge*. Boston: Harvard Business School Press.

Wen, H. J., Schwieger, D., & Gershung, P. (2007). Internet usage monitoring in the workplace: Its legal challenges and implementation strategies. *Information Systems Management*, *24*(2), 185–196. doi:10.1080/10580530701221072

Wen, H., & Gershuny, P. (2005). Computer-based monitoring in the American workplace: Surveillance technologies and legal challenges. *Human Systems Management*, *24*(2), 165–173.

Wertheim, C., & Leyser, Y. (2002). Efficacy beliefs, background variables, and differentiated instruction of Israeli prospective teachers. *The Journal of Educational Research*, *96*(1), 54–64. doi:10.1080/00220670209598791

Wheeler, D. (2007). *Why Open Source Software. Look at the Numbers*. Retrieved January 30, 2010, from dwheeler.com/oss_ls_why_html

Wiig, K. (1993). *Knowledge Management Foundations: Thinking about Thinking – How People and Organizations Create, Represent, and Use Knowledge*. Arlington, TX: Schema Press.

Wilfong, J. D. (2006). Computer anxiety and anger: The impact of computer use, computer experience, and self-efficacy beliefs. *Computers in Human Behavior*, *22*, 1001–1011. doi:10.1016/j.chb.2004.03.020

Williams, C. (2011). *MGMT*. Mason, OH: South-Western Cengage Learning.

Willinsky, J. (2002). Democracy and education: the missing link may be ours. *Harvard Educational Review*, *72*(3), 25–43.

Willinsky, J. (2005). Scientific research in a democratic culture: or what's a social science for? *Teachers College Record*, *107*(1), 38–51. doi:10.1111/j.1467-9620.2005.00455.x

Wilson, R. A. (1999, April). *Revelry, revelation, or research: What are college students really doing on the Internet*. Paper presented at ACRL's Ninth National Conference: Racing toward Tomorrow, Detroit, MI. Retrieved October 28, 2009 from http://ala.org/ala/mgrps/divs/acrl/events/pdf/wilsonr99.pdf

Wise, P. A. (2009). Tweet, tweet, you're fired. *Employment & Labor Relations Law*, *7*(4), 7–12.

Woods, D. R. (1994). *Problem-based Learning: How to Gain the Most from PBL*. Waterdown, ON, Canada: Donald R. Woods.

Wootton, R., Craig, J., & Patterson, V. (2006). *Introduction to telemedicine* (2nd ed.). London: The Royal Society of Medicine Press Ltd.

Wyatt, J., Allison, S., Donoghue, D., Horton, P., & Kearney, K. (2003). *Evaluation of CMF Funded UK online Centres*. DfES.

Yin, R. K. (2003). *Case study research: Design and methods* (3rd ed.). Thousand Oaks, CA: Sage.

Young, J., & Faris, N. (2009). *Akamai delivers record streaming and web content during historic presidential inauguration*. Retrieved November 1, 2010, from http://www.akamai.com/html/about/press/releases/2009/press_012009.html

Young, K. (2010). Killer surf issues: Crafting an organizational model to combat employee internet abuse. *Information Management Journal*, *44*(1), 34–38.

Zocchi, P. (2003). *Internet. La democrazia possibile. Come vincere la sfida del digital divide*. Milano, Italy: Guerini e Associati.

About the Contributors

Antonio Cartelli is a Researcher in Didactics and Special Pedagogy and has recently won a national competition for associated professorship in Experimental Pedagogy. He manages the Laboratory for Technology of Education and Knowledge Management and the Centre for ICT and on line teaching in the Faculty of Humanities at the University of Cassino - Italy. Among his interests are: misconceptions, mental schemes, Information Systems for research and teaching, Web Technologies in teaching research, and their everyday application for the improvement of teaching and learning. He has authored many papers and books concerning the themes he is interested in and is currently chief-editor of the *International Journal of Digital Literacy and Digital Competence.*

* * *

Paola Adinolfi is full Professor of Organization Science; Director of the University Master for Leadership in Healthcare Services (DAOSan), organized by the University of Salerno, the Regional Healthcare Agency (ARSAN), the "Federico II" University of Naples and the University of Sannio; director of CIRPA, Interdepartmental centre for research in law and management of Public Administrations; director of the PhD program in economics and management of public organizations; lecturer in Organization of public administration and companies Evaluation of managerial performances in the degree and PhD courses at the Faculty of Economics of the University of Salerno.

David López Berzosa, senior lecturer at University of León holds a PhD in Telematic Engineering by the Technical University of Madrid and a MBA by I.E Business School. His research interests currently are open innovation and knowledge management. He has also worked for multinationals such as IBM and Vivendi before joining the academia.

Isabel Cantón holds a Doctorate in Pedagogy, and is currently a Professor in the Didactic and Scholar Organization Department at the University of Leon (Spain). She had collaborated in educative innovation and teacher instruction, and research interests include these areas. She has published ten books and several articles on educational topics. He has given conferences on International Congress in Belgium, Sweden, France, Jerusalem, Portugal, Cuba, Argentina, Peru, Venezuela, and Switzerland.

Laura Cervi, PhD in Political Science from Pavia University, Italy, currently is Associate Professor of Political Communication at the Universitat Autónoma de Barcelona, Spain. She is researching about ICTs and new forms of political participation.

Laura Corazza held her PhD in Pedagogy in 2006. Her PhD thesis was entitled Democratic Education and the Knowledge Society. She is actually involved in studies and researches on Media Education, Democratic and Intercultural Education and Video movies. She works closely with professor Luigi Guerra, who teaches Technology of Education in the University of Bologna, and manages the Technology Laboratory "MELA" at the Department of Education in the same university.

Valentina Dagiene is head of Department of Informatics Methodology at the Institute of Mathematics and Informatics as well as Professor at Vilnius University. She has published over 120 scientific papers and the same number of methodical works, has written more than 50 textbooks in the field of informatics and ICT for primary and secondary education. Her main research topics are informatics didactics, especially teaching algorithms and programming, technology enhanced learning, computing education research, localization of software. She is national representative of the Technical Committee of IFIP for Education (TC3), member of the Group for Informatics in Secondary Education (WG 3.1) and for Research (WG 3.3) of IFIP, member of the European Logo Scientific Committee, member of International Committee of Olympiads in Informatics. She is Executive Editor of international journals "Informatics in Education" and "Olympiads in Informatics".

Paolo Maria Ferri is Associate Professor in the Faculty of Educational Sciences of University of Milano-Bicocca - Department of Epistemology and Hermeneutics of Education. He teaches "Technology of Education" and "Theory and application of New Media" in the graduation courses of the Faculty of Educational Sciences. He also taught in after graduation courses and international and interdisciplinary PHD. His main field of research involves didactical technologies and theory and practice of new media. He published many books, essays in books, papers in journals and conference proceedings.

Gerald Futschek has the position of an Associate Professor at the Institute of Software Technology and Interactive Systems at Vienna University of Technology. He works on several initiatives to increase the digital fluency of all people and to prevent the digital divide: European Computer Driving Licence ECDL, Bebras International Contest on Informatics and Computer Fluency, e-Learning for prisoners, etc. His research interests are software verification and informatics didactics. Since 2007 he is president of the Austrian Computer Society OCG.

Carlo Giovannella is currently the scientific and ICT coordinator and chair of the ISIM_garage (Interfaces and Multimodal Interactive Systems - http://www.scuolaiad.it/isimgarage - only Italian) at the IaD School (Distance Learning Center) of the University of Tor Vergata - http://www.scuolaiad.it. He is also teaching at the Faculty of Science, Physics Department. At present he deals with design for the experience (including interaction design), natural computer-mediated communication, augmented places and pervasive computing, collaborative learning and working (environments/ tools/ methods/ strategies/ processes). He is designer and chair of the project LIFE, an innovative learning environment of new generation (http://www.scuolaiad.it/life). He is deeply involved in the research on the definition of a set of experience styles and on the ecological monitoring of experience style's indicators in education at, but not only, cognitive, emotional/affective and social levels.

Maria Gravani is a lecturer in Continuing Education/Adult Education at the Open University of Cyprus. She previously worked in the UK (Bristol University, University College London), in the Republic of Ireland (Trinity College), and Greece (University of Peloponnese, Hellenic Open University). Her main research interests include: continuing professional development, program development in adult education, adult digital literacy, adult teaching and learning in higher education. She has recently published articles in *Teaching and Teacher Education, Learning and Instruction, Compare, Journal of In-service Education.* She is on the editorial board of the new ESREA journal, the European Journal of Research in Adult Education and Learning.

Carmen de Pablos Heredero is a Professor in the Business Administration Area at the Rey Juan Carlos University in Madrid, Spain from 1994. She is specialised in the impact of information technologies over organisational systems and entrepreneurship where she develops main research. She coordinates the Doctoral Program on Business Administration and Entrepreneurship at the Rey Juan Carlos University. She is the main research of the open innovation group, a multidisciplinary research group specialised in open innovation analysis. She has presented communications in different international venues and has published in specialised journals. She has also worked as a consultant in the area of IS management at Primma Consulting.

Athanassios Jimoyiannis is an associate professor in Science and ICT in Education at the Department of Social and Educational Policy, University of Peloponnese, in Greece. He has received his PhD from the University of Ioannina in 1991. Prior to his current position he has been an assistant professor at the Department of Preschool Education, University of the Aegean. His current research interests include e-learning and ICT in education, teachers' preparation about ICT in education, computer science education and science education. He is a co-editor of the international journal THEMES in Science and Technology Education. He is also a member of the Scientific Review Board in various international journals and conferences in the areas of e-learning and ICT in education.

Dimitris Kanellopoulos holds a PhD in multimedia communications from the Department of Electrical and Computer Engineering in the University of Patras, Greece. He is a member of the Educational Software Development Laboratory (ESDLab) in the Department of Mathematics at the University of Patras. His research interests include multimedia communications, intelligent information systems, knowledge representation and Web-based engineering. He also authored many papers on his research field in international journals and conferences. He serves as an Editor in ten scientific journals.

Angelina Kiser is an Assistant Professor and Department Chair for Management and Information Systems in the HEB School of Business and Administration at the University of the Incarnate Word in San Antonio, TX, USA. She teaches management courses to undergraduate students and works closely with the information technology professors to integrate the two fields. She has traveled extensively with both professors and students and has had the opportunity to investigate ethics among various cultures. She has explored the varying ethical attitudes with regards to gender, age, and ethnicity. She has various academic journal publications and presented at academic conferences in areas related to technology ethics, business ethics, and diversity.

Ela Klecun is a Lecturer in Information Systems at the London School of Economics and Political Science and a member of LSE Health. Her research interests include: information policy and strategies for information systems (IS) in health, implementation of IS in healthcare organisations, societal and organisational implications of new technologies, digital literacy and social exclusion. She was a principle investigator for ESRC funded project on digital literacy. Currently she is a member of a team evaluating the National Care Records Service in secondary care, a project funded by the Connecting for Health Evaluation Programme. She has published in various journals, edited books and conference proceedings.

Emilio Lastrucci. Before his permanent position as a Professor of Education at University of Basilicata, Prof. Emilio Lastrucci obtained a degree, two masters and a Ph.D. at University of Rome "La Sapienza", where he worked for several years. He took part in many research projects about literacy, reading comprehension, history teaching, civic education and socialisation processes. He also focused the following topics: learning, teaching planning, achievement evaluation and Open Distance Learning. Prof. Lastrucci participated in many international research programmes organised by I.E.A. (Written Composition, Reading Literacy) and in the European inquiry "Youth and History" as the Italian national coordinator. He also participated in several European projects. In Italy, he was involved in several cross-university national studies. He is a member of several Ministry Committees and is mainly involved in the work of "UNIFAD" committee, aimed at planning university courses created on ODL, a national e-learning platform.

Fotis Lazarinis is a visiting lecturer at the department of Cultural Heritage Management and New Technologies, University of Ioannina in Greece. He authored more than 50 refereed papers in international and national conferences, journals and research books. He has also published several Computer Science educational books in Greek and served as a review member for many conferences and workshops.

Consuelo Morán holds a Master in Resources Humans Management and a Doctorate in Psychology of Stress. She has over eleven years on Work and Organizational Psychology experience. Now is a Professor of Work and Organizational Psychology and Health Psychology at the University of León. She has published three books and several articles on stress, coping, and mobbing at work, and these are the researching topics.

Oralia Paredes is a researcher and PhD candidate in Journalism and Communication Sciences at Autonomous University of Barcelona, Spain. She is a member of the research group Gabinete de Comunicación y Educación, UAB; and has taken part in research projects on media literacy. Her research interests include media education, uses of ICT and the assessment of Media Literacy in order to improve ML levels.

Angela Pascale obtained a degree in Humanities with a final dissertation in Educational Sciences, a Master in E-learning Design as well as a Master in ICTs (Information & Communication Technologies) and a Ph.D. in Educational Sciences. She has significant experience in teacher trainer's role and worked in various Italian projects which focused on ICT, laboratory teaching and e-learning. She took part in conferences and seminars and led several university laboratories in the field of ICT and e-learning. Her main research fields are: teachers' education and training with emphasis on ICTs, e-learning and citizenship education, and has been involved in relevant national and international research projects.

Corrado Petrucco is Associate Professor of Educational Technology at the Faculty of Education in the University of Padua. His main research interest focuses on three areas: Information Literacy and Semantic Web, social software and Digital Storytelling. In the Information Literacy field he developed a new methodology (SEWCOM – Search the Web with Concept Maps) for a meta-cognitive approach to the information seeking process. In the field of social software he has analyzed the use of blogs, wikis, social bookmarking, geo-referencing, etc. to study how to create personalised and collaborative knowledge spaces. His most recent research interest, Digital Storytelling, is strictly connected to the social software focus because it is linked to a participatory media literacy.

Timothy Porter is an Information Systems instructor in the HEB School of Business and Administration at the University of the Incarnate Word in San Antonio, TX, USA. He teaches Information Systems courses to undergraduate students. His has prior vast experience successfully managing information technology departments. Mr. Porter spent the last 12 years in the corporate world prior to teaching. Mr. Porter is introducing University of the Incarnate Word students to building mobile applications across multiple platforms. His research interests include social media, mobile applications and business and technology ethics.

Andrea Pozzali holds a Ph.D. in Applied Sociology and Methodology of Social Research. He is currently research fellow at the QUA_SI Inter-department Centre of the University of Milan-Bicocca (Italy) and collaborates with the Observatory on New Media (nuMediaBios) in the same university.

Luca Tateo, PhD, is social psychologist, research fellow of the Department of Economy, Institutions and Society, University of Sassari (Italy), coordinating the e-learning of the Faculty of Political Sciences. Has been research fellow of the Department of Education Sciences, University of Salerno (Italy), coordinating the research activity of the project LEAD Technology-enhanced learning and problem solving discussions: Networked learning environments in the classroom, funded by the VI-FP. He is researching and teaching in social psychology applied to the following areas: Design of e-learning and CSCL in school and university education; Social Psychology of computer mediated communication; Social Representations and group identity; Teachers professional identity; Education, orientation and vocational guidance.

José Manuel Pérez Tornero is a Doctor in Journalism and Communication Sciences. He is Professor of Journalism at the Autonomous University of Barcelona, Spain; and he is the director of the Communication and Education Department. He has been member of the Digital Literacy-High Level Expert Group and the Media Literacy Expert Group of the European Commission, and has advised and UNESCO and EAVI among other international organisations, in digital and media literacy. He has conducted important studies in media literacy, carried out by international and multidisciplinary research teams.

David G. Vequist IV, PhD is the founder and Director of the Center for Medical Tourism Research (www.medicaltourismresearch.org) - the very first academic Medical Tourism research center in the world. Dr. David G. Vequist IV is also an Associate Professor and tenured member of the Management Discipline in the H-E-B School of Business & Administration at the University of the Incarnate Word. Dr. Vequist is a well-known speaker and presenter on subjects like medical tourism, training, and human resources and is the author of books and chapters on the Management of Technology (MOT), Information Communication Technologies (ICT) and consulting trends, and the globalization of healthcare (in press). He has also had several academic journal and trade publication articles published around medical tourism, Collaborative Knowledge Management (CKM), new technologies in Training & Development (T&D), forecasting of business trends, and business simulations.

Index